Toward a Transnational University
WAC/WID Across Borders of Language,
Nation, and Discipline

Across the Disciplines Books

Series Editor: Michael A. Pemberton

The Across the Disciplines Books series is closely tied to published themed issues of the online, open-access, peer-reviewed journal *Across the Disciplines*. In keeping with the editorial mission of *Across the Disciplines*, books in the series are devoted to language, learning, academic writing, and writing pedagogy in all their intellectual, political, social, and technological complexity.

The WAC Clearinghouse and University Press of Colorado are collaborating so that these books will be widely available through free digital distribution and low-cost print editions. The publishers and the series editors are committed to the principle that knowledge should freely circulate and have embraced the use of technology to support open access to scholarly work.

Other Books in This Series

Marilee Brooks-Gillies, Elena G. Garcia, Soo Hyon Kim, Katie Manthey, and Trixie G. Smith (Eds.), *Graduate Writing Across the Disciplines: Identifying, Teaching, and Supporting* (2020)

Steven J. Corbett, Jennifer Lin LeMesurier, Teagan E. Decker, and Betsy Cooper (Eds.). *Writing In and About the Performing and Visual Arts: Creating, Performing, and Teaching* (2019).

Alice S. Horning, Deborah-Lee Gollnitz, and Cynthia R. Haller (Eds.). *What is College Reading?* (2017)

Frankie Condon and Vershawn Ashanti Young (Eds.), *Performing Antiracist Pedagogy in Rhetoric, Writing, and Communication* (2017)

Toward a Transnational University
WAC/WID Across Borders of Language, Nation, and Discipline

Edited by Jonathan Hall and Bruce Horner

The WAC Clearinghouse
wac.colostate.edu
Fort Collins, Colorado

University Press of Colorado
upcolorado.com
Denver, Colorado

The WAC Clearinghouse, Fort Collins, Colorado 80523

University Press of Colorado, Denver, Colorado 80203

Copyright © 2023 by Jonathan Hall and Bruce Horner. This work is licensed under a Creative Commons Attribution-NonCommercial-NoDerivatives 4.0 International License.

ISBN: 978-1-64215-152-7 (PDF) | 978-1-64215-153-4 (ePub) | 978-1-64642-387-3 (pbk.)

DOI: 10.37514/ATD-B.2023.1527

Library of Congress Cataloging-in-Publication Data

Names: Hall, Jonathan (Professor of English), editor. | Horner, Bruce, 1957– editor.
Title: Toward a transnational university : WAC/WID across borders of language, nation, and discipline / edited by Jonathan Hall and Bruce Horner.
Description: Fort Collins, Colorado : The WAC Clearinghouse ; Denver, Colorado : University Press of Colorado, [2023] | Series: Across the Disciplines Books / series editor, Michael A. Pemberton | Includes bibliographical references.
Identifiers: LCCN 2023000292 (print) | LCCN 2023000293 (ebook) | ISBN 9781646423873 (paperback) | ISBN 9781642151527 (Adobe pdf) | ISBN 9781642151534 (epub)
Subjects: LCSH: Academic writing—Study and teaching (Graduate) | English language—Rhetoric—Study and teaching (Graduate) | Dissertations, Academic. | Translanguaging (Linguistics) | Intercultural communication. | Interdisciplinary approach in education. | Critical pedagogy.
Classification: LCC LB2369 .T69 2023 (print) | LCC LB2369 (ebook) | DDC 808.02071/1—dc23/eng/20230201
LC record available at https://lccn.loc.gov/2023000292
LC ebook record available at https://lccn.loc.gov/2023000293

Copyeditor: Don Donahue
Book Design: Mike Palmquist
Cover Art and Design: "Burning Bush in a Place of Holy Water," by Malcolm Childers, www.malcolmchilders.blogspot.com. Used with permission.
Series Design: Tara Reeser
Series Editor: Michael A. Pemberton

The WAC Clearinghouse supports teachers of writing across the disciplines. Hosted by Colorado State University, it brings together scholarly journals and book series as well as resources for teachers who use writing in their courses. This book is available in digital formats for free download at wac.colostate.edu.

Founded in 1965, the University Press of Colorado is a nonprofit cooperative publishing enterprise supported, in part, by Adams State University, Colorado State University, Fort Lewis College, Metropolitan State University of Denver, University of Alaska Fairbanks, University of Colorado, University of Denver, University of Northern Colorado, University of Wyoming, Utah State University, and Western Colorado University. For more information, visit upcolorado.com.

Land Acknowledgment. The Colorado State University Land Acknowledgment can be found at https://landacknowledgment.colostate.edu.

Contents

3   Introduction. The Transnational Translingual University: Teaching Academic Writing Across Borders and Between Languages
    Bruce Horner

Part 1. Rewriting Writing Disciplines: Trans- Perspectives

13 WAC/WID in the Age of Trans-: Crossing and Re-crossing Borders of Discipline, Language, and Identity
    Jonathan Hall

35 "We are the 'Other'": The Future of Exchanges between Writing and Language Studies
    Christiane Donahue

59 Remapping Writing Instruction at the Borders of Modern Languages, Bilingual Education, and Translation Studies: A Canadian Proposal for a Transnational Conversation
    Guillaume Gentil

Part 2. Professional Development: Trans- Perspectives

87 Advancing a Transnational, Transdisciplinary and Translingual Professional Development Framework for Teaching Assistants in Writing and Spanish Programs: An Update
    Alyssa G. Cavazos, Marcela Hebbard, José E. Hernández, Crystal Rodriguez, and Geoffrey Schwarz

107 Global Business Communication: *Kairos* and Discipline-Crossing along the Path toward Globally Responsive Education
    Gail Shuck

123 Centering Our Students' Languages and Cultures: WAC and a Cross-Disciplinary Collaboration
    Joyce Meier, Xiqiao Wang, and Julia Kiernan

143   Transnational Telephone Games: Collaborations on Writing Education in South Asia
Shyam Sharma and Gene Hammond

Part 3. Trans-ing Institutional Structures

167   Mapping Transnational Institutions: Connections between WAC/WID and Qatar's Engineering Industry
Amy Hodges

189   Challenges in Positioning WAC/WID in International Contexts: Perspectives from a Japanese Engineering Undergraduate Program
Monica H. Kwon

205   Enhancing Science and Engineering Undergraduate Students' Writing in the Disciplines at Chinese Universities
Yongyan Li

221   Dimensions of Transnational Writing Exchange: An Exploratory Approach
Mohammad Shamsuzzaman

239   Transnational Translingual Literacies: Re-thinking Graduate Student Identity and Support
Jonathan Hall and Nela Navarro

261   Afterword. Translingual Lives and Writing Pedagogy: Acculturation, Enculturation, and Emancipation
Federico Navarro

279   Contributors

Toward a Transnational University
WAC/WID Across Borders of Language,
Nation, and Discipline

Introduction. The Transnational Translingual University: Teaching Academic Writing Across Borders and Between Languages

Bruce Horner
UNIVERSITY OF LOUISVILLE

This collection investigates the challenges and opportunities for the teaching of academic writing brought on by the increasing, and the increasing recognition of, the mobility across linguistic, national, disciplinary, and institutional borders of teachers, students, scholars, and institutional programs. As chapters in this collection demonstrate, the teaching, practice, and study of academic writing now take such mobility as their foundation; it is no longer adequate, if it ever was, to imagine academic writing as a subject for teaching or research, or as a practice, that is bound by linguistic, national, or disciplinary borders.

This is not to ignore longstanding borders among all these, nor, importantly, the hierarchical relations among them: there remains a geopolitics at work in the production of academic knowledge that is manifested in "border disputes," as it were, among languages, disciplines, institutions, and nation states. But those disputes themselves demonstrate, and enact, the historical character of those borders as ever emergent, in construction, variable, fluid, and, above all, crossed, hence the shifting, intermingling, and interdependent character of what the borders are meant to maintain, however futilely, as discrete, stable, internally uniform, and independent. Like efforts to "contain" the Covid-19 coronavirus, those disputes bring out the many ways in which, contrary to prevalent notions of discrete and stable entities—sedentary and immobile—mobility across borders is in fact the operating condition of our work.

Of course, many institutions of higher education (hereafter "IHEs") officially claim to be "global" in reach and foundation. But in practice, many of these same institutions maintain curricular structures, placement practices, and support services that were founded on more sedentarist conceptions of academic writing and its teaching—those that mobility scholars would characterize as based on assumptions of these as unchanging and immobile. As the chapters in this collection demonstrate, however, these IHEs are increasingly confronting the actual mobility and fluid character of academic writing and writers: their movement across borders of nation state, discipline, and language, and, in the process of that movement, the continual transformation of these. Against what Christiane Donahue (2009) has critiqued as the "export/import" model of writing programs and writing program expertise, teachers, scholars, and students are increasingly coming to recognize the need to address the inevitable and necessary transformation of themselves as academic writers and their writing as they move across borders, and in the process, their transformation of what those borders are intended to maintain.

Terms like translinguality, transnationality, and transdisciplinarity have emerged to name this alternative model by which to engage in, teach, and study academic writing and its teaching. Rejecting tenets of the language ideology of monolingualism and outmoded models of immigration and assimilation to address and control student and faculty mobility, they pose new questions: How do we address the issue of the language medium to be used for writing and teaching in such partnerships? How do we formulate a transnational and translingual WAC approach? How do transnational perspectives call into question assumptions about disciplinary identities and boundaries? What opportunities do transnational, translingual, and transdisciplinary perspectives afford WAC programs?

It is, of course, possible to take up these terms as simply new monikers for more familiar, and therefore understandable, models for addressing differences: translingual as multilingual, transnational as "global" or "international," transdisciplinary as "interdisciplinary" and/or "multidisciplinary." Such uptakes acknowledge the legitimacy of different practices but, crucially, maintain the borders among these as settled matters. At least some versions of WID, for example, while acknowledging differences among disciplinary writing practices, treat these practices as sets of discrete, stable, internally uniform kinds of writing specific to individual disciplines. And those advocating multilingualism, while acknowledging the legitimacy of the use of different languages, simultaneously insist, in keeping with the language ideology of monolingualism, that each language is discrete from others, internally uniform, stable, and with specific rules governing the locations for its appropriate use. Arguments for adopting "trans" perspectives on language, nation, and discipline are meant to challenge such uptakes as advancing not substantive difference but, instead, surface differences: glossodiversity, for example, papering over uniformity in meaning (see Cameron, 2002), and teaching translation of knowledge across disciplines or between academic and lay genres as a simple matter of recoding rather than rewriting (cf. Donahue, 2021, pp. 26–28). At the same time, such arguments can themselves risk understating the continuing dominance of ideologies that permeate ordinary thinking and practice: named languages, nation-states, disciplines. While it's easy enough to demonstrate the invalidity of the claims of those ideologies for the discrete, internally uniform, and stable character of what they name (see Bazerman, 1992, p. 63), such demonstrations in themselves do not weaken the power of those ideologies (see Lewis, 2018). As Yasemin Yildiz (2012) has argued, for example, we live not in a translingual but a postmonolingual condition, one in which actual practices conflict with what participants believe and claim about those practices and with what policies, official and tacit, and institutions maintain and dictate about them.

The chapters in this collection wrestle with that conflict, navigating between, on the one hand, practices in academic writing and its teaching, and, on the other, the ongoing legacies of ideologies about those practices that shape them and to which those practices inevitably respond. Chapters in Part I, "Rewriting Writing Disciplines: Trans- Perspectives," provide theoretical overviews on this state of affairs, addressing both the challenges and strategies that adopting a trans- approach can entail. In "WAC/WID in the Age of Trans-: Crossing and Re-crossing Borders of Language, Disciplinary, and National Identities," Jonathan Hall draws on scholarship from a range of disciplines taking a "trans" turn to rethink WAC/WID as necessarily engaged in "boundary work" as it confronts and responds to long-standing national, linguistic, and disciplinary borders and the inevitable inability of these, as ideological constructs. This, Hall argues, can enable us to account for and make use of the crossings over and continuous revisions of the distinctions of national, linguistic, and disciplinary identities such borders are meant to uphold. Drawing on Robert Frost's poem "Mending Wall" (1915), Hall argues that in responding to the competing senses that walls "make good neighbors," but also that "something there is that doesn't love a wall," we should think of WAC/WID as engaged not so much in boundary "work" but "boundary play" in which we recognize borders as "porous, fluid, as lines which connect more than they divide."

In "'We Are the Other': The Future of Exchanges between Writing and Language Studies," Donahue explores the broader history of divides between writing and language studies in the US and the opportunity transnationalism offers to think differently about the relation of writing and language studies. Drawing particularly on scholarship and teaching traditions outside the US and the anglophone realm, Donahue suggests that a transnational approach can help teachers and scholars move beyond limited understandings of such concepts as "transfer" and "codes" by adopting and adapting treatments of these in contact linguistics. Donahue thus brings to the fore the ways that a transnational approach to the study and teaching of composition necessarily involves us in transdisciplinary and translingual work. And in "Remapping Writing Instruction at the Borders of Modern Languages, Bilingual Education, and Translation Studies: A Canadian Proposal for a Transnational Conversation," Guillaume Gentil examines the ways that pursuit of bilingual academic writing development in Canadian IHEs can reinvigorate, and "re-map," institutional and disciplinary borders separating modern languages, translation studies, and writing instruction, in particular by redefining curricular arrangements for WAC/WID instruction. Drawing on a case study of a French/English graduate student's cross-lingual and cross-national research and writing, Gentil shows the tensions arising from attempts to draw on a diverse set of linguistic and disciplinary resources in settings where a strong sense of boundaries between these prevails, concluding that a "transnational translingual" approach to teaching academic writing can help students overcome monolingualism's "language-nation-identity" links while drawing on their own particular linguistic and national "moorings."

The chapters in Part II, "Professional Development: Trans- Perspectives," offer accounts of specific challenges at chapter authors' IHEs and their strategies for professional development to meet these. In "Advancing a Transnational, Transdisciplinary, and Translingual Professional Development Framework for Teaching Assistants in Writing and Spanish Programs," Alyssa G. Cavazos and her colleagues describe a cooperative effort among faculty and graduate and undergraduate students from several disciplines to make good on their IHE's designation as an Hispanic-Serving Institution (HSI) and its commitment to becoming a truly bilingual IHE, an effort that led to a series of workshops and continuing initiatives to think through an approach to the teaching and learning of writing and languages that treated students' and faculty's heritage languages and transnational and transborder/transfronterizo experiences as resources rather than barriers to their learning and scholarship. Likewise, Gail Shuck, describing the development of a "global business communication" partnership at her IHE, explains how the tripling of its international student population over a four-year period, primarily from Saudi Arabia and Kuwait, served as a catalyst prompting faculty to develop policies and pedagogies more reflective of the students' linguistic and cultural diversity and, more specifically, to a coordinated effort between various program administrators and instructors to revise her school's business communication course to address and incorporate intercultural communication and global business practices, a change useful to all students, international and domestic. In "Centering Our Students' Languages and Cultures: WAC and a Cross-Departmental Collaboration," Joyce Meier and her colleagues describe similar collaborative efforts at their IHE to draw on the linguistic and cultural diversity of its students. Reporting on a study involving faculty across disciplines at their IHE, they demonstrate the importance of engaging faculty from non-language-focused disciplines as well as in such disciplines as writing studies in efforts to recalibrate teaching to take into consideration and make use of the cultural knowledge and languages all students, from outside as well as inside the US, bring to their academic work, and to defamiliarize their own cultural references by rethinking, as well as translating, common instructional language that is foreign to many students (again, domestic and international). And in "Transnational Telephone Games in Writing Education: Collaborations on Writing Education in South Asia," Shyam Sharma and Gene Hammond describe their and their colleagues' efforts to engage directly in establishing collaborations with IHEs in South Asia. Finding little effect from one-off visits to IHEs outside the global North by U.S. experts in writing, Sharma and Hammond describe both exciting opportunities and humbling challenges experienced through a series of transnational WAC collaborations among Nepalese and U.S.-based faculty and administrators, leading them to advocate for exchanges valuing experience and processes more than the institutionalization of programs and centers.

Chapters in Part III, "Transing Institutional Structures," explore the challenges and strategies for transnational and transdisciplinary work posed by specific institutional conditions, locations, and arrangements. In "Mapping Transnational Institutions: Connections between WAC/WID and Qatar's Engineering Industry," Amy Hodges draws on data from interviews with alumni of TAMUQ (Texas A&M University Qatar), an international branch campus, and learning outcomes statements from course syllabi to show how the "export" of learning outcomes for WAC/WID programs is mediated by the specific conditions, interests, and needs of "local" students hailing from diverse nationalities and bringing diverse language backgrounds despite claims and institutional policies to the contrary that aim to offer "the same" education and educational experience at both "home" and "branch" campuses. As her interview data show, specific needs of students lacking Qatari citizenship to secure employment, and the prevalence of translingual practices of moving among English, various Arabic dialects, and other languages produce simultaneously an apparent reinforcement of beliefs in the value of English monolingualism and a "flexible mindset towards communication" involving continuous invention of new rhetorical knowledge, and an "inevitable slippage between institutional and course policies and the lived experiences of student writers" that WAC/WID program directors can work to realign.

The need to take local considerations and needs into consideration in positioning WAC/WID programs is further highlighted in Monica Kwon's chapter addressing "Challenges in Positioning WAC/WID in International Contexts: Perspectives from a Japanese Engineering Program." Drawing on a study of engineering faculty at a Japanese IHE striving to draw more students from outside Japan as part of the Japanese government's Top Global University Project, Kwon finds that faculty's concern with teaching disciplinary knowledge in Japanese conflicts with that project's aim to increase English Medium instruction ("EMI"), and that the greater importance those faculty place on the ability to speak, but not write, English conflicts with basic tenets of the WAC/WID movement postulating a close relation between writing and knowledge development. Likewise, the faculty's own lack of training in EMI, and their perception of such instruction being culturally different and more conducive to critical thinking than Japanese instruction, leads them to reject EMI as ill-suited to Japanese students (while advantaging non-Japanese students), despite their own belief in the importance of critical thinking to students in their academic and post-academic careers.

In "Enhancing Science and Engineering Undergraduate Students' Writing in the Disciplines at Chinese Universities," Yongyan Li provides a different exploration of the significance of the "local" in grasping WAC/WID practices. Based on her study of a corpus of published scholarship (in Chinese) on Chinese undergraduate disciplinary writing pedagogy (in Chinese and in English), Li identifies three strands in that scholarship that appear to be unknown to scholars of writing outside the Chinese context, and notes that scholars working in any one of the strands are not aware of those working in others—e.g., content teachers and language teachers—despite the fact that both groups appear to agree with Donahue that "writing and disciplinary knowledge are embedded in each other" (2011, 25). That said, Li finds promise in the move toward English for Academic Purposes for greater emphasis on "writing to learn" and increased cross-cultural discussion.

In "Dimensions of Transnational Writing Exchange: An Exploratory Approach," Mohammad Shamsuzzaman describes both quantitative and qualitative differences in the writing produced by U.S. and Bangladeshi undergraduate students and in their comments on one another's texts in a course engaging peer review between undergraduate students at North South University, Bangladesh and the State University of New York in the US. These suggest not only different degrees of familiarity with English-medium academic writing conventions encouraged in the US but also conflicting beliefs about writing development generally.

In "Transnational Translingual Literacies: Re-thinking Graduate Student Identity and Support," Jonathan Hall and Nela Navarro use their study of graduate students currently designated as "international" to argue that these students can be better understood as "transnational emerging scholars" with complex relations to a diversity of languages, disciplinary and professional identities, and socio-cultural affiliations. Focusing on graduate academic support programs ("Grad-ASPs"), Hall and Navarro reveal how, all too often, there is a mismatch between such programs' assumptions about and expectations for the graduate students recruited to U.S. IHEs, on the one hand, and, on the other hand, those students' experiences, interests, and desires. That mismatch leads Hall and Navarro to argue for programs to engage students more directly about their own complex identities and to treat them as emerging transnational professional participants in disciplinary work rather than as outsiders deficient in knowledge and language.

In Federico Navarro's Afterword, "Translingual Lives and Writing Pedagogy: Acculturation, Enculturation, and Emancipation," he reflects on the collection's chapters and cautions against naïve approaches that overlook local constraints and conditions, and those that treat locality as determinative and that overlook commonalities across disparate locations. Instead, Navarro argues for a stance attentive to the specific pressures and conditions obtaining in historical, temporal, and spatial locations. Noting, by way of illustration, differences in how evidentiality is marked in Quechua in comparison to Spanish and English, Navarro highlights the need to be attentive to such structural differences without dismissing the need to challenge center-periphery power dynamics engaged in linguistic negotiations. And, more broadly, Navarro reminds us of the need to extend notions of transnationality, translinguality, and transdisciplinarity beyond those that take as their anchor those conditions and concerns dominating the Anglophone Global North, whereby cross-language relations are defined in terms of English monolingualism only, and the institutional and curricular structures of U.S. IHEs as the presumptive norm, whether to be maintained or challenged.

Navarro's Afterword usefully highlights the friction engaged in the movement across languages, cultures, disciplines, institutions, and nation states in teaching academic writing. As Anna Lowenhaupt Tsing (2005) reminds us, friction is "where the rubber meets the road," necessary to any movement while simultaneously shaping the velocity and direction of that movement—even producing what might seem like stasis (p. 6). While often seen as nothing more than an impediment to movement, that friction, arising from the inevitable encounters with difference, defines and makes possible that movement.

At the same time, such friction itself, as Tsing warns, charges and changes all participants in such encounters (2005): all that meets, as it were, is transformed by the meeting, thereby not so much highlighting what was different previously but making newly different all involved. The transnational, translingual, and transdisciplinary character of contemporary university work, including the character of academic writing it produces, is the ever-emerging product of such encountering. As the chapters in this collection and the collection itself demonstrate, such products mark instances of the confluence of previous movement and the friction causing and resulting from such movement: how and why academic writing and its teaching are moving in the ways they are, and what new movements and changes might result from the encounters to which these lead.

References

Bazerman, Charles. (1992). From cultural criticism to disciplinary participation: Living with powerful words. In Anne Herrington & Charles Moran (Eds.), *Writing, teaching, and learning in the disciplines* (pp. 61–68). Modern Language Association of America.

Cameron, Deborah. (2002). Globalization and the teaching of "communication skills." In David Block & Deborah Cameron (Eds.), *Globalization and language teaching* (pp. 67–82). Routledge.

Donahue, Christiane. (2009). "Internationalization" and composition studies: Reorienting the discourse. *College Composition and Communication, 61*(2), 212–243.

Donahue, Christiane. (2021). Mobile knowledge for a mobile era: Studying linguistic and rhetorical flexibility in composition. In Bruce Horner, Megan Favers Hartline, Ashanka Kumari & Laura Sceniak Matravers (Eds.), *Mobility work in composition* (pp. 17–35). Utah State University Press.

Lewis, Mark C. (2018). A critique of the principle of error correction as a theory of social change. *Language in Society, 47*, 325–384.

Tsing, Anna Lowenhaupt. (2005). *Friction: An ethnography of global connection.* Princeton University Press.
Yildiz, Yasemin. (2012). *Beyond the mother tongue: The postmonolingual condition.* Fordham University Press.

Part 1. Rewriting Writing Disciplines: Trans- Perspectives

WAC/WID in the Age of Trans-: Crossing and Re-crossing Borders of Discipline, Language, and Identity

Jonathan Hall
YORK COLLEGE, CITY UNIVERSITY OF NEW YORK

> What kinds of intellectual labor can we begin to perform through the critical deployment of ""trans-" operations and movements? Those of us schooled in the humanities and social sciences have become familiar, over the past twenty years or so, with queering things; how might we likewise begin to critically trans- our world?
> – Susan Stryker et al., 2008, p. 13

We live in the age of trans-. My focus here will be on transdisciplinary, transnational, and translingual challenges for WAC/WID, but let's take a moment at the outset to see our efforts here as one part—a very small part—of a much broader *trans-* moment. How do these *trans-* phenomena interact with each other and how do they affect WAC/WID pedagogy, administration, and research?

Transing Boundaries

Most prominently, of course, *trans-* in contemporary culture points to *transgender, transsexual,* and related terms. For persons who identify as trans, it is both a deeply personal matter, yet also inevitably a socially-constructed one. Transing requires that social categories such as gender be seen as malleable, as arbitrary and imposed, and therefore subject to change, as opposed to natural, biological, and inviolable. Rogers Brubaker (2016), in a discussion of transgender and transracial intersectionality, argues that trans- may be seen as "part of a much broader moment of cultural flux, mixture, and interpenetration, as suggested by the burgeoning discussions of hybridity, syncretism, creolization, and transnationalism in the last quarter century" (p. 11), and issues a call to "think with trans" (p. 4).

Thinking with trans- in the context of WAC/WID is the challenge for us to take up, working with, as Brubaker has suggested, three basic ways of thinking about this categorical malleability:

1. Trans- as the possibility to migrate, to *transition* from one category to another. This version actually leaves the categories themselves mostly intact, just enables a (usually) one-way transportation between them. Here we might

think about the *across*ness of Writing Across the Curriculum. How would Writing Trans- the Curriculum be different? And what do we mean by "the"? Is "*the* curriculum" a parameter that we must work within, or a contested field that we may negotiate?
2. Trans- as emphasizing the *betweenness* of the journey rather than its endpoints. This version suggests that we are never fully *in* a category, but are always *in transit*, perpetual motion, shuttling between, swimming in a middle condition where the categories themselves are fluid and merge into each other. This meaning of trans- is especially important when we are thinking of a translingual approach to language difference, where languages themselves are understood as always emergent, influencing each other, bouncing off each other, interpenetrating, where the borders dissolve. It is also relevant to notions of transnationalism, where national borders are seen not as fully determinative but rather as places that people can move—and live—between.
3. Trans- as moving *beyond* the categories, *transcending* them. This is easier said than done, of course, and it's not even all that easy to say, because language thrives on oppositions, and much of Western thought is enabled by dichotomies. What if the borders between Writing and Non-Writing were to be eradicated?

As Susan Stryker et al. (2008) have argued, "the time was ripe for bursting 'transgender' wide open, and linking the questions of space and movement that that term implies to other critical crossings of categorical territories" (12). That "time" was fully fifteen years ago, and it was in that interim that "translingual" became an important category in writing studies. This is neither to say that translingualism was derived directly from work on transgender issues, nor that it was something brand new—one of the arguments I will take up here is that translingualism must be situated in a historical transdisciplinary context. Rather, I call attention to work in other types of trans- studies in order to point to a broader intersection of tendencies in widely diverse fields of study and practice. Thus the time is even "riper" now for a new examination of trans- theory and practice, to take up the call to "trans- our world."

Transing WAC/WID: Boundary Work

Robert Frost's poem "Mending Wall" (1915) famously suspends itself between two repeated and contradictory principles: "Good fences make good neighbors" and "Something there is that doesn't love a wall." The speaker's neighbor believes that "Good fences make good neighbors," having inherited a traditional ritual of bonding through separation. This position implies that boundaries are a crucial means of creating social identities, of defining relationships, of removing sources of stress that might stem from ambiguity, and that they are therefore well worth the joint work required to maintain them. The poem's speaker, however, is more skeptical and ironic, musing that "Something there is that doesn't love a wall." From this perspective, boundaries are not natural; in fact, they seem to go against the nature of things; they tend to collapse themselves. The speaker comes to regard them as "Oh, just another kind of out-door game," though also expressing a wish—"If I could put a notion in his head . . ."—to lead the neighbor to a more nuanced understanding of boundaries.

Who is the WAC/WID persona in Frost's "Mending Wall"? Are we the neighbor who believes that "Good fences make good neighbors"? WID traditionally defers to "faculty in the disciplines" and defines the WID role as helping those faculty to articulate their disciplinary values and to develop assignments that implement their disciplinary genres, conventions, and epistemology.

Or is WAC/WID better located closer to the poem's speaker: do we also sense that "Something there is that "doesn't love a wall"?" WAC has always been tasked with crossing departmental boundaries in search of a unified writing curriculum, and WAC professionals find their work routinely intersecting with faculty and courses in multiple disciplines.

To move from Frost's poetic metaphor to a more academic one, we find a similar ambivalence in the concept of "boundary work," which in science studies originally (Gieryn, 1983) addressed ideological definitions of science vs. non-science, that is, a way that scientists patrol the borders of the scientific domain and exclude what they see as not scientific—e.g, creation science, various types of pseudo-science. Steve Fuller (1991), pertinently for us, expanded the notion of boundary work to include negotiations between adjoining social science disciplines, noting that "disciplinary boundaries provide the structure needed for a variety of functions, ranging from the allocation of cognitive authority and material resources to the establishment of reliable access to some extra-social reality" (p. 302).

Put that way, boundary work for Gieryn and Fuller is an act of group self-assertion, often in response to an underlying anxiety: you don't need to say that something is unscientific unless you're worried that someone will think that it is. This kind of boundary work seems defensive and exclusionary, a power move designed to create an in-group and an out-group. But that's not the whole story. Noting that another strain in the boundary work literature focuses on boundary objects (Star & Griesemer, 1989), boundary organizations (Guston, 1999), boundary concepts (Klein, 1996), and boundary discourses (Shackley & Wynne, 1996), Hauke Riesch (2010) identifies a persistent duality in the idea that echoes Frost's poetic meditations on good fences and bad walls:

> A group or a group member can draw a rhetorical boundary
> that excludes other groups' claims to competence in their area,

> thus exerting or trying to exert some sort of control over their epistemic authority. In the other tradition a boundary is seen as a given division between social groups that, while working together, view the world and the object of their collaboration in fundamentally different ways. In this view a boundary is not something created to establish epistemic authority, but rather something to be overcome to create scientific cooperation. (p. 456)

Boundaries, that is, not only exclude but can also connect, and the most fruitful areas for cooperation may lie specifically in the most contested boundary zones. From this perspective, putting up boundaries and taking them down are not opposites but rather simultaneous and interrelated, as mirror twins, aspects of the same action. The apparent act of raising fences can actually be seen as an invitation to collaborate—and perhaps the reverse as well. We may see boundary work of various kinds, complex gestures of rejection and inclusion, ambivalent acceptance and conflicted resistance, often simultaneous, in *trans-* approaches to multiple phenomena: disciplines, languages, nations, identities, and more.

Transing Disciplines

> Dividing up a problem so that it can be addressed by different theories doesn't encourage the dialogue we need. Rather we need to move beyond difference towards overlapping and intruding expertise . . . [O]ur efforts thrived in proportion to the amount of linguistics our educators could learn, and the amount of educational theory and practice our linguists could absorb.
>
> — James Martin, 2000, p. 121

Transdisciplinarity as a concept has a contentious 50-year history, which we may (over)simplify for present purposes by dividing the approaches into the "beyond" and the "between" versions of *trans-* discussed above. The most prominent champion of the "beyond" approach is Basarab Nicolescu, whose "Levels of Reality" approach was summarized by Artur Manfred Max-Neef (2005) in terms that echo the famous mathematical incompleteness theorems of Kurt Gödel: "the laws of a given level of reality are not self-sufficient to describe the totality of phenomena occurring at that same level" (p. 13). Nicolescu's other two axioms are the anti-Aristotelian "logic of the included middle" and an axiom of complexity. Nicolescu (2010) himself cites not only Gödel but also Heisenberg, as well as the phenomenology of Husserl, Heidegger, and Cassirer as reinscribing the Subject as part of the scientific enterprise. Peter Osborne (2015) cites an alternate tradition of transdisciplinary works in the humanities and social sciences, including Horkheimer and Adorno, de Beauvoir, Sartre, Levi-Strauss, Foucault, Derrida, Deleuze and

Guattari, Habermas, and Sloterdijk. Most of the names on Osborne's list are customarily described as participants in various *post-* movements, especially post-structuralism and post-modernism. To be *post-* is to still be trapped in the horizon of what came before, though one can see its fatal limitations; to re-position these thinkers as *trans-* rather than *post-*, as Osborne does, is to emphasize their potential escape from the *post-* trap, to highlight the continuing movement of these thinkers between and beyond various disciplinary spaces and identities, and to begin to offer a more accurate description of the ways that *theory as transing* has exerted profound influence on multiple disciplines, from literary criticism to philosophy to anthropology to linguistics and beyond, without the theorists themselves being clearly located in a univocal disciplinary identity. This potent intersection of science, philosophy, and theory of various stripes suggests that transdisciplinarity as "beyond discipline" is not some pie-in-the-sky future aspiration but rather an existing force that has already been driving widely diverse intellectual endeavors for several decades, if not longer. From this perspective, the tasks of a transdisciplinary researcher go beyond merely applying one's own expertise to a new object of study and certainly beyond just importing aspects of another field into one's own discipline. Rather, the mandate is to seek out areas where similar pressures and influences have already borne relevant fruit in other contexts.

While transdisciplinarity as "beyond," as "theory," might even be described as the mainstream in the humanities and some social sciences—though certainly not without controversy or resistance—a more pragmatic "between" approach to transdisciplinarity has prevailed as the principal discourse in STEM fields. Thomas Jahn et al. (2012) offer a consensus definition of what might be dubbed the "social problem approach" in that it concentrates on issues that are too large for any one discipline to tackle alone: climate change, hunger, globalization, etc.:

> Transdisciplinarity is a reflexive research approach that addresses societal problems by means of interdisciplinary collaboration as well as the collaboration between researchers and extra-scientific actors; its aim is to enable mutual learning processes between science and society; integration is the main cognitive challenge of the research process. (p. 4)

In this version, transdisciplinarity erodes the borders not only between disciplines but between "science and society" by including "researchers and extra-science actors" in a "mutual learning process." The goal of "integration" is also the primary "challenge" of this variety of transing: how to remain indefinitely in that "between," in that mutually created knowledge space without retreating into disciplinary corners.

As Martin (2000) argues, notions of "overlapping" and "intruding" are central to transdisciplinary projects, which otherwise may have hardly anything in common with each other except that they don't allow the participants to remain securely ensconced in their disciplinary silos, but instead to experience friction, discomfort, ambiguity of affiliation, weakening or erasure of boundaries, learning and integration of elements from different disciplines, overlapping of intellectual territories, blurring of academic identities.

Transing Languages

WAC/WID has made some tentative approaches to language issues, from calls for transformative collaboration (Wolfe-Quintero & Sagade, 1999; Matsuda & Jablonski, 2000; Johns, 2001; Hall, 2009) to three special issues of *Across the Disciplines* and an associated edited volume (Johns, 2005; Cox & Zawacki, 2011; Zawacki & Cox, 2014; Horner & Hall 2018). Nevertheless, the field has not yet fully engaged with the questions raised by a translingual approach to language difference. Translingualism contests the idea that languages reside in discrete boxes, or separate systems, that do not touch or influence each other. At the macro level, translingualism points toward the idea that the edges of languages are contested territory, contact zones. At the micro level of individual idiolect, the translingual turn insists that all the languages a person knows can be active in the present moment of reading or writing, that all the components of one's complete communicative repertoire are, at least potentially, simultaneously in play in a mutually re-enforcing manner. WAC/WID theory and practice needs to be attentive to both the macro- and micro- levels of language change and interaction.

The translingual approach actually has at least three major components. One is a theory about relations between languages, especially about language difference, about language boundaries. A second component includes an ideological imperative, because of the pervasive yet often-unconscious cultural assumptions of monolingualism that must be countered. This aspect has sometimes been figured as developing translingual or transcultural "dispositions" (Lee & Canagarajah, 2018; Lee & Jenks, 2016), an ethical obligation of openness to variation within and between languages. A third aspect moves beyond writing to research in translinguistics (Dovchin & Lee, 2019) or what I prefer to call "everyday translinguality" (Robinson, Hall & Navarro, 2020). Here the emphasis is on the ubiquitous, routine nature of translinguality, which only appears to be strange or exotic from the vestiges of a monolingualist perspective.

The original statement of a translingual approach (Horner et. al, 2011) succinctly summarizes the underlying language theory: "A translingual approach takes the variety, fluidity, intermingling, and changeability of languages as statistically demonstrable norms around the globe" (305). Or, rather than a summary, perhaps this is better described as a brief allusion to a complex of existing theories—not original to this translingual approach but rather building on decades of work in critical applied linguistics and other fields. This formulation points toward the investigation of a state of translinguality, presented as "statistically demonstrable norms": that is, future studies of translinguality will aspire to produce verifiable research about languages and language difference. Translinguality as a questioning of linguistic boundaries situates comfortably among developments that have influenced a wide range of disciplines ranging from applied linguistics to anthropology to literary theory across the past forty years. One formulation attributes the recent feverish interest in "linguistic multiplicity" to the influence of

> postmodern, poststructuralist, and postcolonial thought as seen in such notions as multiplicity, heterogeneity, fluidity, hybridity, and constructedness, which expand and blur the fixed boundaries of the social and linguistic categories that are defined in an essentialist binary logic in the previous modernist paradigm (Kubota, 2014, p. 2).

From *post-* to *trans-*: the "*post*" prefix suggests both an awareness of the limitations of a phenomenon and at the same time the condition of remaining trapped within its horizon. Yasmin Yildiz (2011) suggests the term "postmonolingual" for "a field of tension in which the monolingual paradigm continues to assert itself and multilingual practices persist or reemerge." (p. 5). The translingual, as an aspiration, would signal that we are ready to go beyond the monolingualist ideology that coincided historically with the simultaneous rise of the nation-state.

The second main component of the Translingual Statement involves a shift to an ideological presentation of translingualism, which

> confronts, as well, the practice of invoking standards not to improve communication and assist language learners, but to exclude voices and perspectives at odds with those in power. It treats standardized rules as historical codifications of language that inevitably change through dynamic processes of use. A translingual approach proclaims that writers can, do, and must negotiate standardized rules in light of the contexts of specific instances of writing. (Horner et al., 2011, p. 305)

Here the focus is on a translingual analysis, with strong echoes of Foucault and Bourdieu, of the power relations inherent in a monolingualist paradigm. The key word here is "negotiate," a term which will recur again and again in discussions of translingual approaches, introducing a fully rhetorical aspect to linguistic change. It is not only that the "rules" of standardized languages shift and change over time, on a macro level, as power relations within and between language communities shift and change—any modern linguistic theory would agree with this much. But translingualism insists on the agency of each individual writer in each rhetorical situation as participating in that process (Lu & Horner, 2013), if only as one in trillions of such micro-negotiations in every act of language every second of every day all over the world. It's not an either/or matter of choosing whether to follow or to defy the rules of a standardized language, but rather of finding strategies for situating oneself, as a writer, within the already shifting and already malleable repetitions and deviations that constitute the network of differences that form what we call language(s) or dialect(s) or variet(ies)-or subsets such as registers or disciplines.

A third aspect of translingualism points toward researching the ways in which all language users, whether "native" or not, contribute constantly to the moment-by-moment re-production and re-vision of any language they use. This "everyday translinguality" (Robinson, Hall & Navarro, 2020) is both routine and yet potentially transformative, and forms a potent area for future WAC/WID translingual research. Two of the co-authors of the statement followed up with a careful delineation of both the roots of translingualism and its pedagogical application to a student text (Lu & Horner, 2013), focusing most urgently on the issue of agency:

> A translingual approach thus defines agency operating in terms of the need and ability of individual writers to map and order, remap and reorder conditions and relations surrounding their practices . . . (p. 591)

Min-Zhan Lu and Bruce Horner position writers, including student writers of any linguistic background, as active and purposeful negotiators of meaning.

Translingual pedagogy needs to be built on the language theory, the ideological dispositions, and on meeting students where they are in their everyday non-controversial use of multiple language resources, an approach or cluster of classroom approaches that combine linguistic research, instructor raised consciousness, and student agency. One of our jobs as writing professionals is to help both WAC faculty and students reach the consciousness that the particular rhetorical configuration that we call standardized correctness is not written in stone but rather is subject to trillions of micro-negotiations every day, based on the interactions, the rhetorical and linguistic choices, made by speakers and writers all over the world.

Negotiation and Empowerment

It is vital that students understand, both intellectually and viscerally, that they are among those negotiators, those makers of language—that they are co-owners of English, not just renters. Just because they speak English "as a second language," it does not mean that they are second-class speakers of English. But they enter our classrooms already having absorbed the cultural message that a language is owned by its native speakers, and part of our job, in teaching students to write in a second or for that matter in any language, is helping them to develop a critical consciousness of what that enterprise really entails. Students, it is true, may express their desire to master Standard English (and only Standard English) because they can perfectly well read the cultural semiotics that associate a particular register of English with prestige and status. But students' attraction to the "Standard" needs to be contextualized, and if the important task of helping students to understand the power relationships inherent in current cultural beliefs about language difference is not addressed in the writing classroom, it probably will never be done at all. The result would be that students regard themselves as passive recipients of a language which will always remain somewhat foreign to them, rather than as one of the billions of active shapers of the language.

One way of thinking of translingualism is as a rhetoricization of language "correctness," or rather as a recognition that "correctness" is already a rhetorical category, and not a purely linguistic one. A standardized variety of a language describes a particular configuration of writer, audience, and text that has been normalized through social processes, not an inevitable or eternal structure. Suresh Canagarajah (2015) has suggested that "what translingual pedagogies favor is deconstructing Standard English to make students aware that it is a social construct" (p. 425).

Negotiations, of course, are seldom between exact equals, and it would be foolish to underestimate the continuing power of monolingualist ideology or to assert that the hegemony of Standard English can be lightly defied with impunity. Even an established scholar like Canagarajah (2006) remains cautious about how he introduces elements of code-meshing and other translingual practices into his academic prose. But recognition of a power differential does not mean that no negotiation is possible, nor that it is pointless to raise consciousness even if, in the end, a student declines to challenge existing rhetorical or linguistic norms in a given text or embraces common practices. Understanding the contingent nature of current standards can nevertheless empower students to greater rhetorical assertiveness even as they continue to operate within the established constraints of a particular situation, because they begin to think of themselves as agents making active decisions in real rhetorical situations as they write, rather than simply filling in the blanks of a template or memorizing a book of rules. While prescriptivists look for rules and descriptivists look for patterns, translingualists look for choices.

Transdisciplinary Roots and Branches of Translingualism

Translingualism, while it may be the new kid on the block in WAC/WID circles, did not arise ex nihilo, nor does it exist in isolation in its contemporary circumstances. The original Translingual Statement (Horner et al., 2011) included an extensive bibliography, which can stand as a historical representation of what the authors and signatories of that statement saw as their key predecessors, as of 2011, in the fields of second language writing, applied linguistics, second language acquisition, and related disciplines. From a WAC/WID perspective, Terry Myers Zawacki and Michelle Cox (2014) present a narrative of gradual influence from research in all the above fields.

In second language acquisition (SLA), Vivian Cook's conception of "multi-competence," in the 1990s to early 2000s, provides perhaps the most direct precursor to the translingual approach—though Cook was mostly not talking about writing, at that time not a front-row priority in SLA. But multicompetence broke down the idea that languages could be kept separate within the individual speaker; rather, they affect each other and do not stay in silos or walled-off systems; a bilingual does not reside in "two solitudes" (Cummins, 2008). Crucially, the influence could move both ways: not only did the L1 affect the L2, but the L2 affected the L1 (Cook, 2003). Cook's concept of multicompetence was later re-formulated by Joan Kelly Hall, An Cheng, and Matthew T. Carlson (2006) as a much more dynamic and usage based view of language, a model with important implications for WAC/WID (Hall & Navarro, 2011).

If translingualism has multiple roots in the past, it also has multiple fellow travelers in the present, as part of a broader intellectual movement—or perhaps several movements—across all fields involved in language study, and in society at large. From the perspective of applied linguistics, Ryuko Kubota (2014), in describing what she calls "the multi/plural turn," defined as research "which focuses on the plurality, multiplicity, and hybridity of language and language use to challenge a traditional paradigm of understanding linguistic practices in various contexts" (p. 2), captures something of the breadth of these recent developments, even if at times we seem to be drowning in a sea of neologisms: "multilingualism, plurilingualism, world Englishes, English as a lingua franca, codemeshing, metrolingualism, translingual approach, translanguaging, multiliteracies and hybridity" (p. 2).[1]

Kubota locates the translingual approach as one among many examples of "the multi/pluri turn," identifying a fundamental rift that cuts across several disciplines related to language research. Canagarajah (2013a) provides a different list of transdisciplinary phenomena that are parallel with or at least bear a strong family resemblance to translingualism:

> In composition: translingual writing, codemeshing, and transcultural literacy;
>
> In new literacy studies: multiliteracies, continua of biliteracy, and hetero-graphy;
>
> In sociolinguistics: fused lects, ludic Englishes and

---

1   I've omitted Kubota's citations for all of these; see Kubota (2016) for references.

metrolinguistics, poly-lingual languaging, and fragmented, multilingualism;

In applied linguistics: translanguaging, dynamic bilingualism and pluriliteracy, plurilingualism, and third spaces. (p. 9)[2]

In both of these examples of connective boundary work, translingualism is positioned neither as a stand-alone revolutionary paradigm, nor as a provincial development within rhetoric and composition, but rather as part of a broader transdisciplinary wave of critical approaches to language difference. The movement of re-contextualization may be seen as an example of boundary work in its more positive, collaborative sense, a move toward articulating a transdisciplinary nexus where multiple perspectives and multiple disciplines are involved in trying to unravel a complex phenomenon. For WAC/WID, it raises the question of how to respond, however belatedly, to the transdisciplinary, transnational, and translingual challenge.

Transing National Identities

The notion of standard languages is inextricably tied to the idea of national identities. A supposed common language is frequently adduced as a reason for the creation of a nation-state, even as linguistic uniformity is often imposed on language minorities in the aftermath of a nationalist movement. Insistence on "English Only" in the US, for example, is about anti-transnationalism, i.e., maintaining the prominence of borders, and its concurrent division of "In" and "Out" among people on the various sides.

Alastair Pennycook's 2008 essay on "Translingual English" adds a sociolinguistic complement to multicompetence theory's focus on the individual language user. Monolingualism as an ideology has always had both a micro dimension—the expectation that one individual would speak only one language—and a macro dimension, in which a single language is seen as an indispensable unifying factor in a nation-state. Pennycook instead urges a transnational/translingual approach,

[a] move towards an understanding of the relationships among language resources as used by certain communities (the linguistic resources users draw on), local language practices (the use of these language resources in specific contexts), and language users' relationship to language varieties (the social, economic and cultural positioning of the speakers). This is, consequently, an attempt to move away from nation-based models of English and to take on

---

2   I've omitted Canagarajah's citations; see Canagarajah (2013a) for references.

board current understandings of translingual practices across communities other than those defined along national criteria. (p. 304)

For Pennycook, translingualism arises from transnationalism, or, more specifically, from moving beyond the equation of one nation/one language. Language practices are not limited to one geographic location; across the globe, languages are on the move.

The forces of national identity continue, of course, to make claims of family, culture, and patriotism, and so the transnational challenge—for students, for faculty, and for institutions—raises the stakes of *trans-* phenomena. What does a transnational approach have to offer us as WAC/WID professionals? What do we mean, anyway, by "transnational"? Here's one definition:

> . . . many contemporary migrants and their predecessors maintained a variety of ties to their home countries while they became incorporated into the countries where they settled. Migration has never been a one-way process of assimilation into a melting pot or a multicultural salad bowl but one in which migrants, to varying degrees, are simultaneously embedded in the multiple sites and layers of the transnational social fields in which they live. . . . (Levitt & Jaworsky, 2007, p. 130)

Instead of identities defined by national borders, a transnational perspective focuses on the complex relationships that transnational migrants maintain both with the culture of wherever they are physically, and with wherever else they have ties of family, heritage, birth, language, interest, curiosity, or affiliation. It examines the ways that individuals, families, and diasporic communities construct and maintain transnational identities, sometimes through a conscious claim or performance of identity and sometimes through largely unconscious immersion in cultural traces, connections, and memories, often mediated by the ongoing use of a minoritized language in a particular displaced setting. A transnational approach takes multidirectional mobility and the possibility of repeated migration as a given and rejects the notion of an immigrant without a past fully assimilated into a new national identity.

The concept of transnationalism has advanced from early studies in anthropology (Glick Schiller et al., 1995; Duany, 2008), sociology (Levitt & Jaworsky, 2007), mobility studies (Soong, 2016; Wu, 2017) and ethnic studies (Kivisto, 2001; Portes et al., 1999; Vertovec, 1999) to transdisciplinary approaches such as communication flows (Verdery et al., 2018) and superdiversity (Blommaert & Rampton, 2012; Vertovec, 2007). More recent studies of transnationalism have focused on how it functions in particular domains such as health (Villa Torres, 2017), families (Cho & Allen, 2019), sport (Vertovec, 2009), diplomacy (Kuus, 2017) and history (Macdonald, 2013; Körner, 2017).

In writing studies, transnational approaches continue to illuminate aspects of Writing Program Administration (Martins, 2014); TESOL (Solano-Campos, 2014); composition studies (Donahue, 2009); and mobility studies (e.g., Blommaert & Horner, 2017). WAC/WID has made some steps toward engaging with some aspects of this research (e.g., Zenger, Haviland & Mullin, 2013). Nevertheless, WAC/WID as a field has not yet fully engaged with the questions raised by a transnational approach to writing pedagogy and research. Transnationalism may be contextualized as a subset or example of a broader "turn" away from the idea of the nation-state as the main, or at least the initial, reference-point in a student writer's identity.

Transnationalism is not merely the interrelation of one static place with another static place. We need to take into account not only the places and cultures changing moment to moment, but also the ceaseless churning movements between and within them. Whether through physical movement via modern transportation or virtual displacement in the vast nowhere/everywhere of cyberspace, people are on the move, and so are their ideas, their stuff, their languages, their loyalties. In the recent pandemic situation, the key aspiration around the world has been to slow movement, with policies necessitating the enforced immobility of persons aimed at arresting both the worldwide and also local mobility of the virus. But this is of course an aberration from what got us in that situation in the first place: the accelerating and—we thought—unstoppable mobility of people, goods, ideas, money, languages—and diseases.

For academic research in multiple fields, especially in the social sciences, the "mobility studies paradigm" (Steller & Urry, 2006) has challenged "sedentarist" assumptions that phenomena such as nations, families, businesses, individuals, societies would stay still long enough to be studied. Disciplines, too, are unstable and mobile (Blommaert & Horner, 2017), and scholarly identities require constant modification, project by project and moment by moment within "the same" project. For WAC/WID as an ever-shifting network of persons (students, instructors,, administrators, scholars), texts (created daily in multiple virtual locations), and practices (always already adapting on the fly, only now we can see it more clearly), the interruption of mobility in the pandemic environment emphasizes the necessity of interrogating what we mean by academic writing in an environment where instruction is online, where people are on edge, and where the future is on hold. To what degree will this interregnum in mobility force an awareness of all the motion that we were overlooking before, now visible because we miss it?

Transnational Challenges and Opportunities for WAC/WID

In the context of WAC/WID, transnational approaches offer challenges and opportunities for transnational student identities, for universities as transnational institutions, and for faculty as transfronterizo instructors and scholars.

The Transnational Triangle: From Monodirectional Immigration to Transnational Mobility

How are our WAC/WID students affected by a re-thinking of national identity, and especially of immigration, as not a melting pot or a multicultural salad bowl but rather as an ongoing connection to multiple social fields across borders?

The laws of physics say that we cannot be in two places at the same time. The laws of the heart say that often we must be in two places at once. The laws of governments, along with the laws of the marketplace, complicate, mediate, and regulate the operations of the other types of laws. That is to say: transnational identity is composed of the interaction between three points of a triangle: physical location and the events, necessities, and cultural demands of that milieu; continuing ties and activities (legal, economic, familial, linguistic, cultural, symbolic, emotional) to other location(s); and a multitude of external factors which help to determine the specific forms that these connections are allowed to take on.

Steven Vertovec (1999) describes transnationalism as "a social formation spanning borders" in which "the network's component parts—connected by nodes and hubs—are both autonomous from, and dependent upon, its complex system of relationships" (p. 449). The transnational triangle exists in the physical world, in social or cultural spaces, and in individual subjectivity. It can be influenced by the actions of governments, economic actors, cultural groups, or individuals. It may be seen as both voluntary and deterministic: individuals make choices regarding their loyalties and the connections which they wish to maintain (or not), but those decisions take place in a matrix of influences which is not completely in their control.

In the U.S. context, discussions of immigration tend to put the emphasis on the future, which leads us to conceive of immigration as a one-time and final act, a burning of bridges, a blind and irrevocable leap into the unknown. We still think of immigration the way that the Irish did in the wake of the 19th-century famine, when the custom of an "America wake" arose: whenever a young person was emigrating to America, they would hold a party where the unspoken assumption was that this would be the last time that friends and family would ever see that person (Diner 1998). Yet even in the 19th century, it has been argued that the Irish in America never fully assimilated and always thought of themselves as exiles (Diner, 1998; Miller, 1988). So if even the 19th-century Irish emigrant—lamented in song and mourned as dead, and with return trips limited by existing technology and the cost of a journey—can nevertheless be seen as maintaining some degree of transnational identity, what of today's global flows of what we still call "immigration," facilitated by much more advanced transportation and communication technologies?

Still it is not illusory that immigrants of today have a different relationship both to their arrival culture and to their departure culture. A shift from a conception of irrevocable monodirectional immigrants to transnational continuing mobility can help to restore a sense of a two-way (or more) flow of influence and information and ideas. Today's migrants and children of migrants, including many of our WAC/WID students, function as nodes on multiple intersecting networks of language, culture, and identity.

Transnational Institutional Structures: Beyond "International"

Transnationalism tends to erode borders between nations; the best example might be the European Union. Top-level transnationalism—or anti-transnationalism—most directly affects our WAC/WID students and faculty when it comes to policies regarding transnational students (usually referred to as "international" students—see Hall & Navarro in the present volume). The recent actions of the Trump administration attempting to curtail student visas during the COVID pandemic, for example, have had very direct effects on enrollment, programming, support, and all aspects of international student programs in the United States.

The original context of the term "transnational" was in analyzing the organizational structure of large corporations. Companies with operations beyond a single nation were categorized along axes of Integration and Responsiveness. This model of an I-R framework distinguishes among four types of organizational structure. A transnational corporation was to be distinguished from an international one (just import-export), a multinational one (relatively autonomous subsidiaries with limited working arrangements) and from global corporations (think McDonalds) that attempted to reproduce themselves exactly, often with franchises, with the minimal possible adaptation to local conditions (Bartlett & Ghoshal, 1988; Brock & Hydle, 2018; Kordos & Vojtovic, 2016).

This transnational analysis of corporate structure is relevant to the actions of universities as they expand beyond their national borders of origin to position themselves in global, multinational, international, or transnational manners (Chen, 2015). The claims of U.S. universities to be "global" in their reach, or their signing of multinational study-abroad or "sister campuses" agreements with universities elsewhere, or their opening of "branch" campuses in very different national and cultural contexts: all these rhetorical moves need to be evaluated in the context of models of transnational institutional structures.

At the micro-institutional level of "writing programs," WAC/WID has attempted to move beyond its North American roots to at least acknowledge that the teaching of writing and the doing of academic writing may vary across national and cultural locations. The theme of the 2004 WAC Conference was "WAC from an International Perspective," and each subsequent conference has been designated as an "International Conference on Writing Across the Curriculum." In 2012, the results of an extensive worldwide initiative "mapping" writing programs were published (Thaiss et al., 2012), which shed some light on the diversity of the ways in which "writing" is conceived and taught in multiple locations. Included in the recent formation of the U.S.-based Association for Writing Across the Curriculum (AWAC 2021) is a renewed initiative to interact and to collaborate with similar organizations abroad.

But "international" is not transnational: rather, international envisions everyone remaining in their national silos, signing agreements to cooperate. A truly transnational intersection of programmatic structures would result in de-centered models, involving interdependent parts working together across multiple national and cultural locations.

Crossing and Re-crossing Boundaries: Transfronterizo

If transnationalism explores the slow erosion of national boundaries, there remain many contexts in which borders are not disappearing at all but rather serve as a source of constant tension and potential conflict for those who live in proximity. The term "transfronterizo" has emerged to describe those who cross and re-cross borders repeatedly and often routinely, for whom transnationalism is not a subjective connection across great distances but rather a medium in which daily life is immersed (Fránquiz & Ortiz, 2017; Marshall, 2019; O'Connor, 2019; Zentella, 2009). In this volume, Alyssa Cavazos et al. describe the opportunities and challenges of living in borderlands without either the option of or the desire for an escape route—constantly crossing and re-crossing borders that are physical (their institution is located near the U.S./Mexico border), linguistic (the institution is officially bilingual, and a large majority of both students and instructors make use of both English and Spanish), and disciplinary (the authors are all located in a newly-created Department of Writing and Language Studies). In discussing the sometimes uneasy collaborations between instructors in first-year composition and in Spanish language courses in a translingual and transnational context, the authors describe their condition as that of "transfronterizo collaborators." Recognizing that most of their students and, in many cases, themselves are simultaneously living acá y allá, transfronterizo instructors must intentionally interrogate the "multiple daily transactions" across borders that form the basis of complex language, personal, and intellectual identities.

Transfronterizo may be seen as, in one sense, an inescapable condition emerging from situated dichotomies beyond individual control: the physical border is an artifact of history, the stakes of language difference are rooted in ideology, and disciplinary identities are under pressure from institutional reorganization. In such a situation, to retreat from the borderlands into the supposed safety of a stable disciplinary identity would be to ignore language difference and the liminal existence of a borderland residence.

Conclusion: WAC/WID in the Translingual Transnational University

WAC/WID professionals need always to keep in mind that good fences make good language, national, or disciplinary neighbors only so long as both sides are conscious that boundary work is, as Frost puts it, "Oh, just another kind of out-door game" (1915). Perhaps we should call it boundary play. A translingual approach deconstructs the bright-line separation between languages, and between languages and dialects. Academic disciplines, too, attempt to divide up research territory, but their boundary work collapses, as well, under the centripetal forces of transdisciplinarity. National borders try to define through separation, but a transnational approach regards borders as porous, fluid, as lines which connect more than they divide.

For researchers, instructors, and administrators in a transdisciplinary field like WAC/WID, who are operating in the context of an actual or potential translingual transnational university, all three *trans-* phenomena are inescapable factors in everything that we do. For WAC/WID instructors, many of their students will already be living transnational identities which may not be immediately visible in the classroom, but which potentially offer a rich resource for them to draw upon in their academic writing and research. Administrators of WAC/WID programs may find that their university's announced "global" identity falls short of true transnationalism. If a university regards its outreach across borders merely as a way of attracting potential students from overseas, it is missing the chance to really engage with what it would mean for a university to be a fully global citizen in a transnational world. WAC/WID researchers should examine the intersection of translingual practices and transnational identities in all of these areas and suggest what it would mean to truly re-invent the contemporary university as a participant in transnational translingual dispositions across boundaries of discipline, language, and nationality.

References

AWAC. (2021). International Collaborations committee. https://wacassociation.org/committee/international-collaborations-committee/.

Bartlett, Christopher A & Ghoshal, Sumantra. (1988). Organizing for worldwide effectiveness: The transnational solution. *California Management Review*, *31*(1), 54–74.

Blommaert, Jan & Horner, Bruce. (2017). Mobility and academic literacies: An epistolary conversation. *London Review of Education*, *15*(1), 2–20.

Brock, David M. & Hydle, Katja Maria. (2018). Transnationality—Sharpening the integration-responsiveness vision in global professional firms. *European Management Journal*, *36*(1), 117–124.

Brubaker, Rogers. (2016). *Trans: Gender and race in an age of unsettled identities*. Princeton University Press.

Canagarajah, A. Suresh. (2006). Toward a writing pedagogy of shuttling between languages: Learning from multilingual writers. *College English*, *68*(6), 589–604.

Canagarajah, A. Suresh. (2013a). *Translingual practice: Global Englishes and cosmopolitan relations*. Routledge.

Canagarajah, Suresh (Ed.). (2013b). *Literacy as translingual practice: Between communities and classrooms*. Routledge.

Canagarajah, Suresh. (2015). Clarifying the relationship between translingual practice and L2 writing: Addressing learner identities. *Applied Linguistics Review*, *6*(4), 415–440.

Chen, Pi-Yun. (2015). University's transnational expansion: Its meaning, rationales and implications. *Procedia - Social and Behavioral Sciences*, *171*, 1420–1427.

Cho, Eunae & Allen, Tammy D. (2019). The transnational family: A typology and implications for work-family balance. *Human Resource Management Review*, *29*(1), 76–86.

Cook, Vivian J. (1992). Evidence for multicompetence. *Language Learning*, *42*(4), 557–591.

Cook, Vivian. (Ed.). (2003). *Effects of the second language on the first*. Multilingual Matters.

Cox, Michelle & Zawacki, Terry M. (Eds.). (2011). WAC and second language writing: Cross-field research, theory, and program development [Special issue]. *Across the Disciplines*, *8*(4). https://wac.colostate.edu/atd/special/ell/.

DePalma, Michael-John & Ringer, Jeff. (2013). Adaptive transfer, writing across the curriculum, and second language writing: Implications for research and teaching. In Michelle Cox & Terry Myers Zawacki (Eds.), *WAC and second language writers: Research towards developing linguistically and culturally inclusive programs and practices*. The WAC Clearinghouse; Parlor Press. https://doi.org/10.37514/PER-B.2014.0551.

Diner, Hasia R. (1998). Ethnicity and emotions in America: Dimensions of the unexplored. In Peter N. Stearns & Jan Lewis (Eds.), *An Emotional History of the United States* (pp. 197–217). NYU Press.

Donahue, Christiane. (2009). "Internationalization" and composition studies: Reorienting the discourse. *College Composition and Communication*, *61*(2), 212–243.

Dovchin, Sender & Lee, Jerry Won (2019). Introduction to special issue: "The ordinariness of translinguistics." *International Journal of Multilingualism*, *16*(2), 1–7.

Duany, Jorge. (2008) Quisqueya on the Hudson: The transnational identity of Dominicans in Washington Heights. *CUNY Academic Works*. http://academicworks.cuny.edu/dsi_pubs/1.

Fránquiz, Maria E & Ortiz, Alba A. (2017) Who are the *transfronterizos* and what can we learn from them? *Bilingual Research Journal*, *40*(2), 111–115.

Frost, Robert. (1915). Mending wall. In *North of Boston* (pp. 11–13). Henry Holt and Company.

Fuller, Steve. (1991). Disciplinary boundaries and the rhetoric of the social sciences. *Poetics Today*, *12*(2), 301–325.

Gieryn, Thomas F. (1983). Boundary-work and the demarcation of science from non-science: Strains and interests in professional ideologies of scientists. *American Sociological Review*, *48*(6), 781–795.

Glick Schiller, Nina. Glick, Linda Green Basch, L. & Cristina. Szanton Blanc, C. (1995). From immigrant to transmigrant: Theorizing transnational migration." *Anthropological Quarterly*, *68*(1), 48–63.

Guston, David H. (1999). Stabilizing the boundary between U.S. politics and science: The role of the Office of Technology Transfer as a boundary organization. *Social Studies of Science, 29*(1), 87–111.

Hall, Joan Kelly, Cheng, An & Carlson, Matthew T. (2006). Reconceptualizing multi-competence as a theory of language knowledge. *Applied Linguistics, 27*(2), 220–240.

Hall, Jonathan & Navarro, Nela. (2011). Lessons for WAC/WID from language learning research: Multicompetence, register acquisition, and the college writing student. *Across the Disciplines. 8*(4). https://doi.org/10.37514/ATD-J.2011.8.4.21.

Hall, Jonathan. (2009). WAC/WID in the next America: Re-thinking professional identity in the age of the multilingual majority. *The WAC Journal, 20*, 33–47. https://doi.org/10.37514/WAC-J.2009.20.1.03.

Horner, Bruce, Lu, Min-Zhan, Royster, Jacqueline Jones & Trimbur, John. (2011). Language difference in writing: Toward a translingual approach. *College English, 73*(3), 303–321.

Jahn, Thomas, Bergmann, Mattias & Keil, Florian. (2012). Transdisciplinarity: Between mainstreaming and marginalization. *Ecological Economics, 79*, 1–10.

Johns, Ann M. (2001). ESL students and WAC programs: Varied populations and diverse needs. In Susan H. McLeod, Eric Miraglia, Margot Soven, Christopher Thaiss & Susan H. McLeod (Eds.), *WAC for the new millennium: Strategies for continuing writing-across-the-curriculum programs* (pp. 141–164). The WAC Clearinghouse. (Originally published in 2001 by NCTE). https://wac.colostate.edu/books/landmarks/millennium/.

Johns, Ann. (Ed.). (2005). The linguistically-diverse student: Challenges and possibilities across the curriculum [Special issue]. *Across the Disciplines, 2.* https://wac.colostate.edu/atd/special/lds/.

Kellman, Steven G. (2000). *The translingual imagination.* University of Nebraska Press.

Kivisto, Peter. (2001). Theorizing transnational immigration: A critical review of current efforts. *Ethnic and Racial Studies, 24*(4), 549–577.

Klein, Julie Thompson. (1996). *Crossing boundaries: Knowledge, disciplinarities, and interdisciplinarities.* Charlottesville: University of Virginia Press.

Kordos, Marcel & Vojtovic, Sergej. (2016). Transnational corporations in the global world economic environment. *Procedia - Social and Behavioral Sciences, 230*, 150158.

Körner, Axel. (2017). Transnational history: Identities, structures, states. In Barbara Haider-Wilson, William. D. Godsey & Wolfgang Mueller (Eds.), *International history in theory and practice* (pp. 265–290). Verlag Der Österreichische Akademie Der Wissenschaften.

Kubota, Ryuko. (2014). The multi/plural turn, postcolonial theory, and neoliberal multiculturalism: Complicities and implications for applied linguistics. *Applied Linguistics, 37*, 474–494.

Kuus, Merje. (2017). Transnational institutional fields: Positionality and generalization in the study of diplomacy. *Political Geography, 43*(17), 163–171.

Lee, Eunjeong & Canagarajah, Suresh. (2018). The connection between transcultural dispositions and translingual practices in academic writing. *Journal of Multicultural Discourses*, 1–15.

Lee, Jerry Won & Jenks, Christopher. (2016). Doing translingual dispositions. *College Composition and Communication, 68*(2), 317.

Levitt, Peggy & Jaworsky, B. Nadya. (2007), Transnational migration studies: past developments and future trends. *Annual Review of Sociology,* 33(1) 129–156.

Lu, Min-Zhan & Horner, Bruce. (2013). Translingual literacy, language difference, and matters of agency. *College English*, 75(6), 582–607.

Lu, Min-Zhan & Horner, Bruce. (2016). Introduction: Translingual work. *College English*, 78(3), 207–218.

Macdonald, Simon. (2013). *Transnational history: A review of past and present scholarship.* UCL Centre for Transnational History.

Marshall, Miguel. (2019, June 6). El estilo de vida transfronterizo. Foro Económico Mundial. https://es.weforum.org/agenda/2019/06/el-estilo-de-vida-transfronterizo/.

Martin, James R. (2000). Design and practice: Enacting functional linguistics. *Annual Review of Applied Linguistics*, 20, 116–126.

Martins, David S. (2014). *Transnational writing program administration.* Utah State University Press.

Matsuda, Paul Kei & Jablonski, Jeffrey. (2000). Beyond the L2 metaphor: Towards a mutually transformative model of ESL/WAC collaboration. *Academic Writing: Interdisciplinary Perspectives on Communication across the Curriculum, 1.*

Max-Neef, Artur Manfred. (2005). Foundations of transdisciplinarity. *Ecological Economics*, 53, 5–16.

Miller, Kerby A. (1988). *Emigrants and exiles: Ireland and the Irish exodus to North America* (Reprint edition). Oxford University Press.

Nicolescu, Basarab. (2010). Methodology of transdisciplinarity: Levels of reality, logic of the included middle, and complexity. *Transdisciplinary Journal of Engineering & Science*1(1), 20.

O'Connor, Brendan H. (2019). "Everything went boom": Kinship narratives of transfronterizo university students. *The Journal of Latin American and Caribbean Anthropology,* 24(1), 242–262.

Osborne, Peter. (2015). Problematizing disciplinarity, transdisciplinary problematics. *Theory, Culture & Society,* 32(5–6), 3–35.

Pennycook, Alastair. (2008). Translingual English. *Australian Review of Applied Linguistics*, 31(3), 30.1–30.9.

Portes, Alejandro, Guarnizo, Luis E & Landolt, Patricia. (1999). The study of transnationalism: Pitfalls and promise of an emergent research field. *Ethnic & Racial Studies*, 22(2), 217–237.

Riesch, Hauke. (2010). Theorizing boundary work as representation and identity. *Journal for the Theory of Social Behaviour,* 40(4), 452–473.

Robinson, Heather, Hall, Jonathan & Navarro, Nela. (2020). *Translingual identities and transnational realities in the U.S. college classroom.* Routledge.

Sheller, Mimi & Urry, John. (2006). The new mobilities paradigm. *Environment and Planning A: Economy and Space,* 38(2), 207–226.

Solano-Campos, Ana. (2014). The Making of an International Educator: Transnationalism and Nonnativeness in English Teaching and Learning. *TESOL Journal,* 5(3), 412–443.

Soong, Hannah. (2015). *Transnational students and mobility: Lived experiences of migration* (1st ed.). Routledge.

Stryker, Susan, Currah, Paisley & Moore, Lisa Jean. (2008). Introduction: Trans-, trans, or transgender? *WSQ: Women's Studies Quarterly, 36*(3), 11–22.
Thaiss, Chris, Bräuer, Gerd, Carlino, Paula, Ganobcsik-Williams, Lisa & Sinha, Aparna. (Eds.). (2012). *Writing programs worldwide: Profiles of academic writing in many places.* The WAC Clearinghouse; Parlor Press. https://doi.org/10.37514/PER-B.2012.0346.
Verdery, Ashton. M, Mouw, Ted, Edelblute, Heather & Chavez, Sergio. (2018). Communication flows and the durability of a transnational social field. *Social Networks, 53,* 57–71.
Vertovec, Steven. (1999). Conceiving and researching transnationalism. *Ethnic & Racial Studies, 22*(2), 447–462.
Vertovec, Steven. (2007). Super-diversity and its implications. *Ethnic and Racial Studies, 30*(6), 1024–1054.
Vertovec, Steven. (2009). *Transnationalism.* Routledge.
Villa-Torres, Laura, González-Vázquez, Tonatiuh, Fleming, Paul. J, González-González, Edgar Leonel. L., Infante-Xibille, César, Chavez, Rebecca & Barrington, Clare. (2017). Transnationalism and health: A systematic literature review on the use of transnationalism in the study of the health practices and behaviors of migrants. *Social Science & Medicine, 183,* 70–79.
Wu, Xi. (2017). Transnational students and mobility: Lived experiences of migration. *Asia Pacific Journal of Education,* 37(3), 418–420.
Yildiz, Yasmin. (2011). *Beyond the mother tongue: The postmonolingual condition.* Fordham University Press.
Zawacki, Terry M & Cox, Michelle. (Eds.). (2014). *WAC and second language writers: research towards linguistically and culturally inclusive programs and practices.* The WAC Clearinghouse; Parlor Press. https://doi.org/10.37514/PER-B.2014.0551.
Zenger, Amy, Haviland, Carol & Mullin, Joan. (2013). Reconstructing teacher roles through a transnational lens: Learning with/in the American University of Beirut. In Michelle Cox & Terry M. Zawacki (Eds.), *WAC and second language writers: Research towards developing linguistically and culturally inclusive programs and practices.* The WAC Clearinghouse; Parlor Press. https://doi.org/10.37514/PER-B.2014.0551.2.17.
Zentella, Ana Celia. (2009). *Transfronterizo talk: Conflicting constructions of bilingualism on the US-Mexico border.* https://scholarship.tricolib.brynmawr.edu/handle/10066/14611.

"We are the 'Other'": The Future of Exchanges between Writing and Language Studies

Christiane Donahue
DARTMOUTH COLLEGE

Years ago at a biannual Watson Conference at the University of Louisville, in the "wrap-up" final Saturday morning open discussion, luminaries in the field raised the question of language study and teaching in relation to writing study and teaching. In the room were scholars and teachers invested in first-year composition, second-language writing, writing in the disciplines, and other writing domains. "I do not teach 'language,' I teach writing," stated a highly-influential, respected, and thoughtful colleague emphatically, and heads nodded. The lively debate that ensued highlighted a question that we cannot afford to marginalize: what is the relationship, in U.S. writing studies, between scholarship about writing and scholarship about language?[1] What should it be?

The growing transnational work in the US is opening up new ways to answer these questions as well as reminding us of longstanding efforts to do so, in a very complex network of questions about language and teaching and writing and disciplines, disciplinary boundaries, intrinsic goals, and defining the epistemological edges to our work. Attention to these questions is itself transnational.

> La mondialisation de la communication, la multiplication des échanges professionnels entre des personnes appartenant à des communautés linguistiques et culturelles diverses ainsi que la pluralité des supports de diffusion de ces échanges impliquent de mieux connaître les modes de fonctionnement des discours qui émanent de ces communautés et de mettre en lumière les traits spécifiques qui les caractérisent. (von Munchow & Rakotonoelina, 2006, p. 9).

Both A. Suresh Canagarajah (1996) and Mary Muchiri et al. (1995) noted decades ago that compositionists have made claims about academic writing, knowledge, and language from a particularly U.S.-centric position, something simply no longer tenable in this increasingly interrelated world context.

---

[1] I use "Writing Studies" as a term meant to encompass all of the many domains of writing work—research and teaching—today: WAC, WID, first-year composition, multimodal composition, writing didactics, academic literacies, technical-professional writing, and so on.

Bruce Horner (2006) notes that globalization, while increasing what seems to be a monolingual dependence on English, is in fact fragmenting that English in ways that make a focus on single-standard English quite misguided. Claire Kramsch (2014) notes in parallel that foreign language teachers were traditionally prepared to teach a new or different language to students who all shared another language—essentially, a monolingual ideology underpinning foreign language teaching. For Kramsch, it is time to reject the "standard monolingual native speaker as our ideal," embracing instead the "living multilingual subject" in language teaching (Kramsch, 2014, p. 251; see also Heidrick, 2006 and Cook, 1992 among others). And Kramsch points to L2 users' impatience with monolithic "standard" language rules as they play with language across modes, media, contexts, and varieties; their goal is communication. These learner expectations do not mesh with traditional teaching.

Kramsch's point fits into a national trend in which "departments of English and foreign language in particular see the reshaping of their curricula as essential for responding to shifting educational needs and student interests," and foreign language programs can really be affected—the increase in global studies efforts and programs usually calls out more language training, in speech but also in writing (Schultz, 2011, p. 66), and transdisciplinary programs such as the one described by Alyssa Cavazos et al. (2018), (modern languages, applied linguistics, and composition-rhetoric) facilitate exchanges about writing and language coursework. This increased pressure, coupled with new ways of conceptualizing what that teaching does and is, makes the discussions about foreign language writing instruction highly relevant.

"Others"?

The "other" in my title is meant to suggest that there are disciplinary and epistemological domains that have been pitched as oppositional to the detriment of our collective, collaborative work; "we are the other" suggests that perhaps language and writing studies are closer than we think, certainly a proximity that defines work on writing in some countries. There are additional layers to this "other"ness. U.S. writing studies seems to sometimes "other" writing instruction and research in countries outside the US that might have different teaching and research traditions. The field of writing studies has also, at least according to some, seemed for the most part to "other" the language fields of second-language writing, foreign language writing, and linguistics within the US, both for their practices and for the disciplines that inform their scholarship. Those same disciplines, interestingly, are often the ones also shaping writing research and teaching around the world—research that has also been depicted as marginalized (Horner et al., 2011). Translation studies and comparative literature scholarship have treated transnational and translingual subjects for decades but are rarely included in U.S. writing scholarship. World-wide, deeply plurilingual contexts such as in Africa or Europe have driven writing research in ways from which U.S. scholars could draw important insights (*cf.* Arezki, 2018; Belondo, 2011; Kara-Abbès, Kebbas & Blanchet 2011; Kara-Abbès, Kebbas & Cortier 2011; Ndamba, 2018; Peeters, 2011; Prasad 2014; Rasoloniaina, 2011; Reimer, 2018; Rispail 2011). Some of this work raises essential questions in new ways, as for example in French scholarship calling for a "decolonization" of multilingualism in the face of societal interdiction and scholarly hesitancy to take on the "other-ness" of linguistic diversity (Prax-Dubois, 2019). And finally, foreign language writing instruction is perceived as the "other" in L2 writing (Reichelt, 2011).

In thinking about these "others" I do not want to try to address deeply, here, any of the frequently-posed questions about whether second-language writing and writing studies are distinct fields or disciplines (Matsuda, 1999; Silva & Leki, 2004; Silva et al., 1997); whether second-language writing indeed is "situated at the intersection of second language studies and composition studies" (Silva et al., 1997, p. 399); whether the two "intellectual formations" (Matsuda, 1999) should or should not merge; or whether the division is rather between applied linguistics and composition studies (Silva & Leki, 2004). I can say with some certainty, however, that there have been communication challenges among these fields, as suggested also by Guillaume Gentil (2018), within the US and in global interactions, and, in a related debate, more generally among scholars who feel writing faculty teach language, and those who feel we do not, as I noted above. That question has led to the marginalization that scholars like Paul Kei Matsuda (2006) have described, noting that "second-language issues have remained peripheral to composition studies" (p. 571), or to the warnings about the ways L1 scholarship and teaching might negatively impact L2 writers' learning and progress (Leki, 2006).[2] Tony Silva et al. (1997) argued already decades ago for much more interaction between composition and second language studies, to the benefit of both, and Jean Marie Schultz (2011) has suggested that "the potential bi-directional effect of writing instruction in both the L1 and the L2 holds exciting potential for significant linguistic and rhetorical cross-fertilization" (p. 73).

I will put my focus on how *language* and *linguistics* in general have been othered, and how a transnational framing might offer an opportunity that we must not miss to think differently—a path, a prompt, and a provocation—serving as catalyst for exchange and collaboration and making "the language question" essentially unavoidable for U.S. writing scholars, in the way it has already been unavoidable around the world.

---

2   Note that a range of complex questions is linked to this central question, but cannot be taken up here: questions about "2nd" language writing, the field of applied linguistics, whether L2 writing is field of its own or part of composition or Writing Studies, etc. These questions raise further questions about "the field," who "we/us" are when invoked in scholarly works, discipline(s)—see Horner (2018) and Donahue (2018) for further discussion.

International, Global, Mobile, Superdiverse, Transnational . . .

The terms "international" and "global" are sometimes used interchangeably, but differentiating them is useful in the context of writing research and writing program administration. Internationalizing is built from the starting point of "nations" and then imagines "inter"-nation interactions. "Internationalizing higher education" tends towards the idea that U.S. colleges might expand their reach, establish campuses overseas, or draw additional students from other countries. Globalization, on the other hand, generally draws on such questions as increasing economic interdependence, the "shrinking" of the world stage (driven in part by social media and the internet), and the re-hierarchizing of multinational corporations over nation-states. Unlike "internationalization," with no "nation-" in its root, "globalization" focuses our attention on common experiences driven by something other than nation-state configurations.

Another useful concept, this time from social geography, is "mobility." This frame, drawn into writing studies in the past decade or so (cf. Blommaert & Horner, 2017; Lorimer Leonard, 2013; Nordquist, 2017; Ploog et al., 2020), can offer additional insights into the shifting nature of society, a nature that can only influence higher education in multiple interrelated ways, a human geography that serves to make sense of the geographical nature of being-in-the-world today (Verstraete & Cresswell, 2002; see also Horner, this volume). A mobility perspective considers place as radically open and permeable (Verstraete & Cresswell, 2002). In this model, the stability of place and of one's place that we seem to have counted on becomes less foundational, replaced by an expectation that people will move, travel, engage, whether virtually or in person, whether in real time or asynchronously, in every lived context.

While terms such as "global" or "international" have been used frequently in the past couple of decades of attention to writing studies' scope in contexts outside of the US, including by me, perhaps it is "transnationalism" that can best decenter the U.S.-centric perspective, moving us into a "trans" frame, rather than an "inside-outside" one (see Horner, this volume, for a deep exploration of the affordances connected to the "trans" frame). "Transnational" is understood most commonly as "*working across* national contexts." Steven Vertovec (2009), noting the massive expansion of interest in transnational issues, describes transnationalism as "economic, social, and political linkages between people, places, and institutions crossing nation-state borders and spanning the world . . . sustained cross-border relationships, patterns of exchange, affiliations and social formations." Earlier, Vertovec (1999) explored transnationalism as the interaction between country of origin and new country, via migrants and migration, noting that both home country and new country become a site of social action in which migrants operate (cited in Dahinden, 2009). This transnational interaction evolved in intensity and simultaneity (Dahinden, 2009). For Dahinden, two types of transnationalism took shape: diasporic transnationalism, which is grounded in economic investment and close ties between home and new, and an evolving "transnationalism in mobility" which understands transnationalism not as the exploration of movement from one space to another to settle there but a "circular, perpetual, and permanent mobility" (Dahinden, 2009, p. 3) which is in fact part of the strategy of the mobile. "[T]o be transnational involves a mode of acting and performing (i.e. building up transnational social relations and practices) as much as it involves a mode of thinking, feeling and belonging" (Université de Neuchatel, Faculté des lettres et sciences humaines, Laboratoire d'études des processus sociaux, n.d.).

If we take the three prongs of Hall's exploration of "trans" as linked to the transnational (this volume), we can see the richness of the frame: "trans" as transition, as betweenness, and as "beyond-ness" would lead to understanding the transnational as more than only working across, but as working in-between national spaces and eventually working beyond "nation" and "national" while still recognizing the modes in which nations do exist and work. To pick up on the distinction Benedict Anderson made of "imagined communities" that ML Pratt further developed decades ago, nations imagine themselves to be sovereign, bounded, and fraternal—which they both are and are not. We face both the reality of some forms of border (after all, walls, checkpoints, borders, armies, and actions of heads of state who perceive sovereignty exist) and the reality of fluidity, porosity, connectivity that is often beyond the control of agents and institutions. As Gentil (this volume) suggests, there are *both* national/regional challenges and transnational challenges. It is particularly connected to a translingual perspective on fluidity in language and writing (and other) practices, to "translingualism as a diverse and strategic social practice" (Canagarajah and Gao, 2019, p. 3).

These transnational questions do not, of course, uniquely belong to composition studies nor to U.S. scholarship, but are prevalent in other contexts and disciplines. "*Si le transnationalisme est considéré comme une incise épistémologique dans l'histoire des sciences sociales, c'est parce que ce courant de recherche révèle à la pensée sociologique elle-même le nationalisme méthodologique qui l'a habité*" (Lacroix, 2018, p. 7). Transnationalism as a strand of sociology has allowed sociology to see itself as "methodologically nationalistic." This trend allows the home country to be the automatic point of reference and, equally importantly, leaves scholars unable to carry out research outside of a "nation-state" framework; it also seems to me to underscore the frequency with which we tend to say "other than" English or "outside of" the US in this same referential way. (See also Schneider 2019; Shajahan & Kezar, 2013; and Wimmer & Glick Schiller, 2002, who focus in particular on methodological nationalism in higher education research). The social sciences and in particular migration studies have been "epistemologically straightjacketed," which encourages scholars to miss the dynamic in play, "transcending the symbolic and spatial limits of the State, and in particular those brought on by human migration" (Lacroix, 2018, p. 7). Peggy Levitt and Nina Glick Schiller (2004) further note that traditional approaches can obscure the social processes and institutions in play. They call for scholars to rethink and reformulate the concept of society such that it is no longer automatically equated with the boundaries of a single nation state.

But as Ludger Pries and Martin Seeliger (2012) note in their chapter in *Beyond Methodological Nationalism: Research Methodologies for Cross-Border Studies*, while it has become clear that the critique of methodological nationalism is essential, it is also important to remember the weight and influence of national analyses, to not "dissolve the geographic-spatial bonding of the social into the air of deterritorialization, spaces of flows and global cosmopolitanism" (p. 219). This same point is good to keep in mind for our understanding of language(s). Gentil (this volume) reminds us that fluid, mixed, meshed understandings are important, but so is acknowledgement of the reality that even if socially constructed, the discreteness of languages still powers much of our daily linguistic understanding, and Ofelia García and Li Wei (2014) note that the linguistic repertoire that is one comprehensive and dynamic repertoire still works with features that are "socially constructed as belonging to separate languages" (p. x). These conceptual conversations and trends in other disciplines, for example migration studies, are deeply valuable to composition as we make our way into this territory and underscore the degree to which we need to understand and attend to language knowledge in order to be effective participants in the conversation.

Work in transnational writing research thus demands that we think beyond, that we focus on the ways in which language and writing intersect and align in other traditions in the world. In Europe, for example, the linguistics research tradition, cross-pollinated with the tradition in *la didactique* as part of education sciences, anchors higher education writing research firmly in language study as part of writing study, or maybe more as two parts of the same thing. When we start working with transnational assumptions about language, culture, affiliations, patterns of exchange, and the ways they shape literate activity, we end up needing to understand the language relationships as wholly integrated into our questions about literacy, and we thus need to understand language itself, how it functions, what it does.

Transnational movements are making it necessary for us and for our students to engage with language when we engage with writing, whether in terms of writing and English or in terms of writing and any language in the world. Because of their focus on social and economic mixing, inevitability of movement, or heterogeneous communities and communications, the phenomena raise questions about what constitutes "literate competence," a broad term that can be used in any writing domain. Questions can include those about the qualitative difference between people who are (apparently) monolingual vs bi- or multi-lingual: difference in metalinguistic awareness, for example, or in cognitive processes (Cook, 1992).

For years now, scholars have been identifying the changing nature of student writers in those contexts. In the US, Silva and Matsuda (2001), Matsuda, Michelle Cox, Jay Jordan, and Christina Ortmeier-Hooper (2006), Christine Tardy (2011), Irwin Weiser and Shirley Rose (2018), and many others have been pointing to the increasing diversity of U.S. society and higher education landscapes, including of course U.S. writing programs and classrooms. There is no doubt that the population in U.S. higher education is rapidly changing. But this is a change that, it turns out, like so many things, is shared around the globe. European institutions are seeing high rates of international enrollees, from across Europe (encouraged by the Bologna Process) but also from Asia, South America, and Africa; my Korean colleagues report high numbers of students from China seeking to complete their education in Korean universities; and so on.

But this change within our classrooms is only part of the picture. The change is also, more universally perhaps, to the world in which graduates will do their work and live their lives. The workforce of the 21st century is highly mobile and diverse, whether because of employee travel outward (from the migrant farm worker to the CEO) or place-of-work reception of employees from diverse locales and contexts. As research in mobility studies has amply demonstrated, for both positive and challenging or traumatic reasons many people today are on the move in the work world. It remains to be seen how the COVID–19 pandemic will have changed the ways in which people are "on the move," but I believe that change will be in mode rather than in substance, and in some ways we will have seen mobility increase.

That diversity has done nothing but grow, to the point where Vertovec (2007, 2009) and Jan Blommaert (2013) among others have suggested we are in an era of "superdiversity." This evocative term first developed in reference to migration phenomena and their effects on the social, cultural, and linguistic fabric in British metropolitan areas, but it seems clearly adaptable to world-wide trends in movement—both forced and chosen—of people. It has become a term of force in the 21st century. Adrian Blackledge and Angela Creese (2017) recently explored both "diversity" and "superdiversity" to highlight the limitations of concepts such as diversity, multiculturalism, integration, or assimilation in "their power to explain the complexity of contemporary societies" (p. 2) and to sharply remind us that this superdiversity is born of both positive and negative mobilities within and across borders: "migration, invasion, colonization, slavery, religious mission, persecution, trade, conflict, famine, drought, war, urbanization, academic aspiration, family reunion, global commerce, technological advance . . ." (p. 2).

The sociolinguistic transformations in superdiverse contexts include the transformation of dominant languages. English monolingualism may appear to be inevitable, but in fact "our [monolingual] colleagues need *languages* (emphasis mine) to gain a perspective on themselves and to move beyond the comfortable and mobile milieu in which they live" (Tonkin, 2001; cited in Schultz, 2011, p. 72). As language questions move us into new milieux, we (re)discover the other we have been thinking was alien to us in our more recent history. As Mikhail Bakhtin (1986) suggests, "the self comes into existence only by virtue of its relationship to all that is other" (Nystrand et al., 1993, p. 294). This relationship suggests a different way to think about the writing-language dynamic, by looking back at U.S. writing studies via elements of language study.

Language . . .

How did U.S. writing scholarship move from the entrenched trio of literary theory, composition, and linguistics cited by Martin Nystrand et al. (1993) to the "I am not a language teacher" and the marginalization of linguistics research in writing studies?[3] From the late 1970s on, certainly conceptualizations of writing changed in ways that de-emphasized direct interest in language. Nystrand et al. noted in 1993 that "[w]hereas ideas about composition were traditionally limited to analyses of text features, subsequent and more recent models have conceptualized writing in terms of cognitive and social processes" (p. 306), that shift burgeoned into new directions less anchored in linguistics.

"Linguistics" or "linguistic science" is of course not a monolith; Chomskyans are not functionalists or pragmatists, and applied linguists work differently than theoretical linguists. The L2 writing scholarship is grounded, primarily, in applied linguistics, and I would like to explore the relationship to linguistics in other forms.

If we want to use the notion of "other" to explore the ways in which language studies and writing studies interconnect, we need a sense of when these domains became "othered" in the US. The question of language was certainly not always held at arm's length nor divided from writing studies. It is a complicated question I'll simply sketch here. Nystrand et al. (1993), in their detailed analysis of the development in the US of what was at the time understood as composition studies, reference deep interrelated epistemological and research connections involving language and writing in the 1960s–1970s. Every phase of their extensive review is based on theories of and research about *language* and *language use*. Indeed, many of the foundational thinkers they cite are linguists, from Searle or Grice or Austin to Bakhtin, van Dijk, or Beaugrande. They remind us of the essential role played

---

3 This has been the case until quite recently. In perhaps an example of the cyclical nature of trends in research and theory, the effect of "big data" and the availability of very large corpora, alongside technological development in computational linguistics, has ushered in a new period of attention to linguistic methods in composition.

by sociolinguist Labov in turning scholarly understanding from deficit models to speech community models of language variety, enabling the work of many writing scholars, including Mina Shaughnessy.

Another factor was the link between speech, foreign language teaching, and language vs. writing. Eli Hinkel (2010) notes that successful foreign language programs, heavily influenced by structural linguistics, focused on speech. Even though scholars such as Widdowson (1978) pushed against any separation of the four essential skills of reception and production of both speech and writing (cited in Hinkel, 2010), it is possible that linguistics seemed increasingly distant to writing scholars because of its strong connection to speech. Matsuda (1999) clearly notes this challenge in the evolution of work in second language writing, which might suggest the same phenomenon developing in writing studies more broadly. And finally, structuralism itself, a foundation for both linguistics and literary theory (two of the three fields Nystrand et al. take into account), fell out of favor, while U.S. composition studies moved towards its own identity, grounded in social construction and critical theory, both antithetical to structuralist accounts of language, writing, and composing.

And why might it be time to come back? Language has always been inextricably at the heart of writing research and teaching, but it is now so starkly clear in its centrality that U.S. writing studies must reimagine its relationships of exchange. Matsuda's comprehensive review of what he calls the "disciplinary division of labor" (1999, p. 700) provides ample evidence that language questions even in the specific domain of second language writing were rarely present in various signature histories of the discipline to that point, histories that Silva, Ilona Leki, and Joan Carson (1997) call ethnocentric. I do not think this has radically changed since, though there have been many works attending to the history leading to the current landscape (just a quick sampling could include Jun, 2008; Leki et al., 2008; Matsuda 2003, 2005; Santos et al., 2000).

In this framing, inevitably questions about the deep field of *second* language study will arise—the one facet of language that is embedded in writing studies discussions today, even if far less than the second language writing community has argued is necessary. Matsuda (1999) reports an emphasis, in earlier decades, on linguistic training for writing teachers (especially if they were to teach second-language students) and the roots of disciplinary division coming in part at that point. He suggests that structural linguistics encouraged, in the 1960s, the development of separate ESL classes with specifically-trained faculty, a move that ultimately contributed to waning attention to language issues in writing classrooms, programs, or initiatives. While his emphasis is on the declining interest in language issues, he notes specifically that this decline was about second-language components.

Silva et al. (1997) focused certainly on second language writing, but also and significantly on "other" language writing alongside, making a similar philosophical case for "broadening the perspective" of composition studies' work. They predicted decades back that the absence of attention to writing in other languages, in our history, could even have the huge effect of leading to "inadequate theories of composition" (p. 400) overall:

> A theory of writing based on only one rhetorical tradition and one language can at best be extremely tentative and at worst totally invalid. Such a theory could easily become hegemonic and exclusionary; that is, English/Western writing behaviors could be privileged as being "standard" . . . and such a theory could be seen as monolingual, monocultural, and ethnocentric. (p. 402)

Note that this point underscores not only an openness to other languages but also to other traditions and other disciplines. The U.S. focus in the scholarship I have cited here is partly because some parts of what I report here are in fact from particular U.S. traditions that have not taken shape in the same way in other countries or contexts; transnational work helps to bring that into focus. But it is also the case that whatever scholarship *is* available, scholarship that would help build the more complete theory of writing Silva et al. call for, is much broader than the U.S. pool of English-medium scholarship; we just don't often see it. In addition, the writing studies ⇔ language studies split that I've been focusing on here is a U.S.-specific split; many other traditions have divided disciplinary labor and inspired disciplinary liaisons differently, rooted in different grounds, often published not in English, and developing careful attention to disciplinary structures and epistemologies. When we engage with scholarship because the transnational context demands it, we grow the models Silva et al. mention with broader disciplinary contributions, broader concerns about writing, and a much wider swath of research not published in English.

French scholars, theorists, and linguists, for example, have worked on these topics for a very long time. U.S. ethnocentrism and monolingualism (without suggesting the US has cornered the market on these -isms . . .) have enabled ongoing work that does not take these into account, so when we explore topics such as knowledge transfer or the nature of "code," we limit our knowledge base. Transnational approaches to research demand that we grow our knowledge base, including in terms of languages in which we read and disciplines from which we consider drawing. As Cavazos et al. note, transdisciplinary work becomes essential to transnational work as it evolves; "engaging in transdisciplinary conversations with our colleagues [in other disciplines] is critical in responding to the linguistic needs and assets of our students" (2018, p. 21; see also Hebbard & Hernandez, 2020; Hendricks, 2018).

Such a return to language questions entails, as well, attention to English, specifically, in relation to U.S. composition. A progressive view of English, as Englishes, has been amply developed in composition and much more extensively in sociolinguistics (cf. Ives, 2015; Matsuda & Matsuda, 2010; Nihalani, 2010; Tupas & Rudby, 2015; Saxena & Omoniyi, 2010). It directly raises a question that both second language writing and writing in any discipline or context must engage head-on: is writing about English, in the US, and if it is, which English? Here as well, linguists support our inquiry. Ruanni Tupas and Rani Rudby (2015), for example, argue that "There is no one English but many Englishes. No one has exclusive rights to the language; anyone who speaks it has the right to own it" (p. 1). As early as 1985, linguist Dell Hymes was already stating unequivocally that "the functional equality of all languages has been a tenet of the faith from the founders of structural linguistics to most practitioners of linguistics today" (p. v). If we accept this view we must engage in questions of class and power and equity; while both writing research and second-language writing research in the US, each in its own way, have done so, neither has ultimately resolved the fraught question of the role of a particular English in college writing, first-year and, perhaps even more, across the disciplines.

As much as there has been tension in the applied linguistics/second language ⇔ composition/writing studies interactions, heightened by the later-developed translingual scholarship (see for example Atkinson et al., 2015; Canagarajah, 2015; Hall, 2018; and multiple chapters in the 2020 volume *Reconciling Translingualism and Second Language Writing* including those by Matsuda, Tardy, Nancy Bou Ayash, and Brooke Schreiber), there is no question that these interactions are also bringing key attention back to language. Silva and Leki's 2004 treatment of applied linguistics and composition in relation to second language writing underscores essential differences in paradigms, traditions, and scope, and suggests that the separation between second-language work and composition was a mutual moving-apart. But they quite powerfully detail the similarities and argue that "it might be preferable for L2 writing to consider reconciling the differences between its parent disciplines" (2004, p. 10), pulling from both applied linguistics and composition studies.

Translingual and translanguaging scholarship, as well as the MLA with its 2007 report *Higher Education: New Structures for a Changed World*, have pushed new attention on language in writing, the kind of attention L2 scholars have been advocating, by attending to a changing understanding of language and language practices (and as another example of how we sometimes focus with blinders on, the same attention is given in other fields and contexts to translingualism in centuries of history and in all ages and grade levels—it is far from unique to college writing concerns). Horner (2006) asks that compositionists move towards "an explicit policy that embraces multilingual, cross-language writing as the norm for our teaching and research" (p. 570). This kind of call, multiplied across the past decade, cannot leave composition scholars lukewarm and begs us to learn much more about (trans) language—about the rhetorical assets of our students, their "already-sophisticated and diverse language and writing abilities" (Cavazos et al., 2019)—for which we must learn more about language.

The way we use the terms we use becomes part of this attention to language. That is, attention to language also means attention to the language we use, to clarification and differentiation and depth in our terminology, as Gentil (this volume) notes when he talks of translingualism, translanguaging, and the possibilities of terms such as crosslingualism, biliteracy, or transliteracy. "Translingual" and "translanguage" invoke different aspects of language practice, as do codeswitching or codemeshing (see above, Creese & Blackledge, 2017, as well, on terminology and clarity). Terms are introduced, take hold, and can ultimately become indexical or be surpassed, transformed. They also can, like the term "transfer," get cemented in use even as multiple scholars note their shortcomings.

Language Research with Benefits to Composition

We can begin to see that if work on college writing had stayed closer to language questions over the years, we might be more ready to understand some of the new challenges to writing in any discipline for the 21st century. We would have, collectively, the full linguistics background to understand claims made about codeswitching, codemixing, and codemeshing or to embrace the distinctions between translingualism and translanguaging, to account for differences among dual literacy (a literacy in two languages with "the added ability to move confidently and smoothly between languages for different purposes" (Estyn, 2002, p. 1), European *plurilinguisme* models that can not only share key principles of translingualism but also clarify that plurilingual repertoires in transnational mobility must be socially valued (Prasad, 2014), or variants of multilingualism that are not additive but rather models of language production, reception, and meta-linguistic awareness in movement (Gentil, this volume).[4]

As an example, the rich field of "contact" linguistics, a subfield of sociolinguistics that surfaced in the 1970s, provides useful underpinnings to studying language mixture, presenting it as "a creative, rule-governed process that affects all languages in one way or another, though to varying degrees" (Winford, 2003, p. 2). It is, according to Winford, quite normal for speakers and writers in contact situations to bypass communicative barriers and compromise in order to communicate, or to use what Pratt (1991) describes as the "literate arts of the contact zone." Many different factors govern this activity—from range of typological similarity of the languages to the spread, dominance, or prestige of each language involved (p. 2). The results of language contact appear in a range, from linguistic diffusion to structural convergence to the blurring altogether of any boundary between the languages (Pratt, 1991).

---

4 I am fully aware of the distinctions some scholars provide among second language and foreign language learning (see Cimasko & Reichelt, 2011; Reichelt, 2011), but here I am trying to clarify a distinction not everyone makes between ESL and "X"SL (say, for example, French as a Second Language, "FLE," literally translated "French as a Foreign Language").

Another example comes from foreign language writing scholarship. As I've noted, "second" language writing is not equivalent to *English* as a second language writing.[5] Research in *foreign language* writing instruction (instruction in languages that are neither a language someone grew up with nor a language that dominates in the context in which a speaker-writer is functioning, per Melinda Reichelt, 2011) has blossomed in recent decades after a long stretch of neglect. Reichelt (2011) notes that "a great deal of FL writing occurs around the world in various contexts" (p. 4), and it is the object of a range of studies of its writers' texts, processes, strategies, and perceptions, the ways it is taught and learned, and contexts of its use and development.

I will now develop, briefly, two key components of language research with reference to how they might inform existing language discussions in writing studies: one is about "transfer" and is grounded in applied linguistics, and the other is about using the term "code" to reference language and is grounded in French functional linguistics. I hope it will be clear that they could also inspire new conversations. Just as the significant European critiques of "transfer" as the term and frame for how writers reuse, adapt, and transform writing knowledge and know-how (Astolfi, 2002; François, 1998; Le Boterf, 1994; Meirieu & Develay, 1996; Perrenoud, 1999) suggest that we need to broaden our knowledge base, the work in socio- and applied linguistics and foreign language writing on key features like "code" opens up new ways to consider them for writing studies. In a way, they bring us back to a claim made by first language, second language, translingual, and foreign language writing scholars alike: language and writing are inextricably wound together, and the different interests of each research group are more productively seen along a continuum than in discrete oppositions.

I'm going to focus in on two brief examples among many possible ones that suggest unexploited knowledge that could help build fruitful exchange between writing and language research. In the process of considering these examples, we might see how the "inadequate theories" predicted by Silva et al. (1997) could be developed and grow to include theories of linguistic transfer and of linguistic code.

Transfer?

In writing studies, attention to this model of knowledge acquisition and reuse has been rapidly developing, but in education and didactics, it has been studied for a

---

5   "Whereas the concept of multilingualism has traditionally been used to describe a speaker's development of equal levels of proficiency in a number of distinct languages, the emerging plurilingual paradigm suggests that individuals develop an interrelated network of a plurality of linguistic skills and practices that they draw on for different purposes in a variety of contexts" (Prasad 2014, p. 52).

century.[6] In exploring this question here I align myself with Michael-John DePalma and Jeff Ringer (2011; 2014), who have thought about "transfer" through the lens of (second) language learning carefully and thoroughly, in particular in reference to WAC teaching and learning. What I suggest here complements and extends that work, in an effort to show how linguistic understandings of "transfer" layer and complicate current U.S. writing studies understandings. DePalma and Ringer note that (1) the "transfer" discussion was embedded in language-learning before it trended in mainstream composition; (2) this conversation has largely focused on reuse more than adaptation (see also Donahue, 2012; 2016b) and "adaptive transfer" offers a more accurate framing; and (3) L2 transfer research has focused in part on how to help students transfer their rhetorical knowledge from one language context to another (DePalma & Ringer, 2014). They define "adaptive transfer as a writer's conscious or intuitive process of applying or reshaping learned writing knowledge in order to negotiate new and potentially unfamiliar writing situations" (DePalma & Ringer, 2011, p. 141). This version is dynamic and transformative.

The meaning of "transfer" in second-language and in foreign language research and teaching (remembering that second-language writing research is richly developed in many languages, not just in English as a Second Language), compared to recent writing studies work, is different—and potentially inter-informing. Linguists and didacticians around the world study the ways a speaker or a writer uses knowledge from one language (usually an "L1") in another language (usually an "L2"), with positive or negative effect (the negative tellingly considered to be "interference").

For example, the research suggests that:

- L1 literacy abilities and strategies do not *automatically* lend themselves to successful work in L2 writing but they also do not *automatically* obstruct work in L2 writing (see among others Saffari et al., 2017).
- The work in first-year writing is, based on what we know from "transfer" research, often simply too dissimilar from what will be required later in various disciplinary and professional contexts for it to help students in later courses (Leki, 2006). For Leki, in the case of L2 students in particular, this is simply not a tenable practice.
- Language transfer is bi-directional; working with two or more languages in fact enriches writers' competence in both languages, for example in developing their ability to write complex sentences in both languages and their cultural sensitivity towards monolingual writers (Schultz, 2011).
- Writers at earlier stages in language acquisition may have more trouble transferring some writing strategies (Wolfersberger, 2003).

---

6   For an overview of transfer in U.S. conversations, try *Critical Transitions: Writing and the Question of Transfer* (Anson & Moore, 2016).

- Well-developed L1 abilities can have long-term positive effects on developing those same abilities in an L2 (Sparks et al., 2009).
- The practices writing teachers and scholars have seen as multimodal are proposed in foreign language research as multilingual, and thus they are forms of transfer in the domain of foreign language; Kramsch (2014) suggests that they include "translating a poem or a song into a picture, a narrative into a visual, and vice-versa" (p. 253).
- Only when "L2" proficiency is well developed enough will "L1" abilities be positively useful to a speaker or writer (Ito, 2009); competence and writing process are very different for students with different language levels, and different kinds of activity thus support "transfer" differently for different kinds of students (Kobayashi & Rinnert, 1992).

These transfer effects are also being studied in relation to multilingualism. Vivian Cook's (1992) framing of multilingual and multicompetent phenomena has proven illuminating. Other scholars such as Ingrid Heidrick (2006) have shown that in speakers and writers learning additional languages, the second language is actually a stronger resource from which the user draws than the first language. As Heidrick notes, "there is no reason why that existing knowledge [to be transferred] should not include previously-learned non-native languages" (2006, p. 1). Indeed, Heidrick seeks to understand what exactly influences the choices multilinguals make in terms of which language(s) they select from for a given utterance (2006). In this subfield, "transfer" of lexical and grammatical structures from one language to another is a productive phenomenon, not an interference. Deep, fundamental empirical research about the functioning of these various forms has led to linguistic conclusions that could nourish the composition discussion.

This language knowledge transfer scholarship is a resource by and large untapped to date in discussions about university writing and knowledge transformation more broadly, across years and disciplines, in the US. And yet each of these points above offers insights into "transfer" that illuminate more general questions about how it might work and how we might enable it as our students move across years and disciplines. The very model of "transfer" as a progression from one learning experience to another is in fact something that scholars interested in language use have questioned. Canagarajah (2006) argues for a much messier and more dynamic process in which students "shuttle" back and forth among a variety of linguistic and discursive elements, in the process transforming the contexts in which they are communicating. We might think about writing knowledge transfer also as "shuttling" rather than linear trajectory. We could also imagine that the work in contrastive rhetoric offers us cultural layers to "transfer." With this lens, variations in writers' approaches and text features are not failures but alternatives (Silva et al., 1997); "transfer," again, is not a linear progression but a layering of useable options for a writer who we can designate as "rhetorically flexible" across time, contexts, and disciplines (Donahue 2016).

My question for this first example is, how might this extensive body of work on language and transfer help the current and rapidly-expanding thinking about writing knowledge and transfer? Are there clues about writing knowledge re-use and adaptation that this work can offer? Can it help us re-imagine the very nature of "transfer"? DePalma and Ringer (2014) suggest that "Narrow conceptualizations of transfer . . . reduce readers to decoders" (p. 46) rather than, I would suggest, dialogic co-constructors of meaning. Can the broader work on language knowledge "transfer" help us to rethink teaching writing?

Code?

Another richly productive connection is in terms of language as "code" (and its connection to terms built on "code," like codeswitching, codemeshing, or codemixing (though see Woodall, 2002, "Language-switching" for an alternative model). These language activities have provoked some strong debate in recent years, taking center stage in discussions of multilinguality, "trans"linguality, second-language writing, and diversity (Canagarajah, 2011; Guerra, 2012; Lu & Horner, 2013; Matsuda, 2013; Young, 2009; Young et al., 2014; Young & Martinez 2011).

If, however, language research and writing research partnerships had already been more frequent, the exchanges might have been different, because they would be grounded in different initial understandings of both "code" and code interaction in the dynamic models of language structure and language use available. The fact that "code" is at the root of several dynamic language terms in our current debates is actually quite interesting. "Code" has been critiqued in some branches of linguistics for some time. It is seen in French linguistics, for example, as a very limiting term that focuses on fixed structures rather than dynamic language practices; a concept much more appropriate to structuralist assumptions about language that many linguists moved beyond by the 1970s or 1980s, around the same time literature was moving away from structuralist and modernist frames, and composition from positivism and empirical research (Nystrand et al., 1997). Transnational work highlights the degree to which language scholarship, in both U.S. linguistics and world-wide writing research from other disciplines including linguistics, clarifies or otherwise illuminates questions in the U.S. writing studies community.

While not every scholar takes "code" head-on the way that the French functional linguists do, many scholars depict language function in ways that suggest an understanding of language that is far more fluid than the structuralist version underpinning code-based models that dominated European and U.S. linguistics for many decades (Matsuda, 1999; Silva & Leki, 2004). As early as the late 1800s, some linguists were arguing that no language comes from a single source (Winford, 2003), a precursor to hybrid or non-code models. Kramsch (2014) asks how language teaching might focus less on language structures and function and more on the social process of "enunciation" ("énonciation" or the actual putting-into-words production of discourse) (p. 8). Cook's multicompetence model (1992) proposes that individuals with multiple languages may be working with a merged language system rather than separate and distinct languages—"codes"—from which speakers or writers pull discrete pieces. Blommaert (2010, cited in Blackledge & Creese, 2017) talks of "language-in-motion" and sociolinguistic transformation; Garcia and Wei (2014) define "translanguaging" as starting "from the speaker rather than the code or the 'language' and focuse[d] on empirically observable practices" in ways similar to French functional linguistics. Translanguaging "refers not simply to a shift or a shuttle between two languages but to the speakers' construction and use of original and complex interrelated discursive practices that cannot be easily assigned to one or another traditional definition of a language" (Garcia & Wei, 2014, p. 14). Building from Goffman, they note that we might be led away from seeing languages as "distinct codes" and rather see "individuals engaged in using, creating, and interpreting signs for communication" (2014, p. 14). This kind of "communicative competence" (Hymes, 1971, cited in Hinkel, 2010) is a way to focus on the communicative value and function of communication in social contexts.

For French linguist Frédéric François, "code" is restricted to accounting in a limited way for what governs lexicon and syntax. He suggests we might use "language codes" to capture the diverse, pluralized, fluid ways language actually works and to help us unpack communicative competence, and reserve "linguistic code" for the limited structural questions (personal correspondence, 2017). In a superdiverse context, language as "code" simply doesn't make sense. I want to note, then, that proponents of both codemeshing and codeswitching—terms used in more than one of the disciplines mentioned earlier—might want to consider the ways in which "code" (and thus presumably the various terms connected to it) might be, linguistically, a term that runs counter to the fluidity, hybridity, and dynamism they support. The distinctions being carefully drawn and argued between codeswitching and codemeshing could be beside the point if the "code" model on which they are built is not the model that works for the kind of language activity in play.

If we start the discussion at "code" we might find ourselves in a different debate. Initial analyses of the regularity and creativity of code-switching (as well as language shift and language creation) arise out of the contact linguistics research mentioned earlier (Winford, 2003), as does the establishment of "conventionalized" mixed languages. In other words, I suggest we back up from the various debates about codeswitching, codemeshing, and codemixing—debates that would themselves benefit from more attention to years of research in the field of "contact linguistics" mentioned earlier, and the well-established definitions and models provided there—to the root debate about the very nature of language.

If it is language in use that interests us, language that shapes and organizes our perceptions (as noted by Vygotsky, cited in Berthoff, 1999), language as symbolic form, with symbols that "derive their meaning from the force of social convention" (Kramsch, 2014, p. 7), then as Blackledge et al. (2013) have argued, we must move beyond "code" in order to shift away from a focus on "languages as distinct codes to a focus on the agency of individuals engaging in using, creating, and interpreting signs for communication" (p. 193). My question to us all, out of this second body of work, is how might linguistics thinking about the nature of language, its resistance (in some branches) to language as "code," be useful to our explorations of students' language use—all students' language use across disciplines and contexts—in writing today? Thinking about the dynamic nature of language seems to me to be our common interest, and one we must take up in preparing our students for the international, global, mobile contexts in which they work and live.

Conclusion

"Transfer" and "code" are just two examples of the potential for deep exchange. What I draw from these really brief examples (so much more could be said!) is that writing studies across time, contexts, disciplines, and expertises in language as connected to writing have the potential to be highly complementary, in response to transnational pressures and promises. Now is the time to collaboratively deepen the pool of expertise in order to best prepare all students in all disciplines for a superdiverse world. We are the other—or maybe, we are each other.

References

Arezki, Abdenour. (2018, May 22–24). *La place dévolue à la culture, à l'interculturalité dans l'enseignement/apprentissage des langues*. Conférence Voix africaines, voies émergentes. Université de Paris Diderot, France.
Astolfi, Jean-Pierre. (2002). *Savoir, c'est pouvoir transférer*. Cahiers Pédagogiques, 408(9).
Bakhtin, Mikhail. (1986). *Speech genres and other late essays*. University of Texas Press.
Berthoff, Ann. (1999). *The mysterious barricades: Language and its limits*. University of Toronto Press.
Belondo, Sandra. (2011, June 14–16). *Perception de la pluralité linguistique et culturelle de jeunes allophones: d'un "handicap" socio-culturel à une "transparence" égalitariste?* Conférence Dynamiques plurilingues: des observations de terrains aux transpositions politiques, éducatives, et didactiques. Ecole Normales Supérieur de Bouzaréa, Algiers, Algeria.

Blackledge, Adrian & Creese, Angela. (2017). Language and superdiversity: An interdisciplinary perspective. Paper number 187 in the Tilburg Papers in Culture Studies, University of Tilburg.

Blackledge, Adrian, Creese, Angela & Takhi, Jaspreet. (2013). Beyond multilingualism: Heteroglossia in practice. In Stephen May (Ed.), *The multilingual turn: Implications for SLA, TESOL and bilingual education* (pp. 191–215). Routledge.

Blommaert, Jan & Horner, Bruce. (2017). Mobility and academic literacies: An epistolary conversation. *London Review of Education, 15*(1), 1–20.

Blommaert, Jan. (2013). Citizenship, language, and superdiversity: Towards complexity. *Journal of Language, Identity and Education, 12*(3), 193–196.

Canagarajah, A. Suresh. (1996). "Nondiscursive" requirements in academic publishing: Material resources of periphery scholars, and the politics of knowledge production. *Written Communication, 13*(4), 435–472.

Canagarajah, A. Suresh. (2006). Toward a writing pedagogy of shuttling between languages: Learning from multilingual writers. *College English, 68*(6), 589–604.

Canagarajah, A. Suresh. (2011). Codemeshing in academic writing: Identifying teachable strategies of translanguaging. *The Modern Language Journal, 95*(3), 401–417.

Canagarajah, A. Suresh. (2015). Clarifying the relationship between translingual practice and L2 writing: Addressing learner identities. *Applied Linguistics Review, 6*(4), 1–30.

Canagarajah, A. Suresh & Gao, Xuesong. (2019). Taking translingual scholarship farther. *English Teaching and Learning, 43*, 1–3.

Cavazos, Alyssa, Hebbard, Marcella, Hernandez, José, Rodriguez, Crystal & Schwarz, Geoffrey (2018). Advancing a transnational, transdisciplinary, and translingual framework: A professional development series for teaching assistants in writing and Spanish programs. *Across the Disciplines, 15*(3), 11–27. https://doi.org/10.37514/ATD-J.2018.15.3.09.

Cimasko, Tony & Reichelt, Melinda. (2011). Introduction. *Foreign language writing instruction: Principles and practices.* Parlor Press.

Cook, Vivian. (1992). Evidence for multicompetence. *Language Learning, 42*(4), 557–591.

Dahinden, Janine. (2009). *Transnationalisme "diasporique" ou transnationalime en "mobilité"?* In Mériam Cheik (Ed.), *Des femmes sur les routes. Voyages au féminin entre Afrique et Méditerranée* (pp. 199–225). Editions Le Fennec.

DePalma, Michael-John & Ringer, Jeffrey M. (2011). Toward a theory of adaptive transfer: Expanding disciplinary discussions of "transfer" in second-language writing and composition studies. *Journal of Second Language Writing, 20*(2), 134–147.

DePalma, Michael-John & Ringer, Jeffrey M. (2014). Adaptive transfer, writing across the curriculum, and second language writing: Implications for research and teaching. In Terry Myers Zawacki and Michelle Cox (Eds.), *WAC and second-language writers: Research towards linguistically and culturally inclusive programs and practices* (pp. 43–67). The WAC Clearinghouse; Parlor Press. https://doi.org/10.37514/PER-B.2014.0551.2.01.

Donahue, Christiane. (2012). Transfer, portability, generalization: (How) does composition expertise "carry"? In Kelly Ritter and Paul Kei Matsuda (Eds.), *Exploring composition studies: Sites, issues, perspectives* (pp. 145–66). Utah State University Press.

Donahue, Christiane. (2016a.). The "trans" in transnational-translingual: Rhetorical and linguistic flexibility as new norms. *Composition Studies, 44*(1), 147–50.

Donahue, Christiane. (2016b). Writing and global transfer narratives: Situating the knowledge transformation conversation. In Jessie Moore & Chris Anson (Eds.), *Critical transitions: Writing and the question of transfer* (pp. 107–138). The WAC Clearinghouse; University Press of Colorado. https://doi.org/10.37514/PER-B.2016.0797.2.04.

Donahue, Christiane. (2018). Writing, English, and a translingual model for composition. In Kathleen Blake Yancey, Susan Miller-Cochran, Elizabeth Wardle & Rita Malencyzk (Eds.), *Composition, rhetoric, and disciplinarity* (pp. 145–166). Utah State University Press.

Estyn, Cardiff. (2002). *Developing dual literacy: An Estyn discussion paper.* http://www.estyn.org.uk/publications/Dual_literacy.pdfwww.

François, Frédéric. (1998). *Le discours et ses entours.* L'Harmattan.

García, Ofelia & Wei, Li. (2014). *Translanguaging: Language, bilingualism and education.* Palgrave Macmillan.

Gentil, Guillaume. (2018). Modern languages, bilingual education, and translation studies: The next frontiers in WAC/WID research and instruction? *Across the Disciplines, 15*(3). https://doi.org/10.37514/ATD-J.2018.15.3.16.

Guerra, Juan C. (2012). From code-segregation to code-switching to code-meshing: Finding deliverance from deficit thinking through language awareness and performance. In Pamela J. Dunston, Susan King Fullerton, C. C. Bates, Kathy Headley & Pamela M. Stecker (Eds.), *61st Yearbook of the Literacy Research Association* (pp. 29–39). Literacy Research Association.

Hall, Jonathan. (2018). The translingual challenge: Boundary work in rhetoric and composition, second language writing, and WAC/WID. *Across the Disciplines, 15*(3). https://doi.org/10.37514/ATD-J.2018.15.3.10.

Hebbard, Marcela & Hernandez, Yanina. (2020). Becoming transfronterizo collaborators: A transdisciplinary framework for developing translingual pedagogies in WAC/WID. In Lesley Bartlett (Ed.), *Diverse approaches to teaching, learning, and writing across the curriculum: IWAC at 25* (pp. 251–274). The WAC Clearinghouse; University Press of Colorado. https://doi.org/10.37514/PER-B.2020.0360.2.14.

Heidrick, Ingrid. (2006). Beyond the L2: How is transfer affected by multilingualism? *Working Papers in TESOL and Applied Linguistics, 6*(1), 1–3.

Hendricks, C. C. (2018). WAC/WID and transfer: Towards a transdisciplinary view of academic writing. *Across the Disciplines, 15*(3), 48–62. https://doi.org/10.37514/ATD-J.2018.15.3.11.

Hinkel, Eli. (2010). Integrating the four skills: Current and historical perspectives. In Robert Kaplan, (Ed.), *The Oxford handbook of applied linguistics* (pp. 110–126). Oxford Press.

Horner, Bruce. (2006). Introduction: Cross-language relations in composition. *College English, 68*(6), 569–574.

Horner, Bruce, Necamp, Samantha & Donahue, Christiane. (2011). Toward a multilingual composition scholarship: From English only to a translingual norm. *College Composition and Communication, 63*(2), 269–300.

Horner, Bruce. (2018). Translinguality and disciplinary reinvention. *Across the Disciplines 15*(3), 76–88. https://doi.org/10.37514/ATD-J.2018.15.3.13.
Hymes, Dell. (1971). Sociolinguistics and the ethnography of speaking. In Edwin Ardener (Ed.), *Social anthropology and language* (pp. 47–93). Routledge.
Hymes, Dell. (1985). Toward linguistic competence. *AILA Review/Revue de l'AILA* (Association Internationale de Linguistique Appliquée), *2*, 9–23.
Ito, Fumihiko. (2009). Threshold to transfer writing skills from L1 to L2. http://les.eric.ed.gov/fulltext/ED506378.pdf.
Ives, Peter. (2015). Global English and inequality: The contested ground of linguistic power. In Ruanni Tupas (Ed.), *From World Englishes to unequal Englishes* (pp. 74–94). Palgrave Macmillan.
Jun, Zhang. (2008). A comprehensive review of studies on second language writing. *HKBU Papers in Applied Language Studies, 12*, 89–123.
Kara-Abbès, Attika Yasmine, Kebbas, Malika & Blanchet, Philippe. (2011, June 14–16). Introductory conference notes. *Conference Dynamiques plurilingues: des observations de terrains aux transpositions politiques, éducatives, et didactiques.* Ecole Normale Supérieure de Bouzaréa, Algiers, Algeria.
Kara-Abbès, Attika Yasmine, Kebbas, Malika & Cortier, Claude. (2011, June 14–16). *Aborder autrement les pratiques langagières plurilingues en Algérie? Vers une approche de la complexité. Conference Dynamiques plurilingues: Des observations de terrains aux transpositions politiques, éducatives, et didactiques.* Ecole Normale Supérieure de Bouzaréa, Algiers, Algeria.
Kobayashi, Hiroe & Rinnert, Carol. (1992). Effects of first language writing on second language writing: Translation vs. direct composition. *Language Learning, 42*(2), 183–215.
Kramsch, Claire. (1996). The cultural component of language teaching. *Zeitschrift fur Interkulturellen Fremdsprachenunterricht, 1*(2), 1–13.
Kramsch, Claire. (2014). The challenge of globalization for the teaching of foreign languages and cultures. *Electronic Journal of Foreign Language Teaching 11*(2), 249–254.
Lacroix, Thomas. (2018). *Le transnationalisme: Espace, temps, politique. Mémoire d'Habilitation à Diriger des Recherches* [Unpublished manuscript]. Université de Paris.
Le Boterf, Guy. (1994). *De la competence: Essai sur un attracteur étrange.* Editions D'Organisation.
Leki, Ilona. (2006). The legacy of first-year composition. In Paul Kei Matsuda, Christina Ortmeier-Hooper & Xiaoye You (Eds.), *The politics of second language writing: In search of the promised land* (pp. 59–74). Parlor Press.
Leki, Ilona, Cumming, Alistair & Silva, Tony. (2008). *A synthesis of research on second language writing in English.* Routledge.
Levitt, Peggy & Glick Schiller, Nina. (2004). Conceptualizing simultaneity: A transnational social field perspective on society. *International Migration Review, 38*(145), 595–629.
Lorimer Leonard, Rebecca. (2013). Traveling literacies: Multilingual writing on the move. *Research in the Teaching of English, 8*(1), 13–39.
Lu, Min-Zhan & Horner, Bruce. (2013). Translingual literacy, language difference, and matters of agency. *College English, 75*(6), 582–607.

Manchón, Rosa. (2011). The language learning potential of writing in foreign language contexts: Lessons from research. In Tony Cimasko & Melinda Reichelt (Eds.), *Foreign language writing instruction: Principles and practices* (pp. 44–64). Parlor Press.

Matsuda, Aya & Matsuda, Paul Kei. (2010). World Englishes and the teaching of writing. *TESOL Quarterly 44*(2), 369–374.

Matsuda, Paul. (1999). Composition studies and ESL writing: A disciplinary division of labor. *College Composition and Communication, 50*(4), 699–721.

Matsuda, Paul. (2003). Second language writing in the twentieth century: A situated historical perspective. In Barbara Kroll (Ed.), *Exploring the dynamics of second language writing* (pp. 15–34). Cambridge University Press.

Matsuda, Paul. (2006). The politics of L2 writing support programs. In Paul Kei Matsuda, Christina Ortmeier-Hooper & Xiaoye You (Eds.), *The politics of second language writing* (pp. 81–96). Southern Illinois University Press.

Matsuda, Paul Kei. (2013). It's the wild west out there: A new linguistic frontier in U.S. college composition. In A. Suresh Canagarajah (Ed.), *Literacy as translingual practice* (pp. 128–38). Routledge.

Matsuda, Paul, Cox, Michelle, Jordan, Jay & Ortmeier-Hooper, Christina. (2006). *Second-language writing in the composition classroom: A critical sourcebook*. Bedford/St. Martin's.

Moore, Jessie & Anson, Chris (Eds.). (2016). *Critical Transitions: Writing and the question of transfer*. The WAC Clearinghouse; University Press of Colorado. https://doi.org/10.37514/PER-B.2016.0797.

Muchiri, Mary, Mulamda, Nshindi, Myers, Greg & Ndoloi, Deoscorous. (1995). Teaching and researching academic writing beyond North America. *College Composition and Communication, 46*(2), 175–198.

Münchow, Patricia von & Rakotonoelina, Florimond (Eds.). (2006). *Discours, cultures, comparaisons*. Presses Sorbonne Nouvelle.

Ndamba, Josué. (2018, May 22–24). *Quel développement en quelles langues pour les pays africains? Conference Voix africaines, voies émergentes*. Université de Paris Diderot, Paris, France.

Nihalani, Paroo. (2010). Globalization and international intelligibility. In Mukul Saxena & Tope Omoniyi (Eds.), *Contending with globalization in world Englishes* (pp. 23–44). Multilingual Matters.

Nordquist, Brice. (2017). *Literacy and mobility: Complexity, uncertainty, and agency*. Routledge.

Nystrand, Martin, Greene, Stuart & Weimelt, Jeffrey. (1993). Where did composition studies come from? *Written Communication, 10*(3), 267–333.

Peeters, Jean. (2011, June 14–16). *Plurilinguisme, hétérogénéité, et traduction. Conference Dynamiques plurilingues: des observations de terrains aux transpositions politiques, éducatives, et didactiques*. Ecole Normale Supérieure de Bouzaréa, Algiers, Algeria.

Perrenoud, Philippe. (1999). *Transférer ou mobiliser ses connaissances? D'une métaphore l'autre: Implications sociologiques et pédagogiques*. http://www.unige.ch/fapse/SSE/teachers/perrenoud/php_main/php_1999/1999_28.html.

Prasad, Gail. (2014). Portraits of plurilingualism in a French international school in Toronto: Exploring the role of visual methods to access students' representations of their linguistically diverse identities. *The Canadian Journal of Applied Linguistics, 17*(1), 51–77.

Pratt, Mary Louise. (1991). The arts of the contact zone. *Profession*, 33–40.
Prax-Dubois, Pascale. (2019). *Décoloniser le multilinguisme à l'école française. Pour une pédagogie rhizomatique et transgressive. Cahiers Internationaux de Sociolinguistique*, 2(16), 43–74.
Pries, Ludger & Seeliger, Martin. (2012). Transnational social spaces: Between methodological nationalism and cosmo-globalism. In Anna Amelina, Devrimsel, D. Nergiz, Thomas Faist & Nina Glick Schiller (Eds.), *Beyond methodological nationalism: Research methodologies for cross-border studies* (pp. 219–138). Routledge.
Rasoloniaina, Brigitte. (2011, June 14–16). *Réflexions sur le bilinguisme et le modèle d'éducation bilingue dans les écoles primaires malgaches suite au choix du trilinguisme anglais, français, et malgache. Conference Dynamiques plurilingues: des observations de terrains aux transpositions politiques, éducatives, et didactiques.* Ecole Normale Supérieure de Bouzaréa, Algiers, Algeria.
Reichelt, Melinda. (2011). Foreign language writing instruction: An overview. In Tony Cimasko & Melinda Reichelt (Eds.), *Foreign language writing instruction: Principles and practices* (pp. 3–21). Parlor Press.
Reimer, Peter. (2018, May 22–24). *La restructuration des repertoires langagiers de migrant-e-s originaires de la République du Congo en Lorraine. Conference Voix africaines, voies émergentes.* Université de Paris Diderot, Paris, France.
Rispail, Marielle. (2011, June 14–16). *Rencontre de la sociolinguistique et de la didactique: Questions méthodologiques autour des études de cas et des démarches qualitatives. Conference Dynamiques plurilingues: des observations de terrains aux transpositions politiques, éducatives, et didactiques.* Ecole Normale Supérieure de Bouzaréa, Algiers, Algeria.
Saffari, Narges, Noordin, Shahrina, Sivapalan, Subarna & Zahedpisheh, Nahid. (2017). Transfer of mother tongue rhetoric among undergraduate students in second language writing. *International Education Studies*, 10(11), 23–32.
Santos, Terry, Atkinson, Dwight, Erickson, Melinda, Matsuda, Paul Kei & Silva, Tony. (2000). On the future of second language writing: A colloquium. *Journal of Second Language Writing*, 9(1), 1–20.
Saxena, Melindam & Omoniyi, Tony. (2010). *Contending with globalization in world Englishes*. Multilingual Matters.
Schneider, Britta. (2019). Methodological nationalism in linguistics. *Language Sciences*, 76, 1–13.
Schreiber, Brooke. (2020). Opening the door toward a framework for a translingual approach. In Tony Silva & Zhaozhe Wang (Eds.), *Reconciling translingualism and second language writing* (pp. 225–234). Routledge.
Schultz, Jean Marie. (2011). Foreign language writing in the era of globalization. In Tony Cimasko & Melinda Reichelt (Eds.), *Foreign language writing instruction: Principles and practices* (pp. 65–82). Parlor Press.
Shahjahan, Riyad & Kexar, Adrianna. (2013). Beyond the "national container": Addressing methodological nationalism in higher education research. *Educational Researcher*, 42(1), 20–29.
Silva, Tony & Leki, Ilona. (2004). Family matters: The influence of applied linguistics and composition studies on second language writing studies: Past, present, and future. *The Modern Language Journal*, 88(1), 1–13.

Silva, Tony, Leki, Ilona & Carson, Joan. (1997). Broadening the perspective of mainstream composition studies. *Written Communication, 14*(3), 399–428.

Silva, Tony & Matsuda, Paul. (Eds.). (2001). *Landmark essays on ESL writing.* Lawrence Erlbaum Associates.

Sparks, Richard, Patton, John, Ganschow, Leonore & Humbach, Nancy. (2009). Long-term relationships among early first language skills, second language aptitude, second language affect, and later second language proficiency. *Applied Psycholinguistics, 30*(4), 725–755.

Tardy, Christine. (2011). Enacting and transforming local language policies. *College Composition and Communication, 62*(4), 634–661.

Tardy, Christine. (2020). The discursive construction of "translingualism" vs. second language writing. In Tony Silva & Zhaozhe Wang (Eds.), *Reconciling translingualism and second language writing* (pp. 13–24). Routledge.

Tupas, Ruanni & Rudby, Rani. (2015). Introduction. *From world Englishes to unequal Englishes.* Palgrave Macmillan.

Verstraete, Ginette & Cresswell, Tim. (2002). *Mobilizing place, placing mobility: The politics of representation in a globalized world* (vol. 9). Rodopi Press.

Vertovec, Steven. (2007). Super-diversity and its implications. *Ethnic and Racial Studies, 30*(6), 1024–1054.

Vertovec, Steven. (2009). *Transnationalism.* Routledge.

Widdowson, Henry G. (1978). *Teaching Language as Communication.* Oxford University Press.

Wimmer, Andreas & Glick Schiller, Nina. (2002). Methodological nationalism and beyond: nation-state building, migration and the social sciences. *Global Networks, 2*(4), 301–334.

Winford, Donald. (Ed.). (2003). *An introduction* to *contact linguistics.* Blackwell.

Wolfersberger, Mark. (2003). L1 to L2 writing process and strategy transfer: A look at lower-proficiency writers. *TESL-EJ, 7*(2).

Weiser, Irwin. & Rose, Shirley. (2018). *The Internationalization of US Writing Programs.* Utah State University Press,

Woodall, Billy. (2002). Language-switching: Using the first language while writing in the second language. *Journal of Second Language Writing, 11*, 7–28.

Young, Vershawn A. (2009). "Nah, we straight." *JAC 29,* 49–76.

Young, Vershawn. A. & Martinez, Aja Y. (Eds.). (2011). *Code-meshing as World English: Pedagogy, policy and performance.* National Council of Teachers of English.

Young, Vershawn, Barrett, Rusty, Young-Rivera, Y'Shanda & Lovejoy, Kim. (2014). *Other people's English: Code-meshing, code-switching, and African American literacy.* Teachers College Press.

Remapping Writing Instruction at the Borders of Modern Languages, Bilingual Education, and Translation Studies: A Canadian Proposal for a Transnational Conversation

Guillaume Gentil
CARLETON UNIVERSITY

As in the US and other countries, postsecondary institutions in Canada have been enrolling linguistically and culturally diverse student populations through their endeavor both to attract international students in a competitive and globalized academic market and to reach out to increasingly diverse pools of domestic students.[1] At the same time, the politics and policies surrounding such diversity present interesting differences north and south of the border. Notably, the co-existence in Canada of two official languages, English and French, along with federal and provincial policies to promote French as a language of higher education and scholarship, have created demands for bilingual English-French writing in the disciplines, at least in some parts of the country. With these demands come a number of challenges, not only for student writers but also for the institutions and programs that are supposed to support them. Indeed, in many ways the challenges of bilingual academic writing development offer a case in point for the need to rewrite disciplinary and departmental boundaries in academic writing instruction, notably by bringing together modern languages, translation studies, and writing instruction in order to adequately support academic literacy development in two languages or more.

It is from this particular Canadian vantage point that I propose to explore the transdisciplinary, translingual, and transnational challenges for writing across the curriculum (WAC) and writing in the discipline (WID). While each national and regional context of education faces unique exigencies, it is my hope that the arguments and strategies I offer in the Canadian context will resonate with scholars and educators in other contexts as well. A transnational perspective on the teaching of academic writing invites an exploration of problems and solutions that may

---

1   An earlier version of this chapter appeared as Gentil, G. (2018). Modern languages, bilingual education, and translation studies: The next frontiers in WAC/WID research and instruction. *Across the Disciplines*, *15*(3), 114–129. The text was revised and reframed for the transnational theme of this collection.

transcend national borders by attending to the specificities and sensitivities of one's and others' national contexts; ignoring these specificities is a recipe for importing curricular options in unproductive ways. As a member of the Francophonie and the Commonwealth with close ties to the US, Britain, France, and the rest of the English- and French-speaking world, Canada offers an interesting example of the potential and challenge for student writers and teachers of writing to negotiate disciplinary conversations and affiliations across linguistic, national, and geopolitical lines. As a large country with pronounced regional differences, Canada further illustrates that variability can also be found within a national context. Indeed, the complex makeup of Canada as a country problematizes the relations among statehood, nationhood, and language. Canada can be characterized as a polyethnic multinational state (Kymlicka, 1995). For example, the Canadian parliament recognized "the Québécois" as forming "a nation within a united Canada" (House of Commons, 2006), and the term "First Nations" is preferred over "Indians" to refer to "one of the three distinct groups recognized as "Aboriginal" in the Constitution Act of 1982 (Assembly of First Nations, n.d.). A shared linguistic heritage is an important unifying element of such national minorities, and yet can be problematic in itself: Are English Quebeckers, the English-speaking minority of Quebec, part of the Québécois nation? Should French-speaking Canadians living outside of Quebec (e.g., the Franco-Ontarians, the Franco-Albertans, the Acadians) also be recognized as a nation or a group of nations? And to what extent are the very concepts of nations, national identities, and nationhood themselves the means and products of a settler, and rather recent, reading of Canada's history?

While delving into such complexity is beyond the scope of this chapter, it is useful to bear it in mind as a backdrop for understanding the case I make here for redefining curricular arrangements in WAC/WID instruction to better support academic literacy development in more than one language. Therefore, in this chapter, I first elaborate on this backdrop to the extent that it helps to situate the demands and practices of bi- and multilingual disciplinary writing in Canadian postsecondary institutions within the country's broader demographic and legal contexts. I then illustrate the challenges of bilingual English-French WID in a particular institutional context by means of a case study, followed by the description of a pedagogical initiative I recently had the opportunity to develop in order to provide instructional support for bilingual WAC/WID development. These two specific examples will help to anchor a more theoretical discussion on how the biliteracy and translanguaging approach to WAC/WID that I propose here may relate and contribute to a translingual and transnational perspective on the teaching of academic writing.

Before I begin, however, I would like to clarify my use of terminology. Specifically, I will stay away from the use of "translingual" until my more theoretical conclusion. The main reason for this is that this term seems to have created some confusion and even tension, notably in the dialogue that WAC/WID has opened with the field of second language writing (Atkinson et al., 2015; Gevers, 2018; Horner & Alvarez, 2019). Indeed, one goal of this paper is to suggest ways to move this dialogue forward by clarifying terminology and bringing in other terms and associated approaches, such as translanguaging and biliteracy, which I see as more helpful for capturing WID/WAC practices in the Canadian context I describe. Until this juncture, I will simply refer to writing in two languages as bilingual writing, writing in three languages as trilingual writing, and writing in more than one language as multilingual writing. To these terms I will add biliteracy, as a synonym of bilingual literacy or dual literacy—the ability to speak, read, and write with confidence in two languages, and "transliteracy" as "the added ability to move confidently and smoothly between languages for different purposes" (Estyn, cited in Lewis et al., 2012, p. 646). As I will show, it is not uncommon for bilingual academic writers, in the Canadian context, to write in French (e.g., a dissertation) from sources in English (e.g., published research articles), and then to reverse languages (e.g., to publish in English the results of a dissertation composed in French), all the while mixing, switching, or meshing languages when talking about written texts. I refer to this constant shuttling between languages within and across modes as "crosslingual" work. I realize that such terminology oversimplifies the complexity of language interaction and participates in the construction, and some may argue the reification and essentialization, of linguistic resources into well-bounded language systems, a point to which I will return. I offer more nuanced definitions, notably of biliteracy, later on. However, this terminology does help in describing essential aspects of WID practice in the prevailing linguistic orders within which Canadian multilingual university writers seem to operate.

WID Needs and Practices in Canada's Linguistic Landscape

Canada is a country with pronounced regional disparities, making it hazardous to paint a broad-brush picture of its linguistic landscape. Nonetheless, Statistics Canada, the agency that oversees the quinquennial national census, distinguishes three main language groups based on mother tongue (defined as the first learned at home in childhood and still understood, Statistics Canada, 2015): English mother-tongue speakers, or Anglophones (58% of the population), French mother-tongue speakers, or Francophones (21% of the population), and speakers of other mother tongues, or Allophones (23%; Statistics Canada, 2017).[2] The latter group is disparate, comprising a great number of languages, notably Punjabi, varieties of

---

2   The percentages do not quite add up to 100% because they exclude respondents with more than one mother tongue; they are also rounded up.

Chinese, Spanish, German, Italian, Arabic, Tagalog, none of which represent more than 1.5% of the Canadian population but which collectively comprise about 20% of the population. In addition to language groups originating from various waves of immigration, Allophones also include speakers of Indigenous languages (11 language groups and 65 languages and dialects). However, despite recent steps to reverse a long history of language suppression and assimilation policies, less than 1% of Canadians reported an Indigenous language as their mother tongue, with only Cree, Inuktitut, and Ojibway having large enough populations to be considered viable in the long term (Statistics Canada, 2001).

Canada's current demographic makeup reflects the country's history: European settlements decimating Indigenous populations, the persistence of a sizable French-speaking minority after the British Conquest of New France (1763) and the birth of the Canadian confederation (1867), and more recent immigration from around the world (Gillmor et al., 2001). It is thus useful, as Kymlicka (1995) does, to distinguish two main sources of linguistic diversity: the incorporation of previously self-governing "national minorities" (French Canadians, First Nations, Inuit, and Métis), with their own languages, institutions, and cultures, into a large state; and the emergence of "ethnic groups" resulting from individual and familial immigration. This distinction helps to explain the privileged legal status given to English and French as the two official languages of Canada (Official Languages Act, 1985) relative to other languages. The Canadian Multiculturalism Act (1982) aims to "facilitate the acquisition, retention and use of all languages that contribute to the multicultural heritage of Canada" (Section 5(1f)) and yet also seeks to "strengthen the status and use of the official languages of Canada" (Section 3(1i)). Implied in Article 35 the Canadian constitution, rights related to indigenous languages have recently been recognized explicitly by Canadian law, with the passing of the Indigenous Languages Act in June 2019 (https://laws-lois.justice.gc.ca/eng/acts/I-7.85/page-1.html). One key purpose of the act is to "support the efforts of Indigenous people to reclaim, revitalize, maintain and strengthen Indigenous languages" (2019, Article 5b).

Against this demographic and legal backdrop, most Canadian postsecondary institutions offer instruction in only one of the official languages, with the exception of language courses. The language in which students learn to write in their disciplines is thus largely dependent on their university's medium of instruction. That being said, while English-medium institutions offer few opportunities for writing in the disciplines in languages other than English, in the province of Quebec they technically allow submission of written work in either English or French. Although this policy can be difficult to implement when the instructor cannot read French, some Francophone students will claim their right to French, particularly in the humanities and social sciences where disciplinary discourses are still produced in this language (Gentil, 2005). Conversely, Francophone and

Allophone students in French-medium universities will be motivated or pressured to read and write in English, notably in the STEM disciplines as well as in business and administration, given the quasi-hegemony of English as a language of scholarship in these disciplines. These students will thus be exposed to the specialized literature of their disciplines in English, especially in the upper years, while receiving instruction and writing exams (mostly) in French. Graduate students in Quebec's French-medium universities who wish to write a dissertation as a coherent compilation of research publications will generally be expected to write their published papers in English but to contextualize them within a frame (i.e., introducing, linking, and concluding chapters) in French, as per university regulations aimed at preserving French as a language of higher education and scholarship (Dion, 2012). Such practices and policies create great demands on Francophone and French-dominant Allophone students for biliteracy and transliteracy. In contrast, English-dominant students will generally not learn to write in their disciplines in French unless they elect to enroll in a French-medium university or in French studies.

There also exist a handful of officially bilingual universities and colleges. Again, the unequal language balance of power is reflected in institutional linguistic arrangements and individual linguistic choices, with French-dominant students having generally greater motivation and more opportunities to develop bilingual (and sometimes trilingual) academic literacy than English-dominant students (Gentil, 2006b).

What emerges from this picture is that the linguistic demands of writing (and talking, reading, and learning) in the disciplines depend largely on four interacting main dimensions: the student's language background, the institution's language regime, the discipline, and the language dynamics at play within and among regional, national, and international contexts. As is common in asymmetrical situations of language contact, the costs, and benefits, of bi- or multilingualism fall on the linguistic minorities. Indeed, within the country as a whole, English-French bilingualism is more prevalent among Francophones (44%) than Anglophones (8%) or Allophones (12%), whereas the reverse is true for the French-dominant province of Quebec (Anglophones: 66%, Allophones: 50%, and Francophones: 36.6%, as per University of Ottawa, n.d.). One can expect demands and opportunities for bilingual writing in the disciplines to be highest among university students who have already developed bi- or multilingual repertoires at home and in school.

Unfortunately, whether in bilingual or monolingual universities, prevailing institutional arrangements are generally not optimal for bi- or multilingual academic literacy development. Part of the reason for this is the compartmentalization of instruction into departments and programs that sequester available resources away from students (Gentil, 2006a). I illustrate this in the next section, by means of a case study.

A Case Study of Bilingual WID Practice

I have reported on this case study in some detail elsewhere (Gentil, 2005). I focus here only on the aspects that illustrate the participant's multilingual WID practices, challenges, and contexts, in order to later draw theoretical, curricular, and pedagogical implications for the teaching of academic writing in higher education. At the time of the study, from 1999 to 2002, Katia[3] was a Francophone student of cultural studies in an English-medium university in Quebec (henceforth "the University"). What was particularly remarkable was her strong commitment to developing academic biliteracy in both English and French. Indeed, she was determined to make her doctoral dissertation available in both English and French, either by translating it as a whole or by reworking the original English version into a French book for a larger audience. Her motivation for this came from a complex interplay between her desire to learn English to fulfil personal and professional aspirations and equally strong feelings of linguistic loyalty to her French-speaking community. When she began her doctoral studies, she had completed her K–12 education entirely in French but had received her previous postsecondary education in both French-medium and English-medium institutions—a remarkable trajectory considering her modest roots. However, the challenges she experienced while composing three comprehensive examination essays soon put her biliteracy commitment to the test. Availing herself of her student right to submit work in either English or French, she chose to write the first and third essays in English but the second in French (after ensuring that her doctoral committee could indeed read French). After much struggle through the first essay, she expected the second essay to be easier to compose since she understandably felt much more fluent in French. That hope was dashed, however. One reason for this, she quickly realized, was that most of the literature she was drawing on was in English. She thus found herself having to reconceptualize English disciplinary discourse into French, a challenging task for which she was ill-prepared.

This short excerpt from her first draft provides a glimpse into both her writing process and challenge:

> ... l'idéologie liée au développement conçoit celui-ci comme étant neutre au niveau du sex [sic] (gender-neutral).... De nos jours, le développement n'est plus gender-neutral mais la question des femmes est souvent considérée comme étant une catégorie qui doit être ajoutée aux autres catégories. Au Pakistan [...] les programmes qui concernent les femmes se retrouvent surtout dans les programmes de sécurité sociale (welfare) ...

---

3   A pseudonym. IRB approval was received for the research reported on in this chapter.

> Cette tendance est née lors du basic needs approach, philosophie développementaliste élaborée au milieu des années '70.

This text could be variously theorized as an example of codemixing, codemeshing, or translingual practice. I will return to these distinctions later. For now, I will only observe that Katia appears to draw on her entire linguistic repertoire to develop and express her ideas. More specifically, she appears to be using lexical resources that can be labelled as "English language" within an overall textual frame that can be recognized as "French language." Moreover, her use of English seems to be limited to simple or compound terms (*gender neutral, welfare, basic needs approach*), sometimes juxtaposed with their literal translations in brackets (*programmes de sécurité sociale*) or in the main text (*neutre au niveau du sex*).

During the interviews, Katia complained about the French language, notably its relative dearth of terminological resources compared to English:

> Il y a plus de termes exacts en anglais qu'en français... Juste le terme **gender studies**. On dirait qu'en anglais ça veut dire quelque chose, mais en français, études sur les genres, c'est comme... tu sais le concept n'est pas autant connu. Je trouve qu'en anglais, il y a plus de termes qui vont exprimer précisément une idée. En français, peut-être que c'est une impression, mais j'ai l'impression que je suis obligée d'utiliser beaucoup de mots pour mettre en contexte, pour exprimer ce que je veux dire alors qu'en anglais, tu as juste qu'un mot.

> There are more exact terms in English than in French... Take the term *gender studies*. It seems that in English, it means something, but in French, *études sur les genres*, it's like... the concept is not as well known. I find that in English there are more terms that can express an idea precisely. In French, maybe it's just an impression, but I feel that I have to use many more words to contextualize, to express what I want to say, whereas in English, you just need one word.

Rendering the concept of *gender* and its derivatives (e.g., *gender-neutral*) in French proved to be particularly challenging yet essential for Katia because her second essay was a critical literature review on gender studies of relevance to her doctoral project. In order to develop her argument despite these terminological challenges, Katia simply postponed those terminological issues until later in the composing processing, and simply resorted to English terms (and tentative literal translations) while composing her first draft in French. This turned out to be a successful strategy. Had she tried to repress English (in both her text and her mind), she would probably have experienced a writer's block. However, in the later drafts she submitted for assessment, she reworked her text entirely in French, in keeping with her understanding of her professors' expectations.

In the case studies I conducted of French-English university writers, several participants reported similar challenges in finding French equivalents of English terms in their disciplines, which also led to devaluing French as a language of scholarship (Gentil, 2003). A consequence of the dominance of English as a language of science and scholarship is that knowledge and thus terms are developed in English, with terminology in other languages thus lagging behind (Ammon, 1996). At the same time, multilingual terminology development and management is central to the language work of translation specialists working for international organizations such as the United Nations and the institutions of the European Union, and a main area of research within translation studies. Translation specialists have developed a number of resources that could be extremely useful for multilingual writing in the disciplines. Indeed, an entire book has been devoted to the translation of terms related to gender equity in international discourse as a means to illustrate challenges, developments, and resources in multilingual terminology (Raus, 2013). One such resource includes terminology banks, such as TERMIUM and *Le grand dictionnaire terminologique*, which inventory terminological equivalents per domain found by terminologists in well-documented sources.

These terminological banks could have been very useful for Katia, notably in proposing equivalents for *gender* and derived compound terms such as *gender-neutral policy*. Multilingual terminological banks, however, have a number of shortcomings: they are labor and cost intensive to maintain, and therefore are often incomplete and quickly obsolete, not keeping up with fast-paced terminological advances. Bilingual concordancers such as Linguee, Tradooit, and Webitext help to overcome these shortcomings by using algorithms to search the web for bilingual texts and extract not only translation equivalents of search terms or phrases but also paragraph-long bilingual texts ("bitexts") that show parallel language use in context. An added advantage of such bilingual concordancers is thus to assist bilingual writers not only in finding equivalent terminology or lexis but also appropriate phraseology (another challenge of Katia's). Nonetheless, bilingual writers, like students of translation, should also be made aware of the limitations of these tools, such as text alignment and phrase extraction errors, translations or source texts of questionable quality, and the inability to filter searches per domain or expand the corpus to genres and discourses of interest (Raus, 2013). For investigation of specialized terminology and phraseology in their disciplines, academic writers might thus be better off creating their own specialized corpora and research them using monolingual or bilingual concordancers such as Antconc or SketchEngine (see, e.g., Gavioli, 1996).

Other resources routinely used by translation specialists that would have been useful to Katia include awareness of translation strategies at the phrase- and text-level, including the understanding that the primary translation unit is generally considered to be semantic and pragmatic (the idea, the message, and the effect) rather than lexical (the word) (Delisle, 2013). There is also within translation studies a well-established body of work in comparative stylistics that documents English-French differences in syntactic and stylistic preferences (including the pioneering and now classic work of Jean-Paul Vinay and Jean Darbelnet, 1995).

However helpful such translation resources might have been to Katia in her crosslingual WID practices, she did not have access to them despite the existence of a translation program within the University. Her case illustrates the deleterious impact on multilingual WID of the compartmentalization of the curriculum into disciplines, languages, and programs. Because she was not a student of translation studies, she could not take courses in translation studies without additional cost (as a continuing education student). In fact, she wasn't even aware of them and of what they could offer. She could not take courses in French academic writing either, because these were reserved for French-as-a-second-language writers or French majors. Interestingly, while WAC/WID programs are not as well established in Canada as in the US (Graves & Graves, 2012; Turner & Kearns, 2012), the Writing Centre of the University did offer lower-year and upper-year courses in effective written communication for students in disciplines such as education, business, and engineering. However, because Katia's home department had not entered into an agreement with the Writing Centre, these WID style courses were not available to her either. The only writing course that was on offer was an English-as-a-Second-Language course in academic graduate writing open to Francophone and Allophone students from all disciplines. While Katia did benefit from this form of instruction, it was exclusively in English and did not touch on strategies for the kind of crosslingual WID work she was engaged with.

A Transciplinary Experiment in Biliteracy Instruction

Thus far, I have tried to illustrate some of the challenges of WID practice, as well as to suggest how resources and strategies developed in translation studies may help overcome them, provided that they become an integral part of the multilingual WAC/WID curriculum. I now would like to describe what may be considered a transdisciplinary experiment in biliteracy instruction. My hope in doing so is to suggest ways to develop instruction for bi- or multilingual WAC/WID despite institutional and disciplinary strictures that separate out writing instruction in a modern language from English writing in the disciplines and translation studies.

The opportunity for this pilot project arose in the fall of 2016 within my institution, an English-medium university in Ottawa, Canada's capital city. This university is located within a predominantly English-speaking part of the city and serves a mostly anglophone or English-dominant student population, but the proximity of Quebec less than six kilometers away and the central role of the federal service in the local economy make French quite present in the university's regional context. Again because of departmental compartmentalization, as a professor of (English) applied linguistics, I could not teach courses in the French language or through the medium of French unless the Department of French negotiated my release from my home unit, the School of Linguistics (I have since become cross-appointed in order to be able to teach in both English and French annually). As a colleague's sabbatical created a curricular gap that justified the release, I was asked to teach a special topics course in applied linguistics in French at the fourth-year level, and I developed FREN4414 *Bilittératie: Recherches, Pratiques et Pédagogie* (Biliteracy: Research, Practices, and Pedagogy).

The main objective of the course was to draw on biliteracy research at the cross-over of bilingual education, literacy, translation, and writing studies in order to help students develop biliteracy strategies adapted to their own contexts and needs. Specifically, the course encouraged the students not only to read about biliteracy but also to reflect on their own biliteracy practices and experiment with strategies for multi- and crosslingual writing in light of the readings and class discussion. From a theoretical standpoint, the course was informed by Christine Tardy's (2009) integrated model of genre knowledge as reconceptualized within a biliteracy perspective (Gentil, 2011). It was thus structured around different genres (notably, the assignments) and the four components of genre knowledge as identified by Tardy: content, formal, rhetorical, and process knowledge.

Each component was the focus of one or two weeks, with special attention given to bi- and transliteracy considerations. With regard to content knowledge, the course readings provided a common knowledge base for the class and coursework, beginning with an introduction to key concepts in biliteracy studies and a review of research on the crosslinguistic transfer of writing. Readings and activities related to formal knowledge emphasized the lexical, terminological, and phraseological strategies for crosslingual work that I had seen Katia and other bilingual writers needing the most, such as assessing and using terminological banks and concordancers to find terminological and phraseological equivalents across languages (Raus, 2013). The development of formal knowledge also included, at the sentence level, an initiation to comparative French-English stylistics (e.g., Vinay & Darbelnet, 1995) and, at the text level, a crosslingual comparison of coherence, cohesion, and information management in English and French (emphasizing similarities beyond linguistic specificities, drawing on Marie-Odile Hidden's 2013 textbook). The classes on rhetorical knowledge aimed to foster a critical reflection on contrastive/intercultural rhetoric work (e.g., Rozycki et al., 2008) by having students compare instructions given by English and French composition textbooks on how to introduce a paper with actual writing samples. One underlying goal was to raise awareness of the possibility that the textual patterns observed may have more to do with exigencies in genres and rhetorical situations (e.g., introducing an essay for a course vs. a research journal article for a national audience vs. a book chapter for an international audience) than with the language of composing. As for process knowledge, activities drew attention to similarities and differences in L1, L2 (and L3) composing strategies, as well as the strategic use of one's entire linguistic repertoire to write in a language in which one's command was weaker.

To these four knowledge dimensions, a fifth was added, namely technological knowledge—comfort with the computer technologies that commonly mediate academic and professional writing today. To this end, several classes took place in the computer lab. In addition to practice with the terminological and lexicographic online resources and software described above (Antconc, Tradooit, Linguee), the lab sessions also introduced a video screen capture tool, TechSmith Relay, to allow students to share short videos of selected aspects of their writing processes, for instance illustrating a writing strategy such as the use of an online resource while writing.

The main assignments progressed from narrative to expository as well as shorter to longer, more complex genres. First, a biliteracy autobiography, inspired by Diane Belcher and Ulla Connor (2001), prompted the students to narrate how, in what contexts, and what types of texts they had learned to read and write in English, French, and other languages. A second assignment, linked to terminology work, asked students to contribute one entry to the class' bilingual glossary by selecting a term of interest and documenting its definitions, collocations, uses, and translations. Three short reports, distributed throughout the term, required reflective accounts of selected in-class activities, for example assessing the affordances and constraints of selected online lexicographic resources for finding translation equivalents of *gender, literacy*, and derived compound terms (e.g., *gender parity, literacy practices*). These shorter assignments, along with the course readings and workshop-style class activities, aimed to prepare for the term paper, an 1,800-word self-case study research report on a selected aspect of the student's own biliteracy practices. For this final report, students were encouraged to use TechSmith Relay to include links to videos as a way to document and research, and thus become self-reflective of, their writing processes (Hamel et al., 2015). They were free to use other data sources as well, such as a corpus of texts they wrote. The overall intent of these assignments was to foster self-awareness of one's strategies, resources, and challenges as a student writer learning to write in English, French, and possibly other languages in specific disciplinary, professional, and social contexts and genres.

In keeping with a translanguaging (Gentil, 2019; Lewis et al., 2012) approach and to help develop strategies for transliteracy, I would have liked to alternate between English and French for reading, writing, and talking, for example planning a class discussion and a writing activity in English on a French text, and then switching languages for the next sequence. Because the course was part of a BA program in French, however, the language of instruction and evaluation had to be French. Nonetheless, in consultation with the chair of the French department, some course readings were assigned in English, which gave an opportunity to discuss and practice French writing from English sources. Furthermore, students were also encouraged to reflect on their English writing experiences in other courses and bring writing samples from these courses. The use of English as a resource when composing in French was also a subject of class discussion, to the apparent surprise of some students who had been taught to repress it; informal testimonials suggested that this discussion gave students permission to use English more freely in their French prewriting and found it to be helpful (on the use of the L1 while composing in an L2, see, e.g., Manchón, 2013). That being said, given that all the students were much more at ease in English than in French and yet had enrolled in an advanced French class ostensibly with the goal to improve their French, it was important as well to give them opportunities to push themselves in French, in effect asking them to suspend their linguistic privilege as English speakers in an English-medium university. As Roy Lyster (2019) and Susan Ballinger et al. (2017) convincingly argue in the Canadian French immersion context, language status should be an important consideration in crosslinguistic pedagogy. While encouraging minority language users to draw on their whole linguistic repertoire can support learning and biliteracy in English-medium programs, pushing English speakers *not* to use English is equally important in foreign/second language classes and bilingual programs as a means of counteracting the overriding tendency toward increased use of English at the expense of languages of lesser ease and status. For these reasons, while English was allowed and occasionally used in the class, noticeably in small group conversations and to enable conceptual links across languages, instruction and class discussion were predominantly in French.

One challenge in designing the course was to find relevant and appropriate course readings. Reflecting disciplinary divisions of labor, available textbooks were geared at English or French writing, or bilingual education, or translation. In the end, I adopted Hidden (2013) as a course text, a textbook in French writing instruction aimed at teacher development in French as a foreign language. Even if most students did not consider a career as French teachers (although some had plans to teach English in France), my rationale for choosing this text was that drawing attention to research-based approaches to the teaching of writing would contribute to developing students' metacognitive self-awareness as multilingual writers, a key objective of the course. Naturally, the textbook had to be complemented with selected readings in translation studies, biliteracy, bilingual education, and L2 writing studies.

Another challenge was to find French translation equivalents of concepts and terminology needed for the course. In many ways, I found myself in a situation similar to Katia and my students of being exposed to specialized literatures in

English and yet having to write and talk about them in French, a point which I emphasized in class. I thus had ample opportunities to illustrate the translation strategies I aimed to teach. Whenever a question arose that I could not address on the spot (e.g., how to render *creative writing* or *learning curve* into French), this became a terminological problem for us to solve.

Despite these challenges and constraints, the course appeared to have been helpful, at least based on the students' formal and informal evaluations as well as their self-reflective reports. The class turned out to be small, only 10 students (the French BA program itself is fairly small). This allowed for individualized attention. Most students were Anglophones who had learned French in school, but a few had more complex linguistic repertoires and histories, including one student who was already well on his way to developing advanced literacy in Mandarin, French, and English for work. One student commented that the course had been useful not only for French writing but for English writing as well, adding that she had not been aware of stylistic differences between English and French essay writing before. Several students reflected on how they came to appreciate similarities and also differences in their composing processes in English and French (and sometimes other languages as well), such as not to let concerns over accuracy impede their idea development in French. Other students shared their appreciations of translation strategies beyond literal translation, of the potential and limitations of online translation, writing, and editing tools, and of the use of video screen capture as a self-evaluation tool to access and assess their own writing processes. Only one student used video screen capture in his final report to offer a detailed account of his composing processes in English and French while writing a comparable text in each language. Several other students, however, shared interesting analyses of their English and French writing based on writing samples, notably comparing how they structured introductions to argumentative texts in different disciplines.

Together, the students' coursework and reflections suggest that the course helped promote writing development by following two of the main principles of WAC/WID instruction (Kiefer et al., 2021): (1) the use of writing as a means to learn and (2) familiarizing students with the writing conventions and genres of their disciplines. In the context of the course, writing to learn meant using writing (biliteracy autobiography, reflective reports, self-case studies) as a tool for learning about oneself as a strategic multilingual writer responding to specific writing contexts and demands; writing in the disciplines meant learning to write in French for a course in applied linguistics. While students had had opportunities to write literary analyses or essays in French, writing a research report, let alone a self-case study, was an unfamiliar genre to them, in French at least. I also hope that by fostering awareness of genres and composing strategies across disciplinary and linguistic contexts, the course also promoted the students' writing development across their curriculum as well, in both English and French.

Translingual, Transnational, Translanguaging, and Biliteracy Approaches to WAC/WID

The course in biliteracy I just described is but a small pilot experiment. More systematic research is needed to show to what extent and how initiatives of this sort can help promote bilingual writing development in and across disciplines. Such research may in turn help make a case for developing a bi/multilingual WAC/WID curriculum on a larger scale that more fully integrates writing instruction in English with translation studies and modern languages. Nonetheless, I hope to have illustrated the need for such integration to better support academic biliteracy development, especially in national and institutional contexts with sizable language minorities such as Francophones in Canada (Spanish speakers in the US may also have similar needs). With this Canadian example in mind, I would like to conclude with some reflections on a more theoretical level in an attempt to clarify how the biliteracy approach to WAC/WID I just described can relate to translanguaging, translingual, and transnational approaches.

In the introduction, I defined biliteracy simply as a synonym of bilingual literacy, the ability to read and write in two languages. In keeping with more sophisticated characterizations of the construct I have provided elsewhere (e.g., Gentil, 2011), I would add that such ability must be understood as situated within the social, cultural, ideological, national, geopolitical, and historical contexts that construct it as ability. In other words, biliteracy is not only a matter of individual skill over languages in reading and writing, but also the social validation of such savoir-faire across linguistic, cultural, and national contexts. To take a culinary analogy, however skillful, a French chef serving boeuf bourguignon will not satisfy a customer who ordered beef curry in a Thai restaurant. Similarly, as research in intercultural rhetoric suggests, a writer's skill in delivering a given genre in one context may not be appreciated in another; success in exploiting and expanding writing expertise across linguistic, cultural, national, and disciplinary communities is contingent on writers finding contexts that validate their genre knowledge. For example, Connor (2003) reports how a Senegalese student's skill in introducing an argumentative essay by problematizing the question in the prompt, based on a French rhetoric tradition, may be poorly received by an American target audience expecting a thesis statement. To successfully frame her argument for her doctoral committee, Katia came to realize that she needed to be cautious about citing French-medium disciplinary discourse her target audience may not be familiar with, privileging English-medium discourse instead (even when writing in French). Biliteracy thus requires not only the ability to read and write in two languages but also rhetorical flexibility, cultural sensitivity, and brokering skill in negotiating texts and seeking recognition of what may count as skillful writing in a given context.

To bring this point home was a main objective in encouraging my students to compare introductions to term papers and research articles in different languages, disciplines, and national contexts (France and Canada). However, no matter how skillful a biliterate writer may be, biliteracy requires an enabling context. It would thus seem unlikely that Spanish heritage speakers in the US would attempt what Katia did with French unless Spanish gains prestige, recognition, and support in that country in both academic and non-academic settings.

A criticism that may be levelled at the biliteracy approach, from a translingual perspective, is that it tends to consider literacy, even though socioculturally situated, still in binary terms: English and/or French; by treating languages as discrete, a biliteracy approach may be seen as "aligned with the ideology of monolingualism" (Horner et al., 2011, p. 307). It is on this point perhaps that the biliteracy approach may be more closely allied to (some versions of) translanguaging than translingualism or translingual literacy (on the various, weak and strong versions of translanguaging and the rapprochement between biliteracy and translanguaging, see Gentil, 2019; Hornberger & Link, 2012). The term *translanguaging* was first coined in Welsh to refer to a bilingual education strategy aimed at developing dual literacy in both English and Welsh, with "the added ability to move confidently and smoothly between languages for different purposes" by means of the purposeful concurrent uses of two languages in the classroom (Estyn, cited in Lewis et al., 2012, p. 246). However, the term has since been expanded to refer to "an approach to the use of language, bilingualism and the education of bilinguals that considers the language practices of bilinguals not as two autonomous language systems as have been traditionally the case, but *as one linguistic repertoire with features that have been societally constructed as belonging to separate languages*" (García & Li, 2014, p. 2, my emphasis).

This definition captures the tension between the desire to consider the linguistic resources of multilinguals as interacting and mixing in complex, dynamic ways and forming one linguistic repertoire on the one hand, and a prevailing backdrop of assumptions, practices, and discourses that continue to create them as separate languages on the other. I acknowledge the permeability of linguistic boundaries and see much value in a translingual approach to language difference that sees language difference as continually (re)produced in moment-to-moment iterations of language use (Lu & Horner, 2013). At the same time, I would contend that the fluidity of languages and language boundaries may at times be somewhat overplayed in the translingual literature (e.g., Horner et al., 2011) and at odds with the language dynamics that seem to be at play in the Canadian contexts of multilingual WID development that I described in this paper. In the successive moments of meaning making, the use of linguistic resources may aptly be described as a flux of meaning in which language systems are both constantly drawn upon and reshaped in minute ways. However, languages appear to evolve on a different time scale. English and French as we know them today, for example, are the products of several centuries of a codification process that has instituted them into distinct systems despite a long history of contact and reciprocal influence. It is not surprising, then, that in the time scale of a person's life, it may take years for a speaker raised in one linguistic tradition to learn another. It would thus seem important not to conflate the historical, ontogenetic, and moment-to-moment time scales of language change. To take another social category, gender, as an example, while gender categories may indeed be made and remade in the repetition of performative acts (Butler, 1999), transgender testimonials are poignant reminders of how changing or transgressing one's gender in a gendered society can be a long and arduous process in a person's life. Becoming translingual within a well-entrenched order of linguistic nationalism may well be as challenging as transitioning into a new gender within a heteronormative order.

Part of the rigidity of language boundaries derives from the "sedimentation of language practices" (Lu & Horner, 2013, p. 288) into linguistic patterns, systems, and categories that become reified and taken for granted in habitual ways of using and conceiving of language(s)—what Bourdieu refers to as a linguistic habitus. More precisely, language boundaries tend to be produced and reproduced in what Bourdieu (1998) sees as the "ontological complicity" (p. 77) or convergence between *habitus*, conceived as mostly unconscious mental and embodied structures that predispose language users to conceive of languages as bounded, and the objective structures of the social space that construct and reify languages as bounded. Importantly, some of these social structures predate and will likely outlive any given individual language user, which contributes to the enduring codification of languages as bounded systems on a historical scale. Examples of such durable structures include the taken-for-granted use of –ed as a past-tense marker in English, the continued institutional presence of the French Academy since its founding in 1635, and nation states built along linguistic lines (on language as both structure and usage, see also Kecskes, 2010).

To return to Katia's struggles with reconceptualizing American gender theories from English to French, it is interesting that her first draft provides a glimpse into the sort of language meshing that goes on in her mind while composing, unlike the later drafts in which all traces of such meshing are erased. The participant in Suresh Canagarajah's (2011) study of codemeshing in in a U.S. state university context, Buthainah, did the opposite: she codemeshed only in the later drafts, after she had sensed that her professor would be open to it. Whether consciously or not, Katia reproduced the boundedness of English and French linguistic resources in her instance of writing, whereas Buthainah played with and at the language boundaries. The reasons for this difference are open for interpretation but point to student writers' intuitive and mostly tacit sense of the different valences assigned to specific languages and their mixing in their respective Canadian and U.S. contexts. During our interviews, Katia did not bring up her rationale for erasing English traces from her later French drafts, nor did I probe the subject specifically. The focus was on the challenges to find translation equivalents, and the necessity for doing so was just taken for granted. Such taken-for-granted necessity of translation and the resulting unquestioned self-policing of one's linguistic behaviour at the language boundary is precisely what contributes to the reproduction of languages as separate systems. As Nancy Bou Ayash (2016) vividly illustrates in the context of first-year writing instruction at an American university in Lebanon, explicitly interrogating the often unquestioned representations that students and instructors have about languages and language relations can help them realize and thus negotiate how these representations can facilitate or impede their abilities and practices with languages. Raising student writers' attention to the unattended conditions and unintended consequences of their language uses can help them make more informed choices, thus empowering their agency. However, it will arguably not be sufficient to undo the prevailing historical, economic, geopolitical, and ideological conditions that constitute the linguistic order within which they operate.

A case could be made for academic writing to be more open to codemeshing, and to language difference more generally, than it currently is, given the linguistic diversity of student populations and the globalized construction of disciplinary knowledge. At the same time, two lines of arguments could be made in favor of upholding language boundaries. First, from an identity perspective, it can be important for language minorities to preserve the linguistic distinctiveness that helps them index and maintain their identities. The ambivalence toward the use of English words in Quebec and French Canada reflects the power imbalance of French and English, with English being pervasive, appealing, and yet threatening for Francophone minorities. This may explain the relative sensitivity of French speakers in Quebec toward obvious English borrowings, such as *parking, shopping, week-end* (spelled with a hyphen in standard French), which are widely used in France, even though other, often more covert types of English influence can be documented at the level of syntax and semantics as being more prevalent in Canadian than European French usage (Bouchard, 1999). Katia and the other research participants from Quebec expressed their attachment to their French mother tongue in strong affective terms, insisting on how it gave them a sense of identity and belonging and emphasizing the importance of not "drowning it with Anglicisms" for the sake of its "survival" given that Quebec was the "last francophone entrenchment" in North America (Gentil, 2005). These affective valuations fuel the desire to keep language boundaries where they are (or appear to be). While codemeshing may be seen as desirable in some contexts, for communicative expediency or as an act of resistance against monolingualist ideology, it can also exacerbate a sense of threat posed by an overpowering language on one's language of affiliation and allegiance (on the less desirable implications of codemeshing for denigrated language varieties and minoritized language users such as speakers of Jamaican Creole in the Jamaican context or Native Americans in the U.S. context, see Milson-Whyte, 2014).

Second, from a cognitive perspective, one should not underestimate the potential for deeper learning of having to rethink knowledge through two languages. One difficulty in rendering concepts such as *gender* and *literacy* from English to French is that they don't have one-to-one equivalents. It may thus be tempting to borrow the English term, either as is, by keeping its native English form, or by translating it literally (e.g., *littératie*). Another solution is a semantic loan, expanding the meaning of a closely related term. Thus, under the influence of English-based gender theory, the uses of the French word *genre* have expanded from a mere linguistic category in French grammar (masculine vs. feminine) to a more complex sociological concept that developed along with a reconfiguration of feminist studies and politics in France (Parini, 2010). However, it can be productive as well to try to render a concept with the available resources of a given language. For example, in the Swiss context, Laurent Gajo (2007; Gajo et al., 2013) showed examples of how professors helped to deepen understanding of key concepts in law or physics by comparing and contrasting terms and metaphors used by German and French. Similarly, I have tried to illustrate how translanguaging about translanguaging, that is, trying to understand the concept of translanguaging through more than one linguistic lens, by bringing various linguistic resources to bear on, dissect, and expand its multi-layered meanings, can help to deepen one's understanding of this complex notion (Gentil, 2019).

Even when terms are borrowed or translated, they tend to be restricted to specialist use, at first at least, and need to be explicated: unlike *literacy*, which is a common word in English, *littératie* was only recently introduced in one general reference dictionary and remains puzzling to Francophone readers beyond education circles, even though it began to make inroads into French-medium scholarly conversations back in the 1990s (Gentil, 2019). Interestingly, the introduction of the *literacy* concept into French-speaking academic circles, while resisted at first, led to productive discussion as to what it could mean and what its added value could be (see, e.g., Lépine & Hébert, 2013). Furthermore, even if they spread beyond academic circles, borrowed concepts tend to have more limited usage than in the original language. This can be seen in derived compound terms, which do not always translate literally. For example, while *literacy* may be rendered as *littératie* in academic contexts, *literacy campaign* will be rendered as *campagne d'alphabétisation*; similarly, terminological banks may document *genre* as the equivalent of *gender* as a simple term, but *équilibre entre les sexes* (literally *balance between the sexes*) as the equivalent of *gender balance*. Multilingual writers can be puzzled by this, and as Katia did, see their first language as somewhat deficient by its apparent lack of terminological resources. It may thus be helpful, in the context of bilingual WID instruction, to open a discussion about how different languages, each conceived as a set of linguistic systems constituting a certain meaning potential, can offer distinctive yet complementary lenses on the world (on the complex relationship between thought and cognition in multilinguals, see Kecskes, 2010; MacSwan, 2017; Pavlenko, 2005).

As Bruce Horner and Elliot Tetreault (2016) have convincingly argued and illustrated in the context of U.S. college composition, "teaching writing as translation" can be a fruitful strategy to make visible the workings of normative language ideologies and how these produce and reproduce language difference. Julia Kiernan et al. (2016) further illustrate practical strategies for implementing a translation assignment in an English first-year composition course, as well as the practical benefits of translation for fostering audience awareness, metalinguistic skills, and cultural sensitivities while positioning multilingual students as experts in their own languages and cultures. Both papers propose intralingual translation activities (such as paraphrasing or translating into a new style, genre, or register) as a way to address the challenges of instructors or students being monolingual or not sharing common language pairs. I fully embrace these initiatives but propose to extend them in two ways. First, while inter- and intralingual translation (e.g., Jakobson, 1959/2000) share certain similarities as a making-meaning process involving rewording and recontextualizing, the loss at which monolinguals find themselves in working out meaning across languages underscores the additional challenges of interlingual translation that multilingual writers like Katia must overcome. Second, Kiernan et al. (2016) describe how useful it can be for students to explore and reflect on the translation strategies they have found by themselves. However, it could be valuable as well to encourage students to compare the translation strategies they have figured out by themselves with the translation strategies recommended and practiced in professional translation training programs. Indeed, it would seem a pity to have multilingual students in English composition courses reinvent the wheel rather than tapping into the wealth of theoretical and practical knowledge developed over the last 60 years in translation studies.

Admittedly, one difficulty for composition specialists to borrow from translation studies is that they cannot be expected to be translation specialists themselves. Furthermore, a great number of the more practical pedagogical resources are available in languages other than English, for the simple reason that, reflecting the power imbalance between English and other languages, translation has traditionally been more prevalent out of than into English. In Canada, for example, there is more of a need to translate out of English and into French, which explains why programs and materials for translator training were developed first in French (for a staple text with several editions, see Delisle, 2013) and are still more abundant in French (Mareschal, 2005). Similarly, European countries have each developed programs and materials for translation training in and into their respective national language(s). Unless English composition instructors can read other languages, they would not be able to access these resources. However, this challenge may be overcome by means of interdisciplinary collaboration with modern language and translation studies departments, along the same kind of participatory models (e.g., team-teaching, modules, workshops) that composition specialists have adopted with other disciplines in WAC/WID programs. Indeed, the time seems all the more ripe for collaborative, interdisciplinary programs involving modern languages and composition now that translation itself, after being much maligned in second and foreign language pedagogy, is being rehabilitated both as a valuable skill to develop (Cook, 2010) and as a means of developing "translingual and transcultural competence" conceived of as the "ability to operate between languages" and "to reflect on the world and [oneself] through the lens of another language and culture" (MLA Ad Hoc Committee on Foreign Languages, 2007). An added advantage of expanding WID/WAC programs to modern language departments is that it would facilitate the structuring of instruction so as to promote bi- and transliteracy work in language pairs (e.g., Spanish-English, English-Mandarin) and in directions (e.g., Spanish to English and English to Spanish) that are meaningful for the students.

There nonetheless exist a number of interesting resources in English for translating into English, such as Baker (2011), the somewhat dated but still useful Lonsdale (1996), and Routledge's Thinking Translation series. Anthony Pym's (2016) *Translation Solutions for Many Languages* may also be particularly useful for introducing translation into linguistically diverse English composition courses because it offers a framework for seven translation strategies or "solution types" derived from an exhaustive list of such strategies developed independently for a number of language pairs. Whenever using a translation assignment in an English composition course, Pym's proposed typology of solution types could be helpful as a framework for students not only to analyze their spontaneous translation approaches but also to consider other strategies they may not have thought of.

In short, the translanguaging and biliteracy approach to WID/WAC instruction that I have tried to outline here aims not only to help bilingual writers learn to write in their disciplines in and across two languages, but also to harness the potential of bilingual and crosslingual writing for learning (in) the disciplines. In other words, it aims not only to create the conditions of learning to write bi- and crosslingually in the disciplines, but also to exploit the facilitative role of writing bi- and crosslingually to learn. Despite some differences in emphasis, translingual, translanguaging, and biliteracy approaches to WAC/WID have this in common: they aim to develop in student writers a "deftness in deploying a broad and diverse repertoire of language resources, and responsiveness to the diverse range of readers, social positions and ideological perspectives" (Horner et al., 2011, p. 308). The main difference, perhaps, lies in how this diverse repertoire of language resources is conceived, with a biliteracy approach underscoring the value of distinguishing language difference at the level of registers, genres, and languages, and across historical, ontogenetic, and moment-to-moment time scales. It can be practical and valuable in some contexts of monolingual WID/WAC instruction to introduce translation as the recontextualizing of meaning across varieties of one language (e.g., Horner & Tetreault, 2016; Horner et al., 2011). At the same time, I also hope to have illustrated the value for WID/WAC instruction to cross-pollinate and collaborate with modern languages, bilingual education, and translation studies in order for student writers to learn to translate and translate to learn across languages.

Lastly and importantly, I also hope to have illustrated the importance of anchoring a transnational conversation on writing instruction in a deep understanding of national specificities. While some scholars point to a transition toward a postnational or transnational order (as Heller, 2008, 2011, 2015 does in the French-Canadian context), Canadian political philosopher Will Kymlicka (2004) warns against the "myth of transnational citizenship." As he convincingly argues, there is no denying the intensification of transnational exchanges, but what shapes borders are not the increasingly transnational forces people are subjected to, but the communities with which they identify as they respond, and globalization does not seem to have eroded the sense that nation states form distinctive communities of destiny and solidarity when responding to transnational challenges and opportunities (2004). For example, while there is a tempting parallel between English-French biliteracy in Canada and English-Spanish biliteracy in the US, the negotiation and valuation of biliteracy takes place against an entirely different historical, demographic, and political landscape; mobilizing for biliteracy thus requires "context-appropriate" (Ballinger et al., 2017) national strategies. The need to enable biliteracy by creating conditions for its validation and safeguarding a space for the minority language may well transcend national contexts, but the modalities of how this can be done are likely to vary nationally and locally. Furthermore, the condition of being without nationality is no more enviable than having lost the language of one's childhood or Elders. At the same time, Francophone communities also illustrate how affiliations, actions, and discourses can be negotiated by mobilizing around a shared language across nation-state borders. In the academic domain, there is a wealth of research into the transnational circulation of ideas between and within the English- and French-speaking world, notably in language and literacy education (Gentil, 2019; Liddicoat & Zarate, 2009), multilingualism (Moore & Gajo, 2009), gender studies (Parini, 2010), and writing instruction (Brereton et al., 2009). What this research suggests is that writing across national contexts entails negotiating positive reception by translating ideas not only across languages (e.g., French and English), but also across geopolitical communities that may share a language and yet differ in their reference points, rhetorical preferences, and disciplinary conversations (e.g., French-medium scholarship in France, Belgium, or Canada). A transnational translingual approach to the teaching of academic writing in higher education has thus much to offer by helping students identify the conversations they want to contribute to as they learn to problematize the language-nation-identity link while leveraging their linguistic and national moorings to affirm their voices.

References

Ammon, Ulrich (Ed.). (1996). *The dominance of English as a language of science: Effects on other languages and language communities*. Mouton de Gruyter.

Assembly of First Nations. (n.d.). About AFN. Retrieved September 15, 2022 from https://www.afn.ca/about-afn/.

Atkinson, Dwight, Crusan, Deborah, Matsuda, Paul Kei, Ortmeier-Hooper, Christina, Ruecker, Todd, Simpson, Steve & Tardy, Christine M. (2015). Clarifying the relationship between L2 writing and translingual writing: An open letter to writing studies editors and organization leaders. *College English, 77*(4), 383–383.

Baker, Mona. (2011). *In other words: A coursebook on translation* (2nd ed.). Routledge.

Ballinger, Susan, Lyster, Roy, Sterzuk, Andrea & Genesee, Fred. (2017). Context-appropriate crosslinguistic pedagogy: Considering the role of language status in immersion education. *Journal of Immersion and Content-Based Language Education, 5*(1), 30–57.

Belcher, D. & Connor, U. (2001). *Reflections on multilerate lives*. Multilingual Matters.

Bou Ayash, Nancy. (2016). Conditions of (im)possibility: Postmonolingual language representations in academic literacies. *College English, 78*(4), 555–577.

Bouchard, Chantal. (1999). *On n'emprunte qu'aux riches: La valeur sociolinguistique et symbolique des emprunts*. Éditions Fides.

Bourdieu, Pierre. (1998). *Practical reason: On the theory of action*. Stanford University Press.

Brereton, John, Donahue, Christiane, Gannett, Cinthia, Lillis, Theresa M. & Scott, Mary. (2009). *La circulation des perspectives socioculturelles états-uniennes et britanniques: traitements de l'écrit dans le supérieur*. In Bertrand B. Daunay, I. Delcambre & Y. Reuter (Eds.), *Didactique du français, le socioculturel en question* (pp. 51–68). Presses universitaires du Septentrion.

Canagarajah, Suresh. (2011). Codemeshing in academic writing: Identifying teachable strategies of translanguaging. *The Modern Language Journal, 95*(3), 401–417.

Connor, Ulla. (2003). Changing current in contrastive rhetoric. In Barbara Kroll (Ed.), *Exploring the dynamics of second language writing* (pp. 218–241). Cambridge University Press.

Cook, Guy. (2010). *Translation in language teaching*. Oxford University Press.

Delisle, Jean. (2013). *La traduction raisonnée: manuel d'initiation à la traduction professionnelle de l'anglais vers le français*. (3rd ed.). Les Presses de l'Université d'Ottawa.

Dion, Jennifer. (2012). *Le défi de former une relève scientifique d'expression française*. Conseil supérieur de la langue française, Gouvernement du Québec.

Gajo, Laurent. (2007). Linguistic knowledge and subject knowledge: How does bilingualism contribute to subject development? *International Journal of Bilingual Education and Bilingualism, 10*(5), 563–581.

Gajo, Laurent, Grobet, Anne, Serra, Cecilia, Steffen, Gabriela, Müller, Gabriele & Berthoud, Anne-Claude. (2013). Plurilingualisms and knowledge construction in higher education. In Anne-Claude Berthoud, François Grin & Georges Lüdi (Eds.), *Exploring the dynamics of multilingualism: The DYLAN project* (pp. 279–298). John Benjamins.

García, Ofelia & Li, Wei. (2014). *Translanguaging: language, bilingualism and education*. Palgrave Macmillan.

Gavioli, Laura. (1996). *Exploring corpora for ESP learning*. John Benjamins.

Gentil, Guillaume. (2003). *Identity construction and academic biliteracy: Case studies of francophone science writers* [Unpublished dissertation]. McGill University. Montréal, QC, Canada.

Gentil, Guillaume. (2005). Commitments to academic biliteracy: Case studies of Francophone university writers. *Written Communication, 22*(4), 421–471.

Gentil, Guillaume. (2006a). EAP and technical writing without borders: The impact of departmentalization on the teaching and learning of academic writing in a first and second language. In Paul Matsuda, Christina Ortmeier-Hooper & Xiaoye You (Eds.), *The politics of second language writing: in search of the promised land* (pp. 147–167). Parlor Press.

Gentil, Guillaume. (2006b). Variation in goals and activities for multilingual writing. In Alister Cumming (Ed.), *Goals for writing in university: English as a second language students and their instructors* (pp. 142–156). John Benjamins.

Gentil, Guillaume. (2011). A biliteracy agenda for genre research. *Journal of Second Language Writing, 20*(1), 6–23.

Gentil, Guillaume. (2019). Translanguaging and multilingual academic literacies: How do we translate that into French? Should we? *Pour en faire quoi ? (et pourquoi s'en faire?*. *Cahiers de l'ILOB/OLBI Working Papers*, 3–41. https://uottawa.scholarsportal.info/ottawa/index.php/ILOB-OLBI/article/view/3831 .

Gevers, Jeroen. (2018). Translingualism revisited: Language difference and hybridity in L2 writing. *Journal of Second Language Writing, 40*, 73–83.

Gillmor, Don, Michaud, Achille & Turgeon, Pierre. (2001). *Canada: A people's history*. McClelland & Stewart.

Graves, Roger & Graves, Heather. (2012). Writing programs worldwide: One Canadian perspective. In Chris Thais, Gerd Bräuer, Paula Carlino, Lisa Ganobscisk-Williams & Aparna Sinha (Eds.), *Writing programs worldwide: Profiles of academic writing in many places* (pp. 117–127). The WAC Clearinghouse; Parlor Press. https://doi.org/10.37514/PER-B.2012.0346.2.10.

Hamel, Marie-Josée, Séror, Jérémie & Dion, Chantal. (2015). *Writers in action: Modelling and scaffolding second-language learners' writing process*. Higher Education Quality Council of Ontario.

Heller, Monica. (2008). *Repenser le plurilinguisme: langue, postnationalisme et la nouvelle économie mondialisée*. *Diversité urbaine*, 163–176.

Heller, Monica. (2011). *Paths to post-nationalism: A critical ethnography of language and identity* Oxford University Press.

Heller, Monica. (2015). *Sustaining the nation: The making and moving of language and nation*. Oxford University Press.

Hidden, Marie-Odile. (2013). *Pratiques d'écriture: Apprendre à rédiger en langue étrangère*. Hachette.

Hornberger, Nancy H. & Link, Holly. (2012). Translanguaging and transnational literacies in multilingual classrooms: a biliteracy lens. *International Journal of Bilingual Education and Bilingualism, 15*(3), 261–278.

Horner, Bruce & Alvarez, Sara P. (2019). Defining translinguality. *Literacy in Composition Studies, 7*(2), 1–30.

Horner, Bruce, Lu, Min-Zhan, Royster, Jacqueline Jones & Trimbur, John. (2011). Language difference in writing: Toward a translingual approach. *College English, 73*(3), 303–321.

Horner, Bruce & Tetreault, Elliot. (2016). Translation as (global) writing. *Composition Studies, 44*(1), 13–30.

Jakobson, Roman. (1959/2000). On linguistic aspects of translation. In Lawrence Venuti (Ed.), *The translation studies reader* (pp. 113–118). Routledge.

Kecskes, Istvan. (2010). Dual and multilanguage systems. *International Journal of Multilingualism, 7*(2), 91–109.

Kiefer, K., Palmquist, M., Carbone, N., Cox, M. & Melzer, D. (2021). *An Introduction to Writing Across the Curriculum.* https://wac.colostate.edu/resources/wac/intro/.

Kiernan, Julia, Meier, Joyce & Wang, Xiqiao. (2016). Negotiating languages and cultures: Enacting translingualism through a translation assignment. *Composition Studies, 44*(1), 89–107.

Kymlicka, Will. (1995). *Multicultural Citizenship.* Clarendon Press.

Kymlicka, Will. (2004). *Le mythe de la citoyenneté transnationale. Critique internationale* (23), 97–111.

Lépine, Martin & Hébert, Manon. (2013). De l'intérêt de la notion de littératie en francophonie : un état des lieux en sciences de l'éducation. [On the relevance of the notion of literacy in Francophone countries: the situation in the field of education]. *Globe, 16*(1), 25–43.

Lewis, Gwyn, Jones, Bryn & Baker, Colin. (2012). Translanguaging: Origins and development from school to street and beyond. *Educational Research and Evaluation, 18*(7), 641–654.

Liddicoat, Anthony & Zarate, Geneviève. (2009). *La didactique des langues et des cultures face à la circulation internationale des idées. Le français dans le mode,* 9–15.

Lonsdale, Allison Beeby. (1996). *Teaching translation from Spanish to English: Worlds beyond words.* University of Ottawa Press.

Lu, Min-Zhan & Horner, Bruce. (2013). Translingual literacy, language difference, and matters of agency. *College English, 75*(6), 582–607.

Lyster, Roy. (2019). Translanguaging in immersion: Cognitive support or social prestige? *Canadian Modern Language Review/La Revue Canadienne des Langues Vivantes, 75*(4), 340–352.

MacSwan, Jeff. (2017). A Multilingual perspective on translanguaging. *American Educational Research Journal, 54*(1), 167–201

Manchón, Rosa M. (2013). Writing. In François Grosjean & Ping Li (Eds.), *The psycholinguistics of bilingualism* (pp. 100–115). Wiley-Blackwell.

Mareschal, Geneviève. (2005). *L'enseignement de la traduction au Canada.* [The teaching of translation in Canada]. *Meta, 50*(1), 250–262.

Milson-Whyte, Vivette. (2014). Working English through code-meshing: implications for denigrated language varieties and their users. In Bruce Horner & Karen Kopelson (Eds.), *Reworking English in rhetoric and composition: Global interrogations, local interventions* (pp. 103–115). Southern Illinois University Press.

MLA Ad Hoc Committee on Foreign Languages. (2007). *Foreign languages and higher education: New structures for a changed world.* https://www.mla.org/Resources/Research/Surveys-Reports-and-Other-Documents/Teaching-Enrollments-and-Programs

/Foreign-Languages-and-Higher-Education-New-Structures-for-a-Changed-World.

Moore, Danièle & Gajo, Laurent. (2009). French voices on plurilingualism and pluriculturalism: Theory, significance and perspectives [Special Issue]. *International Journal of Multilingualism, 6*(2), 137–227.

Parini, Lorena. (2010). Le concept de genre: constitution d'un champ d'analyse, controverses épistémologiques, linguistiques et politiques. *Socio-logos. Revue de l'association française de sociologie,* (5).

Pavlenko, Aneta. (2005). Bilingualism and thought. In Judith Kroll & Annette De Groot (Eds.), *Handbook of bilingualism: Psycholinguistic approaches* (pp. 433–453). Oxford University Press.

Pym, Anthony. (2016). *Translation solutions for many languages: Histories of a flawed dream.* Bloomsbury.

Raus, Rachele. (2013). *La terminologie multilingue: La traduction des termes de l'égalité H/F dans le discours international.* de Boeck.

Rozycki, William V., Nagelhout, Ed & Connor, Ulla. (2008). *Contrastive rhetoric: Reaching to intercultural rhetoric* (Vol. 169). John Benjamins.

Statistics Canada. (2001). *Aboriginal languages (from Catalogue no. 89–589-XIE: Aboriginal Peoples Survey 2001—initial findings).* http://www.statcan.gc.ca/pub/89-589-x/4067801-eng.htm.

Statistics Canada. (2015). Mother tongue of a person. Retrieved August 16, 2022 from https://www23.statcan.gc.ca/imdb/p3Var.pl?Function=DEC&Id=34023 .

Statistics Canada. (2017, August 31. Proportion of mother tongue responses for various regions in Canada, 2016 Canada. https://www12.statcan.gc.ca/census-recensement/2016/dp-pd/dv-vd/lang/index-eng.cfm.

Tardy, Christine M. (2009). *Building genre knowledge.* Parlor Press.

Turner, Brian & Kearns, Judith. (2012). Department of rhetoric, writing, and communications at the University of Winnipeg. In Chris Thais, Gerd Bräuer, Paula Carlino, Lisa Ganobscisk-Williams & Aparna Sinha (Eds.), *Writing programs worldwide: Profiles of academic writing in many places* (pp. 129–138). The WAC Clearinghouse; Parlor Press. https://doi.org/10.37514/PER-B.2012.0346.2.11.

Vinay, Jean-Paul & Darbelnet, Jean. (1995). *Comparative stylistics of French and English: A methodology for translation.* John Benjamins.

Part 2. Professional Development: Trans- Perspectives

Advancing a Transnational, Transdisciplinary and Translingual Professional Development Framework for Teaching Assistants in Writing and Spanish Programs: An Update

Alyssa G. Cavazos
UNIVERSITY OF TEXAS RIO GRANDE VALLEY

Marcela Hebbard
UNIVERSITY OF TEXAS RIO GRANDE VALLEY

José E. Hernández
UNIVERSITY OF TEXAS RIO GRANDE VALLEY

Crystal Rodriguez
SOUTH TEXAS COLLEGE

Geoffrey Schwarz
UNIVERSITY OF TEXAS RIO GRANDE VALLEY[1]

In 2018, we published a translingual and transdisciplinary collaborative piece that sought to respond to the call for writing and language programs to develop professional development opportunities central to multilingual writers' needs as language learners and writers and their sophisticated and diverse language and writing abilities (Guerra, 2008; Horner et al., 2011; Kells, 2007; Tardy, 2017). We described the design, implementation, and implications of a multilingual

---

1   This work was supported by the UTRGV Graduate College and Department of Writing and Language Studies. We wish to thank the Graduate College and our department chair, Dr. Colin Charlton (who submitted the grant application), for their support and commitment to enhancing multilingual pedagogies and professional development at our institution. Los autores desean reconocer a Analynn Bustamante y a Estela Hernández por su ayuda y colaboración en reunir fuentes secundarias durante la etapa inicial de este proyecto. We also wish to thank Brittany Ramirez, who offered ideas for designing translingual assignments informed by her thesis research. We wish to thank linguistics, rhetoric and composition, and Spanish graduate students, teaching assistants, undergraduate students, and instructors for their insights and willingness to engage in multilingual conversations across disciplines by sharing their personal and pedagogical experiences.

DOI: https://doi.org/10.37514/ATD-B.2023.1527.2.04

pedagogy professional development series for teaching assistants in a transnational and multilingual context (Cavazos, et al., 2018). In this chapter, we provide an update on what has transpired since the series ended. We arrange the chapter as follows: first, we give a brief description of the institutional context where the workshops took place. Then we briefly describe the professional development series for readers unfamiliar with our first piece. After that, we provide an update on what happened after the series ended that emphasizes the impact, affordances, and challenges of implementing this type of workshop and how the authors continue to enact the core components of the proposed workshop in their disciplinary contexts and teaching practices.

Local Context: What Does It Mean to Teach Bilingually?

According to Barry Thatcher et al. (2015), the Mexico/U.S. border is "a dynamic rhetorical space with multiple language varieties (Spanish, English, and Spanglish), and at least four complexly-related cultural and rhetorical traditions" (p. 170). This rhetorical dynamic complicates and challenges U.S. mainstream writing programs because multilingual and multicultural writing in border regions is a constant occurrence in academic environments. Isabel Baca et al. (2019) assert that academic institutions located on the Mexico/U.S. border tend to have a large percentage of students who are bilingual/translingual, and many are Mexican nationals who cross the border frequently. Established in 2015 as a result of a consolidation between two legacy institutions and aware of the region's sociocultural and linguistic context, our institution, the University of Texas Rio Grande Valley (UTRGV) devised a vision of becoming a "highly engaged bilingual university." This vision has led faculty at all levels, from full professors to teaching assistants, to ask: "What does it mean to be a bilingual university?" "What does it mean to teach bilingually?" In the Writing and Language Studies Department, faculty from the units of Linguistics, Rhetoric & Composition, Spanish, Asian Studies, English as a Second Language, and French, among others, have asked critical questions regarding the teaching of writing and language acquisition. Colleagues teaching rhetoric and composition asked: "How should I adapt my pedagogy to help students develop bilingual writing abilities?" Faculty teaching Spanish as a heritage language inquired: "How can we respond to students' diverse levels of language fluency in Spanish heritage?" Faculty teaching modern languages asked: "If I am not bilingual in English and Spanish, how can I effectively contribute to fulfilling UTRGV's vision?" These questions fueled our desire to explore building linguistically inclusive educational environments in writing and language coursework.

In 2016, the Graduate College awarded our newly created department with a grant to develop a Multilingual Pedagogy Professional Development (MPPD) series for teaching assistants (TAs). The rationale behind this initiative was that an MPPD centered on TAs could enhance the quality of writing instruction in undergraduate courses and encourage TAs to build cross-linguistic awareness. Supporting TAs' pedagogical development is of vital importance since graduate students (and non-tenured faculty alike) are usually hired to teach undergraduate courses (Smith, 2018). As a result, TAs serve as primary points of contact for undergraduate students across disciplines (Gallardo-Williams & Petrovich, 2017).[2]

To design and implement this professional development opportunity for TAs, a transdisciplinary, multilingual research team was formed consisting of graduate students and instructors in rhetoric and composition, Spanish, English as a second language, and anthropology. As Shuck (this volume) argues, "dialogue between faculty within and across disciplines is a critical first step toward a more inclusive view of language in the classroom"; we aimed to build a cross-disciplinary dialogue among the research team. The makeup of our team exemplifies the linguistic richness of our border region. Four of us were born in Mexico and moved to the United States of America at different ages. All five of us speak and possess different levels of literacy competence in Spanish. While each one of us joined the project for different reasons, all five of us were committed to exploring what it means to teach writing and language bilingually. (Please see Gentil, this volume, for a similar attempt to bridge multidisciplinary and translingual approaches to writing in a case study set in the Canadian Francophone-Anglophone context.) Although we (and our institution) are still trying to answer that question, by the end of the project back in 2016, we arrived at a point of convergence, which sees the diverse linguistic and rhetorical realities in our region as a site where writing and language fluidity, hybridity and blurring of boundaries is the norm (Brunk-Chavez et al., 2015; Christoffersen, 2019). Furthermore, this convergence treats students and teachers as experts in languaging (Robinson et al., 2020). In the next section, we briefly describe the four components of the MPPD series for readers unfamiliar with our first piece.[3]

---

2   The following is, in part, the original grant proposal Dr. Colin Charlton submitted to the Graduate College: "[The Department of Writing and Language Studies should] explore transdisciplinary TA training with the idea that language acquisition (technical, cultural, or professional) is a concern of all learning situations. WLS is primed to begin integrating a multilingual group of graduate students and leveraging their backgrounds for the development of multilingual lessons and community literacy interventions. For the spring and possibly summer, a small group of graduate faculty and advanced graduate students could study existing graduate training programs, design a multilingual one within the existing UTRGV channels and degrees, and prepare it for launch in fall 2016."

3   We presented our work in March 2017 at the Conference on College Composition and Communication in Portland, Oregon under the title, "A Translingual Approach to Professional Development for First-Year Spanish and Writing Instructors."

Brief Description of the Design and Components of the Multilingual Pedagogy Professional Development

As explained elsewhere (Cavazos, et al., 2018), due to our diverse disciplinary backgrounds, we knew as we began our collaboration that we faced challenges based on disciplinary and personal perceptions of English and Spanish and variations of these languages in the teaching of writing and language. To minimize the risk of advocating for a single perspective, a common problem that those in charge of designing professional development opportunities face, we engaged in cross-disciplinary research and pedagogical conversations. We met biweekly during the spring 2016 semester to discuss our disciplinary perspectives and assigned research areas that included multilingual pedagogy, curriculum design, professional development in writing and Spanish programs, and assessment of professional development effectiveness. We recruited graduate students interested in "language learning and teaching, multilingualism/language diversity, writing studies, feedback on student writing, professional development, curriculum design, and/or assessment." At the end, ten graduate students responded to the call and six consistently attended the sessions. The series consisted of four sessions.

First Session: Self Reflection

The first session focused on providing background knowledge of the series and participants' self-reflection on their linguistic background as learners, writers, and teachers, as Anne Ellen Geller (2011) recommended. As Joyce Meier et al. (this volume) explore the need to foster critical awareness of linguistic differences among multilingual and international students through their transdisciplinary collaboration model, we intended to build a sense of critical self-awareness of linguistic differences among the participants in the series through the following questions:

1. What languages/dialects do you know/use? In what contexts do you use them?
2. To what extent have you used all your language resources in your education/academic work?

The interactions revealed that some TAs and instructors who participated in the professional development series learned English as a second language, others learned Spanish as second language, and yet others learned English and Spanish simultaneously. Subsequently, we asked participants to engage in an interdisciplinary exchange of ideas by reflecting on and discussing the following questions in small cross-disciplinary groups:

3. What do you think is the role of language diversity in the classes you teach and why?

4. What languages/dialects do your students know/use? To what extent do your students use or draw on their language resources in the work they do in your class?
5. Identify two to three questions you have about the presence of language diversity in the classes you teach.

The interdisciplinary exchange of ideas during the first session provided us with opportunities to learn and better understand our disciplinary backgrounds and perceptions of language. As a result, we collectively identified the following questions:

1. What is the role of language difference or extent of language difference within different academic units (e.g., writing program, writing center, language learning programs, institution)?
2. How does a grammar-focused and/or a prescriptive approach to teaching writing and language influence/impact native/non-native speakers/writers?
3. How do we reconcile different expectations (e.g., course, program, department, institution) while valuing different languages while adhering to expectations?
4. How does the presence of language diversity impact assessment practices?

The first session aimed to build a sense of community as we prepared to explore these questions in subsequent sessions.

Second Session: Translingual Assignments

The second session focused on brainstorming potential translingual assignments from a Spanish and writing instructional perspective. For this session, we asked TAs to read "Cultivating a Rhetorical Sensibility in the Translingual Writing Classroom," by Juan Guerra (2016). We worked in small groups to respond to questions on the meaning of "rhetorical sensibility" from a language learning and writing instruction perspective (see Appendix).

TAs and instructors explored what is often valued in writing and language learning courses; particularly, they explored the differences between applying a translingual approach in Spanish for heritage language learners and Spanish for non-native speakers. Spanish TAs explored how a translingual pedagogy might work best in a heritage language class or an upper-level Spanish course rather than in an introductory non-native Spanish language learning course.

In this session, we designed an activity that would convey to all TAs that they possess knowledge based on their personal, scholarly, and teaching experiences, which creates an environment centered on their meaning-making rather than on a prescribed set of pedagogical tips to implement. We asked a former teaching assistant to develop a handout describing linguistically inclusive writing assignments informed by her thesis work. Afterwards, TAs reflected on how they could use or revise the examples provided. As a result of our conversations, TAs and instructors discussed potential linguistically inclusive writing assignments in partners or small collaborative groups. This type of activity aligns with the goals of a translingual approach, which includes encouraging instructors to develop their translingual pedagogy (Canagarajah, 2016) and ensuring graduate students facilitate the conversations (Hall & Navarro, this volume; Worden et al., 2015). Some of the assignments we discussed as a group that might apply both to language learning and writing courses included literacy or language autobiographies, language ethnographies within different discourse communities, and reflective writing activities on language and grammatical choices.

Out of the four sessions, most participants found this one to be the most challenging and transformative as we engaged in conversations not only across different languages and disciplines but also pedagogical values. For most of us, it was the first time we learned about translingualism, and for those outside the discipline of composition, it was the first time they were exposed to the term "translingual writing." As a result of this session, several transdisciplinary and translingual collaborations emerged. Later in the chapter we share the lessons learned from one of the authors as she collaborated with a Spanish-as-a-Heritage Language (SHL) instructor during and after the series ended.

Third Session: Linguistically Inclusive Assessment Practices

The third session addressed how we might design assessment practices that are fair and equitable using a linguistically inclusive approach. We read Paul Kei Matsuda's (2012), "Let's Face It: Language Issues and the Writing Program Administrator." The session was designed in two parts:

1. exploring Matsuda's article and
2. brainstorming the design of linguistically inclusive writing assignments (Appendix).

The purpose of the discussion questions about Matsuda's article was to learn about the participants' existing assessment approaches and their values toward responding to and assessing student writing. We discussed the following questions as a group:

1. What assessment tools do you use in your writing and language class to assess student learning?
2. What specific tools/methods do you use to assess specific student learning outcomes for the course, program, department, and/or university?

3. How does Matsuda's discussion of instructional alignment, formative assessment practices, and metalinguistic commentary/awareness align with and/or offer a new perspective on your assessment methods in your language and writing classes?
4. How do we respond to the growing linguistic diversity in our classrooms through assessment tools and the design of writing and language assignments?

These questions helped us understand assessment practices from a language learning and writing studies perspective as well as how instructors who teach writing and language responded to Matsuda's arguments about writing assessment.

Fourth Session: Reflection and Next Steps

The final session was a reflection session intended for participants to share their writing assignments and offer suggestions for the future of the series. Reflection is critical to professional growth and development of innovative pedagogies, as Manel Lacorte (2016) argues: "Reflective practices should be an essential component of language teacher courses and programs in L2 or general education units for TAs . . . reflective practices may be the foundation for a research component in teacher preparation programs . . ." (p. 111). When we are open and willing to engage in rhetorical dialogue with colleagues from diverse linguistic backgrounds and disciplinary expertise, we create the necessary "contact zone [conditions] valuable for reflection and negotiations of translinguality" (Canagarajah, 2016, p. 268). For this reason, the final session was intended to engage in a reflective and collaborative experience, which enriched our respective pedagogical approaches and enhanced collaborative opportunities within our department. During this final reflection session, participants finalized the collaboration objectives they had started during the second session.

By briefly describing the content and purpose of each of the four sessions above, it is our goal that the reader gain an appreciation of the time and effort it takes to develop cross-disciplinary and cross-linguistic collaborations that encourage and equip TAs and faculty alike to become aware of their language choices and resources as they make sense of their language learning and writing process. In the next section we describe what happened after the series ended.

Looking Back Forward: Lessons Learned from the MPPD

In this section we would have liked to highlight and include reflections from the TAs who participated in this project. Unfortunately, we are not able to do that for two reasons. First, the MPPD series was a pilot and we did not seek IRB approval.

By the time the series ended, and we considered applying to the IRB office, many of the participants had graduated and moved away. Second, not having funding to continue impacted our ability to offer another series where we could gather data. We discuss more about the difficulty and need to implement and sustain such initiatives in the implication for teaching section.

Despite these circumstances, when we developed the series back in 2016, we saw our task as an opportunity to engage in conversations on how the transdisciplinary realities of not only our team, but also our region, influence the teaching of writing and languages. As we designed a four-session series, we recognized that the meaning of translingual practices emerged from our lived personal and pedagogical experiences and our context (Garcia & Kleyn, 2016). We also intended to empower TAs as teachers and scholars with a wealth of knowledge and experience related to language difference. Scholars have argued that while TAs might be new to teaching, they possess knowledge we want to recognize (Canagarajah, 2016), especially their experiences with language difference pertinent to their developing identities as educators. We acknowledged from the beginning that TAs play different roles simultaneously—they are both students and emerging educators. We learned that when we value others' teaching and language approaches and their multifaceted linguistic identities, we create room for reflection, rethinking, and redesign of pedagogical practices that can lead to linguistic inclusivity and equity. Thus, in the next section, we provide an update that emphasizes the impact, affordances, and challenges that implementing this type of workshop has on the research team. Our goal is to show that participating in the creation and implementation of a translingual initiative series transformed us. All of us continue to navigate, enact, and explore the core components of the proposed workshop in our disciplinary contexts and pedagogies.

Lessons from First Session: Self-reflection

Geoffrey's reflection on his participation in the series focused on two overlapping lines of inquiry—first, on the emancipatory potential of translingual pedagogy to disrupt hegemonic notions of language, race, and belonging and, secondly, on the methodological challenges of integrating translingual methods into qualitative research practice. For Geoffrey, the power of translingual pedagogy lies in its emphasis on the colonial ideologies that govern language use in the classroom. Understanding named languages as social constructs that operate in the context of European colonialism was particularly salient for Geoffrey, given the legacy of discrimination and delegitimization of racialized bilingual communities in Valley classrooms.

Geoffrey views translingual pedagogy as a framework to subvert the assimilationist and anti-Latinx narratives embedded in the English-only education that have marginalized the language practices of poor and immigrant communities in the Rio Grande

Valley for decades. Similarly, transnational and transdisciplinary pedagogies have the potential to empower students to recognize and challenge the political-ideological borders between nation-states and academic disciplines that reproduce systematic inequality in and out of the classroom. In this way, the professional development series was a much-needed point of entry for students to engage, deconstruct, and blur the boundaries and divisions that separate languages, disciplines, and countries.

After the series, Geoffrey integrated translingual techniques into his qualitative and evaluation research practice (e.g., participatory focus groups, translation, and storytelling activities). Although many researchers have incorporated a translingual approach into their data collection and analyses, Geoffrey noted a gap in the literature on translingual research methodology, particularly in the context of multilingual focus groups. A translingual focus group approach encourages research participants to engage with important issues by using language practice relevant to their experiences and identities. In this way, translingual focus groups can produce data that are more meaningful to the interests of participants and can help them recognize their needs within the context of their own language practice and empower them to mobilize accordingly.

Crystal Even though Crystal was born in the Valley and learned both English and Spanish as a small child, soon after she started school, English became the primary focus until Spanish was revisited as a language elective in junior high. She remembers that during the initial pilot session—in which most students spoke in Spanish—she refrained from speaking Spanish for fear of "messing up" questions or comments in front of native Spanish speakers. However, seeing writing and Spanish graduate students in the pilot sessions question the pragmatics of language difference in writing and language-learning courses helped her realize there is a continued need to discuss language issues openly to not only gain awareness but also identify ways that assist in recognizing language difference in the teaching of writing and languages.

A few months after the workshop, Crystal began teaching at a junior college also located in the Rio Grande Valley. Most of the college's students tend to transfer to UTRGV after they have completed either an associate degree or equivalent hours. The population at the junior college is made up of a large percentage of traditional (those who attend college after high school graduation) and non-traditional (students who begin college after taking time off after high school) Latinx students. From the start, Crystal knew she wanted to teach students about translanguaging so that they could understand the importance of its application. As a lecturer at the college, she started each First-Year Composition course by sharing a brief lesson on language difference and then asking students to write about their language narratives. The lesson involves short videos on regional language differences throughout America, discussion, and reflection. She believes that starting the semester in this manner helps students see how their attitudes shape their understanding of their and others' language use. For example, Crystal incorporates peer-review sessions where students learn how to critique each other's work, and while this practice can be challenging for all students, it is especially challenging for those who are not English dominant speakers. Without the introductory lesson, she believes some students may not understand how their language attitudes (especially negative ones) can greatly affect the confidence and willingness of non-English dominant students to share their work with others. Furthermore, she hopes the language diversity lesson will help English dominant speakers appreciate and value the linguistic abilities of translingual students. Apart from affecting peer-to-peer relationships, the lesson is Crystal's way of approaching students who are grappling with academic requirements due to varying language proficiencies and serves to welcome those who have felt pressured by prescriptivism.

Esteban During the first session back in 2016, Esteban recalls questioning how this collaboration would help his teaching as he believed that, as a sociolinguist, he was familiar with the ideas discussed. To make sense of the experience, he identified terminology used during the workshop and connected them to concepts he knew within his own field of expertise. Specifically, he remembers being surprised to see instructors of English writing courses accepting translingual approaches; in his mind and personal experience, English writing courses are sites where standard English exerted full hegemony. When asked to think about the extent to which he uses his language resources in the classroom, Esteban is sensitive about promoting language variation present in the local community, often missing in textbooks, because students often resort to their whole linguistic repertoires in real linguistic encounters, including their first or second language or a mixture of the two. For this reason, it is critical to introduce students to different registers, styles, and varieties in heritage language courses, alongside more academic registers. Because students often bring to class forms and varieties that are highly stigmatized at the social level, a standard language ideology serves to reinforce insecurities students have about ways of talking in their community, and standard language ideologies have negative effects on students, such as the invalidation of home varieties and other linguistic modalities and potentially erodes pride in their heritage language and bilingual repertoires.

After the series ended, Esteban has continued to seek ways to promote the teaching of language variation in the language classroom with a particular emphasis on the validation of the local bilingual speech. Through a critical analysis of ideologies of language and attitudes, he fosters a language awareness perspective where students can begin to understand the relationship between language and the power structures that (re)produce social inequalities.

Lessons from Second Session: Translingual Assignments

Marcela Back in the fall 2016, Marcela found this session to be the most challenging and transformative when the group engaged in conversations not only across different languages and disciplines but also pedagogical values. When Marcela paired up to collaborate with a Spanish-as-a-Heritage Language (SHL) instructor, disciplinary differences became visible immediately. To negotiate this situation, Marcela suggested to her SHL collaborator to draw on writing across the curriculum scholarship. They read Justin Rademaeker's 2015 piece titled *Is WAC/WID ready for the transdisciplinary research university?* which talks about the importance of engaging in rhetorical dialogue when conducting transdisciplinary collaborations. Their candid exchange afforded them a basic, yet valuable understanding of their respective disciplinary knowledge and conventions, which they drew on to design a collaborative transdisciplinary and translingual writing activity intended to help students develop linguistic agency.

While the implementation of the activity was not a requirement of the series, Marcela and her SHL collaborator decided to pilot their activity in the spring 2017 semester. Marcela and the SHL instructor revised and implemented collaborative transdisciplinary and translingual student activities over the next three consecutive semesters. In addition, they also presented their work in three academic peer-reviewed national and international conferences and published one chapter in an edited collection where they described in detail their collaborative transdisciplinary and translingual journey and student activity (Hebbard & Hernández, 2020). They framed their collaboration around the concept of *Transfronterizo* because of its applicability to students as well as instructors' linguistic practices and experiences. The purpose of listing these academic activities is to show the impact of the series on teachers' pedagogical intentions. Below, Marcela offers a brief account of her collaboration and examples of students' written responses.

After implementing the pilot activity and reading student reflections in spring 2017, the SHL instructor and Marcela learned they needed to revise their activity and ensure their students engaged in face-to-face rhetorical dialogues to increase opportunities for them to verbally articulate issues of language and identity through translingual and transdisciplinary perspectives. They also applied and obtained IRB approval. When they carried out the revised activity, a total of 53 students (25 = FYW, 27 = SHL) participated in the activity. Students were given the freedom to complete the activities, which included a summary/response to a common reading, written reflections, response to peer's reflection, and a short video describing what they learned from this activity in their preferred language; that is, either English or Spanish (for a description of the activity components see Hebbard & Hernández, 2020).

The following are the written responses that two FYW students made to their SHL peers' reflections. Our purpose is to illustrate students' views of language and language practices from two disciplinary perspectives as well as their translingual/ transfronterizo identities. Two of the five guiding questions students had to answer were: What do you find interesting or surprising in your peer's reflection? And, if you could ask your peer anything about his/her reflection, what would you ask? In her reflection, a female SHL student wrote,

> Personalmente yo creo que debemos de expresarnos como uno piensa y no forzar a alguien a escribir en forma estándar porque eso lleva al individuo a tener un límite en su manera de pensar y creer que la manera correcta para expresarse debe ser formal con palabras profesionales y no debe ser así. Por ello, el método translingual puede ser útil.

A female FYW student responded to her peer in English,

> Even though my peer has a good point when she states that standard writing shouldn't be forced on students since each individual writes differently, one thing I'd like to ask is: Why do you think standardized writing can hinder the way you express yourself? Standard writing can help you express yourself in a formal way; it doesn't stop you from saying what you want to say.

Our second example is from a male SHL student. He wrote in English,

> A translingual approach can be very comfortable for many students because many students, including myself, are used in doing assignments in English and then when we switch to Spanish we can struggle. That's why I believe heritage language courses should value language difference.

A female FYW student responded to him in Spanish,

> Las experiencias de mi compañero son similares pero a la vez varían ya que cuando me vine a estudiar al Valle de Texas, yo estaba acostumbrada a escribir en español y en la universidad tuve que cambiar al inglés. Si le pudiera preguntar a mi compañero algo sería ¿cuales son los beneficios que se pueden encontrar en una comunidad translingual?

While the analysis of these interactions is not the focus of this chapter, it is interesting to note that both FYW students raised questions about the prompt acceptance of translingualism the SHL students' reflections imply. From a pedagogical perspective, these written reflections and interactions are an example of translingual/transfronterizo identities in that these students had to traverse language (e.g., had to read SHL peers' reflection in Spanish or English) and engage in complex cognitive processes to draw and (re)construct meaning as they formulated their written responses (Motha et al., 2012). Furthermore, they also considered their peers' and their own disciplinary and linguistic ideologies, if only briefly, which serves as a glimpse into their expertise in languaging (Robinson et al., 2020).

Regarding assessment, the pilot and revised student-centered translingual activities Marcela and the SHL instructor designed were low-stakes for two reasons: 1) they did not want students to stress over a grade, and 2) they are still considering how to best assess translingual writing in a way that is fair and promotes linguistic social justice (Lee, 2016). How to assess students' writing and language learning was (and continues to be) one of the questions among writing and language instructors.

Lessons from Fourth Session: Reflection and Next Steps

Alyssa For Alyssa, the last session revealed the challenges inherent in advocating for translingual approaches to language and writing instruction, especially within transdisciplinary conversations. As early as the first session, instructors voiced concern on how we should assess writing and language learning within a pedagogy that welcomes and accepts language differences. Particularly, participants were concerned about language and writing standards and the message our pedagogy would send students about language "correctness." However, if our assessment practices privilege a standard variety of either Spanish or English, we continue to send a message that dismisses the linguistic realities that exist within a transborder space. For this reason, assessment practices in writing and language learning coursework should be responsive to students' experiences, knowledge, and beliefs about language difference. In other words, our assessment practices should be rooted from within the transborder student experience rather than imposed by an academic standard, existing outside of or in opposition to those realities.

After the series ended, Alyssa continued to explore assessment practices in relation to language difference in the teaching of writing. She developed a translingual disposition questionnaire as a self-assessment tool for students enrolled in her first-year writing, sophomore writing, and upper-level English courses. The questionnaire can help instructors further understand student learning and meaning-making about writing instruction and language learning. Translingual dispositions refers to both the openness to language difference and enactment of language difference as defined by Lee and Jenks (2016). The questionnaire has been validated as measuring translingual dispositions related to language negotiations, resistance to standard language practices, and questioning language expectations (Cavazos & Karaman, 2021).

Alyssa has used the questionnaire as a pedagogical tool to learn about and better understand students' linguistic experiences. Recently, Alyssa collaborated with a bilingual and literacy studies professor on a project where they assigned the translingual disposition questionnaire to their students in bilingual and English language arts teacher preparation courses. The students took the questionnaire at the beginning and end of the semester and provided a written reflection exploring shifts, nuances, and complexities in their responses. As a result, writing and language instructors can draw on the questionnaire as a self-assessment tool that validates transborder students' linguistic realities and places those realities at the forefront of writing instruction and language learning. Sandra Musanti et al. (2020) claim that "preparing preservice teachers to serve an increasingly culturally and linguistically diverse student population requires considering the criticality of fostering translingual dispositions as content in teacher preparation programs" (p. 84). This implication is crucial as our students, regardless of academic path, will work in increasingly diverse local and global contexts. Therefore, creating opportunities across academic disciplines that encourage reflection and assessment of their and others' translingual dispositions ultimately places the linguistic realities of our transborder context as central to learning and meaning-making, rather than something "foreign" or "different" that opposes often-privileged academic language expectations.

Implications for Teaching

In our first article we wrote that as a result of the multilingual pedagogy professional development series, we learned that engaging in transdisciplinary conversations with our colleagues is critical in responding to the linguistic needs and assets of our students and that in order for such collaboration to be meaningful for all, a professional development series like this needs to be institutionalized at the program, departmental, and university levels. While we believe the updates we incorporated throughout the chapter attest to our commitment to the former statement, institutionalizing or even sustaining a professional series for TAs is a complex process beyond our immediate control that involves multiple divisions, disciplines, priorities, and financial support. A sense of privilege of "standard" languages or "correctness" continues to exist across disciplines despite the university's support to develop linguistically inclusive pedagogies to become a "bilingual" institution. In order to challenge monolingualism as the norm in higher education, Geller (2011) argues for the "need to know about multilingual faculty members' experiences as learners, writers and teachers" (p. 4), including TAs. Furthermore, after the grant ended, TA training that includes topics about language difference only takes place in the graduate practicum course offered in the rhetoric and composition program. TAs in the Spanish program do not take a graduate practicum course; however, they attend a pre-semester training and monthly meetings. If a practicum course existed for Spanish TAs like the graduate course for writing TAs, there would be opportunities for faculty teaching practicum to engage in cross-disciplinary collaboration, particularly with a focus on how writing can also be used in language learning contexts. This collaboration among the TAs can enhance linguistically inclusive practices in their respective courses and build long-lasting cross- disciplinary, cross-linguistic relationships.

We hope that in the future, we can once again offer professional development sessions that facilitate conversation surrounding many of the questions, concerns, and issues raised by the TAs and other instructors during the series. For instance, TAs expressed concern regarding how to design translingual assignments, and although some scholars in rhetoric and composition have discussed implementing pedagogies that embrace translingualism (Guerra, 2016b), they tend to focus on assignments that mostly involve reading about translingualism. Therefore, instructors are left wondering about what a translingual approach might look like in practice. Because a translingual approach involves more of an awareness that students use and draw on all of their language resources while reading, drafting, and researching, course activities should facilitate this awareness of language use for both educators and students. Through our transdisciplinary professional development workshop, TAs had the opportunity to collaboratively brainstorm potential assignments that implemented a translingual approach. Through this collaborative work, they not only identified challenges that come from creating such assignments, but they also recognized how these assignments can enhance writing instruction and language learning. As A. Suresh Canagarajah (2016) explains, "Teacher preparation for translingual writing would focus on encouraging teachers to construct their pedagogies with sensitivity to student, writing, and course diversity, thus continuing to develop their pedagogical knowledge and practice for changing contexts of writing" (p. 266). The multidisciplinary workshop introduces participants to these sensitivities by first creating an awareness of the rhetorical abilities multilingual writers already possess, and by encouraging participants to reflect on their personal attitudes towards translingualism in order to better understand their own views toward a progressive approach to writing and language instruction.

In order to sustain a multidisciplinary translingual approach, the practice of reflection for both educators and students is essential. Even devoted advocates of language difference have grappled with fully embracing the practice because as language users, we are constantly reminded of linguistic hegemony, especially in academia. Therefore, through reflection, we can focus on why translingualism is important for current and future language instruction, since its aim is not just to include the languages and dialects of others, but to change the way we think about language and language use—a constant struggle for many. Bruce Horner (2016) argues that ". . . [W]e can recognize, and help our students learn to recognize and engage in, writing as the occasion for just such action-reflection, posing anew the ongoing challenge of what kind of difference to attempt to make through writing, how, and why" (p. 120). Additionally, as a result of rereading and providing updates on this collaborative work, we also advocate for the importance of continuing to share and reflect on teaching practice and research on translingual practices to further expand conversations and work through challenges across and within disciplinary borders. Through the practice of action-reflection, a translingual approach to writing and language instruction will likely be sustainable because the focus remains on awareness of language negotiations for both educators and students.

Implications for Research

Through our collaboration, we realized that the heterogeneous linguistic nature of multilingual, transborder students is a valuable resource that we should integrate into the writing and language studies curriculum. Multilingual students' differences in their linguistic repertoires can be used to "increase students' fluency" in written and oral communication in their first, second, and heritage language (Horner, Lu et al., 2011, p. 307).

The transdisciplinary aspect of the project helped us identify our different linguistic needs and approaches to achieve more inclusive pedagogical practices grounded on a translingual view of writing and language teaching. Geller (2011) calls for research to "push against the institutionalized and standardized English monolingual norms" by designing WAC programs and support services that "encourage faculty to learn about and reflect deeply on language experiences and language biases." Future research should focus on collecting data on the impact of a multilingual pedagogy professional development by collecting evaluations, conducting interviews and class observations, and analyzing primary documents, such as syllabi and course assignments. Data collection will help us apply a systematic approach to evaluating how our pedagogy is enriched by professional development focused on a translingual view to teaching writing in our disciplines. Empirical data would also allow comparisons within our disciplines to see whether our focus on a translingual approach to teaching writing and language studies has the same or a different impact on our pedagogies and students' language practices, and it could show the particular language practices that influence writing and language acquisition in each discipline, informing future studies and pedagogical practices. We also suggest research that investigates how writing-to-learn or learning-to-write approaches (Manchón, 2011) and service learning (Parra, 2016) can be implemented alongside translingual writing in writing and language learning contexts. While, as a collaborative team, we have not addressed these suggestions for future research as it pertains to the professional development of TAs in writing studies and Spanish, we have engaged in research about our translanguaging pedagogical practices in diverse contexts (Cavazos & Karaman, 2021; Hebbard & Hernández, 2020; Musanti & Cavazos, 2018; Musanti et al., 2020; Sánchez et al., 2019) and Alyssa has also engaged in the design, implementation, and research on the impact that professional development on translingual teaching practices has on instructors' beliefs about teaching across academic disciplines (Cavazos & Musanti, 2021).

Finally, we are interested in engaging in cross-institutional collaboration to explore how different factors, such as institutional context and faculty and student populations, impact how translingual approaches to teaching writing and languages are explored through professional development. In order to advance transdisciplinary and translingual approaches as a new normal in composition studies (Horner, NeCamp & Donahue, 2011; Tardy, 2017), we hope to provide a professional development framework that adapts to the linguistic realities of different institutional contexts and students' lived language experiences. Our respective language backgrounds, language perceptions, and linguistically inclusive pedagogies can impact our students' linguistic agency, academic success, and sense of belonging in higher education; therefore, it is critical to explore how multilingual students perceive the presence of language difference in the classroom and create opportunities where they can use all their language resources as they navigate through changing academic and community contexts.

References

Baca, Isabel, Hinojosa, Yndalecio Isaac & Murphy, Susan Wolff. (Eds.). (2019). *Bordered writers: Latinx identities and literacy practices at Hispanic-serving institutions*. SUNY Press.

Brunk-Chavez, Beth, Mangelsdorf, Kate, Wojahn, Patricia, Urzua-Beltran, Alfredo, Montoya, Omar, Thatcher, Barry & Valentine, Kathryn. (2015). Exploring the contexts of U.S.-Mexican border writing programs. In David S. Martins, (Ed.), *Transnational writing program administration* (pp. 138–160). Utah State University Press.

Canagarajah, A. Suresh. (2016). Translingual writing and teacher development in composition. *College English, 78*(3), 265–273.

Cavazos, Alyssa G., Hebbard, Marcela, Hernández, Jose Esteban, Rodriguez, Crystal & Schwarz, Geoffrey. (2018). Advancing a transnational, transdisciplinary and translingual framework: A professional development series for teaching assistants in writing and Spanish programs. *Across the Disciplines. 15*(3), 11–27. https://doi.org/10.37514/ATD-J.2018.15.3.09.

Cavazos, Alyssa G. & Karaman, Mehmet. A. (2021). A preliminary development and validation of the Translingual Disposition Questionnaire with Latinx students. *Language Awareness*, 1–16.

Cavazos, Alyssa G. & Musanti, Sandra I. (2021). Insights from a faculty learning community on translingual community-engaged pedagogy at a Hispanic serving institution. *Language and Education*, 1–15.

Christoffersen, Katherine. (2019). Linguistic terrorism in the Borderlands: Language ideologies in the narratives of young adults in the Rio Grande Valley. *International Multilingual Research Journal, 13*(3), 137–151.

Gallardo-Williams, Maria Teresa & Petrovich Lori Marie. (2017). An integrated approach to training graduate teaching assistants. *Journal of College Science Teaching, 47*(1), 43–47.

García, Ofelia & Kleyn, Tatyana. (Eds.). (2016). *Translanguaging with multilingual students: Learning from classroom moments*. Routledge.

Geller, Anne Ellen. (2011). Teaching and learning with multilingual faculty. *Across the Disciplines, 8*(4), 11–19. https://doi.org/10.37514/ATD-J.2011.8.4.06.

Guerra, Juan C. (2008). Cultivating transcultural citizenship: A writing across communities model. *Language Arts, 85*(4), 296–304.

Guerra, Juan C. (2015). *Language, culture, identity and citizenship in college classrooms and communities*. Routledge.

Guerra, Juan C. (2016). Cultivating a rhetorical sensibility in the translingual writing classroom. *College English, 78*(3), 228–233.

Hebbard, Marcela & Hernández, Yanina. (2020). Becoming transfronterizo collaborators: A transdisciplinary framework for developing translingual pedagogies. In Lesley Erin Bartlett, Sandra L. Tarabochia, Andrea R. Olinger & Margaret J. Marshall (Eds.), *Diverse approaches to teaching, learning, and writing across the curriculum: IWAC at 25* (pp. 251–273). The WAC Clearinghouse; University Press of Colorado. https://doi.org/10.37514/PER-B.2020.0360.2.14.

Horner, Bruce. (2016). Reflecting the translingual norm: Action-reflection, ELF, translation, and transfer. In Kathleen Blake Yancey (Ed.), *A Rhetoric of reflection* (pp. 105–124). Utah State University Press.

Horner, Bruce, Lu, Min-Zhan, Royster, Jacqueline Jones & Trimbur, John. (2011). Language difference in writing: Toward a translingual approach. *College English, 73*(3), 303–321.

Horner, Bruce, NeCamp, Samantha & Donahue, Christiane. (2011). Toward a multilingual composition scholarship: From English only to a translingual norm. *College Composition and Communication, 63*(2), 269–300.

Kells, Michelle Hall. (2007). Writing across communities: Deliberation and the discursive possibilities of WAC. *Reflections, 6*(1), 87–108.

Lacorte, Manel. (2016). Teacher development in heritage language instruction. In Marta Fairclough & Sara M. Beaudrie (Eds.), *Innovative strategies for heritage language teaching: A practical guide for the classroom* (Reprint ed., pp. 99–119). Georgetown University Press.

Lee, Jerry Won. (2016). Beyond translingual writing. *College English, 79*(2), 174–195.

Lee, Jerry Won & Jenks, Christopher. (2016). Doing translingual dispositions. *College Composition and Communication, 68*(2), 317–344.

Manchón, Rosa M. (Ed.). (2011). *Learning-to-write and writing-to-learn in an additional language* (Vol. 31). John Benjamins Publishing.

Matsuda, Paul Kei. (2012). Let's face it: Language issues and the writing program administrator. *Writing Program Administration, 36*(1), 141–164.

Motha, Suhanthie, Jain, Rashi & Tecle, Tsegga. (2012). Translinguistic identity-as-pedagogy: Implications for language teacher education. *International Journal of Innovation in English Language Teaching, 1*(1), 13–28.

Musanti, Sandra, Cavazos, Alyssa G. & Rodriguez, Alma D. (2020). Embracing a translanguaging stance and redefining teacher preparation practices in a Hispanic Serving Institution. In Janine M. Schall, Patricia Alvarez McHatton & Eugenio Longoria Sáenz (Eds.), *Teacher education at Hispanic-serving institutions: Exploring identity, practice, and culture* (Routledge Research in Higher Education) (1st ed., pp. 69–87). Routledge.

Parra, Maria Luisa. (2016). Critical approaches to heritage language instruction: How to foster students' critical consciousness. In Marta Fairclough, Sara M. Beaudrie (Eds.), *Innovative strategies for heritage language teaching: A practical guide for the classroom* (Reprint ed., pp. 166–190). Georgetown University Press.

Rademaekers, Justin K. (2015). Is WAC/WID ready for the transdisciplinary research university? *Across the Disciplines, 12*(2), 1–14. https://doi.org/10.37514/ATD-J.2015.12.2.02.

Robinson, Heather, Hall, Jonathan & Navarro, Nela. (2020). *Translingual identities and transnational realities in the U.S. college classroom.* Routledge.

Sánchez, Yemin, Nicholson, Nicole & Hebbard, Marcela. (2019). Familismo teaching. In Isabel Baca, Yndlencio Hinojosa & Murphy, Susan Wolff (Eds.), *Bordered writers: Latinx identities and literacy practices at Hispanic-serving institutions* (pp. 105–124). SUNY Press.

Smith, Christian. (2018, January 9). Higher education is drowning in BS: And it's mortally corrosive to society. *The Chronicle of Higher Education.* https://www.chronicle.com/article/higher-education-is-drowning-in-bs/

Tardy, Christine M. (2017). Crossing or creating divides? A plea for transdisciplinary scholarship. In Bruce Horner & Elliot Tetreault (Eds.), *Crossing divides: Exploring translingual writing pedagogies and programs* (pp. 181–189). Utah State University Press.

Thatcher, Barry, Montoya, Omar & Medina-López, Kelly. (2015). Global writing and application on the U.S.-Mexico border. In David S. Martins (Ed.), *Transnational writing program administration* (pp. 163–201). Utah State University Press.

Appendix

Session Two: Discussion Points

Activity T-Chart: Language Learning Class and Writing Class

- What does Guerra (2016) mean by developing "rhetorical sensibility that reflects critical awareness of language as a contingent and emergent" (p. 228)? What does this look like in language learning class and in a writing class? How might we already be doing this with our students?
- Guerra (2016) provides several examples of the type of writing activities he asks his students to work on in class and he also acknowledges the mistakes he made (p. 231). To what extent do you find those examples useful and/or valuable in building rhetorical sensibility? How would those assignments (or revised versions of them) look like in your own courses (Spanish/writing)? What changes would you make and why?

- How does the former TA's document help us think about language difference in language learning and writing courses? What are your thoughts? What kind of assignments can facilitate critical awareness and rhetorical sensibility that accomplish course, department, and university learning outcomes? What are the student learning outcomes for your course?
- Discussion question: Guerra (2016) claims that each one of the approaches to language (monolingual, multilingual, translingual) is informed by specific beliefs, values, and practices and he also provides an example of a teacher who asks students to respond to these approaches based on their lived experiences. What are the beliefs, values, practices of each of the approaches based on your own experiences as scholars and teachers but also as you interact in non-academic contexts?

Session Three: Writing Assignment Design Brainstorming (Part 2)

- What is an ideal writing assignment you would like to assign students in your language/writing class?
  - Why would you like to teach this writing assignment?
- How do you think this writing assignment can be linguistically inclusive by considering all our students' language resources and abilities?
- How does the writing assignment fit with the objectives of the course, program, department, and/or university?
- What is the objective and purpose of the writing assignment? How does the writing assignment connect with course readings and beyond the classroom?
  - What do you want the students to learn or experience from this writing assignment?
  - Should this assignment be an individual or a collaborative effort? Why?
- What do you want students to show you in this assignment? To demonstrate mastery of concepts or texts? To demonstrate logical and critical thinking? To develop an original idea? To learn and demonstrate the procedures, practices, and tools of your field of study? Explain in detail.
  - How will you assess student learning? What makes the assignment effective? How will you evaluate it?

Global Business Communication: *Kairos* and Discipline-Crossing along the Path toward Globally Responsive Education

Gail Shuck
BOISE STATE UNIVERSITY

The Power of a Network in Creating Institutional Change

As writing pedagogy and scholarship continue to evolve in response to global mobility and its educational, sociopolitical, and linguistic impacts, it behooves us as teachers, scholars, and program leaders to forge and sustain partnerships with faculty and staff in units across college campuses, as well as with different constituencies in local communities. Tarez Samra Graban (2018), Michelle Cox (2014), and other writing program leaders have argued that it is critical to build relationships with institutional and departmental agents to transform an institutional culture. Those relationships can lead to sustainable, collaborative curricular initiatives and programmatic changes (Cox et al., 2018).

Identifying allies across an institution in the work of linguistically and culturally inclusive pedagogies is an initial step. A bigger challenge is to support faculty from outside composition studies in wrestling with ideological differences surrounding language and writing. Such differences are brought into sharp focus by Emily Simnitt and Thomas Tasker's (2022) study of transdisciplinary conversations about argument and evidence and Joyce Meier, Xiqiao Wang, and Julia Kiernan's study (this volume) of a faculty learning community called "Enriching the Faculty-International Student Experience." Both studies offer clear recommendations for those who lead professional development initiatives to counter deficit models of language difference and to center multilingual students' linguistic and cultural expertise. Similarly, Lisa Arnold's (2016) study of her seminar at American University of Beirut (AUB) on writing in different fields allowed participants in the multilingual, multicultural context of Lebanon to come to value the full, collective linguistic repertoires of their classrooms, including instructors' and students' daily experiences with negotiating language difference.

The present chapter describes the importance of building a network of such partnerships for creating institutional change while understanding the role that institutional structures and dominant ideologies (of educational goals, linguistic diversity, etc.) play in either hindering or facilitating sustainable change. I also argue for the important role of *kairos* in this process, a door of opportunity that any of us can step through or let close without action. How we build the kinds of relationships that can have transformative results can be kairotic or strategically planned or a combination of both. Jay Jordan (2021), exploring the ways that the field of rhetoric has shaped scholarship in second-language writing and translingual composition, suggests that kairos can be productively deployed as a strategy in language contact situations. He characterizes kairos as "[suspended] between the goal of timely rhetorical mastery on one hand and sensitivity, if not susceptibility, to rhetoric's immediacy, spontaneity, and potentiality, on the other" (2021, p. 26). It is not happenstance that rhetors—in this case, colleagues in different disciplines—become attuned to a kairotic moment. Disciplinary expertise and knowledge of institutional structures also inform rhetors of what and where those Aristotelian "available means" are. The development of the Global Business Communication partnership described in this chapter was the result of several individuals' collective, strategic decision to identify avenues for collaboration, and it was augmented considerably by our attunement to kairos, in particular the "emerging exigencies of diversity" (Kells, 2012, p. 3). The partners were able to pinpoint student and curricular needs, recognize responses to those needs, highlight the ethical responsibility for change, and harness a sense of urgency on campus—all elements of a kairotic moment (Wilber, 2016). What resulted was a redesigned course that took a transnational view of business communication and made some initial progress toward developing "the opportunity [for students] to interrogate their own understandings of the world, to consider how and why others may perceive things differently, and to position themselves and their experiences in the context of the 'other'" (Siczek & Shapiro, 2014, p. 330). Even if, as in the Global Business Communication partnership and in Arnold's (2016) study at AUB, not all participants are ready to challenge their own assumptions about language standards and multilingualism, I maintain that dialogue among faculty within and across disciplines is a critical first step toward a more inclusive view of language in the classroom.

In addition to describing the Global Business Communication collaboration in the context of kairotic moments, this chapter urges a reconsideration of traditional boundaries between scholarship and program administration. Such a reconsideration has long been promoted by Ernest Boyer (1990) and has been taken up in a position statement by the Council of Writing Program Administrators (2019). Program administrators, in the United States at least, have been widely seen by their institutions as merely doing service or management without creating new knowledge or shaping disciplinary questions in their fields. This chapter will illustrate a view of scholarship as administrative praxis, demonstrating how building campus or community partnerships, identifying kairotic moments, and engaging in action-oriented work raises new disciplinary questions and suggests directions for future scholarship.

Institutional Context

Boise State University is a mid-sized, doctoral-granting university with approximately 25,000 students, including undergraduates and graduate students. Boise, the largest city in Idaho, is in a county with 8.4% of residents over five years old who speak a language other than English. The percentage of the population of the neighboring county that speaks a language other than English at home is 18% (United States Census Bureau, 2018). Idaho was receiving an average of 1,000 to 1,100 refugees each year, until President Donald Trump put a temporary hold on refugee resettlement to the US. Nevertheless, formerly resettled refugees are included in Boise State's domestic student population.[1]

An important turning point in Boise State's institution-wide changes was a sharp increase in the number of international students from Saudi Arabia and Kuwait that the university experienced from approximately 2011 to 2017. The international student population (undergraduate and graduate), while still comparatively small, reached a peak of approximately 4% of the total student population (approximately 1,000 students) in 2015. The arrival of over 200 first-year students from Saudi Arabia in 2012 was met with a sense of urgency among many faculty across campus. It could easily be argued that the urgency derived from this predominantly white institution's resistance to a sudden ethnoracial demographic shift, but these new students also had relatively low English proficiency. Many had been admitted with an IELTS (International English Language Testing System) score of 5.0 or 5.5. A score of 5.0 is described by the IELTS organization as indicating a "modest user, with a partial command of the language, coping with overall meaning in most situations" (IDP: IELTS Australia, 2019). For comparison, most universities in the US set 6.5 as the minimum score for undergraduate admission. The top score is 9.0, described as an "expert user." On average, the early cohorts' Arabic academic literacy experiences were relatively limited: a widespread use of social media and a great deal of memorizing and reproducing from memory academic, poetic, and religious texts. Students frequently reported that they did almost no composing in school contexts. It was also unusual to find Saudi students who read longer texts for pleasure.[2] Many started their U.S. education in intensive English programs and, according to informal conversations with many students and their program advisors, were pressured to transition to academic coursework after only a year, no matter how little English they arrived with in the United States.

---

1   What portion of Boise State's student population came to the U.S as refugees is so far unclear. It was only very recently, through another partnership, between English Language Support Programs and the Admissions Office, that the institution began collecting data on refugee-background student numbers.

2   One exception was a student in my first-year writing class for multilingual students who revealed on Day One of the semester that he loved to read. From then on, his classmates called him "The Professor."

Boise State's international student population thus tripled in 4 years, going from having approximately 300 international students overall in 2011 to having over 900 international students in 2015, more than 50% of whom were from Saudi Arabia. This rapid increase seemed to draw more faculty attention to the presence of English learners and to raise faculty concerns about "preparedness." Hands were wrung; committees were formed; support staff were hired. As the Intensive English Program (IEP) instructor in this partnership described it, "The pushback and the panic created—it showed, it exposed a lot of things." The Business Communication Director added, "The [negative] response from faculty pushed me to want to address those issues." In our recorded discussion that is the basis for this chapter, all parties agreed that the influx of Saudi and Kuwaiti students was a catalyst for the desire to act—a kairotic moment.

My work as Director of English Language Support Programs had led me to a desire to act long before the Saudi and Kuwaiti students arrived. The university was experiencing what Jane Hill calls a language panic (2008) as a response to their relatively sudden arrival, but I had already known that we had a linguistically diverse U.S.-resident student population. Surveying over 1,200 students in first-year writing courses (FYW) at Boise State in 2015, we discovered that over 10% of those enrolled in FYW who were born in the US or arrived before the age of 18 (that is, unlikely to be international students on visas) said "no" to the question, "Do you consider yourself to be a native English speaker?" More recently, in spring, summer, and fall of 2019, the number of *U.S.-resident* undergraduate students admitted to the university that year who said English was not their native language was 1,651. Approximately 4,500 new first-year and transfer students are admitted each year. Although many admitted students do not end up matriculating, and although the notion of the "native speaker" is neither stable nor objective (see, for example, Canagarajah, 2013; Leung et al., 1997; Shuck, 2006), this information sheds light on the language diversity present among U.S.-resident students at Boise State.

The Director of Business Communication had long described to me his own sense of urgency and ethical responsibility to help our university move toward linguistically and culturally inclusive pedagogies and educational policies. In our respective contacts with faculty within and outside our respective colleges, we have seen wide variation in faculty receptiveness (or lack thereof) to teaching multilingual students who have not fully developed English proficiency. We also have numerous anecdotes—from students and their instructors—that many second-language learners at Boise State are struggling, even in the most receptive and inclusive classrooms. Identifying ways to respond to this need requires collaboration across units, as the need exists in all areas of the institution, from admissions to classroom teaching and assessment to the amount and structure of co-curricular and extra-curricular support.

The focus of the present chapter is one outcome of this collaboration, which might serve as a model of shared responsibility across an institution for equitably teaching linguistically diverse student populations (see also Shuck, 2006, 2016). I worked with the Director of Business Communication (hereafter, "the Director" or "the BUSCOM Director") to enlist the support of the Center for Global Education, the Intensive English Program (IEP), and two other instructors in the College of Business and Economics (COBE) to orchestrate a redesign of the required, sophomore-level business communication course ("BUSCOM 201," for all COBE majors). The course would set aside its focus only on conventional U.S. genres of business communication and adopt a more explicit emphasis on global business practices and intercultural communication. Described in more detail in the next section, the partnership was the result of a number of kairotic moments that different stakeholders seized at different times.

The Global Business Communication redesign was implemented with this new cohort of Saudi students in mind. However, we also knew that monolingual, U.S.-born students, multilingual U.S.-resident students, and even instructors would benefit from such a globally focused course. The changes happened in two iterations: Iteration I was our first attempt to develop and offer a first-year, preparatory, language-support course, BUSCOM 101, to circumvent the English composition prerequisites and expedite entry into BUSCOM 201. Iteration II involved reflecting on the problems with that preparatory course model and then redesigning the required Business Communication course itself to focus on intercultural communication and global business practices.

Methods

The present chapter was originally intended as a co-authored narrative inquiry—a dialogue among the key members of this Global Business Communication partnership: the BUSCOM Director, the IEP Assistant Director, the two BUSCOM instructors who had most overtly expressed interest in revising the BUSCOM 201 course, and me. One of those instructors had earlier collaborated on developing the BUSCOM course that we thought would support this new Middle Eastern student cohort in learning the language of the discipline (see Iteration 1, below). I had invited all of the partners to co-author this chapter with me, in large part as an opportunity for all of us to reflect on the successes and failures of the revised course, as well as to reflect on the impacts of that redesign on our individual and collective thinking about language, the global nature of business communication, and institutional changes that might allow us to facilitate other such course redesigns.

We met as a group one time for approximately 90 minutes for this collective retelling and reflection, and I audio-recorded it with everyone's permission. One of the instructors, whom I refer to as Instructor #2, was not able to attend the in-person discussion, but she wrote responses to questions I had sent by email in advance to spark everyone's thoughts. These questions included the following:

1. What is your [individual] role in this Global Business Communication partnership, and when do you feel it began?
2. What is your understanding of the reasons why BUSCOM went global?
3. What have you learned from others in this collaboration?
4. What impacts has it had on your thinking about language or language learning?

Results

The data included here are excerpts from that mostly open-ended discussion of the development and impacts of this redesign, as well as a jointly produced narrative of the timeline of each member's role in the partnership. I also included some of Instructor #2's written responses. In the end, although I think a collaboratively authored chapter would have been productive, sparking additional reflection on language ideologies and the partners' responsibility for educating linguistically diverse populations, all of the partners bowed out and gave me their blessing to be sole author and accurately represent the partnership. They have all seen drafts of this chapter, and they have given me written permission to quote their words. Drawing on the framework of translingual dispositions (Horner et al., 2011; Lee & Jenks, 2016) and with a focus on the ideologies of monolingualism (Shuck, 2006) and of Standard English (Horner et al., 2011; Wiley & Lukes, 1996), I identify key kairotic moments and consider the potential of this type of redesign for future ideological transformation.

Iteration 1: Developing BUSCOM 101

English Language Support Programs (ELSP) was created because several faculty and staff wanted to serve English language learners more effectively across the curriculum. As ELSP Director, I had responded to these concerns in numerous ways, one of which was to develop a faculty learning community (FLC) program that allowed for sustained learning and community-building around the goal of developing linguistically inclusive pedagogies. I had led shorter-term workshops on this topic, several of which the BUSCOM Director had attended. He also joined the FLC on working with multilingual students in 2014–2015. He continues to maintain connections with those involved in inclusive education across campus.

In our recorded discussion, as we collectively recalled the timeline of how the Director and I came to see each other as allies in the fight for a linguistically and culturally inclusive campus, the Director added an angle that I had not remembered. He says,

> I think part of that process, too, was my attending the student presentations in the Language and Culture workshops that you even have—isn't it next week? And you know, listening to the students.

The Boise State Conference on Language, Identity, and Culture is a biannual collection of multilingual student presentations, designed to center the experiences and knowledge of multilingual students and, ideally, to educate faculty across the curriculum about their needs and strengths (Shuck, 2004). It pleased me to know that it played a role in the Director's growing understanding of the need for global perspectives on business communication.

The beginnings of an expanded partnership came when another BUSCOM instructor ("Instructor #1") joined a faculty learning community to discuss language and culture across the curriculum, adding that his "lifetime" of international experiences, including hosting exchange students from Taiwan numerous times, made him want to explore more cross-cultural teaching opportunities. Additionally, the IEP had just created a business communication course of its own, as many IEP students hoped to go into business-related majors. The IEP assistant director contacted the BUSCOM director for recommendations for an instructor who might be open to teaching in the IEP, even without necessarily having a second-language teaching background. That instructor later joined the Global Business Communication partnership and is referred to here as "Instructor #2."

Our first attempt to develop curricular support for the large number of Saudi students in business-related majors came during the 2015–2016 academic year, when internal grants became available from the additional funds from the Saudi government that accompanied the students who had received the King Abdullah Scholarship. Those funds needed to be used to support the Saudi students. The BUSCOM Director and I collaborated on a proposal in 2016 to use some of those funds to design an elective course, BUSCOM 101 Intercultural Business Language Development, which would help prepare monolingual and multilingual students alike for the discipline-specific language that would be used in the sophomore-level required business communication course and beyond. Although our first idea was to have it be specifically for second-language English users, we decided before submitting the proposal that BUSCOM 101 should be open to any student, removing the potential "ESL" stigma widely felt by multilingual students. To develop the course, the IEP assistant director drew on her considerable experience teaching in the IEP and coordinating an annual short-term visit by students from a Taiwanese university in a master of business administration program. The BUSCOM Director combined his extensive knowledge of the business communication curriculum with his desire to foster the development of "international-student champions" among the faculty. The new course, BUSCOM 101, was approved and added to the 2017–2018 university catalog.

The fall 2017 inaugural run of BUSCOM 101, however, was unsuccessful. Only three students registered for it, and so it had to be canceled. The partners reflected on the probable reasons for this failure and concluded that, despite what we imagined to be an appealing waiver of a prerequisite for BUSCOM 201 if a student were to take BUSCOM 101 first, the 101 course still did not meet any requirement for graduation. We thus experienced a counterpart of kairos—*metanoia*—which played a significant role in the progress of this partnership. Metanoia is a sense of regret about a missed opportunity, but it is one that allows for reflection, empathy with another, and even transformation of beliefs that makes new kairotic moments possible (Myers, 2011). Kelly Myers argues that when an attempt to seize an opportunity fails, "the emotional impact of a missed opportunity motivates a transformation of thought, advancing a rhetor's understanding of the situation" (2011, p. 11).

Iteration II: Global Business Communication

Our reflections during the fall of 2018 were accompanied by two important developments. First, the members of this partnership increasingly focused our discussions on the ways that a cross-cultural experience would not only support multilingual English learners but also provide opportunities for U.S.-born monolingual students to experience a more globally relevant curriculum and learn to communicate across difference. The second significant development was that Boise State had just created the Center for Global Education. This was a crucial kairotic moment. As a member of the search committee for the director of this new center (hereafter "Assistant Provost"), I was able to let candidates know about the already strong relationship between English Language Support Programs and the IEP. After the Assistant Provost arrived, I arranged for a meeting between him and the Global Business Communication partners. We discussed the importance of drawing on multilingual students' experience with transnational and translingual mobility. The outcome of that meeting was another course redesign: focus the required BUSCOM 201 course not on U.S. business communication genres but rather on intercultural communication and business practices around the world. The BUSCOM Director explained some of the impetus for that redesign in this way:

> One of the things, as I was reading on multicultural, intercultural communication—one thing that just concerned me so much in so much of what I read was pointing out how poorly native English speakers were in intercultural communication, and the tendency not to make any accommodation for [pause] English language learners, nonnative speakers, whatever is the term of preference there. And that just seemed so important.

To persuade his colleagues in the College of Business and Economics of the importance of broadening BUSCOM 201 to be about communicating in global business environments, the Director developed a three-page document, "Why Take BUSCOM 201 Global?" (Appendix). In that document, he effectively illustrated the already global nature of Idaho business, with its growing refugee and immigrant population and its participation in global trade. He also explicitly recognized the need for a global decentering of ownership of English, highlighting the notorious reputation of monolingual, native English speakers for being unable to communicate with speakers of non-standardized varieties of English.

Funding for the second curricular design (focusing on the required 201 course) came this time from the Center for Global Education, bringing Instructor #1 onto the redesign team in the summer of 2017. The revised course description, with the course title, Global Business Communication, was listed in the 2018–2019 university catalog. The following is the previous BUSCOM 201 course description:

> BUSCOM 201 BUSINESS COMMUNICATION. Effectiveness and correctness of writing and psychology of letter and report writing stressed through the preparation of a variety of business correspondence. Specific writing problems used in conjunction with various cases with realistic opportunities to develop writing skills following a designated style. Oral presentation skills included.

The prescriptivism evident in phrases such as "correctness of writing" and "following a designated style" is based on U.S.-centric understandings of what constitutes correctness, who designates the style, and what variety of English may be used.

The revised course description is as follows:

> BUSCOM 201 GLOBAL BUSINESS COMMUNICATION. Develop effective intercultural communication skills for business in the global economy. Expressive (writing and speaking) as well as receptive (reading and listening) skills will be included. Emphasis will be placed on developing credible, persuasive business cases that help guide informed business decisions.

The written comments contributed by Instructor #2 for this project make that shift clear. When asked what changes she had made in her teaching as a result of this partnership, she said:

> I've beefed up the electronic communication section to include a hands-on Zoom assignment to accommodate those participants in different geographic locations. I have two separate assignments to enhance intercultural awareness and sensitivity—creating a Team Building Activity based on an assigned country; and researching a country's communication practices, writing an essay and presenting to the class the similarities and unique differences between the US [and that country].

One can see that she creates space for genres that do not appear to be encompassed by the earlier course description ("letter and report writing"). She also facilitates cross-cultural comparisons of communicative expectations, providing important opportunities for students and instructors alike to reconsider their own perspectives on communicative norms. An example she raised in her comments illustrates this shift well.

> I was talking to the students about creating effective powerpoints [*sic*] and mentioned that humans are naturally drawn to reading the "normal" left to right and that our eyes are trained to view material in this manner. Silly me, having two in the class whose "normal" is Arabic, this concept clearly didn't apply.

Changes to the course also extended to rubrics and learning outcomes. One criterion both the Director and Instructor #1 use now for evaluation of assignments—spoken and written—is the extent to which the writing or presentation "communicates well to multicultural audiences." The Director recounted an incident in a BUSCOM 201 class in which a student team was discussing whether or not "RSVP" is idiomatic and would fail to reach people who acquired varieties of English in different contexts. Instructor #2 specifically pointed out that she now introduces the concept of ethnocentrism to her classes. Indeed, all of the BUSCOM instructors in this partnership mention examples of culturally specific references that they have come to realize might exclude certain audiences. A systematic assessment of the impact of Global Business Communication on students, beyond such anecdotes, will be a future step in the ongoing understanding of this course redesign.

In Support of Serendipity

In Michelle Cox et al.'s (2018) whole-systems approach to writing across the curriculum, the first step in developing what is likely to be a sustainable program is to understand the institutional landscape: who believes what, what concerns faculty and administrators are seeing, how much interest there is in collaboration to find solutions, etc. Actions can be planned from there, once a set of shared goals is negotiated. In my work with English Language Support, I have noticed a tension between my interest in seizing opportunities, on the one hand, and my desire to do a more thorough institutional assessment, on the other. The years-long partnership that the BUSCOM Director and I have built has been a sort of duet of understanding. Our different disciplinary perspectives may lead us to view inclusive education from different angles and to identify different responses to institutional situations, but we share common goals and concerns regarding equity among students of diverse language backgrounds, as well as an understanding of the need to expand U.S.-born, monolingual students' understanding of the world beyond the US (and American English). A duet, however, is still just an echo of the more orchestral planning process that Cox et al. (2018) argue that program directors should implement.

Relying on kairos has been crucial in the transformation of the Business Communication program, keeping an eye out for opportunities when the need, urgency, responsibility, and potential responses align. A number of Boise State initiatives have come to fruition precisely because of the success of a kairotic moment, seized by individual, departmental, and other institutional agents. I did not begin my administrative work with a systematic assessment of all of the gaps in linguistic and cultural inclusion throughout the campus. However, I have brought together "natural allies" (Cox, 2014) across campus to come to a shared understanding and build plans of action. Indeed, kairos, supplemented by considerable disciplinary expertise, allowed us collectively to identify additional campus partners and implement a change. I therefore propose that kairos and whole-systems principles (Cox et al., 2018) can be part of the same recursive process.

Shyam Sharma and Gene Hammond (this volume), describing a transnational exchange that resulted from chance encounters, similarly argue that serendipity can be seized effectively. The disciplinary expertise of potential partners, they observe, can allow them to identify affordances rooted in local contexts. Alyssa Cavazos et al. (this volume) drew on such expertise to develop a four-part professional development series for teaching assistants that highlighted the local knowledge—especially the bilingual expertise—of the series participants. While the Boise State Global Business Communication partnership was on an intra-institutional scale rather than a transnational one, the implications of bringing such expertise to bear on our collaborations are similar. Each of us in the Business Communication redesign felt an ethical responsibility to act in order to serve all students well, and we envisioned different responses to this evolving context. The individual interactions and relationships we had built allowed us to share insights and information, which in turn allowed us to co-create an understanding of where the gaps and opportunities were. To transform ideologies around language, culture, and the scope of educational activity, in other words, requires keeping an eye out for that sly God of Opportunity.

Research as Administrative Praxis: Wrestling with Ideological Contradiction

Taking a global view of disciplinary work beyond the walls of any one institution allows students to "engage profoundly with their own situatedness, motivations, and biases" (Willard-Traub, 2018, p. 49). The building of the Global Business Communication partnership, as well as the documentation and analysis of the ways it came about, exemplifies a kind of research that not only informs institutional practice but that *is* institutional practice. In this case, the recorded interview/discussion about the newly revised BUSCOM 201 course allowed for continued reflection among the BUSCOM faculty, particularly related to applying intercultural awareness to ideas about language. The ongoing reconsideration of language by the BUSCOM Director and the instructors is reminiscent of Nancy Bou Ayash's (2016) work on language representations and Simnitt and Tasker's (2022) study of ideological and pedagogical contradictions that can become visible with disciplinary boundary-crossing. The Director wrestled with his own competing ideological stances on language conventions, while Instructor #1 held firmly for most of the discussion to a dominant understanding of standardized language norms. It was only after the IEP assistant director urged linguistic flexibility, as opposed to what she called "rigidity," that Instructor #1 began to acknowledge different varieties of English.

The topic of cultural diversity and a question about how the members responded to writing led to a discussion of the singular "they" for individuals who have a gender identity outside the dominant gender binary. Bringing up grammatical change regarding gender led to the following comment from the BUSCOM Director:

> I readily confess that I'm struggling much, much more than I used to with how to deal with surface errors. I mean, it used to be that I would pounce on them immediately and pretty rigorously. Now I struggle with it. I don't want to say, "That's wonderful," if it's a fairly big, quote, "error." But on the other hand, I really do find if I can understand the message, I tend to be much more accommodating.

In the lengthy conversation that followed, both the Director and Instructor #1 grappled with their individual stances on language use. The Director was struggling to deal with "surface errors," but he suggested that comprehensibility and clarity were more important. After all, he wrote the following paragraph about the issue of language for the "Why Take BUSCOM 201 Global?" document:

> BUSCOM 201 needs to assist native English speakers to become better communicators in global English, especially when they are communicating with non-native English speakers. At the same time, BUSCOM 201 needs to assist non-native English speakers to improve their use of global English. In this respect, however, the primary focus will be placed upon clarity of the communication, not upon strictly following the rules of Standard American English grammar.

For Instructor #1, non-standard grammar use was not so much a matter of correctness, but rather, a matter of status-marking, echoing long-standing debates in education around language ideologies and *Students' Right to Their Own Language* (CCCC, 1974; Perry & Delpit, 1998; Flores & Rosa, 2015). In the following comment, Instructor #1 describes an approach to grammar that focuses on comma splices and capitalization, which are common complaints among teachers of native English speakers:

> I think I have an obligation in teaching business communication to help our students recognize that those markers exist, and being successful not being—losing credibility based on surface things. So I'm still in the method of, you know, we mark the comma splices, we mark the random acts of capitalization, we mark all these things that are native and nonnative. But the nonnatives are going to have more of that stuff cropping up in their writing and, we're not gonna fix it all, but if I see patterns, then we'll have some interaction to say, "Watch for this, and here's why it is what it is," and hope that we build their skills.

Instructor #1 recognizes the importance of helping students who are still acquiring English to notice grammar patterns. However, the IEP Assistant Director challenges him on the issue of whether those same markers will have the same significance in a context not dominated by U.S. English speakers. This moment seemed to be a critical, pivotal one. Katie Silvester (2022) analyzes a series of such pivotal moments during a faculty orientation in the multilingual composition program she directs, arguing for what she calls a *pivotal praxis*, which can result in a transformative understanding of students' expertise and agency as users of multiple languages. Focusing on English as the primary language of global business communication, my colleagues in this collaboration began to wrestle with standardized English norms as the IEP Assistant Director offered the example of the highly international, multilingual context of Micron's microchip manufacturing headquarters in Boise. She says:

> [I]t's the microchips. It's the science. It's the knowledge of the field. If you get the point across, and you have a brilliant thing to say about the research, then no. It's more—I think there are lots of like government [contexts] and lots of things where that is like judged more harshly, but I think HP [Hewlett-Packard] and Micron? I don't think that's where they are.

To this, Instructor #1 responds, "I think it's a matter of degree." As he continues, he seems to be weighing his sense of responsibility to teach students about power and non-standard grammar against his understanding that English is a global language with diverse and ever-changing norms:

> I think if you use the right terms, not the right—if you use American standard terms, if you use American standard grammar,

> then you're received in a way differently than if you don't use those standard things, but if you're in an environment where there are multiple language backgrounds and multiple usages of English, I think there'd be much more comfort with a wider circle of what's not deemed credibility-hurting language usage.

The back-and-forth about language and grammar among the Global Business Communication partners illustrates the inevitable tensions, at an individual and societal level, between representations of language as fixed and bounded, on one hand, and those that view language as dynamic, malleable, and fluid as it is used between language users (Bou Ayash, 2016). This exchange also highlights how the partnership and the research process are themselves a form of continued professional development. As in Meagan Weaver's (2019) study of shifts in language ideologies among college writing teachers as a result of professional development workshops, the Global Business Communication partners continued to think about their stances on language even during the research process itself.

This ongoing reflection constitutes an important part of what Tricia Serviss and Julia Voss (2019) describe as action-oriented writing program praxis that lies at the intersection of "expert" and "lay" practitioners in different disciplines. They urge us to push back against the false binary of administration and scholarship. Doing so presents a significant challenge for supervisors and promotion and tenure committees, raising issues of the institutional value of "service," a term often interpreted as doing the less valued work required to maintain institutional systems but not to advance scholarship or engage in institutional/community transformation. Boyer's (1990) model of scholarship accounts for such potentially transformative activities because it values the scholarship of application and engagement, in which disciplinary knowledge is constructed in the act of solving real-world problems.

To elicit broad participation, develop partnerships, identify allies and kairotic moments, and get a detailed view of how fertile the ground is for building programs takes significant time that is difficult to document. However, these activities are crucial for transforming education. The principle of equity that Cox et al. (2018) describe includes not only eliminating discriminatory practices but also valuing such work in material ways. Achieving equity also must account for the heavy burden disproportionately carried by women, people from marginalized backgrounds, and faculty and staff at lower academic ranks. The fact that I am the only tenure-line faculty member in the collaboration described here may play a role in whether Global Business Communication is sustainable.

This may signal another moment of metanoia—the regret at a missed opportunity. Although seizing kairotic moments led to the relative ease of getting the revised BUSCOM course through various curriculum committees, we had not done the methodical work of ensuring sustainability. However, we can assess the impact of the course redesign on students and instructors, gathering data to share with prospective new partners from other disciplines. Kairos, then, can still serve as a useful component of a long-term, systematic approach to program development, as long as there is an interplay between those fleeting opportunities and the process of (re)planning and (re)evaluating. Kairos can be extremely effective in helping us identify key institutional moments—a new director, a sudden change in student demographics—and also potential allies who have individual, departmental, or institutional reach. During those moments, program leaders can collaborate with new agents, develop new and broader plans, and ultimately transform education.

References

Arnold, Lisa. (2016). "This is a field that's open, not closed": Multilingual and international writing faculty respond to composition theory. *Composition Studies, 44*, 72–88.

Bou Ayash, Nancy. (2016). Conditions of (im)possibility: Postmonolingual language representations in academic literacies. *College English, 78*, 555–577.

Boyer, Ernest. (1990). *Scholarship reconsidered: Priorities of the professoriate.* Wiley & Sons.

Canagarajah, A. Suresh. (2013). *Translingual practice: Global Englishes and cosmopolitan relations.* Routledge.

Conference on College Composition and Communication. (1974). Students' right to their own language. *College Composition and Communication, 25*, 1–32.

Council of Writing Program Administrators. (2019). *Evaluating the intellectual work of writing administration.* https://wpacouncil.org/aws/CWPA/pt/sd/news_article/242849/_PARENT/layout_details/false.

Cox, Michelle. (2014). In response to today's "felt need": WAC, faculty development, and second language writers. In Terry Myers Zawacki & Michelle Cox (Eds.), *WAC and second language writers: Research towards linguistically and culturally inclusive programs and practices* (pp. 299–326). The WAC Clearinghouse; Parlor Press. https://doi.org/10.37514/PER-B.2014.0551.2.12.

Cox, Michelle, Galin, Jeffrey & Melzer, Dan. (2018). *Sustainable WAC: A whole systems approach to launching and developing writing across the curriculum programs.* National Council of Teachers of English.

Flores, Nelson & Rosa, Jonathan. (2015). Undoing appropriateness: Raciolinguistic ideologies and language diversity in education. *Harvard Educational Review, 85*, 149–171.

Graban, Tarez Samra (2018). Contending with difference: Points of leverage for intellectual administration of the multilingual FYC course. In Shirley Rose & Irwin Weiser (Eds.), *The internationalization of U.S. writing programs* (pp. 97–115). Utah State University Press.

Hill, Jane H. (2008). *The everyday language of white racism.* Wiley-Blackwell.

IDP: IELTS Australia. (2019). IELTS 9-band scale. https://www.ieltsessentials.com/global/results/ielts9bandscale.

Horner, Bruce, Lu, Min-Zhan, Royster, Jacqueline Jones & Trimbur, John. (2011). Language difference in writing: Toward a translingual approach. *College English, 73*(3), 303–321.

Jordan, Jay. (2021). Future perfect tense: Kairos as a heuristic for reconciliation. In Tony Silva & ZhaoZhe Wang (Eds.), *Reconciling translingualism and second language writing* (pp. 25–37). Routledge.

Kells, Michelle H. (2012). Welcome to Babylon: Junior writing program administrators and writing across communities at the University of New Mexico. *Composition Forum, 25.* http://compositionforum.com/issue/25/new-mexico-wpas-communities.php.

Leung, Constant, Harris, Roxy & Rampton, Ben. (1997). The idealised native speaker, reified ethnicities, and classroom realities. *TESOL Quarterly, 31,* 543–560.

Myers, Kelly. (2011). "Metanoia" and the transformation of opportunity. *Rhetoric Society Quarterly, 41,* 1–18.

Perry, Theresa & Delpit, Lisa. (1998). *The real Ebonics debate: Power, language, and the education of African-American children.* Beacon Press.

Serviss, Tricia & Voss, Julia. (2019). Researching Writing Program Administration expertise in action: A case study of collaborative problem-solving in transdisciplinary practice. *College Composition and Communication, 70,* 446–475.

Shuck, Gail. (2004). Ownership of texts, ownership of language: Two students' participation in a student-run conference. *The Reading Matrix, 4(3),* 24–39.

Shuck, Gail. (2006). Combating monolingualism: A novice administrator's challenge. *WPA: Writing Program Administration, 30*(1/2), 59–82.

Shuck, Gail. (2016). What is ESL? In Rita Malenczyk (Ed.), *A rhetoric for writing program administrators* (2nd ed., pp. 78–91). Parlor Press.

Siczek, Megan & Shapiro, Shawna. (2014). Developing writing-intensive courses for a globalized curriculum through WAC-TESOL collaborations. In Terry Myers Zawacki & Michelle Cox (Eds.), *WAC and second-language writers: Research towards Linguistically and culturally inclusive programs and practices* (pp. 329–346). The WAC Clearinghouse; Parlor Press. https://doi.org/10.37514/PER-B.2014.0551.2.13.

Silvester, Katie. (2022). A pivotal praxis: Critical conversations to foster plurilingual awareness. In Kay Losey & Gail Shuck (Eds.), *Plurilingual pedagogies for multilingual writing programs: Engaging the rich communicative resources of U.S. students* (pp. 111–124). Routledge.

Simnitt, Emily & Tasker, Thomas. (2022). Developing inclusive teaching across writing programs through asset-focused inquiry. In Kay Losey & Gail Shuck (Eds.), *Plurilingual pedagogies for multilingual writing programs: Engaging the rich communicative resources of U.S. students* (pp. 125–140). Routledge.

Weaver, Meagan. (2019). "I still think there's a need for proper, academic, standard English": Examining a teacher's negotiation of multiple language ideologies. *Linguistics and Education, 49,* 41–51.

Wilber, Daniel. (2016). *Inventing the wheel: Developing institution-wide support for resident multilingual writers* [Unpublished master's thesis]. Boise State University, Boise, Idaho.

Willard-Traub, Margaret. (2018). Writing programs and a new ethos for globalization. In Shirley Rose & Irwin Weiser (Eds.), *The internationalization of U.S. writing programs* (pp. 44–59). Utah State University Press.

Centering Our Students' Languages and Cultures: WAC and a Cross-Disciplinary Collaboration

Joyce Meier
MICHIGAN STATE UNIVERSITY

Xiqiao Wang
UNIVERSITY OF PITTSBURGH

Julia Kiernan
LAWRENCE TECHNOLOGICAL UNIVERSITY

Cross-Disciplinary Snapshots

The writing department where this research is based has been a leader in developing translingual, transcultural, and transmodal pedagogical initiatives.[1] While the chapter authors remain engaged with pedagogical approaches that can be taken up at the curricular and program level, this contribution builds upon the understanding that the sharing of these experiences with colleagues across the university can be complicated by disciplinary contexts and approaches, as well as institutional and even political forces. Put simply: such an expansive endeavor is bound to be messy and (at times) disconnected, yet, we argue that the potential benefits in terms of student learning *and* improvement in faculty teaching writ large outweigh the various challenges. This chapter, then, begins with the disconnect and challenges felt by teachers across the university, which are captured through the following snapshots.

1. The writing professor who complains of the lack of international student participation in class discussion. They are unaware that international students often come from culturally inflected norms that do not value active engagement.
2. The sociology professor who struggles with time-tested sports metaphors. They have not considered that the explanatory power of these examples does not align with the diverse frames of references their students bring.

---

[1] See. for example, Fraiberg et al. (2017), Gonzales (2015, 2018), Kiernan (2015, 2017, 2021), Kiernan et al. (2016, 2017, 2018), Meier (2018), Meier et al. (2018), Milu & Gomes (2021), Wang (2017, 2019a, 2019b, 2021).

3. The biology professor who fails to unpack expectations to their students. They have not realized that the nuances of many directional words such as "analyze," "synthesize," or "justify" are often lost to diverse students.
4. The anthropology professor who is concerned with lower-order language issues (e.g., subject-verb agreement) in their students' writing. They struggle to integrate an asset-based pedagogy which leverages students' languages and cultures.
5. The business professor who recognizes different levels of language expertise yet struggles to develop differentiated instruction. This results in lack of support for students with varying levels of English proficiency across modes.

We begin with these snapshots because while there has been increasing interest by rhetoric and composition scholars into translingual approaches across the disciplines, particularly in terms of language development and transfer, gaps remain in terms of what this perspective might look like in practice. As Bruce Horner (this volume) explains in the introduction to this collection, while many universities "officially claim to be 'global' in reach and foundation," there are few practical resources that enable complementary (and necessary) shifts in "curricular structures, placement practices, and support services." Moreover, as Jennifer Jenkins (2013) has argued, most academics tend to show international students tolerance rather than acceptance. These snapshots, then, not only indicate a strong need to create cross-disciplinary collaboration, as indicated in chapters in this edited collection (see for instance, Gail Shuck's discussion of the collaborative effort in revising the curriculum for a business writing course), but also inform the ways that our chapter approaches acceptance and critical awareness of difference, particularly linguistic difference. To this end, we provide university educators who seek to move away from monolingual assumptions, which position students' languages and cultures as barriers or deficits, with approaches that value difference as assets and resources for learning. Such posturing, however, is just the most recent in pedagogical discussions of deficit; as Glynda Hull et al. (1991) have noted, throughout the history of American education there has existed the perception that low-achievers are "lesser in character and fundamental ability" (p. 312). While the labelling of *who* these students are continues to shift, there remains an underlying—but often quickly accepted—stigma that certain groups of students have lower intellectual abilities. This work aligns with that of Jonathan Hall and Nela Navarro (this volume) who argue: "Transnational translingual literacies reflect not only how our students read and write, but also how we, as instructors, as staff, as administrators, *read them*. How . . . we conceive of their literacies, their identities, and how . . . these conceptions correspond—or not—to the students' own experiences of academic and personal transnational translingual literacies."

Our approach aims to extend these positionings into the WAC/WID conversation, which to date has examined a number of faculty development contexts, including STEM (Manuel-Dupont, 1996; Zemliansky & Berry, 2017), second language writing (Cox, 2014; Lancaseter, 2011; Rose, 2016), multimodality (Duffelmeyer & Ellertson, 2005; Fodrey & Mikovits, 2020), and portfolio assessment (Peters & Robertson, 2007; Rutz & Grawe, 2009), but has paid less attention to university-wide faculty collaborations that engage translingual approaches and dispositions. We situate our work as a response to WAC/WID calls for transformative collaboration (Hall, 2009; Johns, 2001; Matsuda & Jablonski, 2000; Wolfe-Quintero & Sagade, 1999), including those voiced in various special issues and edited collections of WAC/WID scholarship (Cox & Zawacki, 2011; Hall, 2018b; Johns, 2005; Zawacki & Cox, 2014). Accordingly, this chapter, in examining the place of translingualism in WAC/WID partnerships, pushes back against the many "tried and trusted" assumptions our colleagues across the university bring with them to their teaching, arguing that these approaches are often no longer effective in classrooms populated by increasing numbers of multilingual students. Nevertheless, these outdated approaches remain because there has not been enough attention to how our pedagogies and programs—in every discipline—need to shift in order to provide courses that all students can excel in. Instead, the current monolingual status quo prevails in its maintenance of deficit models of multilingualism, which marginalizes many students (both domestic and international) as incompetent outsiders. Our chapter works to close this gap, providing evidence-based research on various strategies that acknowledge and embrace translingual approaches and dispositions, which, in turn, point to ways to foreground "mobility across borders" as "the operating condition of our work" (Horner, this volume) as teacher-researchers in WAC/WID contexts.

A Transdisciplinary Response to Translingual Exigencies

Institutional Context

Like many institutions of higher learning across the US, the university where this research is situated has witnessed a rapid and drastic increase of international students; for a five-year period, growth in the number of international students rose from 5% to 8% annually.[2] In 2017, roughly 10% of our undergraduate class (and 20% of our graduate class) were from non-U.S. countries (*International Studies*, n.d.). This overall demographic shift is felt most tellingly in the business and engineering departments. However, the writing department, where this research is grounded, is home to large numbers of international and multilingual students, who constitute roughly 80% of the students in our Preparation for College Writing

---

2   In the past year that number slightly declined as a result of anti-immigrant and anti-China rhetoric, as well as tightened visa-granting practices.

(PCW) bridge course. In 2012, supported by a university grant on inclusive teaching, a group of six PCW instructors and two teacher-administrators engaged in collaborative efforts to re-imagine this course. Meeting monthly for a two-year period, the group designed and refined a curriculum now featuring assignments and learning objectives that center the students' languages and cultures as sites of inquiry and resources for learning.

Faculty have worked to develop pedagogical tools that support undergraduate students' sustained examination of language difference; in many ways this work complements Hall and Navarro's work (in this collection), which calls for the development of best practices to support transnational graduate students. The undergraduate context of our research situates our pedagogical work as a way to help students complicate language difference as entangled in drastically different material conditions and contexts. In so doing, writing teachers have invited students—multilingual and monolingual, international and domestic—to recognize negotiation across languages and modes as the norm, and to develop meta-awareness and meta-vocabulary for describing and strategizing their rhetorical moves. By the same token, such pedagogies reposition writers as agents of their learning and call into question what John Trimbur (2016) calls the "unmarked hierarchies in U.S. college composition that have long assumed basic writing and second language writing were ancillary activities and institutions at the margins, orbiting around the mainstream English at the center in first-year composition" (p. 226). Similarly, these approaches invite teachers to rethink their own biases towards certain populations of students, building upon Hull et al.'s (1991) assertion that how teachers view students profoundly affects learning: "students whose teachers expect them to do well, tend to do well, while students whose teachers expect them to do poorly, do poorly" (p. 317).

Faculty Learning Commons

It is amidst such conversations of student success that the two-year Faculty Learning Commons (FLC), "Enriching the Faculty-International Student Experience," emerged. Instructors across the university, including two PCW teachers, met monthly over a two-year period with the goal of discussing the pedagogical challenges and opportunities raised by the presence of international multilingual students, which has subsequently increased the visibility of diverse learners across campus. This study diverges from other recent work in this area (Cavazos et al., 2018; Hall, 2018a, 2018b; Hartse et al., 2018; Hendricks, 2018; Horner, 2018, etc.) concerned with language and transdisciplinarity across language-centric programs (e.g., writing, composition, SLW, applied linguistics, English literature, etc.) in its attention to collaboration across disciplines spanning humanities, life and social sciences, engineering, and business. What these collaborations have surfaced are many of the same challenges colleagues in writing programs have encountered: constraints exacerbated by an inability to engage with students whose diverse cultural and linguistic backgrounds do not fit into the Western post-secondary monolingual norm. What we strive to surface in this chapter is that cultural and linguistic assumptions are regularly "inaccurate and limiting," particularly in their implications that these learners are "cognitively defective" (Hull et al., 1991, p. 299). For example, many university instructors who attended the FLC cited the difficulties of teaching "content" in classes with large numbers of multilingual students with diverse political, economic, historical, and social views; such differences were seen as further compounded by students' diversely inflected abilities in written and spoken Standard English.

Collecting and Analyzing Faculty Narratives

During the two-year FLC, which held monthly meetings, the first and second author, who participated in the conversations, generated a corpus of field notes that captured the broad flow of conversation for each meeting. Our field notes reflected our varied professional interests. Joyce's notes reflected her concerns as a writing program administrator who was leading various programmatic and pedagogical initiatives within the writing department; Xiqiao's notes reflected her interests in pedagogical innovation and teacher training, as she was an active participant of a collaborative teacher research project within the department. Following each FLC meeting, Joyce and Xiqiao met to discuss important themes emerging from the meetings, as we synthesized our notes, reconstructed problematic teaching scenarios shared by faculty across the disciplines, prepared debrief memos (eight in total) that were shared during faculty training events within the department, and worked to develop ideas for faculty development videos. In addition to notes and memos we generated, we also drew on memos (seven in total) created by the leaders of the FLC, which captured other dimensions that were missed in our individual notes.

As a research team, we engaged in triangulated reading of these strands of data (notes, memos, and conversations) to construct compelling scenarios that pointed to exigencies for faculty training in translingual pedagogy across disciplines, to unpack and interpret such teaching scenarios as embodying broader tensions between monolingual ideologies that inform instruction and messy, multilingual realities of our students, and to offer pedagogical recommendations. Our positionalities, as transnational individuals with divergent experiences with not only learning and teaching, but also our experiences with language and language negotiation across disciplinary fields, informed the approaches we take when working through our data. For instance, Joyce's extensive experiences organizing pedagogical workshops that highlight best practices within and beyond the writing program has enabled her to identify common themes and innovative pedagogical practices; Julia's disciplinary border crossing, which was embodied in her teaching a wide array of writing courses (e.g., basic, science, engineering) across various institutional contexts, has given her insights into the unique challenges of integrating translingual principles in disciplinary fields beyond first-year writing; Xiqiao's background as a biliterate scholar and an international student has helped her identify problematic scenarios from the perspectives of multilingual students. Working recursively through our notes and memos, which were segmented at passage levels and coded inductively, we allowed themes to naturally emerge (e.g., American-centric frames of reference, disciplinary jargon, culturally inflected frames of participation, material structure, etc.), which were then interpreted through the lens of translingual theory and pedagogy, with particular attention to the

1. need to disrupt monolingual orientation manifested pedagogically, linguistically, and materially, and
2. the need to listen to students' voices and leverage their languages, cultures, and educational experiences, and
3. the benefits and challenges of not only sustaining collaborative cross-disciplinary conversations, but engaging in collaborative innovation, refinement, and dissemination of pedagogical knowledge generated therein.

This chapter describes and analyzes not only this two-year FLC, but also the subsequent initiatives that emerged from it: including a small "tool-kit" disseminated at two "teaching tailgates"; subsequent conversations between business and writing instructors; and the creation of online materials to be made available on a campus-wide virtual hub offering pedagogical resources and workshops. While the FLC provided the opportunity to discuss challenges and propose solutions across disciplinary lines, institutional responses are just beginning to emerge.

The primary goal of each initiative has been to develop cross-disciplinary pedagogical tools that center students' languages and cultures as sites of inquiry. Each of our responses positions multilingual students' knowledge as a potential learning tool that moves against hierarchical styles of classroom teaching that emphasize blanket "content coverage" over student inquiry and learning—a shift that is "good pedagogy for everyone" (Zamel, 1995, p. 519). While such strategies may seem commonplace in discussions of translingual scholarship, they have rarely moved past the disciplinary boundaries of rhetoric and composition. In positioning our research at this axis of translingual scholarship, we consider how pedagogy that employs students' skills in rhetorical attunement—the "literate understanding that assumes multiplicity and invites the negotiation of meaning across difference" (Leonard, 2014, p. 228)—can exist across disciplines.

We position such considerations against the backdrop of pedagogical theories that argue for the importance of drawing upon students' experiences, languages, and cultures to support their learning. From a neo-Vgotskyian notion of the zone of proximal development (Eun, 2017) onward, educators have recognized that successful learners put new information in relation to what they already know. Leveraging what is known as the "learning edge momentum" (Robins, 2010, p. 40), we stress the value of scaffolding and framing new knowledge in relation to the familiar—including the students' home languages and cultural knowledge. We problematize the conflation of what is taught and how it is taught, especially when content is conceived as culturally and linguistically neutral, or when delivery is imagined through the lens of the "banking metaphor" (Freire, 1968). As Suresh Canagarajah (2016) asserts, people in the communicative process "use all the resources at their disposal . . . such as objects, gestures, and the body, for meaning-making" (p. 450). In particular, we suggest how teachers might create opportunities in their teaching for students to place what is new alongside what is familiar. Echoing Canagarajah (2016) and Laura Gonzales (2015), we emphasize the importance of incorporating alternate modes of communication in the negotiation of meaning. In describing these moves we focus on ideologies of familiarity, and present two themes from our collective sharing of and reflection on the FLC stories of struggle and success.

Situating Cross-Disciplinary Collaboration within WAC/WID Translingual Conversations

This study responds to earlier conversations concerning WAC/WID approaches to translingualism; namely, the FLC illustrates one way to "create opportunities where they [i.e., multilingual, international students] can use all their language resources as they navigate through changing academic and community contexts" (Cavazos et al., 2018, p. 23). Moreover, as Joel Heng Hartse et al. (2018) suggest, curricular development needs to involve instructors across various disciplinary backgrounds reimagining their current monolingual approaches. Despite the many voices in translingual scholarship that argue towards these ends, the prevailing attitude across the university by and large maintains that multilingual international students are coming to us with a variety of deficits. Consequently, one of the primary roles of the FLC was to question deficit models: to explain why there is a "need to sing the praises of 'minimal marking' to sometimes-skeptical instructors in disciplinary courses" (Hall, 2018b, p. 41), and to surface that "the particular rhetorical configuration that we call standardized correctness is not written in stone but rather is subject to trillions of micro-negotiations every day" (Hall, 2018b, p. 42).

In this way, we agree with Alyssa Cavazos et. al (2018) that a "translingual approach not only responds to the 'emerging exigencies of diversity' in the classroom but also provides the framework for offering teacher training across disciplines" (p.

15). Like Jerry Won Lee and Christopher Jenks (2016), however, we understand translingual dispositions as valuable in their openness to individual linguistic and rhetorical choices, which can be transferred within and beyond language learning, specifically seen in critiques of the "division of labor model," where SLW and WAC/WID studies are separate rather than overlapping (Johns, 2000; Matsuda, 1998; Matsuda & Jablonski, 2000). We also acknowledge a translingual perspective's capacity to surface the unique linguistic and cultural abilities that students bring to writing and other communicative practices.

As Hall (2009) notes, the population of international students in U.S. classrooms continues to rise, creating a landscape he categorizes as the "Next America," a place where "living one's whole life in one language seems as odd as eating the same thing for dinner" (p. 35). In Hall's "Next America," multilingualism will be the norm—and in fact, already *is* the norm in many parts of the world as well as communities throughout the US. However, while transdisciplinary collaboration outside the field of composition and rhetoric is still emerging, our FLC work suggests that "engaging in transdisciplinary conversations with our colleagues is critical in responding to the linguistic needs and assets of our students" (Cavazos et al., 2018, p. 21). This is especially important when one considers that diverse learner experiences, particularly linguistic experiences, are regularly regarded as a "marginal, or at least technical, issue by many members of university faculty" (Jenkins, 2013, p. 11). Jenkins goes on to argue that a major driver of deficit models, especially those contingent on the usage of SWE, is the lack of critical reflection and, thus, pedagogical transformation: "A current irony of Anglophone HE [Higher Education] is that the very faculty who criticize international (particularly East Asian) students for a perceived lack of criticality are often the very same faculty who lack critical skills themselves when it comes to reflecting on the linguistic correlates of internationalization" (Jenkins, 2013, p. 13). However, our FLC experiences point to ways that colleagues across our university have opened themselves up to critical reflection and transformation. This chapter, then, offers one example of faculty who have chosen not to "remain securely ensconced in their disciplinary silos, but instead to experience friction, discomfort, ambiguity of affiliation, weakening or erasure of boundaries, learning and integration of elements from different disciplines, overlapping of intellectual territories, blurring of academic identities" (Hall, 2018a).

These translingual, cross-disciplinary collaborations are also exponentially rewarding, both for the teachers involved and the students who will reap the benefits from the hard (and often departmentally unappreciated) work of their professors. Hall warns that "[w]e may see boundary work of various kinds, complex gestures of rejection and inclusion, ambivalent acceptance and conflicted resistance, often simultaneous, in the responses of several disciplines to the translingual challenge" (2018b, p. 29). Moreover, shifts from multidisciplinary and interdisciplinary to cross-disciplinary require collaborative efforts that cannot be bound by traditional academic silo-ing (Hendricks, 2018), and as a result must occur "between disciplinarity and the institutional material social vagaries" (Horner, 2018, p. 78). As we have noted, translingualism has often been regulated to the work of those in language-centric disciplines; however, with Hall's "Next America," there is a need to situate translingualism as also transdisciplinary. What follows are early snapshots of this impending reality.

Disrupting Norms

The following section offers two approaches that can contribute to the disruption of hierarchical monolingual assumptions and norms. We offer snapshots from faculty conversations to reveal the challenges faced when attempts to shift one's stance are made. These are followed by detailed analyses of the monolingual norms embodied in each snapshot, ending with recommendations for practice.

De-Familiarizing Language

Snapshots

Jake from the business college described an instance when he discovered that international students demonstrated a pattern of failure in responding to one essay question in particular. The question, inviting discussions of pricing strategies, relies on a business scenario for setting the prices for hard candy and chocolate candy in a grocery chain store. International students' struggles, he discovered, were not due to a lack of understanding of the business principle, but resulted from failures to distinguish American brand names commonly associated with different types of candy. Jackie, an anthropology professor, reported that she had discovered, entirely by accident, that a multilingual student had interpreted the word "transcript" (a mandatory part of the assignment) to mean his *college* transcript—and not a "transcript" of the field interviews he previously conducted. And, Mishka, a biology professor, shared an episode when she discovered that one of their common terms—"nocturnal"—was actually unfamiliar to the majority of their students. These snapshots make clear the need to examine the role of instructional language that embodies the norms and referential frames of academia, which are grounded in western cultural contexts that are too often out of reach to non-traditional students—both monolingual and multilingual.

Unpacking Language Norms of Academia

Often, classroom practices and expectations assumed as the "norm" may be presented in language that is unfamiliar to multilingual students who come from a variety of educational systems. Indeed, teachers may incorporate discursive tools such as "piggy-back on" or "dovetailing" into classroom practices—words that along with the cultures they reflect may be inscrutable to others. "Dovetailing," for example, may be used to give affirmation to a previously stated opinion, and to gain the floor for oneself; to "piggy-back on" may suggest how one's idea builds on another's. Yet, both words reflect teaching strategies that are often unfamiliar to students with limited experiences or strategies for navigating seminar style classroom discussions that are framed in said linguistic knowledge. Consequently, instructors who use these strategies might encounter confusion and inaction on the students' part due to a profound gap between understandings of discursive and material conventions students and instructors bring to the table.

Such gaps can be informed by culturally inflected educational practices across national contexts, but it could be equally present for novice learners learning to navigate disciplinarily specific discursive conventions and modes of reasoning. Indeed, monolingual students from the US may struggle equally to engage with the type of intellectual moves embodied by instructional language. This insight is well illustrated in an informal research study conducted by graduate students in our writing department, which explored undergraduate students' stated confusion about the directional verbs so frequently used in assignment descriptions, such as "analyze," "synthesize," and "justify." As observed, both multilingual and monolingual undergraduate students expressed considerable bewilderment when asked to interpret the specific tasks required by the directional words that typify so many assignments. Similar concerns surfaced in our FLC, as professors from across campus complained that multilingual students had trouble "following the directions." Further complicating the issue for multilingual students is the lack of instructional theories embodied by such words—to say nothing of disciplinary differences (e.g., "analyzing" might embody different intellectual tasks in supply chain management versus literary studies). Furthermore, translations of directional words such as "synthesize," "summarize," and "annotate" might share the same signifier, have opaque meanings, or carry meanings in students' home languages that diverge from instructor expectations.

Recommendations

Such moments can provide opportunities for the instructor to creatively unpack and disrupt norms of participation, such as explicit instruction and modelling. To facilitate students' navigation of such discursive and material practices, instructors could spend some class time unpacking the meanings of frequently used floor-claiming words, modeling and creating opportunities for practicing such strategies, and explaining behaviors, modes of thinking, and textual practices expected therein (Hall, 2009). Such practices of unpacking can be incorporated into discussions of the instructional language used to frame assignments and activities, which are often interpreted differently by multilingual and monolingual students alike.

Another approach is to introduce a version of Think-Pair-Share that makes space for students to put these new words and practices in relationship with their own prior knowledge. For instance, Joyce, a writing professor, has incorporated a Write-Map-Draw model that highlights the "Think" part, and invites students' perspectives on a given classroom procedure that might be construed as "new" (e.g., what does it mean to "'piggy-back on" a student's comments, to "dovetail" two differing strands of arguments, or to "incorporate" one idea within another?).

Additionally, multimodal examples, such as a visual illustration of a person riding on the back of another, can further clarify the discursive practice of "piggy-back on." Xiqiao, a writing instructor, has also worked with students to construct visual maps of classrooms as culturally inflected spaces, in which spatial arrangements of artifacts, texts, and bodies often reflect cultural conventions for participation. Integrating multiple modes of exploring and representing language practices of the classroom can be particularly useful in facilitating instructors' learning about their students' linguistic, educational, and cultural backgrounds. In this way, leveraging multimodal tools of representation can also help instructors to meet their multilingual students halfway. Moving between modes as well as between languages assumes, as Rebecca Lorimer Leonard and Rebecca Nowacek (2016) put it, a translingual approach that positions "language difference as a locus of meaning rather than a problem. . . . a norm of language-in-practice, one of its meaning-making functions" (p. 260, p. 261). Moving (writing) teachers across the discipline toward such an approach—what Leonard and Nowacek cite as a "more tolerant attitude toward language varieties"—has the potential not only to "affect a writer's sense of options and actual choices" (p. 260), but to deepen their disciplinary vocabulary and knowledge.

Together, these strategies work in concert to provide space for the students' own perspectives or interpretations of such words, as well as class exercises that ask students to imagine what they think the expectations of a given assignment might be. Students could be invited to share their sense of what a given directional word might mean with a partner, and then bring forward an example of how one practices it to the larger class. Such activities make visible the student's understanding, encourage modeling and explicit instruction, allowing students and teacher alike to come to a shared understanding of the given task, and help enable transfer across contexts. Such strategies, which focus on unpacking and demystifying both language and classroom practices, can be especially useful to students who might operate with alternative cultural norms for classroom participation.

Informed by such thinking is a pedagogical theme that our evolving ITeach web resource explores: the collaborative identification and construction of a list of pedagogical language and disciplinary jargon (Gentil, 2018), which can then be used to create a shared baseline that students can refer to, raise questions about, and use to organize their conversations. In the cross-disciplinary examples cited at the beginning of this section, visual illustration of the word "nocturnal," along with an image of night and the collective decision to enter the word into a shared classroom glossary could help cement students' understanding of its meaning, thereby addressing a gap that prevents students from grappling with an important threshold concept in the discipline.

In writing classrooms, we have also found embodied learning a useful pedagogical tool in unpacking and facilitating students' understanding of disciplinary concepts. For example, Joyce now uses the visual symbol of "a chain," both embodied through a frequently recycled gesture of her interlocked hands and a visual illustration of knots in a chain, to introduce the pragmatic functions of transitional strategies. To facilitate students' understanding of tense inflection, Xiqiao uses a timeline activity, which invites students to position their bodies in line to indicate nodes in time. While the class reads a narrative, students step forward and backward to indicate shifts in time and therefore the need for verbs to undergo tense inflection. Doing so allows for collective exploration of what Jody Shipka calls the "potentials of alternative, hybrid, mixed, and experimental forms of discourse" (Shipka, 2011, p. 3).

In turn, students might be invited to use more than one means in communicating their understanding of class material back to the instructor. Jessica, a faculty member from the School of Planning, Design and Construction, discussed her ongoing effort to revise her pedagogy in response to shifting demographics. Working to surface student knowledge in ways that conventional practice (e.g., verbal participation) fails to achieve, Jessica instituted an impromptu speaking component, where students were invited to present their ideas on certain topics. She found upon initial trial that this activity allowed differentiation between the students who exercise high capability in language versus those who do not. Furthermore, such assessment revealed the inherent heterogeneity within a seemingly homogeneous group of students: a reticent student can be a strong writer and a careful reader; conversely an outspoken student might struggle with written modes of communication. Opening up the classroom space to include/mix multiple modes of communication (e.g., inviting short writing before verbal sharing; using drawing to represent procedures and ideas; pairing students with differential levels of speaking, writing, listening, and reading capacities in jigsaw models; inviting students to map/diagram key class concepts) allows for multiple opportunities for students to leverage their linguistic repertoire, and thereby ensure that course grades reflect a realistic assessment of students' level of mastery of a full breadth of required knowledge and competence.

Defamiliarizing Culture

Snapshots

Jessie, an anthropology faculty member, expressed frustration with her Chinese students who struggled to engage with her reference to "kinship" as analogous to the relationship between siblings. For years, Jessie has incorporated such tried-and-true analogies into class lectures, with the understanding that these "familiar" comparisons will aid her students' learning of new (course) concepts. Now faced with an increasing number of international students in her classes, though, Jessie encounters blank stares when she introduces these ideas to her students by way of her familiar analogies. Similarly, Max, a business professor, bemoans the fact that his trusted baseball metaphors—artfully sprinkled throughout his lectures—leave his (now mostly Chinese) students lost. In both cases, the issue is not the professor's well-intentioned desire to build on the students' prior knowledge, and to introduce the unfamiliar by way of the familiar, but rather that their analogies are based on cultural assumptions and practices that may be unknown to non-U.S. students with different cultural backgrounds.

Disrupting Taken-for-granted Academic and Cultural Norms

For many faculty members, the need for pedagogical change is most tellingly felt when familiar cultural references, examples, and allusions stop working. In such moments, students must not only unpack task- and disciplinary-related language, but also cultural allusions and knowledge that is Western-centric. The problem, however, is not that these cultural references are used, but that they go unexplained, when ironically, the teacher using them sees these as the very means by which a particular concept may be clarified. That is, drawing on neo-Vygotskian notions of the zone of proximal development, the teacher chooses these allusions in order to aid student understanding, so that the student may put the new information into relationship with what is perceived as common knowledge. However, in Jessie's case, it was only through conversing with students outside of class that they discovered students' struggles with the concept of "kinship," which were deeply rooted in unique cultural family structures. For students raised in a single-child family typical for Chinese millennials and Generation Z, the notion of kinship may often be experienced differently—as extended family; for many of our Arabic students, kinship may be tribal. Differences such as these also surface in the writing classroom.

When Joyce designed a service-learning component that encouraged multilingual, international writers to share a cultural story in a third-grade classroom, many of her (mostly Chinese) students expressed apprehension about working with the children because of limited experiences with siblings. As a result, Joyce created teams of students, where a self-identified "child-expert" was placed with a group of students who felt less experienced. The point is that cultural assumptions based on Western notions of family structure may cause experiences of unnecessary disjuncture and confusion on the part of students from other cultures. Moments such as these encourage educators to challenge taken-for-granted frames of reference that may be inaccessible. Students learn on the edge of what they already know; the very point of using an analogy or example is to help put the unfamiliar (e.g., course content) in relationship to the familiar (e.g., lived experience). Yet ironically, when instructors rely on cultural allusions that are often unfamiliar to their students, they create a kind of "double learning" challenge—students must master not only the disciplinary content but also the unfamiliar cultural reference.

Recommendations

One solution is for the instructor to make the cultural allusion itself more available to the students through verbal explanation or multimodal demonstration. In the FLC, for example, a biology instructor described how he had brought a rose (a relatively "Western" plant) to class and passed it around for the students to feel. This (in many ways exemplary) multimodal experience was intended to give students unfamiliar with this particular plant the opportunity to feel it (thorns included), before the professor launched into his lecture on the means by which such plants both propagate and protect themselves. Clearly, this is an instance of the teacher taking the time to make a more abstract concept (plant propagation and protection) familiar to his students, vis-a-vis multimodality, especially since he was not sure that the mostly non-U.S. students in his biology class would be familiar with such a plant.

Another suggestion is that instructors learn to shift their frames of reference to include input from the students themselves. For example, in a faculty workshop held on our campus several years ago, an art history professor expressed frustration at how few of their international students seemed to understand the cultural impact of the Renaissance—that is, until they invited them to name their own culture's "Renaissance." Asking her (mostly non-U.S.) students to name a historical moment or time that had changed the trajectory of their home cultures, they then had them make these moments visible on a class timeline marked by the centuries. The resulting class timeline ended up demonstrating a world history that instantly became much more complex and actually quite ancient—predating the Western-based Renaissance by centuries— thus making visible the very "oldness" of the Chinese, African, and Arabic histories thus delineated. Finally, by putting the Western "Renaissance" in relationship to their own prior knowledge and histories, the students were able to more fully grasp the concept at hand.

Thus, we encourage instructors to incorporate students' own examples and analogies. For instance, as writing instructors we have worked to leverage the students' own linguistic, rhetorical, and cultural resources through a translation narrative assignment in first-year writing, which invites students' individual translation of cultural texts from their home language into English (Kiernan et al., 2015). Student-generated cultural idioms, stories, and lyrics as well as disciplinary texts written in other languages become sites of inquiry as monolingual *and* multilingual students examine the intersection of multiple perspectives, interpretative frames, rhetorical traditions, and linguistic forms. In so doing, teachers can support students' development of translingual dispositions and practices by surfacing purposeful movements across languages and cultures. Students in such classes engage in focused analysis of the exigencies and consequences of linguistic and cultural crossing.

Responding to such pedagogical challenges, our team has been working to develop teacher-training modules for faculty members across disciplinary backgrounds and to facilitate sustained pedagogical inquiry. Working in collaboration with a Chinese undergraduate student, hired as co-researcher and videographer over the course of spring 2019, the team produced the first training module in an upcoming series which will feature a fictional scenario (grounded in examples provided by students) that illustrates the urgent need for instructors to shift—or at the very least unpack—their cultural frames of reference.

The scenario depicts a group of international students expressing befuddlement when their economics instructor introduces the classic supply-and-demand curve by making an analogy to football's alternating lines of scrimmage (e.g., where defense players adjust to the shifting offence positions). In the video, the depiction makes visible the "untranslatability" of cultural references in facilitating the learning of a complicated disciplinary concept. The video portrays the layering of these complex, culturally inflected references, and the resulting cognitive confusion of the students, before going on to suggest alternative practices that instead draw more on the students' own cultural perspectives—in other words, drawing on the students' own "funds of knowledge" (Gonzalez et al., 2005; Paris, 2012). Thus, the video argues for the peril of relying on U.S.-centric frames of reference, which not only can cause cognitive overload for students who must juggle two unfamiliar cultural/disciplinary concepts at the same time, but also risks silencing and dismissing students' languages and cultures as irrelevant for disciplinary learning.

When instructors across the disciplines open up their classrooms to include and appreciate the multiple learning-based and identity-based cultures that are embodied by the students' own knowledge, they also make more transparent classroom and learning expectations. Implementing such pedagogies ensures that students have the opportunities to leverage their cultural repertoire as a whole, thereby ensuring that course grades reflect a realistic assessment of students' level of mastery of required knowledge and competence. In other words, once more we second Zamel's (1995) thought here: adopting such practices in the express interest of better teaching of multilingual students translates as "good pedagogy for everyone" (p. 519).

Concluding Thoughts on Recognizing and Challenging Deficit Pedagogy

As we have argued, every department across every university will be impacted by the upswing in undergraduate international students, domestic multilinguals, and non-traditional monolingual students. The shift in student demographics does not, however, need to be positioned as a detriment to our teaching. Instead, reflecting upon and repositioning our pedagogical approaches in light of understanding how to teach to increasingly diverse groups of students, how to identify their goals and aspirations, and how to stay true to disciplinary and institutional traditions, standards, and expectations will enable educators across the university to design classroom spaces that are rich in engagement and inclusivity.

The cross-disciplinary conversations that this chapter has grown out of illustrate how collaborative initiatives that build upon the sharing of pedagogical experiences are able to shape not only the contexts and the exigencies of particular disciplines, but also the larger cultural and linguistic contexts of the university. For instance, while the broad goals of the FLC collaboration were to invite faculty input for extant practices in accommodating international students enrolled in their classes— to discuss benefits and challenges, to identify areas for cross-unit coordination, and to generate best practices—an unexpected advantage of this work was collaborating with colleagues across the university, with whom we rarely engage in our professional lives. Hence, while the siloing of our academic disciplines continues to be a major challenge in disseminating and adopting translingual approaches, our colleagues across the university were open to engaging with pedagogies that expressed a "willingness to explore with students what they care to advance about people, languages and cultures in which they are identified and may identify, and how and why and when to do it" (Lu & Horner, 2013, p. 600). It is this willingness that lies at the center of such collaborative success, and it is this willingness that we suggest you seek out at your own institutions. And, yes, while this process will continue to be frustrating and messy—with many starts and stops—we hold firm that it will be rewarding for both faculty *and* students, which we position as a central tenet of our own engagement with translingual approaches and adoption of translingual dispositions.

References

Canagarajah, Suresh. (2016). First-person singular: Crossing borders, addressing diversity. *Language Teaching*, *49*(3), 438–454.
Cavazos, Alyssa, Hebbard, Marcela, Hernández, Jose, Rodriguez, Crystal & Schwarz, Geoffrey. (2018). Advancing a transnational, transdisciplinary and translingual framework: A professional development series for teaching assistants in writing and Spanish programs. *Across the Disciplines*, *15*(3), 11–27. https://doi.org/10.37514/ATD-J.2018.15.3.09.
Cox, Michelle. (2014). In response to today's "felt need": WAC, faculty development, and second language writers. In Terry M. Zawacki & Michelle Cox (Eds.), *WAC and second language writers: Research towards linguistically and culturally inclusive programs and*

practices WAC Clearinghouse; Parlor Press. (pp. 299–326). https://doi.org/10.37514 /PER-B.2014.0551.2.12.

Cox, Michelle & Zawacki, Terry Myers (Eds.). (2011). WAC and second language writing: Cross-field research, theory, and program development [Special issue]. *Across the Disciplines, 8*(4). https://wac.colostate.edu/atd/special/ell/.

Duffelmeyer, Barb Blakely & Ellertson, Anthony. (2005). Critical visual literacy: Multimodal communication across the curriculum. *Across the Disciplines, 3*. https://doi.org /10.37514/ATD-J.2006.3.2.02.

Eun, Barohny. (2019). The zone of proximal development as an overarching concept: A framework for synthesizing Vgotsky's ideas. *Educational Philosophy and Theory, 51*(1), 18–30.

Fodrey, Crystal N. & Meg Mikovits. (2020). Theorizing WAC faculty development in multimodal project design. *Across the Disciplines, 17*(1/2), 42–58. https://doi.org /10.37514/ATD-J.2020.17.1-2.04.

Fraiberg, Steven, Wang, Wiziao & You, Xiaoye. (2017). *Inventing the world grant university: Chinese international students' mobilities, literacies, and identities*. Utah State University Press.

Freire, Paulo. (2008, 1968). *Pedagogy of the oppressed*. (M. Ramos, Trans.) (1970). Continuum.

Gonzales, Laura. (2015). Multimodality, translingualism, and rhetorical genre studies. *Composition Forum, 31*. http://compositionforum.com/issue/31/multimodality.php.

Gonzales, Laura. (2018). *Sites of translation: What multilinguals can teach us about digital writing and rhetoric*. University of Michigan Press.

González, Norma, Moll, Luis C. & Amanti, Cathy. (2005). *Funds of knowledge: Theorizing practices in households, communities, and classrooms*. Routledge.

Hall, Jonathan. (2009). WAC/WID in the next America: Redefining professional identity in the age of the multilingual majority. *The WAC Journal, 20*(3), 33–40. https://doi.org /10.37514/WAC-J.2009.20.1.03.

Hall, Jonathan. (2018a). Introduction to the special issue: Rewriting disciplines, rewriting boundaries. *Across the Disciplines, 15*(3), 1–10. https://doi.org/10.37514/ATD-J .2018.15.3.08.

Hall, Jonathan. (2018b). The translingual challenge: Boundary work in rhetoric & composition, second language writing, and WAC/WID. *Across the Disciplines, 15*(3), 28–47. https://doi.org/10.37514/ATD-J.2018.15.3.10.

International Studies & Programs. Office for International Students and Scholars: Statistical Report. (n.d.). Retrieved October 14, 2022, from https://oiss.isp.msu.edu/about /statistical-report/.

Heng Hartse, Joel, Lockett, Michael & Ortabasi, Melek. (2018). Languaging about language in an interdisciplinary writing-intensive course. *Across the Disciplines, 15*(3), 89–102. https://doi.org/10.37514/ATD-J.2018.15.3.14.

Hendricks, C. C. (2018). WAC/WID and transfer: Towards a transdisciplinary view of academic writing. *Across the Disciplines, 15*(3), 48–62. https://doi.org/10.37514 /ATD-J.2018.15.3.11.

Horner, Bruce. (2018). Translinguality and disciplinary reinvention. *Across the Disciplines, 15*(3), 76–88. https://doi.org/10.37514/ATD-J.2018.15.3.13.

Hull, Glynda, Rose, Mike, Fraser, Kay Losey & Castellano, Marisa. (1991). Remediation as social construct: Perspectives from an analysis of classroom discourse. *College Composition and Communication, 42*(3), 299–329.

Hynd, Cynthia, Holsehuh, Jodi Patrick & Hubbard, Betty P. (2004). Thinking like a historian: College students' reading of multiple historical documents. *Journal of Literacy Research, 36*(2), 141–176.

Jenkins, Jennifer. (2013). *English as a lingua franca in the international university: The politics of academic English language policy*. Routledge.

Johns, Ann M. (2001). ESL students and WAC programs: Varied populations and diverse needs. In Susan H. McLeod, Eric Miraglia, Margot Soven & Christopher Thaiss. (Eds.), *WAC for the new millennium: Strategies for continuing writing-across-the-curriculum programs*. NCTE.

Johns, Ann M. (2005). The linguistically-diverse student: Challenges and possibilities across the curriculum [Special issue]. *Across the Disciplines, 2*. https://wac.colostate.edu/atd/special/lds/.

Kiernan, Julia, Meier, Joyce & Wang, Xiqiao (Eds.). (2018). "Introduction." [Special issue on transnational pedagogy]. *Journal of Global Literacies, Technologies, and Emerging Pedagogies, 4*(3), 647–654.

Kiernan, Julia, Meier, Joyce & Wang, Xiqiao. (2017). Curricular shifts in reading and writing: Centering students' languages and cultures within reflective practices of translation. *L1-Educational Studies in Language and Literature, 17*, 1–18.

Kiernan, Julia, Meier, Joyce & Wang, Xiqiao. (2016). Negotiating languages and cultures: Enacting translingualism through a translation assignment. *Composition Studies, 44*(1), 89–107.

Kiernan, Julia. (2021). A framework for linguistically inclusive course design. In Julia Kiernan, Alanna Frost & Suzanne Blum Malley, (Eds.), *Translingual pedagogical perspectives: Teaching writing in the North American composition classroom*. Utah State University Press.

Kiernan, Julia. (2017). Translation narratives: Engaging second language learners in transnational literacy practices. In David M. Palfreyman & Christa van der Walt (Eds.), *Academic biliteracies: Translanguaging and multilingual repertoires in higher education settings*. Multilingual Matters.

Kiernan, Julia. (2015). Multimodal and translingual composing practices: A culturally based needs assessment of second language learners. *Journal of Global Literacies, Technologies, and Emerging Pedagogies, 3*(1), 302–321.

Lancaster, Zak. (2011). Interpersonal stance in L1 and L2 students' argumentative writing in economics: Implications for faculty development in WAC/WID programs. *Across the Disciplines, 8*(4), 1–23. https://doi.org/10.37514/ATD-J.2011.8.4.22.

Lee, Jerry Won & Jenks, Christopher. (2016). Doing translingual dispositions. *College Composition and Communication, 68*(2), 317–344.

Leonard, Rebecca Lorimer, and Rebecca Nowacek. (2016). Transfer and translingualism. *College English, 78*(3), 258–264.

Manuel-Dupont, Sonia. (1996). Writing-across-the-curriculum in an engineering program. *Journal of Engineering Education, 85*(1), 35–40.

Matsuda, Paul Kei, and Jeffrey Jablonski. (2000). Beyond the L2 metaphor: Towards a mutually transformative model of ESL/WAC collaboration. *academic.writing, 1*.

Meier, Joyce. (2018). Multimodal, embodied learning and listening: ELLs and intercultural dialogue in two community projects. *The Reading Matrix: An International Online Journal, 18*(2), 147–164.

Meier, Joyce, Gannon, Bree, Caesar, Cheryl & Medei, David. (2018). Translingual pedagogy, rhetorical listening, and multimodal experiences in a first-year writing conference that fosters intercultural learning. [Special issue]. *Journal of Global Literacies, Technologies, and Emerging Pedagogies, 4*(3), 714–740.

Milu, Esther & Gomes, Matt. (2021). "Hay un tiempo y un lugar para todo": Students' writing and rhetorical strategies in a translingual pedagogy. In Julia Kiernan, Alanna Frost & Suzanne Blum Malley (Eds.), *Translingual pedagogical perspectives: Engaging domestic and international students in the composition classroom*. Utah State University Press.

Paris, Django. (2012). Culturally sustaining pedagogy: A needed change in stance, terminology, and practice. *Educational Researcher, 41*(3), 93–97.

Peters, Brad & Robertson, Julie Fisher. (2007). Portfolio partnerships between faculty and WAC: Lessons from disciplinary practice, reflection, and transformation. *College Composition and Communication, 59*(2), 206–236.

Robins, Anthony. (2010). Learning edge momentum: A new account of outcomes in CS1. *Computer Science Education, 20*(1), 37–71.

Rutz, Carol & Grawe, Nathan D. (2009). Pairing WAC and quantitative reasoning through portfolio assessment and faculty development. *Across the Disciplines, 6*(2). https://doi.org/10.37514/ATD-J.2009.6.1.04.

Shanahan, Timothy & Shanahan, Cynthia. (2012). What is disciplinary literacy and why does it matter? *Topics in language disorders, 32*(1), 7–18.

Shipka, Jody. (2011). *Toward a composition made whole*. University of Pittsburgh Press.

Trimbur, John. (2016). Translingualism and close reading. *College English, 78*(3), 219–227.

Wang, Xiqiao. (2021). Writing-theory cartoon: Toward a translingual and multimodal pedagogy. In Julia Kiernan, Alanna Frost & Suzanne Blum Malley, (Eds.), *Translingual pedagogical perspectives: Teaching writing in the North American composition classroom*. Utah State University Press.

Wang, Xiqiao. (2019a). Observing literacy learning across WeChat and first-year writing: A scalar analysis of one transnational student's multilingualism. *Computers and Composition, 52*, 253–271.

Wang, Xiqiao. (2019b). Tracing connections and disconnects: Reading, writing, and digital literacies across contexts. *College Composition and Communication, 70*(4), 560–589.

Wang, Xiqiao. (2017). Developing translingual disposition through a writing theory cartoon assignment. *Journal of Basic Writing, 36*(1), 44–73. https://doi.org/10.37514/JBW-J.2017.36.1.04.

Wolfe-Quintero, Kate & Segade, Gabriela. (1999). University support for second-language writers across the curriculum. In Linda Harklau, Kay M. Losey & Meryl Siegal (Eds.), *Generation 1.5 meets college composition: Issues in the teaching of writing to U.S.-educated learners of ESL* (pp. 191–209). Routledge.

Zamel, Vivian. (1995). Strangers in academia: The experiences of faculty and ESL students across the curriculum. *College Composition and Communication, 46*(4), 506–521.

Zawacki, Terry Myers & Cox, Michelle. (Eds.). (2014). *WAC and second language writers: research towards linguistically and culturally inclusive programs and practices.* The WAC Clearinghouse; Parlor Press. https://doi.org/10.37514/PER-B.2014.0551.

Zemliansky, Pavel & Berry, Landon. (2017). A writing-across-the-curriculum faculty development program: An experience report. *IEEE Transactions on Professional Communication, 60*(3), 306–316.

Transnational Telephone Games: Collaborations on Writing Education in South Asia

Shyam Sharma and Gene Hammond
STATE UNIVERSITY OF NEW YORK AT STONY BROOK

This chapter reports and reflects on transnational collaborations between writing scholars in the US and scholars across the disciplines interested in writing education in South Asia. These collaborations began with the first author conducting a 9-month WAC-based training series virtually for faculty at Midwestern University in Nepal, which culminated in a half-week "education summit" workshop on site at Midwestern at which both authors took leading roles in the summer of 2016. Midwestern University faculty's interest in integrating writing into their teaching led in turn to a number of monthly webinars, followed by summer retreats in subsequent years, focusing on student-centered teaching at Tribhuvan University, the central public university in Nepal, and at private colleges in Nepal, and then in Dhaka, Bangladesh. An emerging grassroots community of scholars in Nepal also gave rise to faculty research and publication workshops for a network of scholars from across Bangladesh, India, and Nepal. In all of these collaborations, even though the interest in writing instruction and writing education always remained high, this interest evolved over the years in unpredictable ways. This chapter illustrates how local institutions and social conditions, as well as curricular demands and professional incentives, shaped our transnational collaboration with respect to writing education. In doing so, it highlights how the affordances of emerging technology, as well as diasporic connections, helped collaborators both to exploit and to counter transnational hegemonies, thereby advancing mutually respectful and beneficial transnational exchange in relation to writing education broadly defined.

A "transnational" turn in U.S. writing studies in the past 15 years has ramped up scholars' interest to internationalize writing education and research (Hesford, 2006; Horner, 2016; Martins, 2015; Ray & Theado, 2014; Rose & Weiser, 2018; Tardy, 2014). But transnational "exchanges" still consist largely of exporting (Donahue, 2009) to other countries, a persistent "provincialism" that "places unnecessary constraints on what can be thought, understood, observed, and taught as writing" (Sanchez, 2016, p. 78). Despite the critical voices of scholars like Donahue and Sanchez, mainstream discourse about internationalization has continued to reflect the US's expansionist impulses, leading both to "intellectual tourism" and to "export" of our form of writing pedagogy and to scholarship rather than to "collaboration or 'hearing' of work across borders" (Donahue, 2009, p. 214). While increasing collaborations, including some class-based (Shamsuzzaman, this volume), technology-mediated, and institution-serving ones have been documented (see Wu, 2018), sustained exchange of research, scholarship, and educational partnerships with colleagues in other countries remains limited, barring a few cases (e.g., Sullivan et al., 2012; You, 2016). Mutually beneficial collaborations among educators and scholars, and especially collaborative explorations of evolving opportunities, are yet to be reported in the scholarship. Attempts to document "writing programs" (Thaiss et al., 2012) in other countries are typically made in our own North American images, rather than in local terms on the ground. Mary Muchiri et al. described a quarter century ago in 1995 several challenges of trying to implement writing programs in Kenya, Tanzania, and Zaire; Mark Schaub (2003) has highlighted similar difficulties at the American University in Cairo; and Chris Anson and Christiane Donahue (2015) have shared challenges based on their visits and collaborations with institutions in Europe and Saudi Arabia. Anson and Donahue have indeed argued that it is unproductive to try to identify or promote "writing programs" and "WPAs" abroad and instead suggest that we should focus our international efforts on scholarly practice. To borrow the words of Rebecca Dingo et al. (2013), "the proliferation of the term 'transnational' has been a substitution for a thin understanding of globalization wherein nation state and neocolonial relationships are dissipated in the name of global exchange" (p. 517). The lack of progress in transnational exchange, or even of understanding of writing education across borders, we believe, comes from a collective unwillingness/inability to learn from collaboration and to commit to exchange beyond unilateral sharing and over time.

The lack of substance and progress in transnational exchange in writing education, as we foreground against the above backdrop in this chapter, is most strongly undergirded by geopolitics as a broader context and force. In spite of sharply critical scholarship by a small number of scholars whose work we overviewed above, there remains a prevalent assumption that the US is the only country in the world that teaches writing as an independent subject; furthermore, living in a country that assumes that "the world" would be better off with our version of writing pedagogy—as well as our capitalism, democracy, and education at large—American scholars are still tempted to go abroad and share what we do in our writing courses with missionary fervor. Too often, what we do on these visits is give a few talks, enjoy a few lunches and dinners, and promise to stay in touch. Then our interest dissipates as we take up, now that we have such work on our resume, a new project in another country. Good will and perhaps friendships have been fostered, but in fact little change has taken place, and even less learning has changed our own practice or perspectives back home. This is not only true for those of us who are cultural outsiders, don't speak local languages, and don't have social or professional relationships with our counterparts on the ground; it can also happen to the globe-trotters among us who grew up and worked in the places we return to. And it happens in spite of our intentions to collaborate as equals, primarily because that is how hegemony functions and we often do not have the knowledge or willpower to counter it adequately. One-time attempts are easier made and with greater commitment; long-term and "unfolding" partnerships (see Theado et al., 2017) are less often or less clearly successful, especially because "visiting partners" seldom create room for adapting to lessons learned along the way. Thus, we built our collaborations on the premise that all knowledge is local (Canagarajah, 2002), and that the terms and processes of collaboration should be localized as well.

Based on our experiences in the past six years of transnational collaborations in South Asia as writing scholars based in the United States, we share in the rest of this chapter a number of lessons about transnational exchanges, including:

- how scholars can acknowledge and even exploit the geopolitics of inequality toward more equitable collaboration;
- what roles emerging technologies of communication and collaboration can play in sustaining and deepening transnational exchanges;
- how individuals and institutions involved in collaboration can create productive exchanges, even when they cannot create or sustain formal programs and structures; and
- what collaborators can gain when they value processes and experiences beyond plan-based outcomes and measurable impacts.

While the perspectives we share focus on writing education, they carry broader implications for educational exchanges at large. This broader contextualization is essential because it is within that context that exchanges over writing across the curriculum work can take place, especially across national borders.

Serendipity, Positionality, and Diasporic Connections

Traveling through Myanmar in 2017 a few days after teaching workshops in Nepal and Bangladesh, this article's second author stopped in for breakfast in a family-owned streetfront shop in Yangon. A few minutes after he sat down, a young local man, roughly 25, dressed impeccably, with a string tie, a fashionable cowboy hat, narrow pants, pointed shoes, and a ruffled shirt, took the second seat at a very small table that they now shared. A few minutes into the small talk that ensued, the gentleman interrupted himself to ask the tourist where he was from. "The United States," the latter responded. The young man leaned back and responded, slowly and significantly, with high drama and seemingly without irony, "Superpower!" Clearly we don't control what people in other countries think of us.

Transnational exchange is inevitably influenced by complex dynamics of power and hegemony and is also shaped by often-magnified dynamics of understanding and interests, patience and tolerance of uncertainty, ego and ambition, rewards and incentives, expectations and abilities, connections and trust, and, quite significantly, chance and serendipity—dynamics we can appreciate but usually cannot control. So in the past six years, we tried to plan our collaboration with cultural and political realities very much in mind. First of all, we and our in-country collaborators pursue the exchange as an extension of our academic service, placing our collaborations on strong footings, even as the projects greatly and often unpredictably evolve. The usual logistical arrangement has been for universities to cover just our local accommodation wherever we don't have family in town to stay with; we bear all other costs including airfare ourselves. As we have sought to foster transnational grassroots communities, we have found informal and evolving collaborations to be much more sustainable and socially impactful than formal programs or partnerships. The first author's knowledge of cultural and academic contexts and the ability to converse in different local languages have contributed to the collaborations, allowing the second author to contribute to months-long and years-long virtual programs, in addition to one-off events that we have led together; the major projects have involved collaborative planning with different local coordinators, locally appropriate application and selection processes, extensive documentation, and reporting of progress to participants and institutional leaders supporting the initiatives.

We will discuss the role of virtual connection and networking later, but we want to first highlight that connections made during our travels have been far more lasting and consequential. The first author had been involved in numerous scholarly collaborations online since leaving Nepal in 2006, but had been seldom able to connect well with influential academic scholars and leaders: when we started visiting Nepal and the South Asian region during summer breaks, in 2016, the dynamics drastically changed. Physical meetings prepared the ground and provided follow-up opportunities online. Especially onsite, many chance meetings played an unusually important role. Among the most significant cases, in the summer of 2016, a serendipitous meeting and discussions with Tribhuvan University's then provost, in the last two days of a forty-day visit to Nepal, led to the creation at that university of an extremely productive platform where we could go on to facilitate many training programs, online and onsite, during subsequent summer visits, involving hundreds of professors from across the national network of 64 colleges within Nepal's oldest and largest public institution that educates nearly 80% of total tertiary education students in the country.

Similarly, our willingness to contribute our expertise as writing scholars/teachers, however that expertise fits local needs, has also played an important role. Our initial focus on writing instruction across the curriculum has evolved: into faculty development projects with a focus on writing integration, then student-centered pedagogy, then research-based writing and publication for emerging scholars; into training and discussion for establishing academic support, including writing center support, for students; and into the explorations of institutional faculty development frameworks. The unpredictable but productive evolutions of collaborative opportunities, for us and later for other U.S.-based writing scholars, undergird the stories, reflections, and perspectives that we share in this chapter.

Our positionalities are also critical factors in our collaborations in South Asia. While the first author was able to work alternately as an outsider (U.S-based) and insider (born and raised in Nepal and India), the second author's positionality is very different. The latter didn't do any teaching abroad until he was 50, when, in 1996, he was invited to go to Djibouti by a former student who had become the information officer in the Djiboutian embassy. Then in 2007, his experience in Djibouti helped him get accepted to teach in a program called Semester at Sea, a study-abroad alternative during which 1,000 students, mostly from the US, sail around the world while taking a full semester schedule of classes, stopping in twelve ports for four days each with the full opportunity to explore. And in turn his experience in Asia during 2007 led him to be invited by the first author in 2016 to Nepal for a series of academic events across the country, and the experiences discussed in this chapter ensued.

Given our positionalities and connections, we have tried to avoid or transcend hegemonic terms of engagement (see Alvarez, 2016) and instead sought to pursue collaboration without seeking to use or promote our terms, program models, and writing practices (see Horner, 2015). Most significantly, we have sought out what LuMing Mao (2003) calls "reflective encounters," or the act of using new experience of other places and practices for self-reflection and self-education, especially by understanding others "on their own terms" and creating "an ongoing dialogue" (p. 418). The approach we took also demanded awareness of the limitations of what Burke (1966) has called the "terministic screen," or the lenses of familiar terminology as analytical and methodological tools (also see Donahue & Moon, 2007). We have found more value in the processes and experiences of exploring mutually beneficial collaborations on academic writing across national and other borders than we had found in our earlier attempts to help establish specific programs or foster specific models based on our American experiences.

Emerging Technology and Evolving Collaboration

Transnational scholarly collaboration and exchange are increasingly mediated by (and dependent on) digital/network technologies. Zhiwei Wu (2018) has documented a variety of transnational collaborations among writing educators, showing a general shift from traditional scholar exchanges onsite toward class-to-class collaborations online. In our case, the majority of collaboration has taken place virtually, with technology facilitating what we did and how we did it. In the course of the nearly six years of our collaborations in South Asia, the digital tools and networking platforms we used (such as Google Drive and Doc, Facebook Group and Messenger, and Skype and Zoom) improved vastly in their affordances. Internet bandwidth improved as well, boosting technology adoption that had started accelerating before the pandemic. From the constantly interrupted Skype calls with scholars at Midwestern (such as a complete failure on a day when Professor Charles Bazerman was invited to run a webinar) to the triumphant end of a multi-year power shortage in Kathmandu in 2017, and from the internet "traffic jam" during evenings in Dhaka to the "breakout rooms" of Zoom meeting tool in 2020, technological advancements have recently felt as smooth transnationally as they do within the US. However, the most important aspect of our use of technology has not been the advancements and affordances of the collaborative platforms and tools themselves. It has been the commitment to find shared interest among collaborators that has driven the uses and benefits of technology for us and our collaborators. Over the past six years, local groups involved in transnational collaborations had been well ahead of their peers in the application of emerging technologies for achieving significant goals; so they had significant leverage and interest to respond to a variety of new academic challenges when the Covid–19 pandemic disrupted teaching, learning, and scholarship, involving us in those responses. Their professional skills for organizing pedagogical, research, and publication support projects garnered greater respect than their technological savvy itself, as they went on to organize local support groups, gradually without our support.

Generally put, as technologies advance—and often serve as alternatives to long-distance travels that are either prohibitively expensive or simply unavailable for scholars across borders—some amount of transnational scholarly collaboration can and should shift to online platforms. Our online collaborations have been more effective when they are complemented with onsite work, and vice versa: when technologies were used for fostering relationships, creating and sharing resources, continuing initiatives and following up on completed projects, we could build much stronger communities and achieve impactful outcomes with our local collaborators. Reviewing technology-mediated research and practice, especially focusing on classroom teaching beyond national borders, Wu (2018) found that the practice (which started in the mid–1990s, probably at MIT) has not only been "international" (because participants come from different countries) but also "cross-national" (because they transcend national borders) and "transnational" (because their identities and the elements of communication emerged from process and interaction); but Wu also pointed out that virtual spaces are "vested in power differentials," adding that current practices perpetuate the hegemony of English language, of written text, and of institutional structures. Our work in South Asia has sought to overcome these pitfalls Wu points out by keeping our exchanges translingual, multimodal, and community-driven. Our collaborations have greatly benefited from the use of technology, but we have remained cautious about over-reliance on technology; substitution of virtual networking for physical co-presence; and issues of access and equity, inclusivity, and power differentials that technology can raise or even magnify in our use of technology for collaboration. This mindfulness, we think, has helped the collaborations empower members of the community, pursuing the collaboration with a sense of fairness and respect. Most importantly, we have exploited emerging technologies to let our collaborations change and evolve along the way, creating diverse possibilities and alternative routes, facilitating the creation and sharing of resources, and sustaining conversations during and beyond the completion of specific projects. Above all, we have used technology to respond to the needs and interests of local collaborators.

Midwestern University and the Pull of Educational Transformation

The first institution we worked with, Midwestern University, is a small public university in remote western Nepal. The origin of the Midwestern program was also characterized by serendipity. In 2015, we developed an online WAC training program through informal conversations during a visit to the US by the university's president and provost , followed by collaborations with a group of faculty members in Nepal. To the usual "writing across the curriculum" (WAC) framework, we added "and in the professions" (WACAP) not only because the university leaders wanted an equal focus on academic writing skills and on professional communication skills but also because the acronym "WAC" sounds exactly like the Nepalese word for "vomit" especially in the western variety (a cross-cultural and translingual issue that serves to highlight the need for localized terminology as well as collaboration). In fact, even our core phrase "writing instruction" has rarely resonated well with our diverse South Asian partners in the many different collaborative projects so far. Continued, technologically mediated, conversations and follow-up webinars for a year helped strengthen relationships and understand what both sides could give and receive at Midwestern.

While technology facilitated collaboration, social and political conditions shaped and reshaped it. Because in 2014 Nepal had just promulgated a new constitution as a federal democracy and Midwestern University had just been situated at the center of an independent state, being often asked to lead policy formulation in education and society at large, the webinar training found itself in the middle of broader discussions about transforming higher education. Responding to the ambitions of Midwestern, a small but rapidly growing institution, we proposed to help establish a writing center and generally promote writing skills among students and faculty toward creating an environment (similar to what Violeta Molina-Natera (2017) describes about Colombia) with improved writing curricula and support in the university. We did not succeed in that goal, or at least not directly and explicitly, because, as we later realized, we didn't understand how susceptible to political and leadership change the institution was—as well as how hard and perhaps unproductive it is to try to graft a foreign concept and institution like the "writing center" into a very different academic setting.

Even before the WACAP webinar series completed its one-year timeline, the participants wished to update it into a faculty development initiative for "modernized" teaching. Ironically, we increasingly realized that the more "modern" (in our colleagues' sense of "American") the focus of a program, the more likely that it would not meet local demands and would therefore have to keep evolving (see Allen, 2014). We first responded by trying to share our writing pedagogies with instructors of writing-intensive courses and to help instructors from content-heavy courses to adapt those pedagogies (see Hodges, this volume). However, as the local coordinator of the webinar initiative wrote in a report for the university a year after completion, some of his fellow trainees wanted "theoretical backup," others "practical writing instruction tips," and yet others wanted to shift away from writing altogether. In one case, an engineering instructor conducted an analysis of an alarming student failure rate and found out that whereas students in his department had been writing exam answers in bullet points (using notes provided by instructors), the examiners gave little or no credit for such writing because they wanted answers in paragraph form, in full sentences. This finding didn't create a demand for teaching writing; it instead led to strategies for better aligning instruction, assignments, and assessment. For instance, if the teachers accepted bullet-point responses, the focus on disciplinary content would allow writing skills to develop gradually. Writing skills among students were a problem but the faculty participants in the training saw causes and solutions in different places. Even those interested in writing instruction wanted more to improve the teaching of content due to the local content-dominated assessment practices.

At the peak of our collaboration with faculty in Midwestern University, we visited Surkhet, the university town 14 hours of mountain roads away from the country's capital Kathmandu, in the summer of 2016. Along with another Stony Brook University colleague (Nobi Nagasawa from the Fine Arts department), we were accompanied by two other colleagues, Krishna Bista of the University of Louisiana at Monroe and Santosh Khadka of the California State University at Northridge. Our three-day onsite program at Surkhet, ambitiously called the "Summer Summit" on "Educational Transformation," was organized by the webinar participants, including a series of highly effective workshops and keynotes. Our second author facilitated a workshop helping a group of administrators and faculty members explore ways to institutionalize the changes envisioned by the "summit"; our first author organized training for writing center director and staff; and the other experts explored the use of art, class-to-class exchange, and academic technology for enhancing higher education.

Energized by this program, we assumed that local scholars would implement a multi-dimensional faculty development initiative and launch a new writing center, as they planned. We also agreed to contribute our expertise as writing scholars to the faculty training, knowing that "writing" instruction would be a key but small component. In the year that followed, though, interest in writing instruction itself faded. So, we further adapted the plan based on discussion with our collaborators. "In order to shift from traditional lecture-and-exam dominated practices to student-centered education," said the description of a broadened program, "we need a constructivist approach to teacher development in which teachers come together to learn, share, and develop increasingly productive and effective ways to teach." Called "The Teaching Excellence Project," the plan was to implement a "three-dimensional initiative launched after a two-day workshop in May 2018" and it was, on paper, a part of a more formal collaboration that would begin between Midwestern University and our home institution, Stony Brook. Unfortunately, due to a leadership change at Midwestern, local scholars were unable to launch or even informally rekindle any collaboration. Instead, we were invited to visit Surkhet during our next visit to Nepal in the summer of 2018, where we facilitated a workshop on faculty publication. The interest was now on faculty writing rather than on writing support for students. Participants of the WACAP program do still report using what they learned from the 2015–2016 webinar series, but no formal curricular integration of writing skills took place. Nor did the writing center come into operation, other than a banner outside a room that was filled with dust-covered, iron-framed, four-seater wooden desks attached to their benches, one pair turned upside down to stack upon another. When we saw this space, after insisting to visit the "writing center," we did not ask whether the furniture was brought there for an unborn academic unit or just for storage, for surplus. This image reminded us of what a scholar in Kathmandu called "the fossils of tourist scholars' dreams to establish academic programs per their model."

At Midwestern, we had to change our expectations and adjust. When initiatives fizzled out, or merged or evolved into something new, online or during our visits, it was at first hard to see beyond the disruption, to be patient, or to see new possibilities. It took time and effort to better understand the context, needs, interests, and especially the push and pull of the broad changes taking place in Nepalese society and education. Programs were difficult to launch, but initiatives far easier to take; goals were harder to achieve than it was simply to make progress. Technology added flexibility and facilitated follow ups, fostered deeper engagements, and kept the community connected. Much more importantly, in retrospect, our flexibility made our expertise most useful for our local partners. We too did more and learned more due to our responsiveness to local demands.

Tribhuvan University and a Shift Toward the Semester-Based System

When we started in 2016 collaborating with scholars at Tribhuvan University, the most prestigious public university in Nepal, our collaborations rapidly increased in scope, productivity, and interest. However, the focus on writing instruction became even less clear and predictable than it had been at Midwestern. The online faculty training program that TU's provost launched evolved into a multifaceted faculty development initiative, showing potential for broadly influencing instructional practice. We held monthly online workshops in 2017–2018 and 2018–2019, followed by onsite retreats in Nepal called summer summits in 2018 and 2019. Once again, technology facilitated continuity of collaboration and community building where physical visits alone had traditionally been aligned with one-way-traffic support/consultation; but it was the physical visits that established recognition and trust, friendship and inspiration.

Year-long participants in the online webinar series were now prepared as trainers and, using a handbook created by compiling resources from the webinar program, went on trips to train hundreds of their colleagues across the country. They also served as facilitators for the summer retreats and organized training programs at their respective institutions and in nearby towns. Onsite programs increasingly balanced the number of male and female participants, also becoming inclusive in terms of disciplines, socioeconomic backgrounds, ethnicity, and culture. At the end of 2019, the participants submitted an official proposal to the university's executive body, urging it to institutionalize the faculty development (online and onsite) initiatives by providing specific plans and operational guidelines for establishing a Center for Excellence in Research and Teaching.

Once again, in the highly productive collaborations involving Tribhuvan University and especially its local offshoots created by our Nepalese partners, local scholars and their institutions have incorporated our expertise and experience as educators in an academic culture (the U.S. culture) that is more student-centered and skills-focused, what the Nepalese understand as "semester-based" education. Since the second author had the experience of witnessing a similar transition from lecture-based to student-based education at Oxford University in Britain in the early 1970s, and as the first author has in his transition to graduate education from Nepal to the US, we contribute our expertise in an area where we do not see ourselves as experts, and yet our experiences have been greatly valued. Instead of helping develop writing programs or even writing-focused initiatives, we have once again let local faculty and administrators put our expertise as writing scholars to its broader purposes. "Institutionalization," if any, has only taken place in the form of better response and more direct participation from academic leaders, as well as broader involvement of the faculty. But no program is likely to be formally implemented, at least not with our continued involvement, even if we wanted such involvement.

When we started our collaboration with scholars at Tribhuvan, the institution had just implemented, with little or no preparation (Khaniya, 2014), the semester-based system in its graduate programs across the country; that implementation had created huge demands for faculty training toward making major shifts in curriculum design, instruction, and assessment (Tripathi et al., 2019). Much like at Midwestern, Tribhuvan University faculty also wanted to fold the teaching and learning of writing skills into a broader framework of "major shifts" in higher education. Writing skills were once again viewed from an "instrumentalist" perspective, rather than disciplinary (fostering identity), epistemological (creating awareness), or political/civic (empowering the individual) perspectives. Writing was a focus of various training programs, as part of assignment design and instruction, teaching research papers and other assignments, and for class activities and diversification of assessment; yet, it was rarely an exclusive focus of instruction or of the faculty training initiatives.

Accordingly, we no longer proposed establishing a writing center (we saw posters advertising defunct writing centers during our visits and heard about other failed attempts). And we either avoided or explained our terminologies from the US (such as "composition" or "rhetoric," "writing center" or "writing course," writing "program" or "pedagogy"). Having better understood how writing education takes up different spaces and shapes in different contexts, we didn't propose a WAC program of any kind. Faculty development initiatives adopted writing as a focus of several webinar workshops, but the position of writing instruction reflected an intriguing ambivalence, which notably came from an improved understanding of and response to local interests and needs. The topics of webinar sessions now included: reforming the classroom (making it more student-centered and interactive), effective instruction (foregrounding writing and communication skills), alignment of teaching with assessment (by creating explicit assignment instructions and providing rubrics), handling academic dishonesty (by teaching research and writing skills), mastering professional development skills (including skills for writing and communication, technology use, and job search), and developing teaching materials (so the group could produce resources to multiply the effects of the initiative). As these topics indicate, writing was simultaneously a high-demand area (it kept appearing in the program) and a marginalized one (it was usually part of or the means of achieving another objective).

Going Regional in South Asia: More Shifts and/in Common Grounds

As our collaboration at Nepal's universities grew, we were invited to contribute to faculty development programs at North South University, a high-ranking private institution in Dhaka, Bangladesh. Here, our local coordinator, Mohammad Shamsuzzaman (Zaman), was a composition scholar with writing and TESOL backgrounds in the United States and New Zealand. While our personal connection with Zaman was virtual yet robust, it was physical visits in 2018 and 2019 by several faculty members from our university to his, then visits by him and his colleague to our university during the latter year, that created strong professional relationships across faculty in our respective departments and institutions. But relationship-building, technologically mediated or not, however, is only one step toward productive cross-border collaboration; it is the creation of shared interest and mutual benefits that makes collaboration productive. In Bangladesh, too, the interests of both the institution (North South) and of the scholars who participated in the early online and onsite programs broadened and diverged due to a unique set of contextual factors. We learned from Zaman immediately (see Shamsuzzaman, 2017) that writing studies has struggled to be recognized as a discipline or even a respectable specialization within English studies in Bangladesh. As Tasildhar (1996) highlights, citing arguments by Viswanathan, English studies scholars in India and the South Asian region in general have been resisting the emerging focus on language and communication as reflecting a "mindless enslavement" to market forces. English literature scholars tend to associate writing instruction with deficits among students and a lower-status task for faculty, and private universities there didn't want to acknowledge any such deficits by starting a writing center, for instance. Yet, even though many instructors who joined the first series of webinars discontinued their attendance, an enthusiastic group completed three different webinar series, focusing on classroom instruction of writing, faculty scholarship, and academic support for students beyond class. By summarizing the achievements made by those webinar initiatives in relation to an MOU that had envisioned them the previous year, faculty webinar groups that emerged at North South developed a proposal for establishing a formal space for writing, research, and communication (WRC) support for students and faculty. Here, too, a change in department leadership disrupted the formal collaboration after our second summer visit to Dhaka in the summer of 2019, which included two other Stony Brook scholars, Cynthia Davidson and MaryAnn Duffy. We have continued to invite colleagues from North South University and beyond in Bangladesh to join webinars, as well as to visit us in the US. And we continue to return to Bangladesh, as well as Nepal, every year.

Our collaborations back in Nepal have not only expanded in scope but have also been adapted locally. For example, Surendra Subedi, a scholar representing the private college network founded by the gentleman who connected us to the Tribhuvan University provost, has created a faculty development framework for Kathmandu Model College (an institution that he is principal of), drawing on the contribution and leadership he provides to the public-private partnership with Tribhuvan. With the first author, he has written several pieces of scholarship and op eds in national dailies on the topics of faculty development and higher education (Sharma & Subedi, 2020). Similarly, in late 2019, the first author piloted a new model of publication-focused webinar series at King's College, a private institution affiliated with an American college; during this webinar, nine out of 12 scholars from King's completed journal article manuscripts based on empirical data, taking them through a month-long process of research, another month of drafting, and a final month of open peer review. In 2019, this research-focused faculty development webinar series gave rise to a more robust program that the first author facilitated along with the former head of the English education department at TU, Prem Phyak. The program supported a selected group of scholars from across the disciplines and across the country in Nepal, half of them women. The two-webinar series have ultimately given rise to a South Asia-wide online collaboration where two dozen scholars from as many institutions and from across the disciplines completed a 3-month long writing support program to produce and publish research-based articles in international journals. Academic leaders of the home institutions of most of these scholars enthusiastically supported this highly successful program, as they did a number of online teaching trainings for hundreds of scholars from across the country while responding to the pandemic's disruption and other professional development training programs organized by the local network of scholars in the next few years.

However, no matter how robust and rigorous the collaborations are, universities have so far been unable to mobilize our service as foreign scholars and of their own faculty by creating any formal institutional structures or programs. While their leaders welcome, support, and greatly admire the collaboration, they seem to understand what many scholars from the West miss: while informal and/or virtual transnational networks among scholars offer a new currency in internationalization, structural changes based on them are too tenuous to match the robust and evolving potentials of communities of practice. While we as outsiders may wish to see events and initiatives involving us becoming a part of the system on the ground, or of change that we help effect, institutions and societies in places like South Asia are changing too rapidly for systems to absorb and consolidate the initiatives of transnational collaborations, not just when they are ad hoc but also when they are formally organized. The grassroots communities of scholars have deployed writing instruction and writing in their own careers in a variety of meaningful ways beyond what we could have imagined six years ago—other than by establishing a formal writing program.

The virtualization of relationships built onsite and the onsite embodiment of virtually thriving networks have both contributed to a collaborative ecosystem that feeds on shared, evolving, and mutually beneficial energies and interests. The semi-virtual and fluid exchanges that this ecosystem facilitates uniquely transcends not only national borders but also norms of institutional and formal exchanges of the past. Both the technological mediation and the social dynamics of this hybrid phenomenon deserve further exploration in future scholarship.

Avenues of Transnational Collaborations

Returning to the questions with which we began, our experiences of collaborating and contributing to higher education in parts of South Asia have taught us some important lessons, some of which we shared through a panel along with Zaman at the 2019 CCCC meeting in Pittsburgh. Here we expand some of the lessons within this chapter's thematic context.

Counter-Hegemonic Strategies

How can we pursue transnational collaborations on writing education and scholarship while acknowledging and perhaps even using geopolitical hegemonies to the advantage of the collaboration? The scholarship on transnational writing has addressed issues of power and inequality to some extent (e.g., Dingo et al., 2013; Donahue, 2009; Hum & Lyon, 2008); transnational collaborations could also draw upon a rich body of scholarship with a focus on postcolonialism (e.g., Alvarez, 2016; Baca, 2009; Sánchez, 2016); and collaborators can find some amount of local scholarship to draw on. In practice, however, most of us seem to assume that "writing programs" can be identified or promoted "worldwide" as they develop, typically following the North American model—even though, in reality, even within the State University of New York system, it is hard to find distinct writing programs. The less we know about another culture or context, the less nuanced our assumptions and understandings. In the course of our collaborations, we have come to realize that whether we like it or not, we "perform" roles that are extant in the colonial/hegemonic order of relations and are shaped by our power relative to that of our collaborators. Even when we try to actively resist them, geopolitical power structures continue to powerfully frame us. Hegemony almost automatically accords the more powerful party more space, voice, and respect; it regards the knowledge from colonial powers with higher esteem or takes it for granted, it doesn't encourage the asking of questions, and it tries despite our best intentions only to help the less dominant societies to learn.

So, we have tried to counter geopolitical hegemony, for instance, by encouraging our collaborators to speak in the language they find most comfortable, not switching to English for our convenience. We "threw the respect back" when we sensed undue regard for us or for our ideas. To mobilize rather than passively work within the hegemonic impulses of our society and profession, we paid attention to colonial roots or dynamics on the ground, sought support and advocacy for our collaborators, leveraged their collaboration with us in their institutions, avoided adding unproductive workload on them, invited them to collaboratively produce scholarship or pursue professional development opportunities, refused to simply respond to institutional pressure for them to publish or perish, recognized and promoted different kinds of "scholarship" that are of value to them and their society, promoted their agency and voice in their institutions, and used ethics and advocacy as impetus for collaboration.

"Fossils of Tourist Scholars' Dreams"

How can individuals and institutions involved create productive exchanges even when they cannot create or sustain formal programs and structures? Our various projects involving Tribhuvan University scholars taught us that transnational collaborations can rarely produce "outcomes" in the same way as administrative or even service efforts may do within our own institutions. We certainly helped our collaborators build a few "structural pieces" such as a faculty training handbook and a report and proposal for a faculty development center at Tribhuvan. The *Handbook for Trainers and Teachers* was developed to provide practical training and teaching guidelines for university educators to shift the focus of higher education:

1. from teaching to learning (demanded by a more student-centered academic culture embodied by semester-based education),
2. from knowing to doing (reflecting the society's demand for more academic skills and professional growth during college/university),
3. from exams to diversified assessment (especially given that the instructors would assign nearly half of the course credit and not just external examinations),
4. from degree to disciplinary identity (or the demand for fostering such identity in an educational culture where exams and grades undermined learning), and
5. from classroom to culture (indicating the need for educators to engage different stakeholders so they could make the other major shifts).

As reflected in the chapter titles of the *Handbook,* the push and pull between our specialty as writing scholars and teachers and the need to utilize that expertise in TU's interest in making broader shifts in higher education remained striking. Once again, we were drawn into the contexts of our collaborators, our skills applied to different purposes than we had foreseen. Even our identities shifted from being writing scholars who believed they could offer more valuable skills as writing scholars into becoming "faculty development experts"; we accepted the invitation and used writing pedagogy as a starting point and catalyst for much broader collaborations as fellow educators.

Our most significant achievement in Nepal has been to develop a community of scholars we have become part of. Departments and disciplinary units have been quick to gather surprising amounts of resources to cover the costs of summer retreats for participants from around the country, to develop and print resources, and to send trainers to constituent campuses around the country. Such responses, however, rarely came from administrators—including those who were personally and informally involved in the projects—who instead helped to create an environment. It is easy for outsiders and even cultural insiders on brief visits to misinterpret hospitality, enthusiasm, and engagement of scholars and their institutions as signs of sustainability. It is easy to miss how local scholars and institutions treat the collaborations with those who jet in and jet out, as one local scholar put it, as ad hoc and one-off events. So, we too shifted our focus and helped to take the collaboration online, to connect with more scholars across the South Asian region, to promote the grassroots movement in our writing and program promotion, and to share resources and expertise more and more openly. We did help local scholars "lobby" administrators and hold the latter accountable for recognition and reward of the former's time and efforts. Everyone involved, however, was keenly aware of many "international" projects that only lasted as long as the individual visitors remained on site, and if their institutions' leaderships or priorities remained steady. At the capital in particular, we were told about course syllabi shelved away for years (which were called "fossils") after exciting and expensive visits by American scholars. Our experiences taught us to interpret initiatives and collaborations in ecological terms, rather than institutional and structural ones; this lesson helped us appreciate opportunities to both share and explore how academic and professional writing skills could be a meaningful impetus for broader changes. We now recognize that the faculty training initiatives at and involving a network of hundreds of scholars across Tribhuvan University—an institution educating more than 400 thousand students across the country—have contributed to an educational "culture" more meaningfully than a formal academic unit within a department would.

Learning from Hosts

On whose terms or combination of terms should we seek to enframe, if at all, our contributions and the collaborations with our counterparts in other countries? We have sought to make our visits and connections a two-way traffic not out of idealism, but because delivery of expertise fails if pursued un-reflexively. Whenever we as visitors work from the premise that writing pedagogy is more advanced on our side, we may share knowledge substantively but ironically prompt little change, create little value—in spite of appearances and surprisingly often in spite of demand. We realized that we must also learn from our hosts in order to be effective; to do so, we must account for vastly unequal geopolitical and economic statuses in the world, especially if we are to overcome intellectual and moral failures of knowledge delivery, for the advancement both of understanding and of global good.

Our scholarly motivation behind the collaboration was to better understand how our counterparts in other parts of the world taught or used writing in their academic work. The key lesson we have learned in this regard, which helps us significantly with our teaching and scholarship back in the US, is that scholars and students anywhere share certain purposes of writing with us and they put it to purposes that we don't. We have found that some common uses to which writing is put are: to communicate ideas (tell the truth), to say what we mean (express ourselves), to use details, to draw inferences, to explore ideas, to organize ideas deliberately, to frame paragraphs, to consciously appeal to our readers, to present thought-through theses, to join academic conversations, to respond to and to challenge existing knowledge, and so on. While writing, our counterparts and their students did many of the above and also tried to be concise, to engage in deeper reflection, to revise for greater clarity, to edit for correctness, and so on. But such interests did not translate into daily teaching and learning tasks, and they didn't find the same priority as they do with us in the educators' scholarly lives. And yet, in all societies, writing is at the heart of active learning, and even though our colleagues teach writing more incidentally than we do, writing serves us in overlapping ways. For example, if faculty members found writing for their own scholarship and publication a more urgent need, the teaching of writing became the focus of one or more publication webinars for the faculty group.

In addition to finding our evolving collaborations abroad productive on the ground, we have found a considerable payoff at home. We return from each experience abroad better informed, more flexible educators and individuals. That payoff is most pronounced in our freshman writing course. Since the second author started teaching abroad, he uses only texts set internationally, currently *West with the Night* by Beryl Markham, set in Kenya, and *This Earth of Mankind* by Pramoedya Toer, set in Indonesia, as key texts to generate analysis in his freshman writing course, which now focuses on global citizenship. Teaching at Stony Brook University classes with students coming from as many as ten different countries some semesters, he is better able to help students write the required research paper by requiring evidence from at least three countries, and asking students to interview transnational peers in class and beyond. When he brings in occasional examples from his outside-Stony

Brook life, those examples are more and more likely now to come from other countries, and so they help normalize the people in other countries for his students. The first author has not only found deep satisfaction in the opportunity to give back to the South Asian region where he had the advantage of public education, but also aligns the collaborations with his research agenda and scholarship here in the US. From new assignments and class activities to new approaches to teaching and mentoring students, lessons learned about writing education from South Asia help him think more creatively and work more productively; those lessons enhance his work with graduate students and faculty colleagues across campus by enabling him to understand different perspectives on writing and to find common grounds.

Beyond Outcomes

What do collaborators gain when they value processes and experiences above outcomes and measurable impacts? Through our collaborations abroad, we have come to realize that there are many more applications of writing education, many more opportunities for cross-campus collaborations, than within our disciplinary silos and programmatic frameworks. Our experiences highlight the importance of understanding local contexts and traditions, sharing common ground, and cultivating mutual respect instead of trying to convert or change others. In his book *After Pedagogy: The Experience of Teaching*, Paul Lynch (2013) argues that writing teachers "need a better question about how we think and talk about the work of teaching in the wake of postpedagogy. How do we untrain our capacity for system and paradigm?" (p. 6). In this chapter, we have reflected on our experience of pursuing educational collaborations beyond the hegemony of the "global" West. What form could transnational academic exchanges take beyond or without American hegemony at play, among scholars across borders, including within the currently hegemonic geopolitical conditions?

The more we worked with scholars in different contexts, the more shared (and broader) interests we found in writing across academic cultures. Because we were open to new opportunities and did not go in with an objective of "producing" anything like this chapter, we learned about writing in the contexts of faculty scholarship, student learning, institutional and curricular change, and social and economic demands. We learned to find common grounds by trying to understand the terms that our colleagues used for describing writing; for instance, they may describe it as an assessment tool, a professional skill, a literacy ability, a means of research and publication for faculty, or a catalyst for educational transformation such as with a shift to semester-based education (Sharma & Subedi, 2018).

More generally put, we learned that writing plays unique sets of roles and serves unique sets of needs in different contexts; writing, we learned, is a means that can be put to much larger purposes than just teaching it as a subject or putting it within a discipline (see Hall, "Transing Disciplines," this volume). If the similarity of purposes that writing served in different academic cultures and societies created common grounds, distinct purposes provided opportunities to learn from one another. We found that writing was used as a skill to teach and an ability to foster among students, an assessment tool and a professional skill for students, reading materials for trainees, documentation and reports that became resources for institutionalization of faculty development (within which writing education would continue to be an objective). These diverse values of writing demanded that we stay open-minded about possibilities beyond specific outcomes of initiatives created along the way. Similarly, while we have continued to try to foster the teaching of writing, the more aware of power dynamics we became about the collaboration between local scholars and their foreign and diaspora counterparts the more uses we saw of our expertise. it must be seen as larger than curricular outcomes or the domain of a specific discipline.

Conclusion

We were sometimes a little disoriented when our collaborations in Nepal and South Asia turned into telephone games, where the message evolves in the process of transmission from team leader to collaborator to administrator to other collaborators. But in retrospect, we are glad that they did. Instead of focusing on writing as a discipline, we have learned to view it more as an education. Instead of looking for writing pedagogy, we learned to look for practices and opportunities, resources and environments in which students learned to write and instructors taught or fostered it. We also learned that, somewhat paradoxically, writing education has advanced more easily without labels like "composition" or "rhetoric" than with them, as we generally observed in both Nepal and Bangladesh.

We have become keenly aware that different societies take different paths to their writing education and that understanding those paths without imposing one group's terms and perspectives can help both/all groups create and join broader conversations across borders, whether the borders are created by disciplines, specializations, academic cultures, or economic conditions and political systems. We can think of such flexible collaborations as happening in layers, with writing as a discipline being the innermost/bottom layer, then writing education that is defined more broadly, then its applications in the disciplines, then its place in the larger society. We have learned to be agonistic about global hegemony of Western education; we question it to generate new perspectives and find new possibilities. We want to advance small narratives in our modes of exchange, rather than just embracing critical views or using broad brushes. We do not want to build our conversations on notions of East and West either; globalization has made things extremely complex. We want to participate in practical exchange that addresses inequalities, rather than just write about them theoretically. Inequality affects lives and professions and societies every day, and we want to use our professional experience and affordances to help counter it, to create more equitable advancement and exchange of knowledge. We have learned that writing-based exchange can become a variety of things, from objective/focus to context to catalyst to side note; it may create more room for engagement for some of us than others, depending on how and how much time, resource, and incentives we can find in it.

The greatest takeaway of our collaborations in Nepal and beyond in South Asia in the past six years is self-reflection. When a collaboration doesn't go as we planned or expected or wished, we ask whether we are being as naive as the gentleman in Yangon about the world. To what extent does our being from a "super power" society boost the demand for our expertise and ascribe ethos to our experience in transnational exchange of educational ideas and practices? What should be mindful about when sharing one kind of expertise from one context (e.g., for teaching writing in the US) toward a different application in a new place (e.g., to assist the training of writing instructors in another country)? How can we avoid matching our inevitable naivete and ignorance about complex realities on the ground with inadvertent condescension about other writing educations around the world? How can we learn as much from unplanned outcomes and serendipitous opportunities for exchange of ideas as we want to move collaborations toward more solid grounds of our expertise as well? From our transnational exchange and knowledge-sharing that extended from a WAC initiative to various applications of our expertise in writing instruction, we have become more eager to learn from our fellow educators across borders, refusing to just jet in and jet out, instead learning as much as we share knowledge through continued collaboration.

References

Allen, Jannie F. (2014). Investigating transnational collaboration of faculty development and learning: An argument for making learning culturally relevant. *International Journal for the Scholarship of Teaching and Learning, 8*(2), 1–26.

Alvarez, Sara. (2016). Literacy. In Iris D. Ruiz & Raúl Sánchez. (Eds.), *Decolonizing rhetoric and composition studies: New Latinx keywords for theory and pedagogy* (pp. 17–29). Palgrave Macmillan.

Anson, Chris & Donahue, Christiane. (2015). Deconstructing "writing program administration" in an international context. In David S Martins. (Ed.), *Transnational writing program administration* (pp. 34–60). Utah State University Press.

Baca, Damián. (2009). Rethinking composition, five hundred years later. *JAC, 29*, 229–242.
Burke, Kenneth. (1966). *Language as symbolic action.* Cambridge University Press.
Canagarajah, A. Suresh (2002). Reconstructing local knowledge. *Journal of Language, Identity, and Education, 1*(4), 243–259.
Dingo, Rebecca, Riedner, Rachel & Wingard, Jennifer. (2013). Toward a cogent analysis of power: Transnational rhetorical studies. *JAC, 33*(3–4), 517–528.
Donahue, Christiane. (2009). "Internationalization" and composition studies: Reorienting the discourse. *College Composition and Communication, 61*(2), 212–243.
Donahue, Patricia & Moon, Gretchen F. (Eds.). (2007). *Local histories: Reading the archives of composition.* University of Pittsburgh Press.
Hesford, Wendy S. (2006). Global turns and cautions in rhetoric and composition studies. *PMLA, 121*(3), 787–801.
Horner, Bruce. (2015). Afterword. In David S Martins. (Ed.), *Transnational writing program administration* (pp. 332–41). Utah State University Press.
———. (2016). *Rewriting composition: Terms of exchange.* Southern Illinois University.
Hum, Sue & Lyon, Arabella. (2008). Recent advances in comparative rhetorical studies. In Andrea Lunsford, Kirt Wilson & Rosa Eberly (Eds.). *The Sage handbook of rhetorical studies* (pp. 153–65). Sage
Khaniya, Tirth Raj. (2014, January 26). Semester system in TU: Promise or peril? *The Himalayan Times.* https://www.educatenepal.com/article_archive/print_it/400.
Lynch, Paul. (2013). *After pedagogy: The experience of teaching.* National Council of Teachers of English.
Mao, LuMing. (2003). Reflective encounters: Illustrating comparative rhetoric. *Style, 37*(4), 401–425.
Martins, David S. (Ed.). (2015). T*ransnational writing program administration.* Utah State University Press.
Muchiri, Mary N., Mulamba, Nshindi G., Myers, Greg & Ndoloi, Deoscoros B. (1995). Importing composition: Teaching and researching academic writing beyond North America. *College Composition and Communication, 46*(2), 175–198.
Molina-Natera, Violeta (2017). The history of US writing centers and the emergence of writing centers in Latin America: An interview with Neal Lerner. *Praxis, 14*(2). http://www.praxisuwc.com/molina-natera-142
Ray, Brian & Theado, Kendall T. (2014). Composition's "global turn": Writing instruction in multilingual/translingual and transnational contexts. *Composition Studies, 44*(1), 10–12.
Rose, Shirley K & Weiser, Irwin (Eds.). (2018). *The internationalization of US writing programs.* Utah State University Press.
Sánchez, Raul. (2016). Writing. In Iris D. Ruiz & Raúl Sánchez. (Ed.), *Decolonizing rhetoric and composition studies: New Latinx keywords for theory and pedagogy* (pp. 77–89). Palgrave Macmillan.
Schaub, Mark. (2003). Beyond these shores: An argument for internationalizing composition. *Pedagogy, 3*(1), 85–98.
Shamsuzzaman, Mohammad. (2017). English literature and composition studies in Bangladesh: Conflict, co-existence, and globalization. *International Journal of Multidisciplinary Perspectives in Higher Education, 2*(1), 35–45.

Sharma, Shyam. (2018). Translanguaging in hiding: English-only instruction and literacy education in Nepal. In Xiaoye You. (Ed.), *Transnational writing education: Theory, history, and practice* (pp. 79–94). CRC Press Book.

Sharma, Shyam & Subedi, Surendra. (2018). Semester system in Nepal: Taking a collaborative, constructivist approach to teacher training. *Tribhuvan University Journal, 33*(1).

Subedi, Surendra & Sharma, Shyam. (2020, June 3). Advancing research for social impact. *The Republica*. https://myrepublica.nagariknetwork.com/news/author/4288

Sullivan, Patricia, Zhang, Yufeng & Zheng, Fenglan. (2012). College writing in China and America: A modest and humble conversation, with writing samples. *College Composition and Communication, 64*(2), 306–331.

Tripathi, Sudha, Sharma, Shyam & Subedi, Surendra. (2019). Making the shifts to change the system: Implementing the semester system through pedagogical training in Tribhuvan University. In Krishna Bista, Rosalind L. Raby & Shyam Sharma (Eds.), *Higher education in Nepal: Policies and Perspectives* (pp. 135–148). CRC Press.

Tardy, Christine M. (2014). Discourses of internationalization and diversity in US universities and writing programs. In David Martins (Ed.), *Transnational writing program administration* (pp. 243–262), Utah State University Press.

Tasildhar, Ravindra B. (1996). English studies in India: Some reflections on the present scenario. *English Studies in India, 1*, 60–76.

Theado, Connie K., Johnson, Holly, Highley, Thomas & Omar, Saman Hussein. (2017). Rewriting resistance: Negotiating pedagogical and curricular change in a U.S./Kurdish transnational partnership. In Lisa R. Arnold, Anne Nebel & Lynne Ronesi (Eds.), *Emerging writing research from the Middle East-North Africa region* (pp. 151–174). The WAC Clearinghouse; University Press of Colorado. https://doi.org/10.37514/INT-B.2017.0896.2.07.

Thaiss, Chris, Bräuer, Gerd, Carlino, Paula, Ganobcsik-Williams, Lisa & Sinha, Aparna. (Eds.). (2012). *Writing programs worldwide: Profiles of academic writing in many places*. The WAC Clearinghouse; Parlor Press. https://doi.org/10.37514/PER-B.2012.0346.

Wu, Zhiwei. (2018). Technology-mediated transnational writing education: An overview of research and practice. In Xiaoye You (Ed.), *Transnational writing education: Theory, history, and practice* (pp. 170–86). Routledge.

You, Xiaoye. (2016). *Cosmopolitan English and transliteracy*. Southern Illinois University Press.

Part 3. Trans-ing Institutional Structures

Mapping Transnational Institutions: Connections between WAC/WID and Qatar's Engineering Industry

Amy Hodges
UNIVERSITY OF TEXAS AT ARLINGTON

To be completely honest, when I heard about a job opening in Qatar, I had to go find a map in order to locate what would become my new home. Located on a small peninsula in the Arabian Gulf, the nation of Qatar has been represented on maps in various ways throughout history. The earliest mention of the "Catara" region was in the collection *Geographia* by Claudius Ptolemy from the 2nd century C.E, which was later printed in 1478 in Rome by Conrad Swenheym, an apprentice of Johannes Gutenberg. Yet early cartographers did not often speak the dialects of Arabic used by the local people, and thus they misunderstood or mistranslated place names. Qatar was "Catura" on a 1782 French map, "Katar" on an 1865 British map, and "Catra," "Gattar," and "Cataragade" on other cartographic records. Western European explorers from 1596 to 1823 removed the peninsula from their maps entirely, showing instead a flat coastline. Differences in maps reflected the aims of empire-builders of Western Europe, impacting the decisions they made about trading with (or conquering) local Arabian tribes. Cartographers rarely acknowledged the limitations of their work, except for the refreshing note found on the 1782 map from Jean Baptiste Bourguignon d'Anville, which wryly notes that the Arabian Gulf is a "Coast little known."

Upon coming to Qatar and attempting to map the writing that was taking place in my new institution, I understood more clearly how this process could reveal my own misunderstandings and biases. In writing studies, we have more recently started to learn about the little known "coasts" of transnational institutions and the people within them. I use the term *transnational* in this chapter to emphasize the power of nation-states and other political actors in drawing up and moving between boundaries, including geographical, cultural, linguistic, ethnic, and other kinds of boundaries. The term *transnational*, with its associated terms *translingual*, *transcultural*, and *hybridization*, "reflects a system of dispositions that provides an alternative to the colonial and neocolonial ideologies reflected, respectively, in a monolingual and a multilingual approach" (Guerra & Shivers-McNair, 2017, p. 23). That is, *transnational* recognizes the very real presence of systems of power in institutions like the one I study in this chapter, but it also recognizes the pockets of resistance or complication within that system. As noted in this edited collection and others (Martins, 2015), transnational writing programs are incredibly complex, both on a macro-level of leadership, bureaucracy, assessment, and placement, and on a micro-level of everyday interactions with students, faculty, staff, and other institutional actors.

Like the task of cartographers mapping the nation of Qatar, the task of writing researchers representing the "lay of the land" and the relationships inside and outside a transnational writing program is a challenging one. This chapter unpacks some of that complexity through the use of institutional ethnography, a method espoused by Michelle LaFrance and Melissa Nicolas (2012) as a critical approach to understanding writing programs' place(s) within institutional systems. They explain how the same institutional system can be experienced by different individuals with different perspectives:

> For example, a *university* is something about which we all share a general macro-level idea. But as soon as we move from this generalized view of the *university*, the screen gets fuzzy. A professor experiences *university* differently from the student, who experiences *university* differently from her parents, who, as well, experience *university* differently from the trustees. Even an individual's micro-level account of *university* changes over time: a first-year student has a different relationship with *university* than a senior, whose definition will change again after graduating. (LaFrance & Nicolas, 2012)

Institutional ethnography is a particularly useful method for transnational institutions in that it accounts for material conditions and previous experiences of the actors in the system, as well as the "far more complex trajectories of participation and identification" (LaFrance & Nicolas, 2012, p. 134) than can be adequately captured by the titles actors nominally assume in transnational institutions, such as "American faculty member" or "L2 student writer." Institutional ethnography "begins from the standpoint of those doing the work and zooms upward and outward" (Miley, 2017, p. 104), an approach that was helpful for me in attempting to "map out" my new transnational institution.

Recent scholarship in the US shows that many have adopted a goal of supporting "Multilingual Learning Across the Curriculum" (Hall, 2009, p. 37), and the question of how to best support L2 writers has been thoroughly documented. However, few have given attention to how WAC's best efforts can be unknowingly harmful to some multilingual and/or transnational students, as Michelle Cox (2011) wonders after surveying L2 literature on WAC:

> Is it possible that WAC administrators and scholars, like our colleagues in L2 writing studies and first year composition, place

the same overemphasis on writing? Have we paid more attention to the potential benefits of integrating writing into curricula than the possible costs to some students? If we are paying attention, what possible costs for L2 students should we be attending to? (p. 5)

Taking LeCourt's (2012) advice that "we might be better served by considering what the consequences of the changes we advocate will be rather than denying our role in such changes" (p. 83), in this chapter I map the consequences of my institution's WAC/WID program by considering the following research questions:

- In what ways do the experiences of engineering professionals in transnational workplaces reflect, resist, or hybridize existing approaches to WAC/WID?
- How might writing programs respond to these experiences and formulate a transnational and translingual WAC/WID approach?

After obtaining IRB approval in 2014, I interviewed working professionals who had graduated from my transnational institution about their experiences in the workplace and the connections they saw to the formal instruction they had received on writing and communication in dedicated English courses and engineering major courses. I conclude this chapter by reflecting on how I used this information to shape the WAC/WID program in a more responsive and localized manner.

Study Context

A. Suresh Canagarajah (2018) argues that "developing transnational identities . . . is an ideological project," a process that can be stimulated or advanced by living in transnational or multilingual spaces (p. 58). Although becoming a transnational subject can be accomplished in one's own home and/or among monolingual speakers, he describes how the liminal nature of transnational spaces can provide "scope for detachment from limiting language ideologies, connect writers with larger horizons for meaning making, identity construction, and writing, and facilitate the creativity that attempts to go beyond existing language systems and monolingual ideologies to construct new textual homes" (2018, p. 58). I experienced a similar process of understanding myself as a transnational subject, which in turn influenced my interpretation of the data in this study, so I explain more about my lived experience below.

After obtaining my Ph.D. and teaching composition and ESL classes in the US, I came to Qatar for two years as a postdoc. During that time, I worked on community literacy projects with students and began this study. I left to work at a writing center in an institution in Singapore for a year and then came back to

Qatar, where I lived for four more years. When I returned to Qatar as a faculty member, I resumed this study and began implementing WAC/WID programming. Throughout my time in transnational institutions, I talked with faculty who, like me, found their previous experience of teaching language and writing helpful but not quite sufficient to meet the needs of the students they saw in their classrooms. I talked with other well-meaning researchers who came over from the US with the intent of studying our student population, but whose methods and analysis seemed—to me—to inadequately represent the complexity of a transnational institution, and more importantly, to fail to account for indigenous principles of research that I felt were important to honor in this context: relationality, respect, and reciprocity (Wilson, 2008). I talked with students who allowed me into their rich worlds of meaning-making (Hodges & Rudd, 2014), and I talked with staff who did a lot of unseen and undervalued work with students to help them through the university. This process of mapping out the experience of transnational lives made me stop describing my own identity as simply American, simply an expatriate. I saw the ways in which, through listening and learning, I crossed boundaries and created a new transnational home and transnational identity for myself.

My study site and part of my transnational home, Texas A&M University at Qatar (TAMUQ), is an international branch campus (IBC) of Texas A&M University in the United States of America. Located in Doha, Qatar, TAMUQ, five other IBCs (Carnegie Mellon University in Qatar, Georgetown University in Qatar, Northwestern University in Qatar, Virginia Commonwealth University School of the Arts in Qatar, and Weill Cornell Medicine – Qatar), two European IBCs (University College London and HEC Paris), and a local university (Hamid bin Khalifa University) form a larger academic unit called Education City. These IBCs are fully supported by the Qatar Foundation, a government entity founded by His Highness the Father Emir Sheikh Hamad bin Khalifa al Thani and Her Highness Sheikha Moza bint Nasser (Qatar Foundation, 2019). Their daughter Her Excellency Sheikha Hind bint Hamad bin Khalifa Al Thani serves as the current Vice Chairperson and CEO of Qatar Foundation.

Each IBC offers specialized undergraduate degrees; for example, TAMUQ provides four B.S. degrees: chemical, mechanical, petroleum, or electrical and computer engineering. These degrees follow the same curriculum of the main American institutions, meaning, in TAMUQ's case, that Doha students are required to take American history and American local and state government courses just like College Station students are required to take these courses by the state legislature back in Texas. The promise made to students that they will receive an education that is a replica of the main campus is extended even to the printed degrees students receive upon matriculation, which say "Texas A&M University," with no mention of the location of the campus. Professionals in student life replicate or adapt traditions common to the College Station experience, and make a "targeted, intentional effort

... to educate both students and employees about institutional values, history, and tradition" (Wood, 2011, p. 38). In light of these facts, it might look as if Texas A&M packed up elements of their institution in a shipping container and plopped the whole thing in the Arabian desert, and indeed, American IBCs like those in Education City have been criticized for their thinly disguised neo-colonialist goals and reinforcement of existing inequalities between different academic systems (Altbach, 2004).

But however strong the replication on the surface, the inherent "messiness" of a transnational system defies simple logics of an export model of higher education, where all of the people in the system adopt the values of the exporting country. I agree with anthropologist Neha Vora's view that "what we see in branch campuses instead is that the university is more of a network, a complex apparatus whose channels carry more than the putatively universal values we associate with it" (Vora, 2015, p. 32). Some students embraced Texas A&M traditions, others ignored them, and yet others met them on their own terms (Rudd, 2018). Faculty members, many of whom shared ethnic or religious backgrounds with the students, frequently discussed with me how they were adapting courses and assignments for our students, sometimes in spite of or in opposition to what they perceived as "mandates" from the main campus.

The engineering faculty I met at TAMUQ also had a different factor guiding their pedagogical decisions than the faculty at main campus: Qatar's engineering industry. The majority of our students with Qatari citizenship (roughly half the student population) were sponsored by local companies for their degree, and thus would go on to work for these companies upon graduation. A significant portion of the other half of the students were residents (non-citizens) who, under the *kafala* laws common in the Arabian Gulf region, needed to have a job upon graduation in order to stay in Qatar. Because most of the resident students were children of expatriates and had grown up in Qatar or other countries in the region, they often had family members in Doha and expressed a wish to stay in the country they regarded as home. However, if resident students did not find employment in Qatar upon graduation, they would potentially have to leave their families and return to their country of origin or passport, which could be a country that they had rarely or never lived in before. Thus, the transnational space of the institution itself intersected with students' citizenship and ethnic heritage; these factors all shaped how students perceived their future role in Qatar's engineering industry.

The pressure to have graduates "work-ready" coincided with the American university structures of the IBC to support student writing in a way that will feel familiar to many U.S. writing program administrators. As "exported" from the main campus engineering curriculum, the writing program consisted of a first-year writing course, a technical and business writing course, and two writing-intensive course requirements. At the time of the study, students took one engineering and ethics course that was writing-intensive, and then they also took one upper-level writing-intensive course in their specific engineering major. Like many WAC/WID programs, a committee approved the writing-intensive course designation. Founded by Texas A&M's then-writing center director Valerie Balester in 2003 (Texas A&M University Writing Center, 2003), the writing-intensive course system provided a strong structure for graduates to become excellent communicators.

Because the curriculum at TAMUQ was the same as main campus, the requirements for writing-intensive courses were also the same. What this meant for TAMUQ engineering faculty is that faculty members in their department on main campus might write course descriptions, describe assignments and feedback procedures in their writing-intensive course application, get the writing-intensive course designation approved—all before faculty at TAMUQ were informed about any changes to the curriculum, learning objectives, or course requirements. Additionally, faculty at the main campus almost certainly did not have in mind a student population who hailed almost entirely from the Middle East, North Africa, and South Asia regions (see Kwon, this volume, for more on challenges faced by engineering faculty implementing WAC). Thus, while the writing-intensive course systems at TAMUQ provided a sound, American-centric base for writing instruction in the disciplines, other faculty members' experiences suggested to me that the program had not adapted for its new home in a transnational space. The purpose of this writing program research was instrumental (Hesse, 2012) in that one of my goals was to shape the campus conversation on writing towards mindsets and abilities that were useful to *our* student population, which might or might not be supported by these American-centered systems.

WAC/WID in the Middle East – North Africa Region

A central tenet of WAC/WID programs is that they "develop for various reasons and may take many different forms" (International Network of WAC Programs, 2014, p. 2). William Condon and Carol Rutz (2012) note that although WAC philosophies and practices are prevalent in higher education, "WAC as a phenomenon does not possess a single, identifiable structure; instead it varies in its development and its manifestation from campus to campus" (p. 358). While this variation has proved troublesome to some researchers hoping for a more "global" model of writing in higher education, WAC's ability to localize can be a powerful tool for transnational institutions. By combining localized practices (particularly language practices) with global scope, emerging writing programs in the Middle East/North Africa (MENA) region offer great potential to formulate a transnational and translingual approach to WAC/WID.

Few English-medium institutions in the MENA region have a designated WAC/WID program; most rely upon writing centers to provide assistance for faculty and students beyond English courses. Writing centers in English-medium institutions tend to focus on support for the first few years of university, when many students (particularly those without experience in English as a language of instruction) are challenged by the transition into academic English (Ronesi, 2011). In IBCs, writing faculty members (often trained in the US) can serve as unofficial WAC/WID specialists who take the lead in adapting assignments and curricula for students, who have often learned in diverse and different educational systems (Weber, et al., 2015). By drawing upon local educational cultures, experienced writing instructors, and American writing program structures such as writing centers, these transnational institutions create new hybrids of WAC/WID programming. As researchers at Carnegie Mellon University in Qatar have noted, "influence within a transnational program need not flow from the 'main' campus only, but rather should be constructed through dynamic, negotiated interactions" (Zawodny Wetzel & Reynolds, 2015, p. 100).

As compared to IBCs, "turnkey institutions" in the MENA region are those universities that originally developed as a collaboration with a foreign institution or government, but over which the local administrators have taken formal control (Miller-Idriss & Hanauer, 2011). Although the name, original curriculum, and accreditation of turnkey institutions are often American, the emphasis on local control also means that these institutions have considerable leeway for creating new models for WAC/WID. At the American University of Beirut, Amy Zenger et al. (2014) detail how their assumptions changed as they worked with students in their English 300 course, a course for graduate students writing in their disciplines. The authors adopted new roles of "literacy brokers" as they invited students' multilingual abilities into the classroom and assigned tasks that encouraged "students' understanding of writing as a social act, rather than a set of discrete skills" (2014, p. 427). This experience led them to build the WAC/WID program at the American University of Beirut on a transnational praxis: asking first what students and faculty know about their languages and disciplines before imposing their own assumptions about writing or English. MENA faculty and students who experience teaching and learning in a translingual and transnational context are changed as a result of that experience. We may not always agree with these changes or think that they will benefit students; for example, a transnational student with a rich and diverse multilingual background may, during her university career, develop a prescriptive approach towards language out of a belief that her future career depends upon her English proficiency. As I document later in this chapter, I encountered some similar, unsettling consequences of my institution's WAC/WID program in alumni perceptions of translanguaging.

The emerging transnational and translingual approach to WAC/WID in the MENA region presumes that the languages in use, such as Arabic and English, "can be understood as cultural conduits that [are] anything but unidirectional" (Arnold, 2014, p. 286). Although different languages, pedagogical methods, and writing program structures are subject to and part of institutional systems of power, the interaction between these elements provides a creative space for transnational WAC/WID approaches to flourish. Through investigating the impact of writing and communication in engineering courses on local alumni, I hoped to have a deeper understanding of the particular nature of transnational WAC/WID at my institution.

Methods

To study the connections between the writing in Qatar's engineering industry and the writing in the WAC/WID program at TAMUQ, I gathered two sets of data: interviews with alumni of the institution and learning objectives in the syllabi from students' engineering courses.

Alumni Interviews

After IRB approval, the alumni office at TAMUQ identified recent graduates who might be interested in participating in a research project regarding their experiences with workplace communication. Ten interviews were conducted over the course of 2014–2016, and each interview lasted around 30 minutes. Undergraduate researchers conducted all of these interviews primarily in English, although I was always in the room and occasionally asked a follow-up question. A list of questions is available in Appendix A, and a list of participants is in Appendix B.

Three out of 10 interviewees were female, which is fewer than the usual gender balance of TAMUQ, where the percentage of female students ranges between 45–50% in any given year. Half of the interviewees were Qatari, which is representative of the student body population, although all of the Qatari interviewees were male. The other interviewees self-identified as belonging to different ethnic and national communities in South Asia and the Middle East, including the countries of Pakistan, India, and Jordan.

After the interviews, the recorded data was transcribed and all identifying information removed. The transcripts were then uploaded to Dedoose, a qualitative research software. After reading the transcripts multiple times, I employed inductive and deductive coding (Purcell-Gates, 2011), looking specifically for where interviewees compared their work experiences to their university training in communication, but also allowing for new themes to emerge from the data. During the entire course of coding, I collaborated with the undergraduate researchers who conducted the interviews, discussed the emerging themes with them, and revised the codes based on their feedback. The themes are presented below in the results and discussion section.

Learning Outcomes for Engineering Courses

In this study, I used a selection of course learning outcomes (LOs) to represent the main campus's American goals for engineering communication. All institutions no doubt experience discrepancies between LOs and the actual teaching practices and student learning that occurs in any given course. Thus, it is perhaps more realistic to view these LOs as goals or ideals rather than the lived experiences that formed the alumni interview dataset. These LOs were required to be consistent across campuses, and they were developed by departments on main campus, although it is possible that some departments collaborated with faculty on the Qatar campus on LOs. I included learning outcomes from all engineering courses in order to capture communication goals that were not part of explicitly designated writing-intensive courses.

All syllabi were obtained for undergraduate engineering courses (mechanical, chemical, petroleum, and electrical and computer engineering) offered in Qatar during the fall 2016 and spring 2017 semesters from the public TAMUQ system website. Overall, there were 103 engineering courses and 807 learning outcomes to analyze, as seen in Appendix C.

In the first pass at the learning outcomes corpus, I developed a coding system based on how relevant each individual learning outcome was to student learning of communication skills. I excluded all outcomes that explicitly referenced mathematical problem-solving, such as "characterize an LTI system using the impulse response, frequency response, and (if possible) a linear constant coefficient differential equation." These outcomes were unlikely to be assessed through communication assignments, and were, therefore, unlikely to impact the developing WAC/WID program.

The second category of learning outcomes was those that explicitly referenced a communication assignment or reading/writing abilities, such as "deliver an accurate and effective ten-minute oral presentation on a technical topic" and "search and gather information from the library and other resources on specific topics." The final major category was learning outcomes that did not explicitly reference communication but that could potentially be assessed through assignments that employed writing to learn, writing in the disciplines, or communication in the disciplines methodologies. The examples from the dataset often employed terminology such as "describe the factors that affect the heating and cooling loads of buildings" and "evaluate uncertainty in reserve estimates and economic appraisal." Many of the LOs in this category focused on discipline-specific knowledge; if used, writing or communication would have been a means to teaching that knowledge.

This early analysis was used to sort learning outcomes into categories that could be compared to the themes in the interview data. Inter-rater reliability was 86% with the first coder and 90% with a second coder, both acceptable ranges for a large corpus (Miles et al., 2014). Sixty-nine LOs (8.5% of the total number of LOs) explicitly referenced communication and/or writing, 162 LOs (20%) were categorized as potential sources of WAC/WID programming, and the remaining 576 LOs focused on quantitative knowledge or were excluded from the analysis because they were unclear. These categories were used to triangulate the data from the interviews and determine what communication knowledge could be traced back to their experience as an undergraduate.

Results and Discussion

Once both sets of data were coded, I looked for important differences between the experiences of alumni in Qatar's engineering industry and the writing and communication goals for engineering students that my transnational institution was supposed to abide by. Below, I unpack the key themes of my analysis and explore the potential for transnational and translingual WAC/WID programs.

Rhetoric and Genre

The first theme that emerged from the interview data was the professionals' rhetorical understanding of genre. In the interviews, alumni mentioned that their employers expected them to compose, develop, and provide feedback on the following workplace communication genres:

- Email Messages
- Excel Documents
- Executive Summaries
- HAZOPs (Hazard and Operability Study)
- Letters
- Meeting Minutes and Summaries
- Memos
- Newsletters
- Presentations
- Progress Reports
- Proposals
- Recommendation Reports
- Sales Reports
- Technical Reports

When asked about how they composed these genres, the professionals mentioned using templates or previous documents composed at the company, but they stressed that these templates were used rhetorically and adapted to fit their purpose and situation. For example, Riya used previous Excel sheets to analyze sales data from her company: "It's the same template, but the content is different every time, so considerable time has to be spent on summarizing the findings and go deeper into analysis if need be." In the oil and gas industry, Tariq also used templates as a starting point to supply parts to reservoirs: "I never actually follow one template and go, 'All right, this is it,' but I try my best to summarize what I can in the memo and then try to forward any questions back to me if I missed anything." Working in a process safety role, Ammar described how he needed to "kind of amalgamate the different proposals and synthesize it into one document to best convey what you're trying to achieve. So a lot of times it's just taking a lot of stuff and manipulating it to make it seem coherent and in line with what you're doing." These professionals' writing processes illustrate how engineering communicators can explicitly discuss their rhetorical practices with workplace genres (Leydens, 2008).

Alumni consistently advised their undergraduate interviewers to think about their audience, situation, purpose, and linguistic choices each time they took on a new communication task. As Ali, who worked for a government ministry, noted, this rhetorical purpose extended also to the writer's place in the larger system: "So you have to also consider your audience, consider the place you are in, and consider also your level, because at this time I was an engineer; now I'm a director, so I have to pick my words carefully." This understanding of a writer's place within an institution or system and the power that the writer accumulates or loses through their writing in that system (Seawright, 2017) were evident in alumni interviews.

In the learning outcomes, the most common genres mentioned were written examinations, technical reports, oral presentations, and lab reports and their requisite parts (introduction, methods, results, discussion). Very few referenced specific genres, and the following genres were mentioned in only one LO each:

- Product Specification Sheets
- Interface Control Documents
- Professional and Legal Codes
- Problem Statement
- Work Breakdown Structure
- Manufacturers' Data Sheets
- Proposal
- Literature Review
- Process Design Report

When LOs mentioned the composition process, the goal of the student was not to analyze and respond to a particular rhetorical situation but to produce a document, such as "Compose an accurate and effective two-page written report on a technical topic." In contract to the professionals' thoughtful consideration of audience, the audience mentioned in the LOs was often unspecified, as in one course, students were expected to develop the "ability to present ideas, prepare technical presentations, and effectively communicate with the audience."

The arhetorical stance implied by many LOs may be reflective of Dan Melzer's (2014) findings that many disciplinary writing assignments used in U.S. universities feature the professor as the only audience. It is also possible that the writers of these LOs feared imposing too much on their fellow faculty members who would be teaching the course in the future, and they wanted to allow for diverse approaches towards communication goals. Regardless, in my interviews TAMUQ alumni exhibited a nuanced understanding of rhetorical writing and familiarity with business communication genres, yet these abilities did not seem to have manifested from the institution's disciplinary writing requirements.

This finding indicates that workplace-oriented transnational WAC/WID programs should include an emphasis on rhetorical genre studies and on the rhetorical nature of translanguaging (Bloom-Pojar, 2018). Because writing is a socially mediated act and genres operate within and across cultures, transnational students could benefit from instruction focused on rhetorical adaptability. From experience, TAMUQ alumni seemed to have learned how to analyze their writing situation and to compose for particular workplace audiences. They may have had an easier transition to Qatar's engineering industry if their disciplinary writing education had more rhetorical approaches to writing and rhetorically-situated tasks.

Language

All of the interviewees indicated that they were more comfortable writing in English than in their mother tongues and other languages they had learned, and they often expressed that this preference was not something they had anticipated before entering university or the workplace. Most of the native Arabic speakers felt more comfortable speaking in Arabic or felt that they were equally comfortable speaking in both English and Arabic. This shift towards becoming more comfortable writing in English was often directly tied to their post-graduate work life, as Hamad indicated that his English was stronger because of the "time I spent out in the States and Norway [for work as a process engineer] because basically that's what I've been using."

The primacy of English in the interviewees' transnational workplaces extended even to audiences of Arabic speakers, as when Ali discussed writing reports for his boss, a minister in the government: "Now I do most of my reports in English and I submit it to His Excellency in English, even though I know we're both Arabic speakers." In January 2019, several years after these interviews were conducted, His Highness the Amir of Qatar passed a law to protect the Arabic language; among other things, the law stipulates that Arabic should be the official language of government meetings, discussions, and correspondence (Tribune News Network, 2019). More research is needed to determine the impact of this law on the language practices of working professionals in Qatar's engineering industry.

Interviewees identified "technical terms" as one of the key reasons they used English instead of Arabic. For Ali, writing for a minister in the government, "if I'm going to discuss this matter with someone from a different country, then if I'm used to using the same terms, it's easier for me to negotiate or to say it." As a project manager, Saad had a similar experience, saying, "Sometimes we meet four or five people and it will be all Arabic-speaking people, but we always talk in English and always do the minutes of the meeting in English. The emails are always in English because all of the terms or the technical terms are in English, as well, so you can't really jump between Arabic and English." Although Abdullah, in the oil and gas industry, mentioned that he occasionally had to write email replies in Arabic, he also emphasized how he preferred to present in English, because "it's much easier because I know the technical terms, while in Arabic I have to translate it and I stutter when I'm speaking."

These views were perhaps influenced by my presence as an American English professor, but because I was present, I could observe that translanguaging between Arabic and English took place before, during, and after these interviews. The written transcripts include our small talk where some interviewees spoke with the undergraduates in Arabic. When interviewees expressed appreciation for their achievements, they thanked God (*alhumdilah*), and they occasionally dipped into Arabic to express an idea or concept. Only Hassan, who worked as an electrical engineer, talked about the presence of languages besides English at the workplace: "English will be the official language; of course, if someone is comfortable speaking something else, off the record or unofficially that person will be speaking that language."

Unsurprisingly, none of the learning outcomes in the engineering courses mention the use of languages other than English. Several indicate that students' written or spoken language should be clear, concise, and correct, which indicates prevalent language ideologies about standardized American English. One petroleum engineering LO indicated that students should be able to communicate "the fundamental forms of ownership of petroleum resources, and laws, fiscal systems and financial interests pertinent to their exploitation in the United States *and internationally*" (emphasis mine), and we can only suppose that international discourse over petroleum resources could potentially involve other languages. The lack of reference to different language forms in the LOs reflects the monolingual "face" that many WAC/WID programs or educational institutions may present. It is a possibility that some of the alumni may have internalized these language ideologies about the importance of English, given their preference for using that language. Further analysis will need to be done to determine more about the professional engineers' experience with translanguaging between English and Arabic and within English itself.

However, as Jerry Won Lee and Christopher Jenks (2016) note, "translingual dispositions, like English, are multifaceted and reflect students' varied and evolving lives" (p. 340), and at the time of the interviews, alumni may not have attributed their success at work to their knowledge of languages other than English. It is also possible that moving back and forth between English and Arabic—as the interviewees did throughout the interview—is simply so normal that it did not occur to the professionals to mention it. Lee (2016) has argued that "continuing to view translingual writing as 'different' runs the risk of it being further marginalized or exoticized" (p. 186), and the unmarked status of Arabic and other mother tongues could be a feature of these former students' translingual dispositions. It is worth mentioning that Arabic is a diglossic language, with most speakers using both a dialect (*khaleeji* in Qatar) and *fusha*, or Modern Standard Arabic. Thus, alumni articulated a complicated perspective that both overlooked translanguaging and utilized it at the same time.

For transnational WAC/WID institutions, this finding may reflect language ideologies that position non-English languages as "unofficial" or "colloquial," in contrast to the official and prestigious status of English. Students and faculty may resist or ignore explicit calls to encourage translanguaging, a reminder that "transnational writing education is ethical and ideological work" (You, 2018, p. 2). But on the other hand, those looking at the institution from the outside may wrongly conclude that English primacy is the only translingual disposition espoused by those within. Instead, perceptions of language are constantly evolving, and no actor is left unchanged by interaction with others in a transnational and translingual space. Even in English-medium institutions, "reintroducing into existing writing curricula, pedagogies, and assessments English in its full complexity and depth" (Bou Ayash, 2019, p. 50) and considering local contexts for writing (Shamsuzzaman, this volume) are potential ways for WAC/WID programs to mitigate the consequences of language ideologies.

Formal Instruction on Writing in Major Courses

Alumni were very positive about their university training for the workplace, and many of the experiences they mentioned as impactful included engineering professors who provided professional training in communication. Riya fondly remembered a course with a chemical engineering professor who "taught us about the skills to use PowerPoint, Excel, Word. This may seem basic, but he taught us some really great shortcuts or some really effective tools to make our work faster and easier." This professor "really worked on our grammar, our language, our diction, and presentation skills."

Others thought that it would have been helpful to integrate communication skills more thoroughly into their engineering major courses (see Li, this volume). When asked if he could have used more training in writing, Ali said

> I don't think we did enough writing in the engineering courses because most of our assignments were very technical problems and solving those problems was mostly with numbers. . . . It's not having more courses of English, it's incorporating those English skills into your engineering courses.

When alumni reflected on their opportunity to practice communication skills, they recalled focusing on how to get the grade they wanted; Tariq joked that he thought his reports were graded according to weight. In contrast to the thoughtful way they were able to draw connections between their workplace writing situations, alumni reported that when they were students, they saw each writing task as taking place in its own unique situation. For example, Maryam explained that she completed each lab report with little reference to previous lab reports:

> Each course would have a different instruction sometimes, so it's not something common for all the process. Some chemistry lab reports are different than electric circuits lab reports. It's different. And we all, like for each course, we used to get the training to write this specific lab report.

The lack of transfer between different assignments and the missing connections between engineering and writing courses likely meant that alumni pieced together this knowledge on the job.

While some alumni suggested that explicit teaching of business communication genres such as meeting minutes and emails would be helpful—which is true—the larger point is that the current WAC/WID program did not help students articulate connections between their previous writing knowledge and the task and situation at hand (see Donahue, this volume, for linguists' contributions that could illuminate future WAC/WID transfer research). As Juan Guerra (2016) notes, in translingual teaching "what we want instead is for [students] to call on the rhetorical sensibilities many of them already possess but put aside because of what they see as a jarring shift in context" (pp. 231–232). Alumni perceived that when they were students, the contexts and the "rules" for writing were too distinct for transfer between courses.

Conclusion

Alumni generally observed that their training in communication at the IBC adequately prepared them for their work on the job, although the transition was not without its challenges. Hamad traced his success back to his ability developed at TAMUQ to adapt and learn in new situations:

> But again, TAMUQ is actually teaching you the right skills that would make you adapt to this kind of communication style in industry. How is that? That's basically they're teaching you how to learn. That's something I've been seeing here every day almost, that every day you learn something new and you just have to keep learning, adapting to the new challenges.

This rhetorical flexibility is closely aligned with multilingual rhetorical attunement, or "how multilingual writers negotiate and adapt to language multiplicity, but also . . . emergent, unstable multilingual practices" (Lorimer Leonard, 2014, p. 231). Because of (and despite) the IBC's American goals for engineering communication, these multilingual writers/engineers displayed an ability to adapt to communication in challenging and diverse workplaces. For Hamad and other interviewees, the transnational lived environment of the writers and the institution supported the development of flexible, rhetorically attuned engineers—a key outcome of most technical and professional writing programs.

Transnational institutions highlight both the potential and the challenges of existing approaches to WAC/WID programs, as well as the inevitable slippage between institutional and course policies and the lived experiences of student writers. Institutions worldwide import learning outcomes and writing program structures in an effort to support student writers during and after their time at the university. Adopting, implementing, and assessing these learning outcomes can certainly benefit students, and as shown in my study, can adequately prepare them for technical communication tasks in a diverse workplace. At the same time, this chapter suggests that the lived experiences of transnational students-turned-professionals lead them to continuously invent their own new rhetorical knowledge of genre and language and develop a flexible mindset towards communication that enables them to do their jobs. This conclusion is an admittedly positive outlook on the consequences of exporting American WAC/WID to the Arabian Gulf in the form of arhetorical learning outcomes for writing and communication. The map of transnational WAC/WID programs contains many such "fossils of American academic tourists' dreams" (see Sharma and Hammond, this volume), and it is a testament to the ingenuity, intelligence, and resilience of our students that they picked up these fossils and used them in service of their own goals as people and professionals.

I initially wrote this chapter and used its findings to advocate for a WAC/WID coordinator in TAMUQ's newly formed Center for Teaching and Learning. Positioned as an arm of faculty development and support for teaching innovation, I was able to talk with other faculty about the use of writing in their classes and to heighten awareness of the importance of connecting engineering to professional communication. We often discussed what I learned from these engineering professionals, and faculty shared what they have learned from their alumni interactions and advisory boards. Like Zenger et al. (2014), I anchored the WAC/WID program in a transnational praxis that asks first what students and faculty know about languages and disciplinary structures.

In fall 2019, I piloted a Writing-Enriched Curriculum (WEC) model for engineering (Durfee et al., 2011) that encouraged engineering departments to reach out to former students for their input. By developing plans for writing and communication specific to our campus, engineering departments would be tasked with localizing faculty development, student learning support, and communication learning outcomes that are responsive to the needs of alumni and Qatar's engineering industry. As an effort to reverse the "export" model of learning outcomes for writing, this WEC program held great promise (Anson et al., in press) but was tabled when the COVID–19 pandemic hit Qatar in February 2020 and I left TAMUQ in June 2020. For all of my regrets in leaving, I was thrilled to see that my colleague Dr. Naqaa Abbas would be continuing the WAC position and adding her vision and skillsets in writing, language, and cultural awareness.

Mapping and remapping the (dis)connections between writing outcomes and writers' workplaces illuminates new knowledge for transnational WAC/WID practitioners to act upon and use as leverage for institutional change, but it also reveals our participation in the act of naming, owning, and claiming the existing landscape of writing. Before I came to live and work in Qatar, my transnational students were already living experiences that taught them strategies of rhetorical communication and writing. By seeking out local knowledge and ethically incorporating it into institutional writing structures, transnational WAC/WID programs can provide meaningful learning opportunities and attempt to mitigate consequences of our map-making.

Acknowledgments

The author would like to thank research assistants Hanaa Loutfy, Rida Ahmed, Mizan Jaffer, Aalaa Abdalla, Midhat Javaid Zaidi, Rinith Reghunath, and Elizabeth Schmidt for their contributions to this project. Special thanks also to Christopher Alario and the heritage exhibits at the Qatar National Library in Al Rayyan, Qatar, for the information about Qatar's place in cartography.

References

Altbach, Philip. G. (2004). Globalisation and the university: Myths and realities in an unequal world. *Tertiary Education and Management, 10*(1), 3–25.

Anson, Chris, Hodges, Amy & Rudd, Mysti. (in press). The writing-enriched curriculum: Transnational prospects and challenges. In Christiane Donahue & Bruce Horner (Eds.), *Teaching and studying transnational composition*. Modern Language Association.

Arnold, Lisa. (2014). "The worst part of the dead past": Language attitudes, policies, and pedagogies at Syrian Protestant College, 1866–1902. *College Composition and Communication, 66*(2), 276–300.

Bloom-Pojar, Rachel. (2018). *Translanguaging outside the academy: Negotiating rhetoric and healthcare in the Spanish Carribean*. National Council of Teachers of English.

Bou Ayash, Nancy. (2019). *Toward translingual realities in composition: (Re)Working local language representations and practices*. Utah State University Press.

Canagarajah, A. Suresh. (2018). Transnationalism and translingualism: How they are connected. In X. You (Ed.), *Transnational writing education: Theory, history, and practice* (pp. 41–60). Routledge.

Condon, William. & Rutz, Carol. (2012). A taxonomy of writing across the curriculum programs: Evolving to serve broader agendas. *College Composition and Communication, 64*(2), 357–382.

Conrad, Susan. (2017). A comparison of practitioner and student writing in civil engineering. *Journal of Engineering Education, 106*(2), 191–217.

Cox, Michelle. (2011). WAC: Closing doors or opening doors for second language writers? *Across the Disciplines, 8*(4). https://doi.org/10.37514/ATD-J.2011.8.4.20.

Donahue, Christiane. (2009). "Internationalization" and composition studies: Reorienting the discourse. *College Composition and Communication, 61*(2), 212–243.

Durfee, William K., Adams, Benjamin, Appelsies, Audrey J. & Flash, Pamela. (2011, June 26–June 29). *A writing program for mechanical engineering*. Presented at the American Society for Engineering Education Annual Conference, Vancouver, BC, Canada.

Ferris, Dana & Thaiss, Chris. (2011). Writing at UC Davis: Addressing the needs of second language writers. *Across the Disciplines, 8*(4). https://doi.org/10.37514/ATD-J.2011.8.4.27.

Guerra, Juan C. (2016). Cultivating a rhetorical sensibility in the translingual writing classroom. *College English, 78*(3), 226–233.

Guerra, Juan C. & Shivers-McNair, Ann. (2017). Toward a new vocabulary of motive: Re(con)figuring entanglement in a translingual world. In Bruce Horner & Elliot Tetreault (Eds.), *Crossing divides: Exploring translingual writing pedagogies and programs* (pp. 19–30). Utah State University Press.

Hall, Jonathan. (2009). WAC/WID in the next America: Redefining professional identity in the age of the multilingual majority. *The WAC Journal, 20*, 33–49. https://doi.org/10.37514/WAC-J.2009.20.1.03.

Hesse, Doug. (2012). Writing program research: Three analytic axes. In Lee Nickolson & Mary P. Sheridan (Eds.), *Writing studies research in practice: Methods and methodologies* (pp. 140–157). Southern Illinois University Press.

Hodges, Amy & Rudd, Mysti. (2014). Teaching plagiarism IS teaching culture. In Leslie Seawright (Ed.), *Going global: Transnational perspectives on globalization, language, and education* (pp. 192–217). Cambridge Scholars Publishing.

International Network of WAC Programs. (2014). Statement of WAC principles and practices. https://wac.colostate.edu/docs/principles/statement.pdf.

LaFrance, Michelle & Nicolas, Melissa. (2012). Institutional ethnography as materialist framework for writing program research and the faculty-staff work standpoints project. *College Composition and Communication, 64*(1), 130–150.

LeCourt, Donna. (2012). WAC as critical pedagogy: The third stage? In Terry Myers Zawacki & Paul M. Rogers (Eds.), *Writing across the curriculum: A critical sourcebook* (pp. 69–84). Bedford/St. Martin's.

Lee, Jerry Won. (2016). Beyond translingual writing. *College English, 79*(2), 174–195.

Lee, Jerry Won & Jenks, Christopher. (2016). Doing translingual dispositions. *College Composition and Communication, 68*(2), 317–344.

Leydens, Jon A. (2008). Novice and insider perspectives on academic and workplace writing: Toward a continuum of rhetorical awareness. *IEEE Transactions on Professional Communication, 51*(3), 242–263.

Lorimer Leonard, Rebecca Lorimer. (2014). Multilingual writing as rhetorical attunement. *College English, 76*(3), 227–247.

Male, Sally A., Bush, Mark B. & Chapman, Elaine S. (2010). Perceptions of competency deficiencies in engineering graduates. *Australasian Journal of Engineering Education, 16*(1), 55–67.

Martins, David S. (Ed.). (2015). *Transnational writing program administration*. Utah State University Press.

Melzer, Dan. (2014). Assignments across the curriculum: A national study of college writing. Utah State University Press.

Miles, Matthew B., Huberman, A. Michael & Saldaña, Jonny. (2014). *Qualitative data analysis: A methods sourcebook (Vol. 3)*. Sage Publications.

Miley, Michelle. (2017). Looking up: Mapping writing center work through institutional ethnography. *Writing Center Journal, 36*(1), 103–129.

Miller-Idriss, Cynthia & Hanauer, Elizabeth. (2011). Transnational higher education: Offshore campuses in the Middle East. *Comparative Education, 47*(2), 181–207.

Patton, Martha D. (2011). Mapping the gaps in services for L2 writers. *Across the Disciplines, 8*(4). https://doi.org/10.37514/ATD-J.2011.8.4.26.

Purcell-Gates, Victoria. (2011). Ethnographic research. In Nell K. Duke & Marla H. Mallette (Eds.), *Literacy research methodologies* (pp. 135–154). Guilford Press.

Qatar Foundation. (2019). About Qatar Foundation. https://www.qf.org.qa/about.

Ronesi, Lynne. (2011). "Striking while the iron is hot": A writing fellows program supporting lower-division courses at an American university in the UAE. *Across the Disciplines, 8*(4). https://doi.org/10.37514/ATD-J.2011.8.4.25.

Rudd, Mysti. (2018). "It makes us even angrier than we already are": Listening rhetorically to students' responses to an honor code imported to a transnational university in the Middle East. *Journal of Global Literacies, Technologies, and Emerging Pedagogies, 4*(3), 655–674.

Seawright, Leslie. (2017, March 15–18). *Genre of power: Police report writers and readers in the justice system*. Conference on College Composition and Communication; National Council of Teachers of English, Portland, Oregon, United States.

Shuck, Gail. (2006). Combating monolingualism: A novice administrator's challenge. *WPA: Writing Program Administration, 30*(1–2), 59–82.

Texas A&M University Writing Center. (2003). Faculty Senate Resolution 20.108. https://writingcenter.tamu.edu/Faculty/W-C-Course-Facts/Faculty-Senate-Resolution-20-108.

Tribune News Network. (2019, January 15). Amir issues law to promote and protect Arabic language. http://www.qatar-tribune.com/news-details/id/152201.

Vora, Neha. (2015). Is the university universal? Mobile (re)constitutions of American academia in the Gulf Arab States. *Anthropology and Education Quarterly, 46*(1), 19–36.

Weber, Alan S., Golkowska, Krystyna, Miller, Ian, Sharkey, Rodney, Rishel, Mary Ann & Watts, Autumn. (2015). The First-year writing seminar program at Weill Cornell Medical College – Qatar: Balancing tradition, culture, and innovation in transnational writing instruction. In David. S. Martins (Ed.), *Transnational writing program administration* (pp. 72–92). Utah State University Press.

Wilson, Shawn. (2008). *Research is ceremony: Indigenous research methods*. Fernwood.

Wood, Cynthia H. (2011). Institutional ethos: Replicating the student experience. *New Directions for Higher Education, 155*, 29–39.

You, Xiaoye. (2018). Introduction: Making a transnational turn in writing education. In X. You (Ed.), *Transnational writing education: Theory, history, and practice* (pp. 1–17). Routledge.

Zawodny Wetzel, Danielle & Reynolds, Dudley. (2015). Adaption across space and time: Revealing pedagogical assumptions. In David. S. Martins (Ed.), *Transnational writing program administration* (pp. 93–116). Utah State University Press.

Zenger, Amy, Mullin, Joan & Haviland, Carol P. (2014). Reconstructing teacher roles through a transnational lens: Learning with/in the American University of Beirut. In Terry Myers Zawacki & Michelle Cox (Eds.), *WAC and second-language writers: Research towards linguistically and culturally inclusive programs and practices* (pp. 415–437). The WAC Clearinghouse; Parlor Press. https://doi.org/10.37514/PER-B.2014.0551.2.17.

Appendix A: Interview Questions

1. What kind of writing are you doing for your job right now? Who is the audience for this writing? How much writing do you do for oral presentation purposes?
2. Can you walk me through the process, from beginning to end, of how you completed X? When you sat down at your laptop to write X, did you start typing at the beginning of the document? How did you decide on this process?
3. Have you been asked to do this kind of writing before? Did you write X when you were in undergraduate or graduate school? Did you do any writing in your science or engineering classes? Where did you receive training on how to do this kind of writing?
4. Did you expect coming into this profession that you would be doing this amount of writing?
5. How much time (percentage) do you spend writing every day?
6. How much of your writing for your job is written by groups of people? Do

you enjoy these types of projects? Why or why not? How many people contribute to the final form of this document?
7. What language(s) do you write in and speak in? Do you speak any other languages besides (the languages you mentioned earlier)? Do you use these languages often when you are working?
8. Can you think of an example of when your writing was particularly effective or ineffective?
9. What kind of training on writing did you receive as part of your formal education (secondary school and/or university and or postsecondary)? How did it help you or not help you?
10. What kind of support do you receive for your own writing now that you're out of TAMUQ?
11. What writing habits should our engineering students develop now that will help them in their future profession? What advice would you offer to them with regards to writing? What can TAMUQ do to better support these kinds of writing experiences?

Appendix B: Alumni Participants in Interviews

Pseudonym	Gender	B.S. Degree Received from TAMUQ*	Spoken and Written Languages
Abdullah	M	CHEN	Arabic, English, some Spanish and French
Ali	M	ECEN	Arabic, English
Ammar	M	MEEN	English, Urdu
Dana	F	ECEN	Arabic, English, some French
Hamad	M	PETE	Arabic, English, Norwegian
Hassan	M	ECEN	Urdu, English, some Arabic
Maryam	F	ECEN	Arabic, English
Riya	F	CHEN	English, unidentified "mother tongue"
Saad	M	Unknown	Unknown
Tariq	M	MEEN	Arabic, English, some French

CHEN (Chemical Engineering); ECEN (Electrical and Computer Engineering); MEEN (Mechanical Engineering); PETE (Petroleum Engineering)

Appendix C. Learning Outcomes from Engineering Courses

Department	Number of Courses Offered in 2016–2017 Academic Year	Number of Total Learning Outcomes on Syllabi
Mechanical Engineering	27*	259
Electrical and Computer Engineering	22	198
Chemical Engineering	28	179
Petroleum Engineering	26*	171

*These numbers include required courses cross-referenced with other departments, specifically an industrial and systems engineering course required for mechanical engineering majors and a geology course required of all petroleum engineering students. Because Qatar does not have faculty members from these particular departments, at TAMUQ these courses are taught by qualified faculty members in mechanical and petroleum engineering, respectively.

Challenges in Positioning WAC/WID in International Contexts: Perspectives from a Japanese Engineering Undergraduate Program

Monica H. Kwon
KANAZAWA UNIVERSITY, JAPAN

This chapter introduces a small-scale study that empirically investigated the perceived challenges of positioning WAC/WID approaches in an engineering program at a large public university in Japan through interviews with faculty members. By identifying the issues observed in the interviews, I discuss how translingual practice can enrich pedagogical resources in an EFL (English as Foreign Language) context and address the challenges that administrators and teaching practitioners might face as they try to meet the interests of the current government initiatives designed by the Ministry of Education, Culture, Sports, Science and Technology (MEXT), Japan. I first briefly touch on the backgrounds of WAC/WID programs and how translingual practice is being discussed in the teaching of writing, and then, I explain the government initiative, Top Global Universities Project in Japan to contextualize the present study and further discuss how various English writing programs have been developed for the purpose of internationalization of Japanese higher education.

The data reported in this chapter came from formally interviewing faculty members; however, the knowledge and information that supports my insights and arguments come from both formal and informal conversations with my colleagues and students, as well as my own ethnographic insights into a large public institution in a Japanese context. The insights gained from informally interacting with my colleagues and students in a Japanese institution helped me interpret the interviews with the engineering faculty members and discuss the future directions in pedagogical interventions and options in this chapter, specifically in a Japanese university adopting English Medium instruction ("EMI") policies across departments and colleges.

One of the reasons I decided to explore the engineering department was because engineering students in particular did not seem to be strongly motivated in classroom discussions and conversations to learn EAP writing and speaking. I worked as a member of an academic writing curriculum committee to develop an academic writing program for all first-year students. While developing the curriculum and teaching academic writing, I observed that engineering students in particular seemed to lack interest in learning academic writing entirely in English under EMI polices. For this reason, I wanted to know what engineering faculty members think about the recent changes in the institution and the dynamics between new policies, administrative decisions, and their own perceptions and thoughts on adopting EMI policies.

WAC/WID programs in the U.S. context have been implemented as a way to help facilitate the construction of knowledge and socialization into the discipline through writing (Bazerman, 1994). WAC/WID approaches are typically culturally embedded literacy scholarship and activities in primarily North American contexts (Russell, 1990, 1991; Thaiss & Porter, 2013), making it difficult to adopt in international settings. Moreover, building transnational partnerships between writing programs across national borders or importing WID/WAC approaches in an international settings have encountered several challenges, such as different institutional beliefs and constraints, first language and medium of instruction, personnel management, as well as different cultural assumptions and educational systems (Martins, 2015). The WAC approaches in higher education have taken the form of note-taking, short-answer responses, essay writing, reflections, and journal writing as a mode of learning. Many discipline-specific WAC approaches have been introduced in disciplines such as sociology, science, engineering, etc. (Bazerman et al., 2005; Dannels, 2002; Hanson & Williams, 2008). WAC approaches are a reflective process of learning through writing and identifying any ideas and concepts learned on the writer's own terms in order to reach a closer, clearer understanding of an application of a concept, and, largely, advancement of academic knowledge.

In an international context, while the concept of WAC/WID is not widely known, it is understood as an approach to teach content knowledge in a second language. Often in institutions adopting EMI policies in academic programs and in current discussions of teaching academic writing in EFL contexts in Japan and a few European countries such as Sweden, Finland, Sweden, and Norway, Content and Language Integrated Learning (CIL) is becoming an area similar to WAC/WID (Pérez-Cañado, 2012). In the Japanese context, CLIL is actively being employed (mostly in bilingual modes), practiced, and researched in numerous institutions as a way to teach content knowledge through a second language. CLIL refers to an instructional approach that integrates content knowledge and an additional language, which is a "dual-focused" approach that is "content-driven" and focuses on both content knowledge and learning an additional language that is often a foreign or second language to learners (Coyle et al., 2010, p. 1). The language used in the CLIL approach is called "vehicular language," a term that is employed in CLIL to reflect its "inclusive" meaning that is not necessarily English only but encompasses other languages that can be used to teach both content and language. There are two types of instructional models in CLIL that utilize vehicular language. One model is "extensive instruction through the vehicular language," in which the focus is on both acquisition of high-level content knowledge and language proficiency. In this model, there would be "limited switches" to the mother tongue to explain the subject in class (Coyle et al., 2010, p. 18) and would be supported by one content teacher in collaboration with a language teacher who can teach linguistic structures and vocabulary about the subject before students learn the content knowledge. The other model is "partial instruction through the vehicular language," in which code-switching between first and second language can be more clearly implemented by a bilingual teacher through a bilingual mode of instruction. This model uses both CLIL language and first language as a medium of instruction. The type of code-switching used in this model can be called "translanguaging" that employs "systematic switches" between students' first and second (foreign) language in order to reduce the burden of learning content and additional language at the same time (Coyle et al., 2010, p. 19).

As the definitions and practices of "translanguaging" develop further, current discussion of "translanguaging" goes beyond code-switching and code-meshing as natural phenomena. Instead, "translanguaging" is becoming a conscious decision informed by the awareness of language hierarchy and power dynamics in various educational contexts and classroom contexts (Lewis et al., 2012) According to A. Suresh Canagarajah (2018), the prefix "trans" connotes the transformation of existing norms and relationships of a language, meaning that "translingual" makes it possible to use linguistic resources available to create new meanings, even if the linguistic resources have multiple languages. In a way, "translingual" goes beyond the traditional meaning of a medium of communication that only one form and structure of language can be a means of communication in a communicative context. Using mother tongue together with the target language in the classroom is not only a natural phenomenon but also an ideologically-aware decision. Canagarajah (2018) also defines "transnational" as a space in which one's identities are not bound by one's nationality; instead, it transcends the physical locations of where people are and extends their relationships and experiences (p. 42).

Given these definitions and descriptions of "translingual" and "transnational" and the term "translingualism" in the context of teaching writing, English classrooms in current Japanese higher education should be considered transnational spaces where issues beyond national borders can be discussed and more than one form of language can be considered as a means of communication. Both learners' and teachers' linguistic repertoires consist of multiple languages including English, Japanese, along with other languages such as Chinese, Hindi, Korean, Malay, and Portuguese, which can be used as a way to negotiate their own identities in order to create and produce new meanings in spoken or written words. Unlike what has generally been understood in the public sphere, Japan is increasingly a multilingual and multicultural context due to history and immigration (Gottlieb, 2012). Together with this particular context, as an additional layer, I chose an undergraduate engineering program as a context of the study because it presents a unique challenge in integrating academic content and English as a Medium of Instruction (EMI) in a classroom context in an EFL context. With the Top Global University Project of the Ministry of Education, Culture, Sports, Science and Technology (MEXT) in Japan, selected universities are building global partnerships and innovative teaching environments that promote internationalization (Top Global University Project & MEXT, 2014). Many of the selected universities are actively adopting courses that use English as Medium of Instruction in order to create opportunities for students to learn and engage in an English-speaking environment to foster their English language skills and global leadership (Bradford & Brown, 2018). Study abroad programs for Japanese students, culture exchange programs for non-Japanese students, and degree programs offered in English only or English and Japanese are part of this initiative. Based on the Top Global University Project by MEXT in Japan, various academic programs in Japanese higher education are actively adopting EMI courses and programs to internationalize the universities to attract more students and faculty members from outside Japan by creating more Western academic environments that take more active learning approaches and use students' productive skills in language by learning academic contents in academic English.

Although there is a push for globalization and building academic English programs from the administrative sector, since English is not a medium of instruction in Japanese high schools, teachers and students face many challenges in managing EMI classes in higher education settings, as many students have never been exposed to EMI environments. Communicating the needs of students and untrained teachers becomes a difficult task as the Japanese government and administration sectors tend to assume that English-speaking staff are already prepared to teaching academic writing and that, therefore, students will perform well as long as teachers are teaching them "how to" write an academic paper in English. For this reason, teaching academic writing through EMI courses in Japanese universities is becoming one of the major topics of discussion in teaching and researching Teaching English to Speakers of Other Languages (TESOL) in Japan.

Various studies have demonstrated the potential and value of translingual approaches in teaching and learning writing in the field. In regards to cultural differences and ideologies in teaching writing to second language learners, scholars have addressed challenges in negotiating these ideologies, particularly in understanding the different structures and modes of argumentation and rhetorical strategies (Mao, 2018; Qu, 2014; You, 2005). For example, LuMing Mao (2018) argued that insights from comparative rhetoric and translingual practices can inform the field of teaching writing in a way that can create a space for discussing underrepresented modes of argumentation and empower writers' voice and agency.

As a specific example of using a writer's linguistic repertoire that involves two languages in English-medium higher education settings, Guillaume Gentil's (2018) case study situated a translanguaging approach in a Canadian academic context in which English and French are used. By observing a case where a graduate student who is proficient in both English and French works on a dissertation project on gender studies at an English-medium university in Quebec, the study showed unique challenges the student experienced in the process of translating her ways of perceiving and using lexical resources in English and French, negotiating the gap between the academic terms created in English and French, and issues with finding equivalents in French, while trying to produce new knowledge and arguments for her study. The study indicated that the current lexical resources that are translated from French to English or from English to French by translators are quite limited for discussing the subject in depth, which requires the student in this study to be creative in making meaning across languages. Based on the study, Gentil (2018) noted that translanguaging and biliteracy can "help bilingual writers learn to write in their disciplines in and across two languages, but also harness the potential of bilingual and crosslingual writing for learning (in) the disciplines" (p. 126).

The present study situates engineering faculty members' perceptions and attitudes of implementing WAC approaches in a Japanese undergraduate engineering program. Through interviews with faculty members at a Japanese undergraduate engineering program, I identified possible challenges writing faculty might experience in the process of introducing and localizing WAC approaches in content-area disciplines such as engineering in an international context.

Context and Method

With the support of Top Global Universities Project by the Japanese government, the target institution is currently on a 10-year internationalization plan to increase the number of international students from outside Japan and create more courses that are taught in an English-only environment. Five faculty members in an engineering undergraduate program at a Japanese university were interviewed, who were assistant or associate-level professors, in various disciplines: bio-mechanical engineering (1), chemical engineering (1), and electrical engineering (3). The researcher contacted faculty members at this university via email based on the faculty profile pages of the engineering department and asked for an interview regarding the project. The email explained the purpose of the research and the nature of the project. Five faculty members responded back and agreed to participate in the interview. At the time, using English as a medium of instruction was strongly encouraged in class because the university was aiming to adopt EMI within the next five years. Faculty members were informed by the university about the goals and globalization prospect and were supposed to prepare for teaching content-based EMI courses. Upon interviews, I introduced myself to my participants and the purpose of this small-scale study, and showed a list of questions that would be asked first, and they were also asked if they would feel comfortable providing their insights on this topic. A verbal agreement was obtained, and the interviewees were allowed to stop the interview at any point of the interview. All participants were given pseudonyms.

Findings

Due to the extent of the participants' unfamiliarity with the concept of WAC or writing studies and approaches from North American contexts, the researcher explained this in both English and Japanese, and helped them understand the purposes of this type of approach, typical goals and outcomes expected in writing programs and undergraduate programs in American contexts. In addition to this, I explained ways students learn content knowledge from their early years from primary school to college in the US The interviews were transcribed and coded based on the themes developed through an open coding method that identifies emerging themes in the process of data analysis. The preliminary findings indicated that professors believed that disciplinary knowledge in their mother tongue was more valuable for engineering students, primarily in order to understand the theories and concepts which they needed in advanced-level courses and individual research projects in their program. Interviewees stated that students would benefit from writing in the engineering discipline in the long run; however, the current infrastructure of the institution and different needs and demands of the industry in Japan make it difficult to embed writing activities in English in their current undergraduate curriculum.

Faculty Member's Own Literacy Activities and Perceived Importance of Literacy Skills

Participating faculty members were asked what literacy activities they engage in in their professional lives. As the participants were faculty members in engineering, their literacy activities involved reading and writing in English mostly for research publications; however, they also use documents written in Japanese if they are available to them. The following are the excerpts from the interviews with the five faculty members in the engineering department. The names of the faculty members are pseudonyms given by the researcher.

> Ohashi: Most documents I use are English journal paper, more than 90%, Japanese ones are very few.
>
> Yamada: Reading skill is most important. We use it when I read papers, books, and manuals.
>
> Yaguchi: I often read technical documents to understand a new technology. They are mostly in English, but I read if there is the Japanese edition.

> Tanaka: Writing skill was the most important in my field, especially, in publication of journal papers.
>
> Kimura: I have to write ronbun [articles for journals] in English, so I read and write in English for my research. I need to practice and get better (laugh) too.

Their own literacy activities in English seem to be mostly related to their research in the engineering discipline. It is, however, unclear how much of their work is in English, or if there are any other tasks they do on a regular basis in English. Below are excerpts from the interview in which each faculty member expressed their thoughts on what types of communication skills their students might need.

> Ohashi: Critical thinking skill must be included. However, students should learn it in Japanese before learning English.
>
> Yaguchi: I think that skill for accurate communication is necessary.
>
> Tanaka: Enthusiasm and activeness to learn what they need from other people are essential communication skill (if they already have basic knowledge about the field).
>
> Yaguchi: Required time. I will need time to prepare for the course in English.

It can be seen that different ideologies and perceptions work together in thinking about communication skills and attitudes that are perceived to be needed in such classes. These perceived differences in what English and Japanese might bring into class seems to make the faculty members not only resistant to changing their class formats and styles but also anxious about teaching disciplinary knowledge to students in English either partly or as a main medium of instruction. Some faculty members seem to associate values such as "critical thinking," "enthusiasm," and "active" with English communication skills, which are often contrasted with the values considered important in the way students learn in Japanese contexts, for example, listening without interrupting the teachers (Harumi, 2010; Samimy & Kobayashi, 2004). As Weiguo Qu (2014) rightly noted in his study, different power structures within a given society may "prioritize some items or modes of argumentation" in writing, rather than cultural differences (p. 71). The ways faculty members in the present study see the classroom in English and Japanese may be coming from their perceived cultural differences that seem to give a clear distinction between how classes should be conducted in English and Japanese. And these perceived differences can prevent them from understanding how the actual English-medium content-based classes can be taught. As shown in the interview, one faculty member (Yaguchi) mentioned that preparing the engineering course taught in English using English literacy activities will simply require too much time for faculty members.

Opinions on English as Medium of Instruction Policy and WAC Approaches

Engineering faculty members were asked how they feel about implementing English as Medium of Instruction and WAC approaches in engineering courses. The WAC approaches and how they have originated in the Western educational contexts were explained, as well as how they are used in some university engineering programs in the US. We asked the faculty members how those approaches could work in the engineering program in Japan. Many of them suggested a form of bilingual class as a better way, although it is not clear how exactly both languages can be used in writing tasks for students.

> Tanaka: Yes, of course. This is very good opportunity to obtain theoretical thinking ability, which is useful in all kinds of work. But both the languages should be used in the learning.
>
> Yamada: I think that students should be taught in both. Japanese and English. For example, we use a language suitable to learning purpose.

A faculty member (Yamada) mentions "using a language suitable to learning purpose" by using both Japanese and English, which seems to mean that they are familiar with the instructional language of Japanese; however, they might not be familiar with the style and convention of instructional language in English. Another faculty member (Tanaka) is positive towards the idea of implementing WAC approaches and thinks it can help students' ability to understand theoretical thinking; however, this faculty member thinks that both Japanese and English should be used in this type of learning environment.

I asked them to explain why both languages should be used in the engineering courses, if WAC approaches were to be used in class. A faculty member (Tanaka) explains that using both languages in writing will help students understand differences, which can help them better understand international communication. He also noted that students who are not familiar with critical thinking, especially those who might lack experiences in writing practices with critical thinking, may not benefit from WAC approaches. This is worth noting as it is possible to see that faculty members link English writing practices with critical thinking, acknowledging that it is not widely practiced in Japanese secondary school settings, and at the same time, seeing the benefits of literacy activities that WAC approaches might bring to the students.

> Tanaka: They can understand differences in thinking way and culture between these two different languages, English and Japanese. This experience promotes their ability of international communication? Most Japanese, maybe, and Asian people are

not good at, or do not like critical thinking. The lack of this ability affects all the aspects of Japanese, including writing and communication.

Some faculty members, however, are hesitant about both using English as medium of instruction and implementing various writing tasks from WAC approaches, because they believe it might only benefit non-Japanese students who are more competent in English literacy skills.

> Ohashi: Students from foreign countries will benefit, but not Japanese students.
>
> Yamada: Benefit is foreign students will be able to understand it more easily. Problem is Japanese students cannot understand it much.

The above two faculty members seem to contrast Japanese students with foreign students in their abilities to engage in English literacy activities. As the engineering program at this institution tends to have international students who come from outside Japan, faculty members teach engineering courses that have a somewhat more diverse demographic than in the Department of Humanities and Social Sciences. The international students enrolled in the undergraduate engineering program at this institution range from south Asian countries such as India, Indonesia, and Malaysia to East Asian countries such as China and South Korea, and more rarely, there are some students from Europe. The above two faculty members (Ohashi, Yamada) consider that foreign students are more competent in English language skills, which makes them think that Japanese students might not benefit from learning disciplinary knowledge in English that implements various writing tasks.

Practicalism of Learning English Skills

As with many higher education settings, one of the important goals of the engineering program at this institution is to help students find career opportunities at engineering-related companies or research centers. For this reason, much of their focus is on helping students reach their end goals through credit-bearing engineering courses that could teach them necessary disciplinary knowledge and provide practical training in the field. We asked the faculty members whether implementing writing activities for the purpose of learning the disciplinary knowledge would be helpful in acquiring the knowledge and advancing their writing skills in English for the future workplace. Faculty members seem to think that "conversation skills" are more important than writing skills when engaging in international collaboration or business, and that this skill can be learned in focused training sessions after they enter the workplace. The companies in Japan will provide employees with training needed to improve their conversation skills.

> Yamada: It is difficult to learn practical writing skills related to workplace in their college, because, which so differ depending on type of workplace. This skill should be learned after entering a company.

A faculty member (Yamada) notes that it is hard to say that English writing skills learned in college will help students in their workplace because workplaces vary and the companies will offer additional training opportunities. Another faculty member (Kimura) also mentioned that English skills can be learned more after students graduate and enter workplaces. He also noted that many companies train their employees to communicate better with international workers in international branches for businesses and research. For this reason, engineering students often seem to have a pre-decided idea of which skill areas in English to improve, and whether they would like to spend more time on learning English language skills or furthering their disciplinary training.

> Kimura: Intercultural communication, critical thinking and writing skills are important, but these skills can be learned after they are employed. Companies train employees for international branches and international businesses and projects. Mostly focused on conversation skills. I once worked as a researcher at a company and they gave me one-on-one conversation class with a native speaker. I learned speaking quite a lot in that class. I think conversation skills is important when you want to work for international business at that company.

Interestingly, the above faculty member (Kimura) mentioned that this English skill the companies provide training in is mostly conversation skills. Due to the demands of the professional environments in Japan that put more emphasis on employees' ability to orally communicate with non-Japanese in international businesses than on written communication, writing skills receive little attention in the undergraduate engineering program. As noted in the earlier interview excerpts, "active learning" and "enthusiasm" seem to be more associated with talking and speaking in class, which may influence the way faculty members think about English communication skills as well. This part of the interviews shows us that adopting EMIL policies together with writing-intensive approaches might require a shift in the current learning paradigm in the engineering program. The current learning paradigm in the engineering department seems to focus heavily on the learning of necessary content knowledge to prepare graduates for the job market mostly in Japan. It is more practical to learn English literacy skills after learning and understanding the content knowledge, and preferably after students enter the workplaces of their choice, if they wish to work for international sectors. This is due to a difference in the culture of the Japanese corporations and job market, and the influence of these on the current engineering programs in Japanese universities.

Discussion

From the interviews with faculty members at a Japanese undergraduate engineering program, it is possible to see challenges in introducing WAC approaches in the Japanese context due to different understanding of literacy skills and demands of the current job market in Japan. Faculty members of the engineering department seemed to agree with the general direction of the globalization of Japanese higher education, such as increasing the number of courses that implement English skills; however, teaching of disciplinary knowledge should be in both Japanese and English for effective instruction and students' preparation for careers in Japan. In this section, I will present a few points in furthering the interpretation and discussion of the interviews. In this section, I discuss how WAC programs can be negotiated and localized in an international context where the use of native language is unavoidable in learning disciplinary knowledge. In addition, I discuss how writing programs can be localized with sustainable infrastructure at higher education in international contexts.

Contextualizing WAC/WID and Medium of Instruction

In order to localize an academic writing program that adopts a writing-intensive approaches like WAC/WID, it seems necessary to adjust our expectations of English usage in the classroom, as well as the extent to which a medium of instruction can benefit students to learn disciplinary knowledge. When it comes to engineering disciplines in Japan, use of mother tongue in delivering disciplinary knowledge seems inevitable because faculty members in engineering prefer to use Japanese, for which they already know the forms of language that are "suitable for learning purposes." Deeper consideration should be given on the way to define and apply medium of instruction in the local curriculum and content-based academic programs. The current EMI policies are generating a lot of pushback from faculty members and students, which seems to pose challenges in actually implementing the use of English as a medium of instruction with writing-intensive approaches for content-based academic degree programs in Japan, unless there is specific support for pedagogical approaches and resources available for both faculty members and students. Although engineering faculty members may be capable of teaching content knowledge to students in English, they seem to feel pressure to re-conceptualize and re-purpose their classroom, as well as their teaching approaches and philosophies.

Translingual approaches can potentially have a place in this junction of medium of instruction and content knowledge in degree-based programs in Japan. I have introduced CLIL as one of the instructional approaches being used in the Japanese context earlier in this chapter. The current CLIL approaches do not clearly explain how "translanguaging" can be used specifically, and whether it should be used. However, it is understood that bilingual teachers would systematically switch between students' mother tongue and a second language while teaching content knowledge. In order to fully understand the content and engage in class activities, students may need to have acquired some content knowledge and necessary vocabulary in a second language in advance. In other words, as is often the case that the majority of the students do not already have the content knowledge or content-specific vocabulary in a second language, there will be many gaps to fill. The process of filling these gaps will require time and additional labor from both students and faculty members, which calls for a specific pedagogical intervention specifically designed for this particular academic context. This process may be facilitated by understanding translingual modes and bilingual thinking, and accepting that learning new content knowledge in a second language requires forming knowledge in the first language as well, at least at the beginning. If faculty members and students can understand this process of knowledge acquisition in the first and second language, and if students are allowed to use their first language in their collaborative activities or writing tasks, it can be more efficient to achieve learning goals and objectives.

Despite the current debate in the US (Canagarajah, 2011a, 2012b, 2013; Lu & Horner, 2013), translingual practices seem to be important resources for both teachers and students to learn content knowledge and second language, at least in non-U.S. contexts. It is my belief that use of translingual practices can help students' initial adjustment to the courses that are taught in English and employ WAC principles. The notion of translingualism provides insights in reconceptualizing communicative competence from another angle. A translingual writing program model can allow students and teachers in international contexts to ease their way into "more English" in general. When students' first language is allowed for resources, this further enriches their understanding of the discipline and advances their academic language repertoire, especially in an EFL context when English is not actively used on a daily basis or for education in general.

Translanguaging is a conscious decision accepting it as a natural process for second language learners and for how multilingual learners understand and think (Lewis et al., 2012). Translingual classroom practices may facilitate more meaningful interactions among learners that share a first language and getting access to the second language and content together collaboratively. In his research in a Malaysian primary school, Shakina Rajendram (2021) posits that translanguaging is a naturally occurring phenomenon (Canagarajah, 2011) that occurs in the learning process. His research showed that students used their first language "agentively" and effectively in the collaborative learning process (Rajendram, 2021, p. 189).

Writing studies scholars in other contexts in this book provide insights into the way writing programs can be localized and how the teaching of writing becomes an ideological process in international contexts (Hodges, this volume; Li, this volume). The findings and discussion of this chapter echo those in Li's chapter on building a writing-intensive program in a science and engineering department at a

Chinese university. L1-oriented WAC/WID approaches are generally understood as a category of EAP, and this understanding may differ from the way WAC/WID programs are constructed in the US; however, administrators and faculty members will continue to seek ways to teach academic writing. This process can sometimes take the form of collaboration by fostering a community of scholars working on writing program administration and teaching and assessment in the international context (Sharma & Hammond, this volume).

Looking at the trend in the global sphere, it seems that teaching academic writing will continue to be an important step to include in the internationalization of higher education, not only in Japan but in any other contexts in which English is not the first language. Learning academic literacy in international contexts is increasingly becoming unavoidable for both undergraduate and graduate students. While this trend will continue, the discussion on the specific pedagogical approaches under EMI policies in individual classrooms will become more specific and important. The discussion will generate questions such as "How much are we going to allow translanguaging in the classroom?," "How do we inform policies and administrators about the value of first language?," "How do we help students achieve literacy both content and the second language in a different educational and cultural context?," and "What level of academic literacy do we expect students to achieve?"

In the course of preparing for further globalization of Japanese higher education, teaching academic writing will continue to be a means in the globalization process and enhancing the quality of academic programs. It seems necessary to explore various options in teaching and learning content knowledge in English. Many of these decisions will be made based on practical reasons, but it will be difficult to avoid in-depth discussion on whether to use mother tongue in EMI classrooms. More research on current EMI policies needs to be conducted to find more insights from faculty members and students teaching and learning in content-based academic programs under EMI policies in Japan. And in this process, it is important for policy makers and institutions to collaborate to support "multilingualism as a norm" to create better resources and infrastructure for teaching academic writing in an international context (Rajendram, 2021, p. 196).

Sustainable Infrastructure

Adopting WAC approaches will require much more sustainable infrastructure that can support both faculty members and students. Writing centers, for example, can be one of the ways to help build connections between English writing programs and engineering departments, as well as give individual or group support for the students in need. There can also be additional resources such as instructors specializing in science writing or courses that can foster an understanding of what writing does and how writing can facilitate the knowledge-building process. The internationalization movement towards globalization in Japan is actively encouraging more use of English and more productive skills in English in a way that could promote the global visions that meet the national interests. However, as can be seen in the interviews, there is some resistance toward adopting Westernized methods of teaching in English in the content area courses, and more importantly, there is misinterpretation and disagreement on what literacy can do in the process of acquiring, learning, and using knowledge for advancing scientific knowledge. English literacy, for now in Japanese contexts, seems to be perceived as another barrier to teaching disciplinary knowledge, rather than a means to facilitate teaching and learning of disciplinary knowledge. In order to effectively build and implement an academic writing program for other disciplines such as engineering, there needs to be sustainable infrastructure such as instructors knowledgeable in EFL contexts, writing specialists in second language writing, effective use of translanguaging, and instructors who can demonstrate an in-depth understanding of cultural and national identity in the context they teach. Understanding the motivation and backgrounds of national and institutional globalization initiatives and how certain academic writing programs are established in an institution can extend the knowledge of ways to develop pedagogical approaches for the students, set more realistic goals, and help students reach their full potential.

Conclusion

Writing program localization does not come with manuals for each country and context. The local context significantly informs practice, as each context has a distinctive language policy agenda based on different motivations. Japan is a unique context in which national agendas and global standards are co-dependent. Understanding the context can benefit the way to think about steps to take in writing program localization. Although it seems highly challenging for WAC/WID approaches to be used in a context of Japanese engineering programs, interviewees shared a general agreement that productive language skills are important for participating in globalization and internationalization movement in order for the discipline and industry to grow.

To better localize WAC/WID approaches in international contexts, there needs to be negotiation of the goals and outcomes that take into account students' mother tongue as well as the knowledge and skills required in the Japanese engineering industry. When localizing a writing program, or teaching EAP in a global context, we as writing practitioners need to first discuss what teaching and writing academic English means, why we do it, how we do it, what we expect from the students, and what level we want to achieve and accomplish. Although it might be a challenge, I believe that the discussion on "writing to learn" can benefit the university programs and policies in Japan that are actively adopting EAP, EMI, CLIL as research in EAP in the global context advances further. Research in WAC/WID can inform the practices of EAP in a way that can foster the idea of learning English not as a product but as a process. This process can involve teaching in bilingual modes, making use of students' biliteracy, and translingual approaches as students attempt to make sense of meaning making process in academic language.

References

Bazerman, Charles. (1994). *Constructing experience*. Southern Illinois University Press.
Bazerman, Charles, Little, Joseph, Bethel, Lisa, Chavkin, Teri, Fouquette, Danielle & Garufis, Janet. (2005). *Reference guide to writing across the curriculum*. Parlor Press; The WAC Clearinghouse. https://wac.colostate.edu/books/referenceguides/bazerman-wac/.
Canagarajah, A. Suresh. (2011a). Codemeshing in academic writing: Identifying teachable strategies of translanguaging. *The Modern Language Journal, 95*(3), 401–417.
Canagarajah, A. Suresh. (2011b). Translanguaging in the classroom: Emerging issues for research and pedagogy. *Applied Linguistics Review, 2*, 1–28.
Canagarajah, A. Suresh. (2013). Negotiating translingual literacy: An enactment. *Research in the Teaching of English, 48*(1), 40–67.
Canagarajah, A. Suresh. (2018a). Translingual practice as spatial repertoires: Expanding the paradigm beyond structuralist orientations. *Applied Linguistics, 39*(1), 31–54.
Canagarajah, A. Suresh. (2018b). Transnationalism and translingualism: How they are connected. In Xiaoye You (Ed.), *Transnational writing education: Theory, history, and practice* (pp. 41–60). Routledge.
Coyle, Do, Hood, Philip & Marsh, David. (2010). *CLIL: Content and language integrated learning*. Cambridge University Press
Dannels, Deanna. (2002). Communication across the curriculum and in the disciplines: Speaking in engineering. *Communication Education, 51*(3), 254–268.
Gentil, Guillaume. (2018). Modern languages, bilingual education, and translation studies: The next frontiers in WAC/WID research and instruction? *Across the Disciplines, 15*(3), 114–129. https://doi.org/10.37514/ATD-J.2018.15.3.16.
Gottlieb, Nanette. (2012). *Language policy in Japan: The challenge of change*. Cambridge University Press.
Hanson, H. James & Williams, M., Julia. (2008). Using writing assignments to improve self-assessment and communication skills in an engineering statics course. *Journal of Engineering Education, 97*(4), 515.
Harumi, Seiko. (2010). Classroom silence: Voices from Japanese EFL learners. *ELT Journal, 65*(3), 260–269.
Horner, Bruce. (2018). Translinguality and disciplinary reinvention. *Across the Disciplines, 15*(3), 76–88. https://doi.org/10.37514/ATD-J.2018.15.3.13.

Lewis, Gwyn, Jones, Bryn & Baker, Colin. (2012). Translanguaging: Developing its conceptualisation and contextualisation. *Educational Research and Evaluation, 18*(7), 655–670.

Lu, Min-Zhan. & Horner, Bruce. (2013). Translingual literacy, language difference, and matters of agency. *College English, 75*(6), 582–607

Martins, David S. (Ed.). (2015). *Transnational writing program administration.* Utah State University Press.

Mao, Luming. (2018). Thinking through difference and facts of nonusage: A dialogue between comparative rhetoric and translingualism. *Across the Disciplines, 15*(3), 104–113. https://doi.org/10.37514/ATD-J.2018.15.3.15.

Ministry of Education, Culture, Sports, Science and Technology (MEXT). (2014). *Top global university Japan.* https://tgu.mext.go.jp/en/index.html.

Pérez-Cañado, L. Maria. (2012). CLIL research in Europe: Past, present, and future. *International Journal of Bilingual Education and Bilingualism, 15*(3), 315–341.

Qu, Weiguo. (2014). Critical literacy and writing in English: Teaching English in a cross-cultural context. In Bruce Horner & Karen Kopelson (Eds.), *Reworking English in rhetoric and composition: Global interrogations, local interventions* (pp. 64–74). Southern Illinois University Press.

Rajendram, Shakina. (2021). The affordances of translanguaging as a pedagogical resource for multilingual English language classrooms in Malaysia. In Kathleen M. Bailey & Donna Christian (Eds.), *Research on Teaching and Learning English in Under-Resourced Contexts* (pp. 185–198). Routledge.

Russell, David R. (1990). Writing across the curriculum in historical perspective: Toward a social interpretation. *College English, 52*(1), 52–73.

Russell, David R. (1991). *Writing in the Academic Disciplines, 1870–1990: A Curricular History.* Southern Illinois University Press.

Samimy, K. Keiko. & Kobayashi, Chiho. (2004). Toward the development of intercultural communicative competence: Theoretical and pedagogical implications for Japanese English teachers. *JALT Journal, 26*(2), 245–261.

Thais, Chris & Porter, Tara. (2010). The state of WAC/WID in 2010: Methods and results of the U.S. survey of the international WAC/WID mapping project. *College Composition and Communication,* 534–570.

You, Xiaoye. (2005). Conflation of rhetorical traditions: The formation of modern Chinese writing instruction. *Rhetoric Review, 24*(2), 150–169.

Enhancing Science and Engineering Undergraduate Students' Writing in the Disciplines at Chinese Universities

Yongyan Li
UNIVERSITY OF HONG KONG

Following a research-intensive short visit to Nankai University in Tianjin, northern China in the early summer of 1999, Marty Townsend (2002) concluded: "writing instruction—as we understand it in the US—does not exist at Nankai University." (p. 139). Dan Wu (2013), in her doctoral dissertation (completed at Clemson University, the US), perhaps the most serious engagement with the American notions of WAC/WID in relation to the Chinese context to date, echoed Townsend's finding on a larger scale of Chinese tertiary education. Given the traditional fervor of Chinese higher education for learning from U.S. writing pedagogies (You, 2010), it may be somewhat surprising that the American WAC/WID has not taken root in the Chinese soil insofar as tertiary-level writing education is concerned. Yet despite the absence of WAC/WID in the Chinese context, as to be shown in this chapter through a survey of Chinese literature, discipline-oriented academic writing has been taught to science and engineering undergraduate students at Chinese universities by both content teachers and English teachers. Townsend (2002) pointed out that "American teacher/researchers must understand much more than just WAC principles to engage in cross-cultural discussion about teaching and learning" (p. 148). With the present chapter, together with an earlier mapping of the landscape of teaching English academic writing to graduate students at Chinese universities (Li & Ma, 2018), I aim to provide a Chinese perspective, to facilitate "cross-cultural discussion about teaching and learning" in the long run.

Although the pedagogical practices to be surveyed in the present chapter are "local" practices reported of various classroom contexts at Chinese universities at specific points of time, we are reminded that "remote literate practices shape and constrain local literacy practices" (Baynham & Prinsloo, 2010, p. 4). That is, the local practices are potentially "translocal and transnational" (Baynham & Prinsloo, 2010, p. 5), in light of the New Literacy Studies scholarship (e.g., Street, 2004). This perspective echoes writing studies scholars' championship for translingual and transnational writing education, whereby WAC/WID professionals are challenged to both move beyond a monolingual mindset in working with international students, and to look beyond national borders to understand how pedagogical traditions of other nationalities may inform new practices

(Donahue, 2018; Hall, 2016; Horner & Hall, 2018; You, 2018). In this vein, a perspective from the Chinese context can be a useful contribution to this collective endeavor in writing studies.

The Chinese Context

In the existing Chinese literature on English language teaching, sporadic references to the notion of "writing across the curriculum (WAC)" started to be found in the 2000s, usually in introductory pieces on the American WAC, either as part of book-length introductions of composition research in the West (e.g., Qi, 2000) or individual introductory texts on WAC (Luo, 2009). Notably, although the theme of the 5th International Conference on Teaching & Researching EFL writing in China (held in Guiyang, China in September 2007) was on "Teaching and Researching EFL Writing Across the Curriculum in China," apparently the phrase "Writing Across the Curriculum" was borrowed only to imply a broad coverage of the theme of the conference (Li, 2009).

More recently, there have been proposals among English language specialists for introducing WAC into Chinese higher education (Liu, 2016; Wu, 2013). In addition, calls for learning from the American WAC/WID have also been raised in the context of the traditional College Chinese (*daxue yuwen*) and College Writing (*daxue xiezuo*) (writing in Chinese) courses. These courses tend to be taught by Chinese language/writing specialists in the tradition of Chinese rhetoric studies and have a liberal arts education orientation, but they have been on decline or have been dropped off the course list at many universities (Zhang, 2008). Some calls to revive the courses have suggested that the College Chinese course be re-oriented to "writing in the disciplines," in light of Cornell University's freshman writing seminars (FWS) (Zhuang, 2014), and that the College Writing course should also be both re-positioned to "write to learn" (or *yi xie cu xue* in Chinese) in line with the American tradition (Li, 2007), and should be consolidated with establishment of degree programs on writing studies, after the American model (Ke, 2007).[1]

There seems to be no strong evidence that such calls for incorporating the American-style WAC/WID into Chinese higher education have come to fruition.

---

1   In the realm of undergraduate English language education at Chinese universities, "writing to learn" (*yi xie cu xue*) has long been championed, concerning the teaching of both English majors (e.g., Wang, et al., 2000) and non-English majors (Zhang, 2011). The emphasis conveyed by the slogan of *yi xie cu xue* falls on a "length approach" (*xie chang fa*), which encourages students to write at length, and thus improve their ability of expression through writing. Recently, the call for *yi xie cu xue* has picked on a writing-in-the-disciplines orientation, in the context of enhancing doctoral science students' ability to write English research papers (Yu, 2015).

However, several factors would suggest that an exploration of how instruction on discipline-oriented writing has taken place in tertiary education in China is a worthwhile undertaking. Firstly, there has been no shortage of books on scientific paper writing (SPW) (*keji lunwen xiezuo*) in China (one example being Zhu, 2004). Secondly, specialist English (*zhuanye yingyu*) courses, which typically focus on reading, vocabulary and translation, are often taught by content teachers within their schools/departments (in particular in science disciplines) at Chinese universities (Cai & Liao, 2010). Such courses, together with the trend of policy-prompted bilingual/English-medium instruction of subject courses implemented to various degrees at some universities, as well as the pressure for academics and research students to write for international publication, would provide a context for content teachers to facilitate students' English writing ability. Thirdly, a paradigm shift from general English to academic English or English for Academic Purposes (EAP), initiated in the 2000s, is becoming a major trend at Chinese universities (Cai, 2019; Cheng, 2016; Li & Ma, 2018). The EAP-turn would increasingly justify the installation of English academic writing instruction for students across disciplines at all levels. Finally, at the national policy level there has been a growing emphasis upon enhancing education in academic norms and academic ethics (*xueshu guifan/ xueshu daode*) in recent years. Universities have been responding with new courses designed accordingly. Such courses are offered by content teachers or language teachers to undergraduates or postgraduates.

It is against this backdrop that in the study to be reported below I aimed to deduce from a survey of the existing Chinese academic literature what discipline-oriented academic writing instruction targeting science and engineering undergraduate students has been like at Chinese universities.

Methods

Compared with a questionnaire survey or interviews, the method of surveying relevant existing Chinese-language publications (journal papers) brings two benefits. Firstly, the fact that the authors of the papers have chosen to publish on their pedagogical interventions indicates that they took those interventions seriously and considered them worth sharing with a large audience. The practices reported in the papers thus form a kind of purposeful sample as a result. Secondly, the surveyed papers, by reporting from different parts of the country (rather than from a few elite institutions, for example), imply greater representativeness of the wider practices.

To identify a target sample of Chinese publications, the China Academic Journals Full-text Database (CJFD), a sub-section of CNKI (China National Knowledge Infrastructure) (http://www.cnki.net/), was searched, using a variety of search terms and their combinations, in order to find (Chinese-language) articles that report on discipline-oriented writing pedagogy to undergraduate students. Searching based on the Chinese equivalents of "writing in the disciplines," or combinations of "writing" with "college chemistry," "college physics," etc., was not fruitful. Searching on the Chinese equivalents of "English-medium instruction," "bilingual teaching," "scientific paper writing," "specialist English," "course paper," "academic writing," "English for academic purposes," "education on academic norms" in varied combinations with "teaching," "undergraduate students," etc. led to large sets of hits.

I then went through the full texts of the numerous hits, looking for papers that reported on teaching discipline-oriented academic writing (in Chinese or English) to undergraduate science and engineering students, with at least a moderate amount of detail on the pedagogy provided. Discussion papers, which typically consisted of commentary on a problematic situation followed by recommendations, and indeed accounted for the vast majority, were excluded. A total of 34 papers, comprised of 20 papers on content teachers teaching scientific paper writing in Chinese (see Appendix 1), six on content teachers facilitating their science and engineering students' English writing ability (see Appendix 2), and eight on English teachers teaching English academic writing to science and engineering students (see Appendix 3), were selected as a result. Altogether 29 universities' cases are featured in these 34 papers. The papers are mostly reports of teaching practices, rather than empirical research papers. They range from two to nine pages (with a weight on the shorter side) and commonly include the following sections: introduction, current problems, pedagogical innovation implemented, and reflection and conclusion. The level of detail provided of the pedagogical practices varies and is often quite limited. In examining the short reports, I focused on culling from each report such information as the disciplinary areas of the students, the timing, duration, and content of the pedagogical intervention, and the instructors involved.

Findings

Content Teachers Teaching Chinese Scientific Paper Writing (SPW) to Science and Engineering Students

Twenty papers (shown in Appendix 1) authored by content teachers report on their teaching of Chinese scientific paper writing (SPW) to undergraduate science and engineering students at 19 universities located in 17 Chinese cities, with engineering, agriculture and chemistry being in the majority of the disciplines covered. Two-thirds of the papers were published from the year 2015 onwards, indicating a growing and ongoing interest amongst content teachers in enhancing SPW training for their students. The aim of such training was captured by this statement in one of the papers: "developing students' knowledge in the structure and composition of various types of scientific writing and raising their ability to write research articles and the degree thesis" (Xu & Yang, 2012, p. 93).

In terms of the timing, other than a few unspecified cases, SPW training typically occurred in Years 3 and 4. In one special case, the training was offered to 78 undergraduates preparing to participate in mathematical modeling contests in the years from 2019 to 2020 (Sun & Jing, 2021). The featured SPW training was either in a separate course (14 papers) or integrated into a specialist content course (six papers). When SPW was a separate course, the emphasis was placed upon preparing students to write up their research project, which was either a university-funded project or their graduation thesis project (Bian, et al., 2016; Han & Yang, 2016; Liang, et al., 2016; Liu, et al., 2014; Zhang, et al., 2016), and there was sometimes joint teaching with a content course (Guo, et al., 2017; Lei & Chen, 1998; Zhang & Ge, 2016). When SPW was integrated into a specialist content course, the course involved tended to be compulsory and foundational courses (Chen & Huang, 2012; Liu, et al., 2016; Yan & Sun, 2012; Zhang, et al., 2000), located earlier in time in the curriculum. In one case (materials science), the writing requirement spanned across three modules in Years 3–4 (Li, et al., 2015). There thus in this case seems to be a stress upon sustained SPW training as part of the content learning.

Published journal articles in Chinese or in English, and sometimes previous degree theses too, were incorporated into class teaching, and analyzed by the teacher and the students (Bian, et al., 2016; Li, 2017; Liu, et al., 2014; Xu & Yang, 2012). The teaching could be organized around the different sections of a research report (Gao & Zhang, 2016; Xu & Yang, 2012) and when the timing of the course paralleled students' graduation thesis research, students could be expected to draft their graduation thesis over the duration of the course (Gao & Zhang, 2016). A range of benefits of such "application-oriented" teaching (Bian, et al., 2016; Liu, et al., 2014) were cited: that it would motivate students and enhance their confidence, hone their independent thinking, strengthen their research ability through first-hand experience of the research process, and raise the quality of their degree theses (Guo, et al., 2017; Jia & Zhuo, 2016; Lei & Chen, 1998; Zhang & Ge, 2016; Zhang, et al., 2000).

Content teachers single- or co-authored all 20 papers (as can be seen in the affiliations of the authors), except for the earliest paper in the collection, Zongming Lei and Jie Chen (1998), which had a content teacher (in oil drilling) as the first author and a Chinese language specialist colleague as the second author. Lei and Chen (1998) did not specify the roles of the authors in the teaching, except mentioning that at the end of the featured SPW course, students should submit two copies of their papers—one to the "specialist teacher" who would assess the scientific soundness of the work, and the other to the "writing teacher" who would assess to what extent the presentation of the work conformed to the conventions of academic paper writing (p. 94).

Finally, only one comment on the qualification of the instructors was found in the collection of papers. Xihui Bian, et al. (2016) pointed out that the course teacher should be "familiar with literature searching systems, the conventions of SPW, excellent grasp of English in the relevant specialist area, having conducted in-depth research in an area, and having published high-level research papers" (p. 151). Overall, it seems language teachers were almost entirely out of the consideration of the content teachers who reported on their Chinese SPW instruction.

Content Teachers Facilitating Science and Engineering Students' Ability in English Writing

Six papers reported how content teachers (also authors of the papers) facilitated their students' ability in writing in English. Four of the papers featured the context of a compulsory specialist English (*zhuanye yingyu*) course (Chen, 2003; Liu, 2015; Wang, et al., 2009; Zhang & Jiang, 2010). In Guifang Wang, et al.'s (2009) course, apart from a focus on vocabulary, reading, and translation, students were expected to write paper abstracts. The other three papers all mentioned the use of English journal articles during teaching. In addition, Chen's (2003) students of geosciences were required to draft a short research paper in English based on their own graduation thesis topic, targeting a specialist journal; they were given 10 minutes to present it at the end of the course (with Q & A). Yuanfu Zhang and Zaixing Jiang's (2010) students were required to write short segments on discipline knowledge, paragraphs, and different sections of a research paper; a three-level scale of achievement was designated for each item: basic, intermediate, and advanced. Debao Liu's (2015) students were expected to read native-English-speaking authors' papers in high-impact journals and note down useful expressions for different sections of a paper and for describing figures, categorization, and hypotheses.

In addition to the four papers featuring specialist English courses, two papers concerned a context of a bilingual SPW course (Li, 2011) or a bilingual specialist course (Liu, 2012). Of the two, Xiangli Liu (2012) emphasized writing short pieces in Chinese or in English to facilitate learning and cultivate students' analytic ability: outlining key issues during lesson preview, recalling key points covered at the end of a lecture session, and summarizing the highlights of each unit. This, and to some extent the writing tasks given by Yuanfu Zhang and Zaixing Jiang (2010) (cited above), seem to constitute rare examples in the focal Chinese literature that echo the American notion of "write to learn," with content teachers advocating the use of more informal writing to facilitate students' learning in the disciplines (Townsend, 2018).

Like the literature on content teachers teaching Chinese SPW, this modest collection of papers on content teachers facilitating students' English writing ability does not mention any involvement from language teachers. However, there is one reference to content teachers "observing the writing classes taught to English majors [by English language teachers]" for the sake of "absorbing teaching experience" to inform their own teaching of SPW in English (Zhang & Jiang, 2010, p. 112).

English Language Teachers Teaching English Academic Writing (EAW) to Science and Engineering Students

Eight papers, authored by English teachers, reported on the authors teaching English Academic Writing (EAW) to science and engineering students. In contrast to the Chinese or English writing instruction provided by content teachers which often took place in Year 3 or Year 4, the EAW instruction offered by English teachers tended to occur in Year 1 or Year 2.

Two papers (Liu, 2010; Yang, 2013) specifically indicated target students as those who have passed CET 4 (College English Test, Band 4) (see Zheng & Cheng, 2008). The EAW course described by Bin Liu (2010) focused on information gathering, problem-solving and the writing process. The EAW component in the academic English course described by Feng Yang (2013) introduced skills on note-taking, the writing of the different sections of an AIMRaD paper (Abstract, Introduction, Methods, Results, and Discussion), and avoiding plagiarism. The remaining six papers demonstrated a stronger connection with students' disciplines, with a variety of approaches implemented to make EAW instruction discipline-oriented. For example, Yanjiang Teng (2016) subscribed to an instructional mode of "language plus disciplinary content" (p. 45). Thus, a teaching plan of a writing course for engineering students shows a list of topics, each mapping onto a set of writing skills. Under the topic of "Data," the writing skills focused on the use of academic vocabulary, graphs, writing of descriptive paragraphs, tenses, and sentence patterns (Teng, 2016). As another example, Jin Yan and Yafei Ge (2011) reported that geosciences students, in fulfilling a project-based assessment task in their English for Professional Purposes experimental class, should complete a 2,000-word research paper in a specialist field that they would expect to pursue in the future.

Compared with content teachers, the English teacher authors were able to draw upon various theoretical/pedagogical notions from the applied linguistics literature, such as content-based (Teng, 2016; Yao & Han, 2016), collaborative learning (Yan & Ge, 2011), project-based (Yan & Ge, 2011; Yang & Han, 2012), task-driven (Yan & Ge, 2011; Yao & Han, 2016), the prototypical IMRD structure of research articles (Wang, 2013; Yang, 2013), and academic literacies and learning autonomy (Teng, 2016). In addition, while content teachers hardly considered engagement with English teachers, there was evidence that the latter aspired to work with their counterparts in disciplines (Teng, 2016; Yan & Ge, 2011; Yi, 2015). Yet overall, despite the aspiration, evidence of such partnership in practice is not seen in any of the eight papers, in contrast to such collaboration sporadically occurring in graduate-level EAW instruction (see Li & Ma, 2018).

Discussion

In the foregoing section, three strands of Chinese literature were reviewed: on content teachers teaching Chinese scientific paper writing (SPW) to science and engineering students, content teachers facilitating such students' ability in English writing, and English language teachers teaching English academic writing (EAW) to such students. Due to the traditional separation of language and content subjects, as well as the separate publication venues of content teachers and language teachers in China, it may be safe to suggest that within the country, content teachers' work, reported in the first two strands of literature, has been largely unknown to English teachers; likewise, the latter's work reported in the third strand of literature may have also been hidden from content teachers. Together, all three strands of literature may have been largely unknown to the outside world.

It can be suggested that all three strands of literature reviewed in this chapter, by focusing on the teaching of discipline-oriented writing to undergraduate science and engineering students, illustrate forms of writing-in-the-disciplines pedagogies. It can also be suggested that the content and English language teachers who engaged in their reported pedagogical practices subscribed to the notion that "writing and disciplinary knowledge are embedded in each other" (Donahue, 2011, p. 25). These Chinese forms of writing-in-the-disciplines pedagogies will continue to evolve in the coming years, in light of the paradigm shift from general English to EAP at the tertiary level, local institutional contexts, and their policy-led drive toward creating courses to teach academic norms and academic ethics. Yet it seems hard to foresee an interbraiding of the Chinese writing education and English writing education in the curriculum. Separate bodies of scholarship, connected to separate disciplines, exist; cross-disciplinary fertilization, while desirable, will not be easily achievable. Nevertheless, under the banner of EAP, interdisciplinary collaboration between English language teachers and content teachers can be cultivated, despite potential challenges that come from institutional structures and the traditional separation of their lifeworlds (Li, 2021; Li & Cargill, 2019). Language-content partnership is growing in the context of teaching EAW (or more specifically, English for research publication purposes) to graduate students at Chinese universities (Li & Ma, 2018). Systemic establishment of such partnership, which is likely to be a long-term process, will lead to the growth of "writing to learn" at both undergraduate and graduate levels.

The study reported in this chapter relied on relevant Chinese literature found in the China Academic Journals Full-text Database (CJFD). Needless to say, the numbers of papers in the three strands found to meet the selection criteria do not necessarily correspond proportionately to the amount of relevant work actually going on along these lines in the country. The third strand in particular, on English teachers teaching EAW to science and engineering students, although only represented by eight papers in the study, is taking on a variety of forms as the EAP enterprise continues to boom in China. Two examples are prominent, both concerning events hosted by the China EAP Association (CEAPA) (whose members are mainly EAP teachers) for university students. The first is the 5-Minute Research Presentation (5MRP) contest. The inaugural contest was held in 2018, attracting 871 student contestants from 64 universities. In the competition, student contestants were expected to present on their research in English within 5 minutes.[2] The second example is the International Conference for Students (ICS). The 5th ICS, addressing the theme of "Sustainability and Innovation: Human, Environment, Economy and Development of Technology," was held concurrently (on May 25, 2019) at 16 conference sites, involving over 200 Chinese universities.[3] Informal interviews (conducted by myself and several research students) at one site of the 5th ICS indicated that the university students were keen to enhance their academic communication abilities and receive training from the early years of their study programs. Students' needs seem to point in particular to the value of discipline-oriented research project-based EAW pedagogy, exemplified in the third strand of literature reviewed in the present chapter (Yan & Ge, 2011), and advocated both in the wider Chinese literature (e.g., Zhou, 2011) and sometimes in the English literature on academic writing instruction (Levis & Levis, 2003). The participation of content teachers or supervisors, working in collaboration with language teachers, would obviously be immensely valuable.

Conclusion

Focusing on three strands of published Chinese-language literature, this paper offers only a glimpse of a range of cases of discipline-oriented writing instruction to science and engineering undergraduate students at Chinese universities. I was not

---

2 The 5-Minute Research Presentation (5MRP) competition is modeled after the 3-Minute Thesis Competition. The latter was developed in 2008 by The University of Queensland, Australia and has become popular in many universities around the world.

3 Nearly 7,000 students (including occasional participants from overseas) submitted presentation proposals to the conference. Three forms of presentation (in English) were featured: research paper presentation (20 minutes, including Q & A), research proposal presentation (10 minutes, including Q & A), and poster presentation (via electronic boards at the conference sites).

able to, for example, examine closely textbooks or teaching materials used in the instruction (such information is often lacking in the literature surveyed). Ethnographic research of pedagogies—beyond Townsend's (2002) short research visit at one Chinese university—would be a promising line of investigation to undertake in the future, given that such research in relation to writing in the disciplines seems surprisingly lacking in the Chinese context. At a theoretical level, ethnographies of literacy in local contexts would both shed light on the relationship between the local and the global (Baynham & Prinsloo, 2010; Street, 2004), and feed into the reimagination and practice of writing education from translingual and transnational perspectives (Donahue, 2018; Hall, 2016; Horner & Hall, 2018; You, 2018).

Overall, with this chapter, it is shown that in the Chinese enterprise of teaching writing at the undergraduate level in science and engineering disciplines, both content and language specialists are found to be the bearers of responsibilities; yet there has been little evidence of joint endeavor between the two parties. Nevertheless, such interdisciplinary collaboration is urgently needed and is likely to develop, against the backdrop of the EAP-turn in China. Earlier in the chapter, calls of Chinese authors to introduce the American-style WAC/WID and the American tradition of "write to learn" into China were mentioned (e.g., Li, 2007; Wu, 2013). Yet while "writing to learn" should be enhanced at Chinese universities, it is perhaps EAP, rather than the American-style WAC/WID, that will continue to be the driving force of the process in the years to come. Against this backdrop, it is the right time for the language and content teachers in China to exchange with their international counterparts, to "engage in cross-cultural discussion about teaching and learning" (Townsend, 2002, p. 148).

Acknowledgment

I would like to thank Xiaohao Ma for research assistance.

References

Baynham, Mike & Prinsloo, Mastin. (2009). Introduction: The future of literacy studies. In Mike Baynham & Mastin Prinsloo (Eds.), *The future of literacy studies.* (pp. 1–20). Palgrave Macmillan.

Cai, Jigang (Ed.). (2019). *You tongyong yingyu xiang xueshu yingyu jiaoxue fanshi zhuanyi yanjiu* [Transitioning from general English to academic English]. Shanghai Jiao Tong University Press.

Cai, Jigang & Liao, Leichao. (2010). ELE haishi ESP: Zailun woguo daxue yingyu de fazhan fangxiang [ELE or ESP: More on the orientation of college English teaching in China]. *Waiyu Dianhua Jiaoxue* [Technology Enhanced Foreign Language Education], September, 20–26.

Cheng, An. (2016). EAP at the tertiary level in China: Challenges and possibilities. In K. Hyland & P. Shaw (Eds.), *The Routledge handbook of English for academic purposes* (pp. 97–108). Routledge.

Donahue, Christiane. (2011). Cross-cultural approaches to writing and disciplinarity. In Mary Deane & Peter O'Neill (Eds.), *Writing in the disciplines: Universities into the 21st century* (pp. 14–29). Palgrave Macmillan.

Donahue, Christiane. (2018). Rhetorical and linguistic flexibility: Valuing heterogeneity in academic writing education. In Xiaoye You (Ed.), *Transnational writing education: Theory, history, and practice* (pp. 21–40). Routledge.

Hall, Jonathan. (2016). Encountering difference on U.S. campuses: From "international students" to transnational WAC/WID [Conference paper]. International Writing Across the Curriculum Conference, Ann Arbor, MI. https://www.researchgate.net/publication/304539316_Encountering_Difference_on_US_Campuses_From_International_Students_to_Transnational_WACWID.

Horner, Bruce & Hall, Jonathan (Eds.). (2018). Rewriting disciplines, rewriting boundaries: Transdisciplinary and translingual challenges for WAC/WID [Special issue]. *Across the Disciplines, 15*(3). https://wac.colostate.edu/atd/special/trans/.

Ke, Fang. (2007). Daxue xiezuo ke haiyao jixue *jiaqiang, xiezuoxue yinggai sheli xueweidian—Lin Fei, Xiao Feng fangtanlu* [College writing courses should be strengthened, and degree programs should be established for writing studies—interviews with Lin Fei and Xiao Feng]. *Guangbo Dianshi Daxue Xuebao* [Journal of Radio & TV University], (1), 41–43.

Levis, John M. & Levis, Greta Muller. (2003). A project-based approach to teaching research writing to nonnative writers. *IEEE Transactions on Professional Communication, 46*(3), 210–220.

Li, Binglin. (Ed.) (2009). Kuakecheng de zhongguo yingyu xiezuo jiaoxue yu yanjiu—diwujie zhongguo yingyu xiezuo jiaoxue yu yanjiu guoji yantaohui lunwenji [Teaching and researching EFL writing across the curriculum in China—Proceedings of the 5th International Conference on Teaching & Researching EFL writing in China]. Waiyu Jiaoxue yu Yanjiu Chubanshe [Foreign Language Teaching & Research Press].

Li, Ying. (2007). Zhongguo daxue xiezuo jiaoxue de chongxin dingwei—"*yi xie cu xue jiaoxuefa*" yu xiezuo de renzhi zuoyong [Repositioning the teaching of college writing in China—Training students' thinking ability through the "write to learn pedagogy"]. *Keji Xinxi* [Science & Technology Information], 116–117.

Li, Yongyan. (2021). Collaboration between EAP teachers and content teachers: Insights from the literature for the Chinese context. *International Journal of English for Academic Purposes: Research and Practice, 1*(1), 37–55.

Li, Yongyan & Cargill, Margaret. (2019). Seeking supervisor collaboration in a school of sciences at a Chinese university. In Ken Hyland & Lillian Wong (Eds.), *Specialised English: New directions in ESP and EAP research and practice* (pp. 240–252). Routledge.

Li, Yongyan & Ma, Xiaohao. (2018). Teaching English academic writing to non-English major graduate students at Chinese universities: A review and a transnational vision. In X. You (Ed.), *Transnational writing education: Theory, history, and practice* (pp. 222–243). Routledge.

Liu, Lihua. (2016). Meiguo kuakecheng xiezuo jiaoxue gaige dui zhongguo gaodeng jiaoyu gaige de qishi [Enlightenment of the American WAC movement for Chinese higher education reform]. *Haiwan Yingyu* [Overseas English], 2016 (December), 17–19.

Luo, Yuqing. (2009). Kuaxueke xiezuo lilun yu waiyu jiaoxue lilun de pengzhuang [Connections between WAC theories and foreign language teaching theories]. In Binglin Li (Ed.), *Kuakecheng de zhongguo yingyu xiezuo jiaoxue yu yanjiu—diwujie zhongguo yingyu xiezuo jiaoxue yu yanjiu guoji yantaohui lunwenji* [Teaching and researching EFL writing across the curriculum in China—Proceedings of the 5th International Conference on Teaching & Researching EFL writing in China] (pp. 96–107). Waiyu Jiaoxue yu Yanjiu Chubanshe [Foreign Language Teaching & Research Press].

Qi, Shouhua. (2000). *Xifang xiezuo lilun, jiaoxue yu shijian [Western writing theories, pedagogy and practice]*. Shanghai Education Press.

Street, Brian (2004). Futures of the ethnography of literacy? *Language and Education, 18*(4), 326–330.

Townsend, Marty. (2002). Writing in/across the curriculum at a comprehensive Chinese university. *Language and Learning Across the Disciplines, 5*(3), 134–149. https://doi.org/10.37514/LLD-J.2002.5.3.08.

Townsend, Marty. (2018, December 4–5). Using informal writing to save teachers' time and improve student learning [Pre-conference workshop]. 2nd International Conference on English Across the Curriculum, Hong Kong, China.

Wang, Chuming, Niu, Ruiying & Zhen, Xiaoxiang. (2009). Yi xie zu xue—yixiang yingyu xiezuo jiaoxue gaige de shiyan [Writing to learn—an experiment on reforming English writing instruction]. *Waiyu Jiaoxue yu Yanjiu* [Foreign Language Teaching & Research], *32*(3), 207–212.

Wu, Dan. (2013). *Introducing writing across the curriculum into China: Feasibility and adaptation*. Springer.

You, Xiaoye. (2010). *Writing in the devil's tongue: A history of English composition in China*. Southern Illinois University Press.

You, Xiaoye. (2018). Introduction: Making a transnational turn in writing education. In Xiaoye You (Ed.), *Transnational writing education: Theory, history, and practice* (pp. 1–17). Routledge.

Yu, Wansuo. (2015). "Yi xie cu xue" tigao ligongke boshisheng yingyu keji lunwen xiezuo nengli ["Write to learn" to enhance doctoral science students' ability in writing English research papers]. *Xuewei yu Yanjiusheng Jiaoyu* [Academic degrees and Graduate Education], 4, 41–45.

Zhang, Ailing. (2008). Daxue xiezuo de xueke bianyuanhua yu shehui xiezuo rencai xique [The marginalization of college writing courses and the scarcity of writing talents in the society]. *Suihua Xueyuan Xuebao* [Journal of Suihua University], *28*(6), 10–12.

Zhang, Hongjun. (2011). Yi xie cu xue: Fei yingyu zhuanye xuesheng xiechangfa jiaoxue shiyan yanjiu [Write to learn: Length approach for non-English majors]. *Changchun Jiaoyu Xueyuan Xuebao* [Journal of Changchun Education Institute], *27*(4), 96–97.

Zheng, Ying & Cheng, Liying. (2008). Test review: College English Test (CET) in China. *Language Testing, 25*(3), 408–417.

Zhou, Mei. (2011). Lun xiangmu qudong xia yanjiusheng yingyu lunwen xiezuo nengli de peiyang [Project-driven approach to developing English academic writing performance among graduate students]. *Xuewei Yu Yanjiusheng Jiaoyu* [Academic Degrees and Graduate Education], *3*, 41–46.

Zhu, Yuezhen. (2004). *Yingyu keji xueshu lunwen—zhuanxie yu tougao* [English scientific writing—Composition and submission]. Central China Science &Technology University.

Zhuang, Qinghua. (2014). "Daxue yuwen" huo ke xiang "Xueke xiezuo" zhuanxing—yi meguo Kangnai'er Daxue de FWS wei jiejian fanli [College Chinese may re-orient to writing in disciplines—Cornell University's FWS as a reference]. *Fujian Shifan Daxue Xuebao* [Journal of Fujian Normal University], *4*, 166–172.

Appendix 1. Content Teachers Teaching Chinese Scientific Paper Writing (20 papers)

Bian, Xihui, Tan, Xiaoyao, Liu, Peng & Chu, Yuanyuan. (2016). "Keji lunwen xiezuo" kecheng jiaoxue chutan [Explorations in teaching a course on "scientific paper writing"]. *Jiaoyu Jiaoxue Luntan* [Education Teaching Forum], *34*, 151–152.

Chen, Libo & Huang, Jiangli. (2012). Dui "keji lunwen yu gongcheng sheji gailun" kecheng de jidian gaige [On the reform of the course "scientific paper writing and introduction to engineering design"]. *Jilin Huagong Xueyuan Xuebao* [Journal of Jilin Institute of Chemical Technology], *29*(12), 21–23.

Gao, Xin & Zhang, Baojun. (2016). "Keji lunwen xiezuo" kecheng jiaoxue gaige dui tigao benkesheng biye lunwen zhiliang de jiji zuoyong chutan [Exploring the positive effects of a "scientific paper writing" course on the quality of undergraduates' graduation thesis]. *Jiaoyu Jiaoxue Luntan* [Education Teaching Forum], *37*, 92–93.

Guo, Jianming, Su, Shulan & Shang, Erxin. (2017). Keyan sheji xiezuo yu zhongyaoxue zonghe shiyan kecheng ronghexing jiaoxue sikao [Integrating the teaching of research design writing and of experiments in traditional Chinese pharmacology]. *Zhongguo Zhongyiyao Xiandai Yuancheng Jiaoyu* [Chinese Medicine Modern Distance Education], *15*(3), 4–6.

Han, Xiaoqiang & Yang, Desong. (2016). Zhiwu baohu zhuanye "keji lunwen xiezuo" kecheng jiaoxue gaige tansuo [Explorations in reforming a course on "scientific paper writing" in plant protection studies]. *Keji Zhanwang* [Technology Outlook], *18*, 197–198.

Jia, Zhixun & Zhuo, Yajuan. (2016). Keji lunwen xiezuo zai zhuanye kecheng jiaoxue zhong de shijian [Teaching scientific paper writing in a content course]. *Jiaoyu Jiaoxue Luntan* [Education Teaching Forum], (1), 82–83.

Lei, Zongming & Chen, Jie. (1998). *"Keji lunwen xiezuo" yu "zuanjing xingongyi xinjishu" shixing lianhe jiaoxue gaige de changshi* [Integrating "scientific paper writing" with "introduction to new developments in drilling technologies"]. *Heilongjiang Shiyou Gaodeng Zhuanke Xuexiao Xuebao* [Journal of the Heilongjiang Petroleum Institute], *1*(5), 93–94.

Li, Bo, Xiao, Hui, Xu, Wenfeng, Liu, Xue, Yang, Xiaoling & Liao, Xiaoling. (2015). Cailiao zhuanye kaishe keji lunwen xiezuoke de "sixing" tantao—Yi Chongqing Keji Xueyuan wei li [Exploring a "four-dimensional" model in designing a course on scientific paper writing in materials science: A case of the Chongqing University of Science and Technology]. *Chongqing Keji Xueyuan Xuebao (Shehui Kexue Ban)* [Journal of Chongqing University of Science and Technology] (Social Sciences Edition), *10*, 76–78.

Li, Ximei. (2017). Benkesheng kaishe "Keji lunwen xiezuo" kecheng de biyaoxing ji jiaoxue moshi chutan [Offering a "scientific paper writing" course to undergraduate students: Necessity and feasibility]. *Keji Chuangxin Daobao* [Science & Technology Innovation Herald], (1), 253–254.

Liang, Yonghou, Liang, Chunxia, Xu, Min & Wang, Gui. (2016). Benke yuanxiao keji lunwen xiezuo kecheng de mokuaihua jiaoxue fangfa tantao [Designing modules in teaching a scientific paper writing course for undergraduate students]. *Heilongjiang Xumu Shouyi* [Heilongjiang Animal Science and Veterinary Medicine], *12*, 259–261.

Liu, Changjian, Ma, Gaofeng & Zhang, Xiguang. (2016). Cehui gongcheng zhuanye benkesheng keji lunwen xiezuo nengli peiyang de shijian yu sikao [Cultivating undergraduate students' ability in scientific paper writing in Surveying and Engineering]. *Gaojiao Luntan* [Higher Education Forum], *7*, 46–50.

Liu, Youqin, Yan, Yun & Xu, Yuehua. (2014). *Yingyong wei daoxiang de "Huaxue wenxian jiansuo ji lunwen xiezuo" jiaogai tansuo* [Pedagogical reforms in an application-oriented course on "Literature Searching and Paper Writing in Chemistry"]. *Neimenggu Shiyou Huagong* [Inner Mongolia Petrochemical Engineering], *8*, 89–91.

Sun, Xiaoguang & Jing, Peng. (2021). Benkesheng xueshu lunwen xiezuo peixun de shijian yu fansi [Academic writing training for undergraduates: Practice and reflection]. *Jiaoyu Jiaoxue Luntan* [Education and Teaching Forum], *33*, 5–8.

Xing, Hucheng & Jie, Yucheng. (2014). Caoye kexue zhuanye keji lunwen xiezuo kecheng de jianshe ji jiaoxue gaige tansuo [Designing a course on scientific paper writing in pratacultural science]. *Shidai Jiaoyu* [Time Education], *21*, 202–204.

Xu, Jie & Yang, Jihe. (2012). Keji lunwen xiezuo kecheng jiaoxue zhi shijian daoxiang moshi de jiangou [Creating a practice-oriented model for teaching scientific paper writing]. *Jiaoyu Yu Jiaoxue Yanjiu* [Education and Teaching Research], *26*(12), 93–95.

Yan, Xuxian & Sun, Guoqiang. (2012). "San jieduan" Kecheng lunwen jiaoxue moshi tansuo—Yi benke "xitong gongcheng" kecheng jiaoxue wei li [Building a "three-phase" model of teaching course paper writing: In the context of a "systems engineering" course for undergraduates]. *Gaodeng Caijing Jiaoyu Yanjiu* [Journal of Higher Education Finance], *15*(3), 33–37.

Zhang, Fangfang. (2016). Daxuesheng "keji lunwen xiezuo" jiaogai tansuo [Exploring pedagogical reforms in teaching scientific paper writing to undergraduates]. *Shandong Huagong* [Shandong Chemical Engineering], *45*, 128–129.

Zhang, Ling, Zhang, Kemeng & Cai, Jianzhong. (2000). Kexue suzhi keyan xunlian keji xiezuo [Academic literacy, research training, and scientific writing]. *Xi'an Jiaotong Daxue Xuebao* [Journal of Xi'an Jiaotong University] (Social Sciences Edition), *S1*, 28–29+71.

Zhang, Wenjing, Wu, Liquan, Wang, Chengyu, Ma, Shangyu & He, Haibin. (2016). Anli yantao xing jiaoxue fangshi zai keji lunwen xiezuo kecheng zhong de yingyong

[Applying a case study approach to teaching scientific paper writing]. *Anhui Nongye Kexue* [Journal of Anhui Agricultural Science], *44*, 233–234.
Zhang, Yuanxin & Ge, Yakun. (2016). Shengwu jishu zhuanye keji lunwen xiezuo kecheng jiaoxue gaige tansuo [Pedagogical reforms in a course on scientific paper writing in biotechnology]. *Keji Zhanwang* [Technology Outlook], *33*, 178.

Appendix 2. Content Teachers Facilitating Their Students' English Writing Ability (six papers)

Chen, Yuelong. (2003). Diqiu huaxue benkesheng zhuanye yingyu jiaoxue de ji dian tihui [Reflections on teaching specialist English to undergraduates in geochemistry]. *Zhongguo Dizhi Jiaoyu* [Chinese Geological Education], *2*, 31–33.
Li, Hualan. (2011). Huaxue zhuanye keji lunwen xiezuo shuangyu jiaoxue de shijian yu tansuo [Teaching a bilingual course of scientific paper writing in chemistry]. *Xin Kecheng Yanjiu* [New Curriculum Studies], *6*, 23–25.
Liu, Debao. (2015). Yejin zhuanye yingyu jiaoxue zhong de keji lunwen xiezuo nengli peiyang [Cultivating scientific paper writing ability in teaching English for metallurgy]. *Tianjin Yejin* [Tianjin Metallurgy], *5*, 63–66.
Liu, Xiangli. (2012). "Duoyangxing xiezuo" zai xinjian benke yuanxiao shuangyu jiaoxue zhong de yingyong [Using "diverse forms of writing" in bilingual instruction at newly founded teaching institutions]. *Henan Huagong* [Henan Chemical Engineering], *29*, 62–64.
Wang, Guifang, Mo, Wei & Ma, Shaojian. (2009). Jiehe zhuanye tedian peiyang xuesheng de yingyu zonghe nengli—Kuangwu ziyuan gongcheng zhuanye yingyu kecheng jiaoxue gaige yu shijian [Discipline-integrated English proficiency development: Teaching specialist English to students in mineral resources engineering]. *Guangxi Daxue Xuebao* [Journal of Guangxi University] (Philosophy and Social Sciences Edition)], *31*(supplementary issue), 118–119.
Zhang, Yuanfu & Jiang, Zaixing. (2010). Yi keji lunwen xiezuo wei daoxiang de zhuanye waiyu jiaoxue moshi jiangou [Specialist English instruction with an orientation to teaching scientific paper writing]. *Zhongguo Dizhi Jiaoyu* [Chinese Geological Education], *2*, 112–114.

Appendix 3. English Teachers Teaching English Academic Writing to Science/Engineering Students (eight papers)

Liu, Bin. (2010). Xueshu yongtu yingyu xiezuo kecheng sheji [Course design for college EAP writing]. *Zhongguo ESP Yanjiu* [Chinese Journal of ESP], *1*, 136–143.
Teng, Yanjiang. (2016). "Xueshu duxie suyang" fanshi yu xueshu yingyu xiezuo kecheng sheji ["Academic literacies" and academic English writing course design]. *Dangdai Waiyu Yanjiu* [Contemporary Foreign Languages Studies], *1*, 41–47.

Wang, Li. (2013). Guocheng xiezuofa zai IMRAD yixue yingyu lunwen xiezuo jiaoxue zhong de yingyong [Applying a process-based approach to teaching the IMRAD model in medical English paper writing]. *Shanghai Zhongyiyao Daxue Xuebao [Acta Universitatis Traditionis Medicalis Sinensis Pharmacologiaeque Shanghai]*, *27*(6), 10–12.

Yan, Jin & Ge, Yafei. (2011). Dixue benkesheng xueshu yingyu xiezuo kecheng tansuoxing yanjiu [Teaching academic English writing to undergraduates in geology]. *Hubei Di'er Shifan Xueyuan Xuebao* [Journal of Hubei University of Education], *28*(11), 105–107.

Yang, Feng. (2013). Yixiang jiyu xueshu yingyu xiezuo jiaoxue de xingdong yanjiu [An action research study teaching academic English writing]. *Zhongguo Waiyu Jiaoyu [Foreign Language Education in China]*, *6*(4), 32–41.

Yang, Liping & Han, Guang. (2012). Jiyu xiangmushi xuexi moshi de daxue yingyu xueshu xiezuo jiaoxue shizheng yanjiu [A project-based approach to teaching English academic writing]. *Waiyujie [Foreign Language World]*, *5*, 8–16.

Yao, Jing & Han, Guang. (2016). Feiyingyu zhuanye benkesheng xueshu yingyu xiezuo jiaoxue shijian yu sikao [Teaching academic English writing to non-English major undergraduates]. *Kaoshi yu Pingjia (Daxue Yingyu Jiaoyan Ban)* [Examination and Evaluation (College English Teaching and Research)], *2*, 70–73.

Yi, Lan. (2015*)*. "Tongyong yingyu" zhuanxiang "xueshu yingyu"—Jiaoyu guojihua beijing xia de daxue yingyu jiaoxue gaige yu shijian [From EGP to EAP: College English teaching reform and practice in the context of internationalization of higher education]. *Chongqing Shifan Daxue Xuebao* [Journal of Chongqing Normal University] (Philosophy and Social Sciences Edition], *6*, 74–81.

Dimensions of Transnational Writing Exchange: An Exploratory Approach

Mohammad Shamsuzzaman
NORTH SOUTH UNIVERSITY, BANGLADESH

পশ্চিমি আজি খুলিয়াছে দ্বার, সেথা হতে সবে আনে উপহার, দিবে আর নিবে, মিলাবে মিলিবে যাবে না ফিরে, এই ভারতের মহামানবের সাগরতীরে! – রবীন্দ্রনাথ ঠাকুর, ১৯১০	All bring gifts from everywhere Giving and taking, mingling and meeting They won't ever return And will remain in Indian shores Magnanimous souls all! – Rabindranath Tagore, 1910[1]

When Tagore (1910) envisioned and welcomed a transnational collaboration between the West and the Indian sub-continent in 1910, the latter had already been a British colony for 57 years. Tagore was aware of and resistant to the British Empire's unidirectional vision for transnational exchange of knowledge. A British politician, Thomas Babington Macaulay, in his "Minute on Indian Education" in 1835 brazenly lauded the superiority of the English language to such local vernaculars as Arabic and Sanskrit. He claimed, "We have to educate a people who cannot at present be educated by means of their mother-tongue. We must teach them some foreign language" (p. 349). And the "foreign language" in that colonial context was the English language. He also explained the purpose of educating "a class of persons, Indian in blood and color, but English in taste, in opinions, in morals, and in intellect" (p. 352). English as a language during and since the colonial era in the Indian subcontinent was somewhat predatory, and the promotion of English as well as the knowledge in English was politically and ideologically contentious. Given the emergence of the English language in the Indian subcontinent, it is apparently a tool that isolates and excludes rather than connects and collaborates. The deduction here is that any transnational collaboration mediated through the English language in the Indian subcontinent is always, already dubious–perhaps ineffective.

Despite its political and ideological moorings, the English language continued to reign supreme post-colonially in the Indian subcontinent because of its intellectual,

---

[1] I am sincerely grateful to Fakrul Alam, UGC Professor, Department of English, University of Dhaka, Bangladesh, for translating Tagore.

DOI: https://doi.org/10.37514/ATD-B.2023.1527.2.11

social, and economic potential. The promotion and the consumption of the language, however, assumed a unidirectional trajectory, which has critical bearing for composition studies in the Indian subcontinent in general, and in Bangladesh, in particular. One of the oldest universities in the Indian subcontinent, the University of Dhaka, was launched in 1921 with only twelve academic departments (Rahman, 1981). English was one of the twelve academic departments. Until 1985, the intellectual activities of the department used to revolve only around literature (Alam, 2011). In 1985, the department started to offer an MA in English language testing (ELT). In the meantime, though, literature became the default discipline of English studies in Bangladesh. The physical and intellectual infrastructures of English studies concentrated so much around literature that literature dominated—perhaps diminished—all other branches of English studies in Bangladesh. Besides physical and intellectual infrastructures, the popular culture in general is also complicit in preferring literature to the other subdisciplines of English, composition studies in particular.

Bangladesh has a sovereign writing culture, but unlike in North America, writing is considered as a gift, not a learned skill in Bangladesh. The notion of writing as a gift is always uncontested here in Bangladesh given that the writing icons of Bangla literature such as Nobel Laureate Rabindranath Tagore and the national poet of Bangladesh, Kazi Nazrul Islam were autodidacts. They hardly had any formal education, let alone learned the craft of writing as an outcome of schooling or training in a sustained period. They were poets, and the genres of writing they practiced and excelled in were so-called creative writing. Therefore, Bangladesh is steeped in a Dionysian or creative writing (Calonne, 2006) culture. Shamsuzzaman (2014) claims that, in such a culture, writing is considered so inductive and idiosyncratic that it is not open to analyses and intervention, let alone teaching. As a result, the steps and stages of writing reified in the North American discipline of composition studies are culturally contested—even inappropriate—for conceiving and constructing writing that the culture admires. Because of the cultural predisposition toward writing that requires no teaching, there is hardly any intellectual motivation to institutionalize the teaching and learning of writing in Bangladesh. Composition studies could not occupy any space in the landscape of English studies in Bangladesh yet as such.

Of course, the (lack of formal) education of Tagore and Islam does not pit composition studies vis-à-vis writing in South Asia—and Bangladesh, in particular—to establish a sovereign writing culture. Neither is the perspective—writing is a gift—unique to Bangladesh, for there is a strong view and long tradition in the West that writing arises from individual geniuses, as Francis-Noel Thomas and Mark Turner (1994) claim about French classic writing culture, for example. Yet the existential differences between composition studies and the cultural framing of writing in Bangladesh are critical. Composition studies mandates a specific way of thinking and languaging. It advocates for prose that is more reasoned and objective than intuitive and subjective. It values prose that is top-down, linear, and sequential. The discipline stipulates the mechanical, semantic, syntactic, and rhetorical options and restrictions of prose, and it expects writers to learn and follow those options and restrictions. It cultivates writers' voice, autonomy, and creativity within a framework of convention. The assumption that underpins the discipline is that writing is a skill that can be acquired, and that the acquisition of writing skill presupposes instruction. In South Asia including Bangladesh, on the other hand, the teaching and learning of writing has traditionally revolved around the conviction that writing is a natural endowment rather than an intellectual achievement. Writing is not structurally rigid. Writing, instead, is perceptions transcribed. Because perception is idiosyncratic, writing always tends to be atypical. Conventions do not dictate the production of writing. Neither does instruction contribute to creating a writer as Canagarajah (2001) contends that explicit teaching of writing was not a component of his education in Sri Lanka. Writing in South Asia is apparently indirect, layered, and subtle. The process of writing is not artificially segmented, and writing transpires in a non-linear, non-sequential way. It has its own grammar, unlike the discipline of composition studies. This apparently accounts for why teaching writing is not one of the active agendas of English studies in Bangladesh.

However, after the 1990s the paradigm of English studies in Bangladesh seems to have been shifting apace. The government of Bangladesh sanctioned the establishment of private universities in 1992 in Bangladesh (Alam, 2011), and when the first private university started its operation in 1993 based on the North American model of education (Shamsuzzaman et al., 2014), it first used the word *composition* as GED courses offered by the Department of English and Modern Languages prerequisite for undergraduate programs across disciplines. Following the lead of the first private university in Bangladesh, the private universities around the country which were launched subsequently incorporated some composition courses with such various titles as EAP, FYC, and FC (Foundation Courses). Arguably in 1993, the word *composition* was included in the landscape of English studies in Bangladesh. To date, though, it is a discrete academic subject. It is a "service course" pigeonholed into the roster of courses offering students foundational academic skills. Composition studies lacks disciplinary autonomy, in that no university in Bangladesh offers BA or MA in composition or writing studies yet. The marginal inclusion of *composition* in English studies in Bangladesh signaled, nonetheless, the diversity of English studies following the establishment of private universities when the focus of English studies in Bangladesh shifted from literature to ELT (Alam, 2011). Perhaps because of the ontological tensions between English literature and composition studies that Elbow (1996) discusses, the promotion of ELT somewhat seemed conducive to the development of composition studies in Bangladesh.

Globalization—and its cognate, internationalization—also seems to be a favorable force for composition studies in Bangladesh. As it seems, globalization pertinent to writing studies leans more toward Tagore's vision of transnational collaboration than Macaulay's version of linguistic and cultural colonization. Because of the arguments and activism by some scholars—Suresh Canagarajah, for example—the geopolitics of academic writing is fiercely contested to diversify and democratize it further. Writing studies is becoming more inclusive and expansive. The discursive patterns and policies are more divergent and equitable these days to benefit scholars and their affiliated institutions across contexts. An inevitable outcome of such undercurrent of writing studies is apparently transnational collaboration happening around the globe including Bangladesh. Universities in Bangladesh—private universities, in particular—have been vying for international space and prestige in recent years. They have been attempting to recruit more and more international students, and to cater to their writing needs at universities based on a North American model, universities must draw upon the knowledge base of composition studies. To globalize the universities, the administrators also motivate faculty members to publish in reputable international outlets. Publication in such outlets presupposes strong writing skills. Administrators and stakeholders are leveraging resources to establish writing centers at universities around the country. Composition professional are also sought-after in Bangladesh considering that "writing strategies developed in composition and rhetoric departments of the US must also be incorporated" (Alam, 2011) in Bangladesh. Under such circumstances, universities in Bangladesh often invite and sponsor foreign scholars—composition professionals, in particular—for transnational collaboration, though most of those initiatives seem like what Christiane Donahue (2009) characterizes as "intellectual tourism." However, the collaboration between North South University, Bangladesh, and one of the State Universities of New York is apparently a different one because of its unique vision and unyielding commitment to transnational collaboration. Sharma and Hammond in this anthology detail some of the dimensions and benefits of this transnational collaboration, both as participants and contributors.

Class to Class Collaboration

Back in 2018, two academics from one of the State Universities of New York, US, visited Bangladesh to conduct a two-day long workshop on professional development of faculty members for the Department of English and Modern Languages at North South University, Bangladesh. At the end of the workshop, an MoU was signed between North South University, Bangladesh, and Stony Brook University, US. Since then, the engagement between North South University and Stony Brook is current in research, pedagogy, and professional development. Throughout 2019, some of the faculty members from the Department of English and Modern Languages from North South University, Bangladesh, participated in a weekly meeting moderated by a faculty member from the State University of New York. The outcome was exceptional—some teachers professionally developed remarkably; some teachers published in peer-reviewed journals, and some teachers advocated for developing further resources for both students and teachers at the universities across these two contexts. We initiated and continued with this transnational collaboration to demonstrate that despite critical context-specific constraints such as class overload, limited resources in instruction and research as well as institutional policies and politics driven by market forces, effective transnational collaboration can potentially empower faculty members.

As an extension of the engagement already underway between these two contexts, I and my counterpart in the US embarked on a class-to-class collaboration between two undergraduate classes at North South University, Bangladesh and at one of the State Universities of New York in spring, 2019. We paired up 33 students from Bangladesh with 33 students from New York. One student from Bangladesh was linked with another student in the US on Google Docs, where they could post their essays for their peer to review and to provide feedback. On our course website, we posted a short video vignette to demonstrate the procedures to post their essays. We conducted a workshop across the contexts on a sample essay to help students apply the rubric that we designed.

Peer Review Rubric

The class-to-class collaboration fundamentally revolved around guiding students to write essays in order to have feedback from their counterparts situated either in Dhaka for the students in New York, or in New York for the students in Dhaka. As composition professionals, both of us were aware of the affective and intellectual blindspots of peer feedback. We, therefore, designed a peer review rubric (see Appendix A) to help them avoid making insensitive and irrelevant comments. We wanted them to comment on five specific areas of essays from their peers: context, idea, research, perspectives, and language and presentation. Two drafts of the essays they wrote both in Dhaka and New York, were also specific to the prompts (see Appendix B) that we created. We were not teaching identical courses across these to contexts. That accounted for why our essay prompts were different. We wanted to align our essay prompts to the courses we were teaching.

Features of Some of the Essays Submitted

As I juxtaposed the essays of my students in Dhaka with the essays of my colleague's students in New York, I noticed some common patterns across two transnational contexts.[2] Compared to the essays of my students from Dhaka, the essays of my colleague's student in New York seemed to look more formal given that they were properly indented, spaced, paginated, punctuated, and referenced. On all these fronts, most of my students seemed to have fallen short. It was a moment when I experienced déjà vu. I remembered the first paper that I submitted as a graduate student in the US at a state university in California. While I knew about all these visual dimensions of formal academic discourse, I was inadvertently disinterested in these dimensions of writing. I was never taught about the mechanics of writing the way it is taught in the US. I did teach my students about these visual aspects of writing, but they seemed to have been culturally so conditioned—as I was—that instruction was not strong enough to disabuse them of their cultural perceptions and conventions of writing. My teacher in the US wrote at the end of the paper, "Go to the Writing Center." I did and incorporated the visual codes of academic discourse practiced in North America. I could, however, never write such a comment on my students' papers, because the university I worked at did not have a writing center.

All my students in Dhaka, Bangladesh, were second language writers of English. Compared to the students in New York, who were mostly native speakers, resident immigrants, and multilingual foreign students, my students were the basic second language writers of the English language. And the basic second language writers in English in Bangladesh are indeed basic given that Bangladesh "is a mono-lingual nation-state and does not need a second language for internal communication" (Islam, 2001, p. 19). The writing practices they had in their native language, Bangla, would hardly complement their skills in writing in English, for the conventions of academic writing in English were incompatible to conventions of writing in Bangla. Despite having had feedback from me as well as from their peers in the US, their essays were riddled with fractured syntax, inappropriate shifting between tenses and pronouns, awkward lexical choices, abrupt shifting from one sentence to another, from one paragraph to another, and from one viewpoint to another, and comma splices. Compared to their counterparts in the US, they preferred short sentences and compound to complex sentences; they used simple diction, non-figurative language; they avoided passive voice; and most of their paragraphs were underdeveloped. Tony Silva (1997) claims that these are exactly some of the characteristics of basic second language writers. While some of their counterparts in the US fell short on all these fronts, the frequency of these errors was not as usual with them as with the Bangladeshi second-language writers.

Perhaps the most critical differences between these two groups of students was that the essays of the Bangladeshi students were not rhetorically as fine-grained as was expected of academic discourse, whereas most if not all of their counterparts in the US demonstrated rhetorical awareness. They maintained a formal tone and texture;

---

2   We have followed formal protocols across the contexts to collect data.

avoided first person; consulted sources to locate and incorporate information pertinent to their topics; maintained cohesion between sentences and paragraphs; and seemed to have a sense of audience. Besides incorporating these general rhetorical features, several of the essays from the students in New York were outstanding, and they read like dissertations. Their essays embodied typical hallmarks of academic discourse such as critical intelligence, factual diligence, and semantic sophistication as Steven Pinker claims (2014). Despite some outstanding essays, several essays from the students in New York were truly what Maxine Hairston (1984) calls "blue sky papers." They padded their prose with jargons, pretentious diction, and unduly complex sentences to impress their reader, that is, the teacher. Students from Bangladesh, on the other hand, wrote narrative, but their prose was so much spattered with "I" and "we" that it was more "egocentric" (Lunsford, 1980) than academic. They did not seem to have any sense of audience. They did not seem to have consulted the sources to locate information pertinent to their topic despite the explicit instruction that they had to align their narrative with some theories. They generalized and personalized their narratives so much that occasionally they flouted the convention of objective academic discourse. Also, contractions abounded in their prose. Apparently, these are features of so-called creative writing, and because Bangladesh is predominantly a creative writing culture, their writing style was culturally compatible.

Never do I, however, default to the perception that hailing from a so-called creative writing culture is akin to lacking critical intelligence, factual diligence, and semantic sophistication. I appreciated some of the rigidly structured essays from the students in New York as much as I enjoyed some of the essays from students in Dhaka with unique and arbitrary turns and twists. The essays from both contexts suggested that such convenient labels as creative and critical are misleading and can complicate appreciation of writing that transpires across contexts. If writing does what it needs to do, its linguistic features and cerebral patterns must not restrain readers from appreciating as well as enjoying it. Such writing warrants no judgment about writers' intelligence and linguistic sensibility. When detailing the features of good writing, Sword (2012) argues that discourse has never been uniform and stable across disciplines. Neither is, of course, discourse across cultures. Students from Dhaka and New York wrote to order, when they were conditioned by culture(s) and shaped the teaching of writing. I learned an important lesson from this transnational collaboration as I was reading the essays: writing professionals must be open to diversity and change as they teach and evaluate writing.

Peer Feedback

There are both quantitative and qualitative differences in feedback provided to the peers between these two contexts. As I investigated the feedback provided by the students of my colleague in the US, I discovered that they all provided marginal comments, and none of them cared about providing a summative comment. On the other hand, none of the Bangladeshi students provided any marginal comment. They provided only summative comments. Despite my instruction and insistence, some of my students in Bangladesh even refrained from providing any feedback at all. I had the apprehension that my students here in Bangladesh were overwhelmed by the detailed and extensive feedback they received from the students from my colleague in the US. The peer feedback practice may have renewed and reinforced the native speaker (NS)-non-native speaker (NNS) dichotomy, when native speakers are the default models of linguistic perfection. My students praised their counterparts in the US, and hardly had any critical suggestions to fine-tune their essays further. My colleague's students in the US also praised my students in Bangladesh for their research and writing skills, but they provided extensive feedback to improve the quality of their writing and content. While feedback in general is a "thorny issue" (Raimes, 1991), it is even thornier in transnational contexts given the differences in intellectual, cultural, and linguistic dynamics involved. As they provide feedback on each other's writing, they do not draw from the same intellectual, cultural, and linguistic repertoires. They are physically disembodied and are innocent to the debates and discussions of peer feedback. They are expected to accomplish something they hardly have had adequate experiential and professional capital with. Peer feedback in transnational contexts as such is more complex and chaotic than peer feedback in general.

The feedback that my students received from their U.S. counterparts ranged from language to style to mechanics to rhetoric, which Appendix C demonstrates.

Problematizing Peer Feedback in Transnational Context

Peer feedback is undoubtedly one of the critical aspects of composition pedagogy, but this transnational empirical engagement demonstrates that no assumption and instruction can predict how students will act and react while providing feedback on their peers. The students in the US assume that there is a generalized ESL student despite Raimes' (1991) insistence that there is no entity as such. Therefore, the students from the US assume the persona of acting experts for their Bangladesh counterparts, who, they seemed to believe, are mere linguistic creatures because they are meshed in the syntax, semantics, and mechanics of the English language. Their thoughts and language were hardly transparent and formal. Apparently, there is merit in such an assumption regarding most basic ESL writers across contexts; essentially, however, this assumption is seriously problematic to appreciate the complexity of writing in Bangladesh. Writing is culturally conceived as an autonomous endeavor, and writing transpires beyond such binaries as right or wrong, or correct or incorrect. More importantly, writers are not culturally considered as fallible creatures. Writers are entitled to visions, inconsistencies, and idiosyncrasies. Unless someone has considerable cultural capital pertinent to conceiving and constructing texts in Bangladesh, she might not appreciate the nuances of texts written by Bangladeshi writers in the English language. To provide feedback in an informed fashion on texts written by Bangladeshi students, teachers—in this context, peers—must understand the primacy of the local over the global.

The errors identified by the students in the US in the texts of their Bangladeshi peers are apparently performance errors rising from such factors as unfamiliar tasks, topics, audiences, and genres (Matsuda, 2006). Two of these factors—audiences and genres—are critical criteria in understating the theories and philosophies of writing in Bangladesh. Audiences for writing in Bangladesh are not apparently taxonomized as they are in North America, and writing is appreciated independent of preconceived principles and parameters. Writers are agentive, as are the readers. Such a culture renders the assessment of writing redundant, which feedback underpins. Writing that stands the test of time touches and transforms the audiences, who are connoisseurs of texts. They are not critics of texts. Writing that does not conform with and add to such a legacy generally does not endure. In a culture such as this, no one is conditioned to separate so-called good writing from so-called bad writing by looking into its structural and mechanical properties. This may account for why Bangladeshi peers did not provide any feedback between the margins specific to structure, mechanics, and language contrary to their counterparts in the US. Peer feedback, as it happened with the students in the US, is a learned activity, which is critically informed by a sense of audience. For the Bangladeshi students, peer feedback is low stake commentary (Canagarajah, 2006) hardly informed by a sense of audience.

An arbitrary demarcation of writing between pragmatic (EDNA-expository, descriptive, narrative, and argumentative) and aesthetics (PDF-poetry, fiction, drama) so widespread in North America does not capture the complex writing culture that permeates the landscape of writing in Bangladesh. Genre is an abstraction that hardly has any real-life application beyond academic contexts in Bangladesh. The genre of writing that they call essay in North America is locally called "প্রবন্ধ." The Bangladeshi students in this study wrote a "প্রবন্ধ" in the English language, which is structurally, conceptually, and linguistically different from its North American version. A typical North American essay, as Robert Kaplan (1966) seemed to have claimed, is top down, linear, and sequential, where the language is formal, hedged, and objective. While Kaplan overgeneralized the hybridity and complexities of writing cultures across languages and cultures, his assumption that composing is a cultural construct merits careful consideration. In Bangladesh, for example, "প্রবন্ধ" is another form of story without plots and characters with a fair amount of intuition, subjectivity, and peculiar diction. It has its own character and conventions that combine creative abandon and rational control. It doesn't fit in the mold of any genre; it, instead, falls in a hybrid genre. Providing feedback on a "প্রবন্ধ" with the criteria suitable for an essay ignores "the need to attend to and engage local, institutional, and national differences in thinking about writing and writing instruction" (Horner et al., 2011). Likewise, the Bangladeshi students who are mostly innocent about the North styles and structures of essay, did not have the linguistic and intellectual capital to provide effective feedback on the writing of their U.S. counterparts. Therefore, despite their best intentions, peers from both the sides provided feedback that was not completely responsive to the complex cultures of writing both of these contexts steeped into and had preference for.

Fakrul Alam (2011) claims that most writing teachers in Bangladesh are not writers themselves. Virtually any teacher is a writing teacher in Bangladesh if she has some advanced studies in one of the subdisciplines of English studies. This relegates the instruction of writing to a lesser light position in Bangladesh to align writing studies with the "low status of writing instruction in the modern university (Horner & Trimbur, 2002). What is unique about writing instruction in Bangladesh is that most writing instructors in Bangladesh enact only the linguistic dimension of composition pedagogy. The rhetorical dimension of composition pedagogy is all but missing. What passes off as composition pedagogy in Bangladesh is explicit grammar instruction, and most writing teachers are but error hunters. Peer feedback is always an imitation—and sometimes, extension—of instructor feedback on students' writing. Besides language, rhetoric is critical to composition pedagogy in North America. The North American peers while providing feedback on their Bangladeshi counterparts always indicated shortcomings in cohesion, transition, and flow on top of grammar. The Bangladeshi peers were almost non-responsive to the rhetorical dimensions of texts of their counterparts in the US.

What is apparently puzzling when it comes to providing feedback by the Bangladesh peers on their counterparts in the US is absence of any feedback on language at all, even though the linguistic feedback is almost always the only feedback they receive in Bangladesh. This is an interesting twist that perhaps echoes across contexts regarding any transnational collaboration. The transnational collaborations that transpire between the Anglophone and non-Anglophone countries are incongruous on many grounds. Canagarajah (2006) claims that all speech events are language games, but the rules of the games are not identical across contexts for participants. The Bangladeshi participants in this study, for example, knew that their counterparts were native speakers of English. They are from the US—the site of intellectual, economic, and political prowess—and they are some of the best students attending one of the state universities in the US. The Bangladeshi peers are already overwhelmed by the superiority of their U.S. counterparts. Therefore, instead of a critical approach to the texts, they had a colonized engagement with the texts. As such, while providing feedback on the texts of their counterparts in the US, they assumed the persona of active cheerleaders. They heaped gratuitous praise on their counterparts in the US. Apparently, then, any transnational collaboration, including this one, has profound psychological implications that transcend language as well as the restrictions and options of providing peer feedback.

Given the quantity and quality of feedback provided by the peers across these two contexts, this transnational engagement apparently renews and reinforces the ontological differences between "prototypical students" (Matsuda, 2006) in the US and so-called basic writers of multi-lingual and multi-cultural origins. The basic Bangladeshi writers in this study, however, are not basic thinkers. They all can think critically and write coherently—as expected of typical undergraduate students across contexts—in their first language, বাংলা, (Bangla). The fractured syntax, slipshod semantics as well as underdeveloped and incoherent paragraphs of the Bangladeshi peers in this study do not straightforwardly imply that they are cognitively deficient compared to their counterparts in the US. They are victims of what Kasia Kietlinska (2006) calls "double hats problem," when language learners are performing writers. The English language is a compulsory component in all the stages of formal education in Bangladesh: primary (grades 1–5), secondary (grades 6–10), higher secondary (grades 11–12), and tertiary (university education). Until tertiary education, English is just a subject and its learning and teaching is mostly restricted to grammar drills and rote learning. The exposure to the language is severely limited, and learners do not develop a critical and creative engagement with language, for বাংলা (Bangla) is the medium of instruction. At the tertiary level, however, the medium of instruction is mostly English, and students also have to accomplish assignments in English that must demonstrate critical and creative intelligence. They can hardly transfer any linguistic capital when they shift from higher second to tertiary education. Therefore, they perform poorly in English as did the Bangladeshi peers in this study.

Besides being the victims of the "double hats problem" at the tertiary level, they are also the victims of genre theory and genre pedagogy. At the tertiary level, students in Bangladesh are oriented to the North American version of academic discourse that taxonomizes writings and writers in various categories. These categories are presented in composition primers as if these are invariant to always lead to cold and objective discourse of scientific precision and directness (Zamel, 1996). Such an approach to conceiving and constructing discourse strips writing of individual passion and panache along with requiring a formulaic way of thinking and languaging. While in Bangladesh scholars and critics theorize writing, writing hardly emerges from reified theories. Writing is thoughts transcribed and language approximated with abandon. Genre always meshes and clashes to bleed creativity into criticality. Converting students at the tertiary level, who already have defaulted to such an understanding of writing is time-consuming and consequential, both intellectually and emotionally. The peers in the US in this study are apparently immune to such dilemmas of writing. The finished products that this study investigated came out of processes where different sets of factors and forces intersected and interacted. The peers in this study from both the ends were not aware of such complexities inherent in texts and contexts. Therefore, while the peers both in Bangladesh and in the US read the texts correctly, they understood partially as their feedback reflected.

For all these complexities and contradictions between these two contexts of transnational engagements, one critical common phenomenon emerges about peer feedback. Peers across these two contexts seemed more sensitive to and respectful of each other. Students from Bangladesh as well as from the US demonstrated a fair amount of cross-cultural capital so as not to crush the ego and smash the confidence of their peers. We suggested that our students from both the contexts forge an ethical, intellectual engagement with their peers. Never have we had a comment that could hurt and humiliate their peer at other end; never has anyone reported any objectionable behavior. Peer feedback in this study seems more humane unlike the "hostility and mean-spiritedness of most of the teachers' comments" (Sommers, 1982). This dimension of this transnational collaboration is somewhat intriguing given that our identical rubric for providing feedback across these two contexts of transnational engagement yielded different outcomes. Our guidelines for behavior yielded the same outcomes across contexts. They seem to have common "structures of feeling" (Orram & Williams, 1954) in transnational engagement, even though I would not vouch for such an assumption. As it seems, our guidelines for providing peer feedback perhaps were linguistically more formidable and cognitively more challenging than following the principles of behavior. The structures of mutual feeling are perhaps a fortunate accident emerging out of this transnational collaboration. If this phenomenon holds out across contexts, it might be utilized to optimize pedagogical outcomes in transnational collaborations replicating such a model.

Conclusion

Understanding a human behavior as complex as writing is hard, and understanding transnational writing behavior is even harder, as Wendy Hesford (2006) claims that the field doesn't have the methodological foundation to study transnational rhetorical practices. This experimental approach to studying transnational writing between the US and Bangladesh concerning peer feedback evinces that the profiles of so-called advanced or so-called basic writers are cultural constructs and that they don't equally apply across contexts. Writing is apparently critical to any literate society, whether it is taught or absorbed. Bangladesh has a sovereign writing culture developed over centuries, and the assumptions that underpin that writing culture are idiosyncratic and inscrutable. Writing is shrouded in a mysterious complexity. Parsing writing is not yet an academic agenda, but savoring it is. To provide feedback or to write to have feedback is a cultural anathema. However, the sub-culture of academe influenced by composition studies seems to have challenged that culture to consider critically such stipulation as every writing is autobiographical to some extent; for it is an intellectual activity carried out in an emotional environment (Murray, 1982). The Bangladeshi peers in this experiment revealed their identity and intentions as they provided feedback on their peers from the US. So did the peers from the US as they wrote and provided feedback on the writing of their Bangladesh peers. They acted and reacted as unique cultural, cognitive, and linguistic creatures. And this experimental engagement yields some critical information on all these fronts pertinent to peer feedback in transnational contexts. This transnational engagement doesn't propose any grand theory regarding peer feedback in transnational context; it, instead, contributes to clarifying the "intersection between the global and the local" (Lu & Horner, 2009) so as to approach transnational writing engagement in a more informed fashion.

Bangladesh, for example, is a post, postcolonial country because of multiple occupations. For all its economic, political, and intellectual potential, the English language is a colonial artifact. It is at once embraced and denigrated. Growing up academically in a postcolonial Bangladesh warrants being cognizant of such undercurrents involving the English language. Learning to write in the English language knowing and enacting specific styles and strategies smacks of further colonization. The discipline of composition studies, as originated and flourished in North America, falls out of favor in Bangladesh as such. The way the Bangladeshi students reacted to the writing of their counterparts in the US may have profound psychological dimensions unaffected by literacy in a second language reflected in writing. Writing is a discursive behavior, which is often impervious to instruction in that it is already shaped by inveterate autochthonous forces across contexts and languages. Every transnational collaboration brings to the fore some of those forces, as does ours. As our experimental study suggests, classrooms practices as well as students, genres, and contexts need to be redefined by creating an epistemic tension between local and global. Our preparation as transnational educators on that front to facilitate writing studies is still inadequate, or why does Canagarajah (2016) contend that teacher development in composition studies is not well advanced? Teacher development, however, is an ongoing and unfinished undertaking, which is sometimes complemented by insights and information gleaned from such studies.

References

Alam, Fakrul. (2011). The commodification of English. In H. Lahiri (Ed.), *Literary transactions in a globalized context: Multi-ethnicity, gender and marketplace* (pp. 250–274). Worldview.

Calonne, David. (2006). Creative writers and revision. In A. Horning & A. Becker (Eds.), *Revision: History, theory, and practice* (pp. 142–176). Parlor Press; The WAC Clearinghouse. https://wac.colostate.edu/books/referenceguides/horning-revision/.

Canagarajah, Suresh. (2016). Translingual writing teacher development. *College English, 78*(3), 265–273.

Canagarajah, Suresh. (2006). The place of World Englishes in composition: Pluralization continued. *College Composition and Communication, 57*(4), 586–619.

Canagarajah, Suresh. (2001). The fortunate traveler: Shuttling between communities and literacies by economy classes. In Diane Dewhurst Belcher & Ulla Conner (Eds.), *Reflections on multiliterate lives* (pp. 23–37). Multilingual Matters.

Chowdhury, Serajul. (2001). Rethinking two Englishes. In F. Alam, N. Zaman & T. Ahmad (Eds.), *Revisioning English in Bangladesh* (pp. 15–26). Dhaka University Press.

Donahue, Christiane. (2009). "Internationalization" and composition studies: Reorienting the discourse. *College Composition and Communication, 62*(2), 212–243.

Hairston, Maxine. (1984). Working with advanced writers. *College Composition and Communication, 35*(2), 196–208.

Hesford, Wendy. (2006). Global turns and cautions in rhetoric and composition studies. *PMLA, 121*(3), 787–801.

Horner, Bruce., NeCamp, Samantha. & Donahue, Christiane. (2011). Toward a multilingual composition scholarship: From English only to a translingual norm. *College Composition and Communication, 63*(2), 269–300.

Horner, Bruce & Trimbur, John. (2002). English only and U.S. college composition. *College Composition and Communication, 53*(4), 594–630.

Kaplan, Robert. (1966). Cultural thought patterns in intercultural education. *Language Learning, 16*(1), 1–20.

Kietlinska, Kasia. (2006). Revision and ESL students. In Alice Horning & Anne Becker (Eds.), *Revision: History, theory, and practice* (pp. 63–87). Parlor Press; The WAC Clearinghouse. https://wac.colostate.edu/books/referenceguides/horning-revision/.

Lu, Min-Zhan. & Horner, Bruce. (2009). Composing in a global-local context: Careers, mobility, skills. *College English, 72*(2), 109–29.

Lunsford, Andrea. (1980). The content of basic writers' essays. *College Composition and Communication, 31*(3), 278–290.

Macaulay, Thomas Babington. (1979). *Speeches: With His Minute on Indian Education.* AMS Press.

Matsuda, Paul. (1999). Composition studies and ESL writing: A disciplinary division of labor. *College Composition and Communication, 50*(4), 699–721.

Matsuda, Paul. (2006). The myth of linguistic homogeneity in U.S. college composition. *College English, 68*(6), 637–651.

Murray, Donald. (1982). Teaching the other self: The writer's first reader. *College Composition and Communication, 33*(2), 140–147.

Orrom, Michael & Williams, Raymond. (1954). *Preface to film.* Film Drama Limited.

Pinker, Steven. (2014). *The sense of style: The thinking person's guide to writing in the 21st century.* Viking.

Rahim, Muhammad. (1981). *The history of the University of Dhaka. Dhaka, Bangladesh*: The University of Dhaka.

Raimes, Ann. (1991). Out of the woods: Emerging tradition in the teaching of writing, *TESOL Quarterly, 25*(3), 407–430.
Silva, Tony. (1997). On the ethical treatment of ESL writers. *TESOL Quarterly, 31*(2), 359–363.
Sommers, Nancy. (1982). Responding to student writing. *College Composition and Communication 33*(2), 148–156.
Sword, Helen. (2012). *Stylish academic writing*. Harvard University Press.
Shamsuzzaman, Mohammad, Everatt, John & McNeill, Brigid. (2014). An investigation of the relationship between teachers' backgrounds and the teaching of second language writing in Bangladesh. *International Journal of Innovation in English Language Teaching and Research, 3*(1), 51–72.
Shamsuzzaman, Mohammad. (2014). Crossing borders: Writing in a second language. In Christopher McMaster & Caterina Murphy (Eds.), *Postgraduate studies in Aotearoa New Zealand: Surviving and succeeding* (pp. 219–228). NZCER Press.
Tagore, Rabindranath. (1910). *Gitanjali*. Macmillan and Company.
Thomas, Francis-Noel. & Turner, Mark. (1994). *Clear and simple as the truth: Writing classic prose*. Princeton University Press
Zamel, Vivian. (1996). Transcending boundaries: Complicating the scene of teaching language. *College ESL, 6*(2), 1–11.

Appendix A

Context: Is the essay context-specific and focused? Are there any additional contextual issues that the writer may need to consider when revising this draft?
Idea: Is the writer's main idea, argument, or research question/objective clearly stated in the draft?
Research: Does the draft reflect that considerable research was done? Are the sources reliable? Are they engaged well by the writer?
Perspectives: Does the draft indicate any misunderstanding or oversight about something—or are there one or more perspectives that the writer should consider in order to refine the paper's key argument/idea?
Language and Presentation: Do the language and presentation of the draft follow the codes of standard academic discourse?

Appendix B. Prompts

Prompt for Students in Dhaka: Literacy Narrative of an L2 Learner

PART 1: Find one of your peers to interview about their journey as an L2 learner in English. When interviewing, ask questions to be able to cover issues like the following in your narrative about their second language acquisition. Does your peer remember when he/she was first exposed to the language? What piqued his/her passion in the language? What obstacles did he/she face and to what factors and issues does she attribute those difficulties? How did he/she overcome (or is overcoming) the challenges? When writing, go beyond simply reporting/describing to making sense of the story. When describing their language acquisition, draw upon theories of second language development, using themes and issues about language learning in Bangladesh or similar contexts.

PART 2: In the second part of your essay, shift focus to your interviewee's development of academic literacy skills (reading, writing, communication) in English. When and how did she/he develop literacy skills? What were her/his challenges with it and how did she/he overcome them (or is overcoming)? When writing this part of your essay, pick one of the "literacy narratives" from this set of samples, written by native and nonnative English speakers in the United States, through some online research. Read it carefully and compare your classmate's literacy development with that of the student in the US. How do language acquisition and the development of literacy skills seem to compare/differ in Bangladesh and the United States? Again, develop issues and themes out of the comparison.

You can blend the two areas above into one or use two subheadings: language development and literacy development. In both areas, you should develop and use your own argument about language acquisition to frame your narrative and discussion, supporting your argument with compelling explanations and relevant sources.

Ideally, the assignment should not exceed 1,000 words.

Prompt for the Student in New York: Writing Across Cultures Essay

DRAFT 1: Write a 800–1,200 word expository/persuasive essay about an educational, intellectual, cultural, social, economic, or other significant topic in the context of the country of Bangladesh. For best credit, your writing must reflect a solid understanding of guidelines provided throughout this document. Also draw on readings and discussions from class, as well as exercises on conducting research, developing and supporting argument, writing in a thesis-driven manner, and engaging sources substantively and responsibly that you'll be learning in the course.

DRAFT 2: After exchanging feedback, via Google Docs, with an assigned peer reviewer, a fellow student at the North South University in Dhaka, Bangladesh, revise your paper using his/her feedback and the same rubric (in this doc) that he/she has provided to review your paper draft. You should also use feedback by your peer in class and your instructor, as well as notes from class activities. If you add words while revising your first draft, you must condense the draft (meaning you're expected to practice condensing skills, as needed, with this paper).

Appendix C

One of my students wrote in her essay, "Bangladesh is very much amorous about the English language." Her U.S. counterpart underlined the word "amorous" with a marginal comment: "word choice." Another of my students wrote, "He ended up being pathetically interested with the English language." The marginal comment from her peer in the US was, "pathetically typically has a negative connotation." Having read the sentence "She always felt intimated, and will be judged in front of the class," her peer from the US underlined "intimated" and corrected in the margin "intimidated." Another student from Bangladesh wrote, "She had to face lots of difficulties." Her peer from the US underlined, "lots of" and corrected in the margin with "many." As one of my students in Bangladesh wrote, "In the school his teacher used to speak English consecutively," her peer from the US underlined "consecutively" with the marginal comment, "very frequently." Similarly, another of my students in Bangladesh wrote, "It also varies learners to learners." Her peer from the US corrected her with the following marginal comment, "add the word 'from', and 'leaner' should be singular." These are some of the many examples when the students from the US identified and fixed errors with linguistic infelicities.

Some of the recommendations from the students in the US are straightforward instruction. For example, underlining the title of one of the essays from a student in Bangladesh, her counterpart in the US wrote, "center," along with the instruction, "indent every paragraph." Other widely used instruction by the students in the US on the essays of the Bangladeshi students were "delete; rephrase the sentence as it not clear; you should clearly point out your topic sentence in the beginning of the paragraph; need citations and bibliography for researched information; central argument? Keep in the first paragraph; don't start sentence with 'and,'; don't start sentence with 'but,'; no need to use colon; go more in depth in regard to the questions asked; make sure to cite your sources; you can skip this; and connect these two sentences to make it sound more sophisticated."

When the students from the US were confused about the ideas and arguments proposed by their counterparts in Bangladesh, they asked for further information, or they asked questions directly. For example, having read "Thinking the part of grammatical rules basically hinders their production, because they are very much are of it," her counterpart in the US commented, "Not sure what you are trying to say here." One of the students in Bangladesh wrote, "He properties the challenges he looked with on himself, conceivably he ignored certain things and there for he has these deficiency in English," and her counterpart in the US commented, "I don't understand what you are trying to say here." On the following sentence, "When she started to talk it was not the beginning of her language verifying, it was the eventual outcome of the conceivable data," appearing in one of the essays of a student in Bangladesh, the student from the US commented, "The sentence is little hard to understand. Could you rephrase it in a simple way?" Some of the direct questions from the students in the US as they provided feedback on their counterparts in Bangladesh were, "So are you going to mention the topic of the essay here?; what are you trying to convey here?; Is this common in Bangladesh?; How can this issue be addressed?; "what do you mean by this phrase?"; how does this show extroversion?; Is there a better way to start this sentence?"

Besides these comments and questions for further information, there were also some positive and motivating comments on the essays of the students from Bangladesh from their counterparts in the US—for example, "I really like your introduction. It has lots of information and sets up the topic well"; "Even though you don't speak English every day, your ability to write complex ideas and convey how Israt was feeling in this language is very impressive. Keep it up"; "This is a great essay to show how your friends experience to acquire a new language"; "I believe this is nice way of framing the thesis, clear and concise"; "This paragraph has a really nice flow"; "Loved these few sentences"; and "This paragraph was very clear."

As I mentioned earlier, students from Bangladesh did not comment on the margin for linguistic and rhetorical correction and clarification from their American peers. Instead, the students from Bangladesh had one summative comment on the essays of their American peers. These one-off summative comments apparently lack details and directions, as demonstrated by feedback from the students in the US. One such comment was, "I think this paper is very well written. I feel the claim is very relevant as it addresses a very important issue. And this is true that Bangladesh has dealing with this overpopulation issue for long time and it's still very much concerning for the current and the next generation of the nation. Here it is clear that the evidences provided by my peer doesn't acknowledge any counter argument. But I still believe this paper is fine work because it is organized very impressively. The quality of the language is excellent. It is very simple, making it easy for the reader to clearly understand the author's intention."

Transnational Translingual Literacies: Re-thinking Graduate Student Identity and Support

Jonathan Hall
YORK COLLEGE, CITY UNIVERSITY OF NEW YORK

Nela Navarro
RUTGERS UNIVERSITY, NEW BRUNSWICK

Transnational graduate students—often referred to as "international students" on U.S. campuses—inhabit contested linguistic identity spaces. They generally enter U.S. academic departments with considerable background in their discipline, having read a wide range of academic texts and engaged in academic practices, often in multiple languages and transnational contexts. They have also developed accomplished identities as writers, readers, speakers and thinkers in multiple languages. We will report on a series of interviews with seven such students on a U.S. state university campus in which we asked them about their language and cultural backgrounds, as well as their academic and professional identities since arriving in the US and their future ambitions. This ethnographic approach turns a translingual lens on how U.S. institutional structures (mis-)identify such students, and provides an opportunity to suggest alternate pedagogical practices and support. These interviews encourage our graduate students to interrogate the liminal space that they occupy by virtue of their transnational status, situating their experiences transnationally and translingually, and illuminating a complex range of language backgrounds and identities.[1]

For many U.S. graduate academic support programs (Grad-ASPs) and for transnational students, careful attention to this multiplicity of identities potentially creates a discursive space necessary for negotiating difference, and, if properly supported, for promoting the aspirations and values of a global university for the 21st century. We articulate an approach to Grad-ASPs—and to the students they serve—that we will call *transnational translingual literacies*. This builds upon an academic literacies approach (Lea & Street, 1996, 2006; Lillis, 2003) but adapts it for translingual re-conceptions across language differences, and for transnational developments in studies of migration and identity. A transnational translingual

---

1 This project was judged "Exempt" by CUNY IRB. Participants were compensated for their time. This project was supported by a PSC-CUNY grant.

DOI: https://doi.org/10.37514/ATD-B.2023.1527.2.12

literacies approach necessitates shifts in the ways that we conceive of student language, disciplinary, national, and cultural identities. It also requires a shift in the ways that disciplinary faculty, support staff, and program administrators approach their support for these students.

Reconceiving Graduate Academic Support Programs
Transnational Students, Translingual Literacies

Transnational graduate students on U.S. college campuses are impacted by a daunting array of academic bureaucracy. A global outreach or admissions office may have recruited them originally, often by means of agreements with institutions in the students' country of origin. Even before they leave they may have been in contact with a "testing" office that focuses on the TOEFL or other measure of English proficiency. There will almost certainly be an "international students" office, which usually focuses on securing visas, work permits, housing, etc. A student's academic department has its own academic and procedural requirements, often mediated by a faculty advisor with whom they may have had previous contact.

Our focus here will be on graduate academic support programs (Grad-ASP), sometimes referred to as Graduate Communication Programs. Michelle Cox and Nigel Caplan (2014) surveyed such programs and found that the services available, the institutional location, the approaches to graduate support, and the professional affiliation of directors and staff varied widely from campus to campus. A Grad-ASP may be a free-standing program, or located in a particular academic department, in the international students' office, as part of a writing center, a writing across the curriculum program, an ESL program, a language institute, or, as is the case with the particular program we'll focus on here, housed in the writing program within the English department. There are advantages and disadvantages to all these locations, but wherever they are located institutionally, their mission is to support transnational graduate students as they negotiate the language, academic, social, and cultural challenges that are an integral part of their in-between transient state. A detailed understanding of the transnational graduate student experience is critical to conceptualizing the basic functions of a Grad-ASP:

- How to structure support services for transnational graduate students
- What kinds of pedagogical recommendations to make to graduate faculty through professional development outreach
- What role the Grad-ASP program plays in supporting a transnational translingual mission and vision for the university.

There are a number of possible variables (see Figure 12.1) influencing the language identities of transnational graduate students, and their academic, professional and personal identities as well. We will focus on what our transnational graduate students told us when we asked them about their language practices, and explore tentative conclusions—or better, questions and potential shifts in approach—for effective practices in academic support programs for transnational graduate students. We draw upon a series of in-depth, semi-structured interviews with seven graduate students who agreed to discuss their translingual and transnational literacies. These subjects were compensated for their time (each interview took about an hour).

Figure 12.1. *Variables influencing the language identities of transnational graduate students.*

Our transnational graduate students, or, as we call them, emerging scholars, have a great deal to share about elements affecting their language identities, sometimes affirming our hypotheses, sometimes complicating or contesting our initial assumptions. We have reported elsewhere (Robinson, Hall, and Navarro, 2020, Chapter 6) on students' experiences before coming to graduate study in the US In this chapter we will examine their experiences after they arrive on campus, and examine a range of effective interventions on the part of programs for "international" graduate students and on the part of faculty supervising them to support transnational graduate students.

The questions that we asked in our interviews (Robinson, Hall, and Navarro, 2020, Appendix D) attempted to take a 360-degree view of graduate student literacies (Figure 12.1), taking into account their past language affiliations, their present identity as transnational graduate students on a U.S. campus, and their future professional and personal ambitions:

- Their often complex language backgrounds, including relations both to the standardized language affirmed by official language policy in their country of origin context but also to other language(s) and dialects
- Their history of English language learning, beginning in their primary, secondary, and undergraduate education in their country of origin and continuing as they make the transition to an English-medium campus in the United States
- Their relation to disciplinary language(s) in their graduate studies and in their emerging scholarly and/or professional identities
- Their relationship to the U.S. context where they physically live at present, to their "home" culture, and to their identities as global, cosmopolitan citizens, including an articulation of their plans, ambitions, attitudes toward their future as transnational professionals

Transnational translingual literacies reflect not only how our students read and write, but also how we, as instructors, as staff, as administrators, *read them*. How do we conceive of their literacies, their identities, and how do these conceptions correspond–or not–to the students' own experiences of academic and personal transnational translingual literacies?

In order for Grad-ASPs to fulfill this mission, we will argue, it will be necessary to re-conceptualize "international" graduate students as transnational emerging scholars, to listen to their experiences and their concerns, and to develop support structures and interventions that respect their status as emerging transnational professionals. The first step in developing effective support services for a given population is to examine and discuss their goals and aspirations. Especially when students come from a different national and linguistic background than prevails on the target campus, it is important to avoid assuming that we already understand who they are and what they want. Even brief interviews reveal a possible lack of alignment between U.S. university assumptions and expectations and the actual experiences, aspirations, and expectations of the students themselves.

From Academic Literacies to Transnational Translingual Literacies

When we look at these academic support programs, we should do so through a critical translingual and transnational lens. We need to examine not only the students' interview responses but also the institutional context surrounding them–international students program, language and academic support services, curriculum structure, and pedagogical professional development for faculty—by asking questions that promote linguistic justice and engage with issues of mobility.

Mary Lea and Brian Street (1997; 2006) describe their influential concept of "academic literacies" as both encompassing and going beyond two earlier (and yet continuing) approaches to writing and literacy, and we can apply their model to conceptions of international graduate student literacies and Grad-ASP programs. For Lea and Street (2006), the "study skills" approach sees writing and literacy as primarily an individual and cognitive skill. This approach focuses on the surface features of language form and presumes that students can transfer their knowledge of writing and literacy seamlessly from one context to another.

In Grad-ASP programs, this approach translates to a desire to create parallel courses—sometimes described as English for Academic Purposes (EAP)—for transnational graduate students that contain exercises and materials designed to develop individual skills. An example of such an approach may be found in Liying Cheng et al. (2004), who asked graduate students to rank 31 "study skills" in terms of "most difficult" and "most important." Based on overlaps in these lists, they recommend an EAP "course including *Leading class discussions, Giving presentations, Small group discussion, Writing long or short reports,* and *Understanding a writer's attitude and purpose*" (2004, p. 60). These "skills" are seen as generalizable across disciplines and professions, and the EAP program, as an independent entity, will take responsibility for implementing this course, choosing common examples, and thus for preparing graduate students to deal with their coursework reading and writing, their teaching assistantships, their research, and ultimately their dissertation writing and professional preparedness.

The attraction of the "study skills" model for faculty is obvious: they have some place to *send* the students who are conceived as "problematic," as "other." Cox and Caplan (2014) summarized some faculty attitudes in their survey as "Disciplinary faculty see any type of writing instruction or support as 'inoculation services'—so they assume that students' writing will be 'fixed' if they attend only one writing center consultation."

Going beyond this deficit model, Lea and Street identify a second widespread approach, "academic socialization," as

> concerned with students' acculturation into disciplinary and subject-based discourses and genres. Students acquire the ways of talking, writing, thinking, and using literacy that typified members of a disciplinary or subject area community. The academic socialization model presumes that the disciplinary discourses and genres are relatively stable and, once students have learned and understood the ground rules of a particular academic discourse, they are able to reproduce it unproblematically. (2006 p. 369)

In the Grad-ASP context, such an approach would take students' emerging disciplinary identities as primary, and the program would attempt to defer to disciplinary experts. Based on student surveys and interviews, Swathi Ravichandran, et al. (2007) identified promising strategies as more feedback from faculty, a peer mentor program with mentors from the same discipline, more discipline-based writing center tutors, and department-specific English language support. From a writing center perspective, Tallin Phillips (2013) advocates a "holistic approach" that would "recogniz[e] the role of disciplinarity" in graduate student texts by employing discipline-specific graduate tutors (as opposed to generalist undergraduates), by considering "research methodology" as "in essence an act of pre-writing for many graduate writing projects."

One of the ways in which graduate students differ from undergraduates is in their more nuanced, sophisticated, and deeper commitment to their disciplinary identities. For transnational emerging scholars, closer cooperation and collaboration between Grad-ASP programs and academic departments form an indispensable element in better support. But acknowledging and incorporating disciplinarity will not be enough if disciplinarity itself and student disciplinary identities are conceived as standardizable or stable. Lea and Street's (2006) academic literacies approach

> is concerned with meaning making, identity, power, and authority, and foregrounds the institutional nature of what counts as knowledge in any particular academic context. It is similar in many ways to the academic socialization model, except that it views the processes involved in acquiring appropriate and effective uses of literacy as more complex, dynamic, nuanced, situated, and involving both epistemological issues and social processes, including power relations among people, institutions, and social identities. (p. 369)

Applying the academic literacies approach to Grad-ASP programs would entail a critical scrutiny of all aspects of the transnational graduate student experience:

recruitment in their country of origin, qualification through testing and other means, the assumptions underlying language support initiatives, the pedagogy of graduate courses, the process of developing and approving dissertation topics, the structure and procedures of writing center and other support programs, and a critical approach to disciplinary discourses, seeing them as ongoing negotiations rather than fixed templates, among other possibilities. An academic literacies approach focuses on the institution, situating particular interactions of students with instructors, administrative offices, admissions and testing standards, visa status, language proficiency support, and disciplinary discourses in a context of "power relations." But as Lillis (2003) noted,

> Whilst powerful as an oppositional frame, that is as a critique of current conceptualizations and practices surrounding student writing, academic literacies has yet to be developed as a design frame . . . which can actively contribute to student writing pedagogy as both theory and practice. (p. 192)

That is, an academic literacies approach is good at describing, analyzing, and critiquing current practices in terms of power relations, but does not always clearly point towards enhancing the student experience.

In the most comprehensive study of Grad-ASP programs to date, Shyam Sharma (2018) suggests two key shifts that potentially go beyond critique and an oppositional frame: "fostering student agency" (Chapter 4) and "support driven by advocacy" (Chapter 5). Sharma argues that support for international graduate students needs to undergo a shift beyond its traditional focus on language issues and toward "issues of politics and power, policy and ideology, local and global political economies, diversity and intersectionality of the student identities" (2018, p. 191). Such approaches are starting to emerge, for example in a recent intersectional study of African students on U.S. campuses (Mwangi et al., 2019) or in studies exploring the intersection of transnationalism and gender (Eldaba & Isbell, 2018; Le, 2016).

English language development is one of the most challenging aspect of transnational student success—it is certainly the most visible—but Sharma suggests that we need to approach it in a different, more translingual manner, arguing that

> We must ask new questions. What writing cultures do international students bring with them? How do they build on prior knowledge and why do they discard or repurpose their past skills as they transition and adapt to the new academe and its disciplines and the professions? (p. 191)

Building on Sharma's emphases on student agency and Grad-ASP advocacy as the keys to moving beyond the current quagmire in international graduate student support, we suggest the next logical development in the hierarchical series of encompassing approaches: from study skills, to academic socialization, to academic literacies—then on to what we are calling here, drawing on recent developments in writing and language studies, transnational translingual literacies. That is, not only disciplinary discourses and institutional structures need to be analyzed, as academic literacies would argue, but languages themselves, in the translingual conception, are neither stable nor independent entities. Dynamic student identities, always in flux, are influenced transnationally by complex interactions between ideologies about language and knowledge internalized (or resisted) during experience and education prior to the United States, and students' more recent academic, linguistic, and personal explorations once they arrive.

What do we mean by using a translingual lens when discussing transnational emerging scholars? What do we mean by translingual transnational literacies? What kinds of questions might we ask about a course, a syllabus, a classroom, a curriculum, a support program, a professional development workshop? Or about transnational student experiences, as expressed in the interviews, in any of the above? Here are a few:

- How are language hierarchies constructed, deconstructed, reaffirmed, reconstituted in this particular institutional context? What models of language(s) and language difference are implicitly assumed in the existing policies and procedures of the program? How do students' previous language experiences, affiliations, and cultural conceptions of language and language difference impact their academic progress and their personal interaction with the surrounding campus and societal context?

- What assumptions are implicitly made by the program about students' language identity (including language background, expertise, and affiliation), disciplinary and professional identity, national/cultural identity, and personal identity? How do these correspond (or not) with students' own articulations of identity?

- Do the pedagogical choices, processes and practices in the local courses and classrooms reinforce, resist, or silently acquiesce to the continuing influence of monolingual ideologies? What kinds of professional development approaches may lead to a more reflective practice? What forms of academic support do the graduate students themselves see as most helpful?

- Do our evaluation and assessment practices include our graduate students as active metacognitive participants and reflective agents of their own linguistic and intellectual development? That is, is assessment something that is done to the students by us or (even worse) by outside testing agencies, or is it a process that students themselves participate in and, as emerging professionals, ultimately control?

The common thread in all these questions is the issue of student agency. Traditionally, programs for transnational students, chronically underfunded and often overwhelmed by sudden unexpected bursts of enrollment, have resorted to a one-size-fits-all model, based on hasty and unexamined assumptions about what "international students" are thought to "need" and want in terms of support. A more inclusive approach that we have had time and opportunity to pursue is to ask the students about their experiences: what has happened, what they wanted and whether they got it, what campus programs might have done to make things easier, or at least more transparent, for them.

Experiences of Transnational Emerging Scholars

Even more than undergraduate "international" students, graduate students inhabit a conflicted linguistic territory. While 18-year-old first-year students face considerable challenges in adapting to U.S. academic conventions and assumptions, they also, in common with their U.S.-born classmates, usually come to the classroom with little previous disciplinary knowledge or expertise in writing. Graduate students arrive on U.S. campuses with considerable disciplinary knowledge; with more experiences reading complex texts, often in multiple languages; and with a more developed identity as a writer in one or more languages.

Functioning in a new cultural context often brings previously unconscious assumptions from one's native culture into focus, while at the same time the new local culture also makes multiple assumptions about "international students" in general, as well as more specific stereotypes about particular nationalities or ethnic groups. With experiences from the past taking on new significance in a U.S. milieu, and facing new categorizations in the present from the U.S. academic institution and from U.S. culture in general, some kind of response on the part of transnational emerging scholars to these attributed identities cannot be avoided, though that response can encompass a wide, complex continuum ranging from passive acceptance to ambivalent questioning to active resistance.

The result, for many transnational students, is a sustained liminality. Students with transnational identities (Levitt & Jaworsky 2007) continue to build and sustain networks of connective meaning across physical distances, language interactions, and cultural contexts. Rather than imagining a linguistic identity—whether professional or personal—exclusively in English, translingual approaches (Canagarajah, 2013; Horner et. al 2011) invite us to attend to the continuing interplay of multiple languages during the course of varied communicative activities. Liminality can be acutely uncomfortable, a condition of being neither fish nor fowl, but it can also be the opener of doors to the future, if one can (re)create and sustain an identity as, for example, still Chinese but envisioning a future life lived largely in the US or a third country.

Student Experience: Academics

The academic adjustment of transnational graduate students has been approached usually as an issue of "study-related stress" (Brown, 2007) or "academic stress" (Wan, et al., 1992). More recently Shi Pu and Michael Evans (2018) explored critical thinking through positioning theory, while Shakil Rabbi and Suresh Canagarajah (2017) have turned a critical lens on "socialization in the neoliberal academy" as an important factor in transnational student identity and adjustment.

The transition to U.S. academic culture, and the stresses and often pain of that transition, began before our interviewees even left China or Taiwan: the first hurdle was the dreaded Test of English as a Foreign Language (TOEFL). What those of us who have never taken it might not understand is that it is not a pure language exam, but instead assumes a rather broad academic background. Student #7, an aspiring professional musician, described the sacrifices necessary to pass the exam

> And how I prepare it I actually I finally passed my TOEFL exam. . . . I prepare for it like a four-month. I didn't even play cello for four months and I only study and surprisingly my speaking part scores super high when I took that my last TOEFL exam. So yeah, that's how I prepare it.

Students who grew up in the Chinese educational system are often used to high-stakes tests, but they would discover that in some cases these did not stop coming once they reached the US The music students faced a particularly difficult exam, made more perplexing for transnational students because of the way that it was written and structured. The music exam was developed by a team of senior faculty members who expressed concern about the graduate students' alleged inability to "perform" successfully in their written assignments. They did not explain to the students which "assignments" they did not complete successfully, what the exam was assessing, or how it related to their specific academic program concentration. The exam consisted of several pages of a western-centric reading, written by a scholar decades ago. The question was written in a way that seemed to invite summary rather than analysis and, after discussions with the senior faculty members, they decided that the students would be "better" off simply summarizing, although, by the end of the semester, the students had analyzed the readings, incorporated readings from scholars from the East, made nuanced transdisciplinary connections with arts, literature, and intellectual history, and engaged with the more complex ideas of the texts in ways that "surprised" some of their professors. As student #5 noted,

> I think they forgot, we have read these texts before, in our own languages, we understand our field and we are committed to going outside of our language, our country, our discipline, and our 'comfort zone' to pursue our academic ideas and dreams. We are not "nobodies."

An accomplished musician who had no problem performing in front of large audiences, Student #5 found speaking to small groups of English speakers to be extremely anxiety-provoking. It was Student #5, who, punning on a frequent grammatical barrier, articulated "we're not regular students. We're the Irregulars." This student pointed out that her entire trajectory, experience, and identity was othered from the moment she began the application process. She noted that the very fact that there were so many different types of evaluation tools employed to "assess" her skills, and to ultimately accept her, her talents, her contributions, and her money were still "not enough." Student #5 noted that "it seems we international students were never intended to be 'regular' and if being regular means having one language, one identity, one way of being professional, then I am happy being 'irregular.'" She shared this during an office hour and then expressly recounted her thoughts to her fellow classmates, who later decided to subvert the term and call themselves the "Irregulars."

Enrolled in a joint MSW/ Ph.D. program in social work, Student #4 faced a double whammy of improving her English while also learning a new disciplinary language:

> Because I'm in the Ph.D. program. So there for me statistics, advanced statistic itself, is a new language because I have to learn the software and then for the Ph.D. readings or the assignment. I think the reading are challenging and difficult because they are more conceptual that that is challenging for me. And then also, you know, more sophisticated I think those writing and the concepts.

WAC/WID advocates have often compared learning a discipline to learning a language—though this tendency has been criticized as leaving out the issue of language per se (Matsuda & Jablonski, 2000)–and Student #4 suggests something similar here.

Student Experience: Social Stress and Socialization

In a survey by Jenny Hyun, et al. (2007), 44% of the international graduate students reported emotional or stress-related issues, but they made use of counseling services at a much lower rate than U.S. students. Raquel Chapdelaine and Louise Alexitch (2004) examined the social skills of international graduate students in the context of a culture shock and cultural learning model, arguing that social interaction with hosts was a key determinant of adjustment. Similarly, Andrea Trice (2004) found that students who interacted most often with U.S. students faced less social stress—though this just seems to say that students who were successful at socializing were less stressed than those who found it more difficult or impossible. Yu-Wen Ying (2005) found that academic adjustment was the most challenging stressor, and that issues of emotional and social life tended to emerge after the first stress of academic immersion had passed.

Our interviewees reported a wide range of experiences of life outside the classroom as an international student, ranging from isolation to a select network of friends to a deep immersion in American life. Student #1, for example, came to the university with a network of friends already in place,

> I will because most of my friends are in the US. How? Oh, that's my high school kind of they have like separate program for the for high school students, like preparing [for international study] and so they choose they pay more money to choose that road. So for me, it's like "oh, you're here."

In China, Student #1 had been prepared academically for international education from an early age by participating in special academies, and found that alumni of that school lived all over the United States on various campuses or were already employed. Student #2, by contrast, had attended two years of college in China before coming to the US, and while he remains in touch on social media with his friends from that time, he also feels that their present experiences are more different than similar:

> I don't have any friends [in the U.S.] that I know like before I was coming to America. Yes it's just a surprise for me because like if you are going to go into the social network of your like your University friends—I mean the Chinese one. I mean those friends you will see that they are like they're hanging out here and there in China and you will feel that Oh we are in a different country and we are in different place. We're doing different things.

On this university campus, Student #2 states that his social contacts are mostly with other international students, specifically Chinese ones, partly owing to his continuing lack of confidence in his English—despite his fluency and even volubility throughout our interview. Similarly, Student #5, a violinist, blamed her intensive practice and performance schedule for living a somewhat isolated life on the campus:.

> Outside the classroom my social life here is pretty small. But I mean I have to make regular contact with one of my American friend here. This one Chinese friend, one Korean friends, but mostly I will hang out with my church friends. They're all Taiwanese. Okay.

Another musician, Student #8, asked "do you feel like you're living in two places?" replied:

> No, but something interesting happens to me when I am here I think I should be there (China) and when I am there, I really want to be back here. Is that strange do you think? It is cool that I am sometimes in two places but I think this is interesting to me, I see my experience as bigger now maybe even more interesting, I get this feeling when the other language pops in my mind. Does this sound OK? I mean is what I say now clear?

After first dismissing the idea, Student #8 seems to later embrace the quintessential translingual and transnational experience noting that "the other language pops in my mind," Mandarin, when in the US or English when in China.

While Student #8 feels his "experience as bigger" because of his complex transnational translingual identity, Student #3 experiences her extensive time in the US and impressive English skills as part of a zero-sum tradeoff:

> I tried to like create a resume in Chinese version. I had a really hard time. I had no idea about how to create a resume in Chinese, but I know how to create a resume in English. And now I after I took that us to deal with the present and the future and I feel that also now, I'm bad at don't like Chinese academic words writing really now.

Her comfort in English and in American culture has come, in her mind, at the cost of skills and comfort in her native language and country.

Student #3 feels that her American experience has changed her, while Student #7 situates the source of change elsewhere, specifically back in China. Unlike Student #3, he doesn't feel that his Mandarin skills have deteriorated, noting that he uses his first language for "an hour while I talk to my cousin every day. So yeah, okay once a day." The rapid pace of change in China can be disorienting for those who live there through it, but for expatriates only occasionally returning, like Student #7, the experience is even more disconcerting:

> If you stay U.S. for four years and you go back to China after that you feel so strange, everything new and you know, Yeah, and my dad told me like it's four years ago that the lines of the

> subway only have two. Right now, like they almost have 20 lines so, I'm like . . . all that in just four years! In China nobody uses their wallet everything they pay by phone. You know, I don't even have a credit card in China or bank account in China! So, I don't I don't know. How can I deal with that? But I'll try.

Of course, the change is not only on the Chinese side: everything there may have changed, but the person has changed as well as a result of the American experience. Student #4 was the interviewee most deeply immersed in American life, and fully intending to stay in the United States permanently.

> In the first year, I didn't . . . make a lot of phone call because I am not just here by myself. So right have to take care of that because the second year my children came to stay with me. Oh, yeah, so I need to negotiate with their school in the Intermediate School and Middle School. Another time. I need to take them to see the doctors. So . . . I remember it. You have to schedule appointment on the phone. Yeah, and then I didn't know what is called because when they ask me, what's your insurance?

> It was really challenging because my kids they started learn English from elementary school. And they and so they had some English back home, but it must have been quite difficult for them when they first got here. Yeah, really challenging for them.

> I remember my younger son told me that he wished he was an American because he thought if he was if he were American he couldn't have problem with this homework and I told him that you won't unfortunately, you won't be American in your life because you won't be born here. I mean you did you didn't have the chance but I mean, I told him that in the future you will be bilingual have both advantages. You have the best of both worlds.

> So for my kids they catch up quickly then then I do so now they are teaching me so they make fun of my pronunciation. yes, I would say my life is kind of different from single students because I have family responsibilities. I have to expose to other like I'll get it more involved in the community life.

Student #4's story takes us all the way from the confusion of first arrival, through anxiety about English language proficiency, to moments of clarity and comprehension, and, at least for Student #4, to a more profound connection to and immersion in American life. Because she was not, like all the other interviewees, operating as a single individual, but rather as mother of a family, she could not limit herself to academic English or choose the safety of an enclave of international students. Rather she is "more involved in the community life."

Student #8 wants to "make it here" in the United States, but also envisions a future that might include performing and teaching in multiple countries: he wants to be "in the world," rejecting the idea that he has to be limited geographically. Similarly, Student #3 rejected the dichotomy in the question of returning to China or staying in the US:

> Because my major is engineering I need to know what's going on in the real world so that I can keep myself in the state of art stage and never lose the track. I don't know. I pray I think I hope because I'm not a person like have to stay in one place. I always loved moving. Yeah, and so you may want be one of these people where there's a project here and next year there's a project somewhere else. Look, they're working you ask or come back to China or another that different countries to work. I don't know what it's like now. I don't have a clear plan about that. You just feel like I think I just want to pick a place where I feel comfortable right now.

Like Student #8, Student #3 expresses a desire to encounter "the real world" and to "never look back." She envisions a future of working project to project, with perhaps multiple home ports. Perhaps the most telling phrase here is "I always loved moving"—and she plans to keep it moving.

Student #7 also expresses his willingness to follow his profession wherever it may take him:

> Well, I guess well, as a musician there are two ways for us after we finish the DMA to doctoral degree. The first one is go to teaching in the University or conservatory. And the second one is played in the professional Orchestra. So my well, you know, I'm preparing my Orchestra audition. So I guess for me like wherever accept me as a musician in a university or in you know, orchestra, I will go it doesn't matter where you know, my father favorite country is New Zealand. I don't know why I don't ask me why but so she's so weird. He loved their he asked me like, oh you want to go that far? Well, if they accept me as a musician the orchestra, I'm there.

Basically Student #7 will go wherever he can obtain a position either at a university or as a performer in a professional orchestra. The only country he mentions specifically is New Zealand, for some reason a favorite of his father's. He doesn't mention China at all.

Discussion: Four Programmatic Shifts for Grad-ASP Programs

Programmatic Shift #1: From Imposing Institutional Identities on Students to Supporting Students' Dynamic Identity Processes

The questions that we asked get at notions of identity: the institution's, the instructor's, and most importantly the students'. How is identity constructed and what role does language play in this process?

Traditionally we—as an institution, as a profession—have *given* students identities, sorted them into predetermined institutional categories. But what was revealed in these interviews is that there is a richness, a complexity, to how transnational emerging scholars construct and come to those identities. They were given imposed identities before they came to us, and they chose multiple aspects of their identity in their culture of origin as well. But one of the key things that emerged during the interviewees is that identity is conceived by these students—and, more importantly embodied by them through their actions and through their self-constructions at many levels—as a dynamic and emerging process, rather than a fixed label or a permanent social role. These students, in different ways, resisted the idea of a monolithic or static identity. They came to the US in order to change, in order to let themselves explore multiple layers and levels of identity formation. They are not going to return to China unchanged, if they return there at all. When identity is changed, the notion of "home" is challenged as well.

Programmatic Shift #2: From Asking What Teachers Should Do to Focusing on What They Should and Must Support and Empower Their Students to Do

If we conceive identity of various kinds—language, national, professional, personal—as malleable and dynamic, we need to reflect this shift in thinking in our administrative structures and in our approaches to questions of pedagogy, including what we present in our professional development workshops for our faculty. Faced with graduate students who might struggle with aspects of English—especially listening—in their seminars, faculty in fields that are not focused on language may feel frustrated or just puzzled: How can they intervene to help these students? What can they do?

We propose a shift in approaches to professional development work which traditionally have suggested that faculty "intervene" and address "issues" in other words, that faculty must do something. Perhaps most importantly, a translingual and transnational approach to pedagogy invites faculty to focus on what they can, should, and must empower their students to do by creating learning environments in which students feel safe, encouraged, and heard.

Instructors are often in search of quick fixes, looking for tips or prescriptions. But if we accommodate that approach, we risk having instructors engage in the discourse and practices of the deficit model, and they can easily become trapped in their own desires to fix "deficiencies" or to "solve problems." And this is among people of immense good will, who genuinely want to help the students, but who instead end up inadvertently embracing the very logic that they claim to be dismantling. They put students in the same kinds of categories and spaces that they claim to want to free the students from. But nobody can free anybody else: what we can do is to create a context that is supportive of experimentation and innovation, and that offers not pedagogical tools for instructors but rather metacognitive tools for students.

When we asked the students about their academic journeys in graduate school, we noted that agency was the key. The students articulated ways in which they transform challenges and difficulties into opportunities. They were happily challenged by those difficult moments. They have deployed skills across languages that allow them to construct meaning in complicated situations and contexts where meaning perhaps was lost, where meaning-making or the language exchange was breaking down. They had intervention techniques to address these kinds of situations, to resolve them favorably.

Programmatic Shift #3: From Diagnosis and Proficiency Testing to Assisted Self-Placement and Discipline-specific Language Development

For graduate directors and administrators of international student programs, probably the most important change they can make is to move away from a diagnosis and testing model. Many graduate programs are fixated on "proficiency," an approach that does not acknowledge students' linguistic and cultural competencies. Our interviews underlined the need to recognize how the students were capable of reflecting and evaluating themselves as readers and writers, and especially as professionals in their discipline. Our interviews led us to stories and narratives that showed that students were already engaged in the process of developing unique ways to think about ideas of self-reflection and assessment—like the work of faculty who use literacy narratives in their classrooms. When they realize the power of language, of their languages, they understand themselves to be empowered by language.

Programmatic Shift #4: From International Graduate Students to Transnational Emerging Scholars

Transnational graduate students constitute a class of students on U.S. university campuses who are usually not considered full members of the student body, not fully present, or only temporarily or provisionally present, or who will at some deferred time in the future be present, once they have been "fixed," once they have been acculturated to "our" campus, once their difference from our "regular" students has been defeated, solved, overcome. This process of identifying a deficit and looking for fixes is familiar to anyone who has looked at students enrolled in "basic writing" or other remedial courses, but in this case the students under study are more accurately described as emerging transnational professionals.

Those who U.S. universities, and the U.S. government, categorize as "international students" carry a particular legal status. They must navigate a complex bureaucratic system of testing and (sometimes) support, and are subjected to numerous assumptions on the part of U.S. staff, faculty, and fellow students about their language background, their cultural structures, their teaching abilities, and even their intelligence.

"International" is an obsolete term. As Ruby (2005) points out, higher education is a "good" under global trade negotiations such as GATS, and "international students" are covered by agreements between governments, with an economic impact of international students on the U.S. economy on the order of $30.8 billion in 2014–2015 (Institute of International Education, 2016). In business, an "international" company is basically an import/export entity, with its principal operations only in one country. This would contrast with a multinational company, which has agreements with a network of companies in multiple countries, or with a global company (think McDonalds) that attempts to reproduce itself in multiple countries with as little adjustment as possible to the local context (Bartlett & Ghoshal, 1988; Harzing, 2000; Kordos & Vojtovic, 2016). These models have analogues in the ways that U.S. universities have adopted a global model (e.g., the university described by Pi-Yun Chen, 2015), where, in the example Amy Hodges describes (this volume), the curriculum in the Middle East must be the same as in Texas, right down to American civics courses, or a multinational model (many "study-abroad" or "sister campuses" programs). All of these (international, multinational, or global) may be contrasted with a truly transnational model, where there is no recourse to a central administrative site but rather the network *is* the company, or, in this case, the university.

Grad-ASP programs cannot alter the business model of their institutions, but working within these structures, they can look for opportunities to re-direct the resources of faculty and staff away from a deficit model and toward recognizing emerging transnational scholars as important full members of the university.

Conclusion

Re-thinking "international" graduate students as transnational emerging scholars can lead to Grad-ASPs re-thinking their visions, missions, policies, and programs. U.S. institutions must begin from where students are in terms of their linguistic and cultural backgrounds and recognize the critical role they can play in a truly global university.

We have focused on a few elements that U.S. campuses directly impact: initial placement and evaluation, continuing academic assessment, and support for graduate communication and other academic issues. Improving our support for transnational students requires thoughtful listening to what translingual transnational emerging scholars say about the ways they develop disciplinary and professional identity. It is our responsibility as U.S. faculty and Grad-ASP program administrators to understand and to consider the effects of U.S. academic practices through a translingual lens, and to develop transnational perspectives and practices that illuminate the ways that our assumptions and our actions significantly impact the structuring of the "international student" experience, and what it will take to design effective support for transnational emerging scholars.

References

Bartlett, Christopher A. & Ghoshal, Samantra. (1988). Organizing for worldwide effectiveness: The transnational solution. *California Management Review*, *31*(1), 54–74.

Brown, Lorraine. (2007). The incidence of study-related stress in international students in the initial stage of the international sojourn. *Journal of Studies in International Education*, *12*(1), 5–28.

Canagarajah, A. Suresh. (2013). *Translingual practice: Global Englishes and cosmopolitan relations*. Routledge.

Chapdelaine, Raquel Faria & Alexitch, Louise R. (2004). Social skills difficulty: Model of culture shock for international graduate students. *Journal of College Student Development*, *45*(2), 167–184.

Chen, Pi-Yun. (2015). University's transnational expansion: Its meaning, rationales and implications. *Procedia - Social and Behavioral Sciences*, *171*, 1420–1427.

Cheng, Liying, Myles, Johanna & Curtis, Andy. (2004). Targeting language support for non-native English-speaking graduate students at a Canadian university. *TESL Canada Journal*, *21*(2), 50–71.

Cox, Michelle & Caplan, Nigel. (2014). The state of L2 graduate communication support (Consortium on Graduate Communication). Symposium on Second Language Writing, Arizona State University, Tempe, Arizona, United States. https://www.gradconsortium.org/resources/conference-presentations/.

Eldaba, Abir Aly & Isbell, Janet Kesterson. (2018). Writing gravity: International female graduate students' academic writing experiences. *Journal of International Students*, *8*(4), 1879–1890.

Harzing, Anne-Wil. (2000). An empirical analysis and extension of the Bartlett and Ghoshal typology of multinational companies. *Journal of International Business Studies; Basingstoke, 31*(1), 101–120.

Horner, Bruce, Lu, Min-Zhan, Royster, Jacqueline Jones & Trimbur, John. (2011). Language difference in writing: Toward a translingual approach. *College English, 73*(3), 303–321.

Hyun, Jenny, Quinn, Brian, Madon, Temina & Lustig, Steve. (2007). Mental health need, awareness, and use of counselling services among international graduate students. *Journal of American College Health, 56*(2), 109–118.

Institute of International Education. (n.d.). *Open doors report on international educational exchange*. Retrieved June 4, 2016 from http://www.iie.org/en/Research-and-Publications/Open-Doors/Data/International-Students#.V1M01uRvBb0.

Kordos, Marcel & Vojtovic, Sergej. (2016). Transnational corporations in the global world economic environment. *Procedia - Social and Behavioral Sciences, 230*, 150–158.

Le, Anh T. (2016). International female graduate students' experience at a Midwestern university: Sense of belonging and identity development. *Journal of International Students, 6*(1), 128–152.

Lea, Mary R. & Street, Brian V. (1998). Student writing in higher education: An academic literacies approach. *Studies in Higher Education, 23*(2), 157–172.

Lea, Mary R. & Street, Brian V. (2006). The "academic literacies" model: Theory and applications. *Theory into Practice, 45*(4), 368–377.

Lillis, Theresa. (2003). Student writing as "academic literacies": Drawing on Bakhtin to move from critique to design. *Language and Education, 17*(3), 192–207.

Matsuda, Paul Kei & Jablonski, Jeffrey. (2000). Beyond the L2 metaphor: Towards a mutually transformative model of ESL/WAC collaboration. *Academic Writing, 1*.

Mwangi, George, Changamire, Nyaradzai & Mosselson, Jacqueline. (2019). An intersectional understanding of African international graduate students' experiences in U.S. higher education. *Journal of Diversity in Higher Education, 12*(1), 52–64.

Phillips, Talin. (2013). Tutor training and services for multilingual graduate writers: A reconsideration. *Praxis: A Writing Center Journal, 10*(2).

Pu, Shi & Evans, Michael. (2018). Critical thinking in the context of Chinese postgraduate students' thesis writing: A positioning theory perspective. *Language, Culture and Curriculum, 32*(1), 50–62.

Rabbi, Shakil & A. Suresh Canagarajah. (2017). Socialization in the neoliberal academy of STEM scholars: A case study of negotiating dispositions in an international graduate student in entomology. *Humanities, 6*(2), 39.

Ravichandran, Swathi, Kretovics, Mark, Kirby, Kara & Ghosh, Ankita. (2017). Strategies to address English language writing challenges faced by international graduate students in the US. *Journal of International Students, 7*(3), 764–785.

Robinson, Heather, Hall, Jonathan & Navarro, Nela. (2020). *Translingual identities and transnational realities in the U.S. college classroom*. Routledge.

Ruby, Alan. (2005). Reshaping the university in an era of globalization. *Phi Delta Kappan, 87*(3), 233–236.

Sharma, Shyam. (2018). *Writing support for international graduate students: Enhancing transition and success*. Routledge.

Trice, Andrea G. (2004). Mixing it up: International graduate students' social interactions with American students. *Journal of College Student Development, 45*(6), 671–687.

Wan, Teh-yuan, Chapman, David W. & Biggs, Donald A. (1992). Academic stress of international students attending U.S. universities. *Research in Higher Education, 33*(5), 607–623.

Ying, Yu-Wen. (2005). Variation in acculturative stressors over time: A study of Taiwanese students in the United States. *International Journal of Intercultural Relations, 29*(1), 59–71.

Afterword. Translingual Lives and Writing Pedagogy: Acculturation, Enculturation, and Emancipation

Federico Navarro
UNIVERSIDAD DE O'HIGGINS

The Local and the Transnational: Between-ness, Beyond-ness

Transnational scholarship on teaching academic writing across borders and between languages is a contradictory endeavor. As Christiane Donahue (this volume) explains, national spaces and borders do exist, as checkpoints and armies dramatically remind us. Nations and regions have recognizable linguistic, cultural, educational, and research practices, as well as policies and traditions. Nevertheless, nations are also imagined communities (Anderson, 2006) that include hybridization, mobility, and connectivity beyond the social narratives of homogeneity and institutional control and categorization. According to Jonathan Hall (this volume), a transnational take "regards borders as porous, fluid, as lines which connect more than they divide." Therefore, transnational scholarship simultaneously fosters cross-fertilization as "between-ness," working across nations and regions, but also as "beyond-ness" (Donahue, this volume), working to surpass and transform artificial border restrictions and mono(lingual, cultural, and racial) conceptions.

Several chapters in this collection make the point that the varied features of languages, cultures, and nations challenge common assumptions and need to be acknowledged by translingual writing pedagogy and research. From a transnational perspective, these local considerations can help to prevent the positioning of English/Western theories, practices, and settings as hegemonic and exclusionary (Silva et al., 1997), naturalized as a zero point of observation (Castro-Gómez, 2015). Such a position reinforces a colonial relationship across borders that create patterns of neglect (Donahue, 2009) of worldwide scientific initiatives and traditions.

Amy Hodges (this volume) embodies this theoretical claim in the account of her experience in a transnational writing program in Qatar: the well-meaning methods and analysis put in place by U.S. scholars often seem inadequate in that context. Similarly, the coexistence in Canada of two official languages and active bilingual policies (see Gentil, this volume) responds to needs, offers opportunities, and creates demands that are quite different from those emerging from, for instance, the linguistically, racially, and culturally (super)diverse classrooms in the US, where penalizing the use of vernacular language varieties (such as

African American English) may promote segregation and (self-) stigmatization (Young, 2014). In particular, teaching writing in Canada requires institutional support for academic literacy development in two (or more) national languages. This challenge is similar, but also different, to what happens in countries where national academic language instruction coexists, sometimes problematically, with English as a second language, as Hall and Nela Navarro (this volume) explore in their article for U.S. settings.

Another local contrast, reported by Gentil, is the difference between undergraduate syllabi that promote disciplinary interchange and fluidity between programs (as in the US) and syllabi that compartmentalize the curriculum and aim at early disciplinary specialization (as in Canada). The smaller space of the classroom also presents complex contrasts regarding power structures and learning roles in pedagogical practices. Take Japan, where learning is understood as listening without interrupting the teachers (Kwon, this volume), compared to a learner-centered, socio-constructivist approach where writing/speaking is considered to promote the reorganization and transformation of knowledge. The prevalence of content-dominated assessment practices in Nepal and elsewhere is another example of local constraints for those interested in writing instruction (Sharma, this volume).

Finally, languages, cultures, and nations may also have their distinctive writing habitus or "writing sovereignty," as Mohammad Shamsuzzaman (this volume) puts it when he refers to writing being treated as an idiosyncratic, individual gift in Bangladesh. These practices and shared views may not comply with rhetorical expectations and criteria naturalized elsewhere as universal, as contrastive/intercultural rhetoric has studied for more than half a century (Connor, et al., 2008). Is the primary goal of writing instruction to produce error-free, well-polished papers in English, as Monica Kwon shows for Japan? Or should teachers focus on higher-level cognitive and rhetorical practices and concerns? Is writing prioritized, intertwined (as in the LSP approach explained by Kwon), or separated from the teaching of other skills/modes of communication (as in the "specialist English" reading-translating approach common in China, according to Yongyan Li, this volume)?

These different national, cultural, linguistic, institutional, and educational contexts have an impact on the theoretical take on translingual writing. Each national and regional educational context does not merely face unique exigencies. Theoretical principles—together with blank spots, which we consider underlying assumptions beyond dispute—are often facilitated by the very social, historical, and institutional conditions of specific settings. That is, varied exigencies have determined much of what we—or some of us, or they (cf. Adler-Kassner & Wardle, 2015) —consider threshold concepts of writing studies, composition, and language teaching. However, given that program diversity (see Hodges) and the flexibility/ hybridization of research design (Bazerman, 2011; Prior & Thorne, 2014) are at the very core of writing across the curriculum and writing studies, it is not an easy matter to recognize how epistemic paradigms (Lincoln, et al., 2017), theoretical traditions, and sociohistorical restrictions constrain our view of reality.

As Tony Silva et al. (1997) point out, culturally-situated pedagogical practices, implicit learning-teaching theories (Pozo, et al., 2006), and social narratives and values must be taken into account when teaching writing. Gentil, for instance, establishes a difference between minorities and their nationally recognized languages, such as indigenous peoples in Canada, and diverse minority groups resulting from migration—a dichotomy A. Suresh Canagarajah (2006) has labeled *national/ethnic* minorities. There are several different implications for this distinction in terms of institutional recognition, validation, and promotion of some languages over others. If a particular language is involved in people's identities and political participation, as Gentil points out regarding French for Francophone Canadians (but also Català for Catalans or Mapuzungun for southern Chilean/Argentinean indigenous people), the inclusive effort to fight monolingual/monoglossic ideologies might be counterproductive. In the words of Gentil, "It can be important for language minorities to preserve the linguistic distinctiveness that helps them index and maintain their identities."

In sum, local, national, or regional constraints must be taken into account because they may represent actual barriers or identity values, as Gentil's case clearly illustrates. A translingual/transnational perspective cannot mean a naïve internationalization or globalization ethic, where the ethnocentric perspectives of the privileged are to be considered universal. As Kwon puts it, "the local context significantly informs practice" based on differentiated instructional expectations, experiences, opportunities, constraints, and agendas. These contextual considerations are especially relevant for WAC/WID approaches that have long acknowledged that rhetorical, pedagogical, and curricular transformations and innovations depend on institutional restrictions and opportunities. The same applies to the expectations, alliances, and resistance of stakeholders and disciplines (McLeod, 2000). At the same time, adaptation to local expectations should be negotiated rather than simply accepted. As shown by Joyce Meier et al. (this volume), writing initiatives may include, as part of their goals, the gradual and collaborative transformation of certain conceptions that may be contrary to writing pedagogy.

Interestingly, this transnational diversity coexists with common challenges across contexts. Complaints about time restrictions to incorporate a writing-to-learn approach to disciplinary instruction emerge as a typical comment from faculty across the world, as Kwon demonstrates for Japan. In addition, reading and writing teaching is often perceived as another barrier to teaching disciplinary knowledge, understood as core learning outcomes in higher education, and often delinked from literacy practices. Similar complaints about time restrictions and the pressure to cover "content" opposing time to writing have been found across the disciplines (Scheurer, 2015).

The lack of explicit goals related to teaching writing, including advanced academic/professional genres in course syllabi, is also shared across countries, as Hodges shows for Qatar; Kwon for Japan; and others for Canada (Graves et al., 2010), the US (Melzer, 2009), Lebanon (O'Day et al., 2013), and Chile (Navarro et al., 2020). Research and teaching agendas may exhibit common, global goals, often fueled by center-periphery dynamics. For example, in 2000, the Accreditation Board for Engineering and Technology (ABET) shifted its focus to student learning outcomes and promoted technical communication (Williams, 2001). This created local institutional opportunities and financial support to create initiatives to teach writing in the US (Plumb & Scott, 2002), Chile (Ávila Reyes et al., 2013), and Egypt (Golson & Holdijk, 2012).

Translingualism as People's Choice

People's resistance—a notion explored by Hodges in this volume—and self-identifications are central concepts to consider when discussing frameworks to interpret data or actions for teaching writing. As Hodges illustrates, the same institution or field may well be interpreted, experienced, and embodied differently by diverse individuals, and these experiences might be in conflict within a single community or social group.

Similarly, the same rhetorical issue may be experienced differently. For Gentil's interviewees, to explore how an English technical term is translated/transformed into French promotes metacognitive and rhetorical skills, while for Hodges' interviewees, keeping technical terms in English is one of the critical pragmatic reasons why they have become more comfortable with communicating in English as a supposed "lingua franca" in multilingual settings. A critical discussion of monolingual/monoglossic ideologies in translingual scholarship must accommodate contrasting tendencies on what people do and value in their use of languages. Distinguishing between original, liminal, and adopting identities—whether racial, linguistic or cultural—is a complicated endeavor, as *transfronterizo*/transborder students demonstrate (Cavazos et al., this volume). What students say about their identities and preferences—or what they embody in their language performances—may complicate or contest our initial assumptions, as Hall and Navarro recognize.

The role and attached values of dominant languages, especially English, are also a key differentiator for translingual/transnational pedagogical and research approaches. Is English considered an unavoidable means to address foreigners and survive in a highly globalized economy (Kwon)? Is it a professional lingua franca for professionals who sometimes speak the same local language (Hodges)? Is it a teaching lingua franca (medium of instruction) to attract overseas STEM students that speak a variety of languages (Kwon)? Is it a national language that has a predominant role and threatens other national or migration-related languages and attached identities and histories (Gentil)? Is it a learning goal in itself to be used in the future to broaden employment opportunities, as for STEM higher education students in Japan (Kwon)? Or is it a dominant language variety that undervalues other varieties of the same language, discriminates against users, and restricts their use to less-prestigious contexts (Canagarajah, 2006; Young, 2014)?

Translingual research seems to accommodate two different overall traditions that respond to different linguistic, cultural, and national needs and roles. On the one hand, scholarship that draws from teachers of English to speakers of other languages (TESOL), languages for specific purposes (LSP), and applied linguistics is mostly fueled by the need to teach additional languages in transnational contexts. On the other, scholarship that draws from cultural and critical studies is mostly fueled by the need to vindicate vernacular/undervalued varieties of the same language and fight racism and segregation in multicultural contexts. A Chinese undergraduate student acquiring English as a second or foreign language might actively demand feedback on (standard) English language issues. In contrast, a first-generation, national minority student in an elite university in an English-speaking country might actively resist such feedback. This broad distinction is more of a continuum and a permanent dialogue —Hall and Navarro's chapter is an excellent example of such complexity and complementarity. However, it may help to explain different emphases, theoretical choices, and pedagogical preferences.

Interestingly, the authors in this volume also show how they relate differently to languages other than English in their scholarly writing. Note, for instance, that Donahue uses non-translated French quotations for an article in a U.S.-based publisher. Although French can hardly be considered a peripheral language (or culture), this decision is a statement; it challenges the expectation of translated-into-English quotations while gently inviting readers who do not read French to use now powerful and free translation tools, such as Deepl or Google Translator. After all, the sociolinguistic right to speak the language of one's choice is a threshold concept in translingual scholarship (Horner, et al., 2011a; Navarro, et al., 2022).

Translingual Lives to Transform Writing Pedagogy: from Deficit to Assets

The translingual/transnational lens helps to conceptualize "international students" and "(long-term) English language learners"—a euphemism used to refer to language-minoritized, low academic-achieving, low-socioeconomic status students (Flores & Rosa, 2015)—not from a remedial perspective, but from a perspective that considers students' complex linguistic and cultural background unique *learning incomes* and discursive resources (Guerra, 2015), as well as their dynamic and emerging identity processes, as Hall and Navarro explain. A remedial, hegemonic perspective on "non-traditional students" (Woolf et al., 2019) assumes a naïve view of language and identity as isolated from the dynamics of power within and among diverse languages and discourses, as Min-Zhan Lu pointed out some thirty years ago (Lu, 1991); linguistic stigmatization is not only, nor mainly based on—decontextualized—language use, but on the speakers' racial and class positions (Flores & Rosa, 2015).

In contrast, a perspective on students' learning incomes changes the conversation: it is now up to faculty and institutions, and to the pedagogical principles they draw from, to adapt to and learn from the current scenario of higher education (Ruecker et al., 2017) or, as Hall and Navarro programmatically state, "from imposing institutional identities on students to supporting students' dynamic identity processes" (this volume). Otherwise, the celebrated "global identity" of the present-day university would "fall short of true transnationalism" (Hall, this volume). A more practical—although complementary—argument claims that monolingual and hegemonic writing pedagogies do not prepare students for contexts of linguistic pluralism (Canagarajah, 2006), which are common in many professional and social contexts nowadays.

Thus, it is not a responsibility of non-traditional students to adapt to the traditional university and the monolingual/monoglossic imperative, but a responsibility of traditional universities to adapt to new learning needs and opportunities (O'Shea et al., 2016), as well as new cultures, languages, identities, and trajectories. Students viewed as "problematic" can no longer be sent somewhere out of the classroom to have their language—and their world view—"fixed," as Hall and Navarro point out. Without neglecting the language or study support some students may need, the central question should be "what writing cultures do international students bring with them?" (Sharma, 2018, p. 192), as these approaches "value difference as assets and resources for learning" (Meier et al., this volume). In the case of multilingual speakers, assets and resources include—but are not limited to—metalinguistic awareness and terminology learned through employing multilingual and multicultural knowledge and performance, as well as through extended formal training. This awareness and terminology can be useful to identify the goals, structures, and audiences of various genres; to plan, monitor, and revise multimodal texts; and to provide feedback to peers or respond to reviewers (see Cox, 2014).

This Copernican turn—from deficit to resource (Canagarajah, 2002; Horner et al., 2011a), from acculturation to transculturalism (Guerra & Shivers-McNair, 2016; Lu, 1992)—is inextricably linked to a paradigm change on crucial educational and literacy issues that have long been explored by the writing-across-the-curriculum approach: What is good writing? Who is responsible for teaching writing? What is the connection between writing and learning? What role do students' identities and agency have in writing and learning? What are the implicit expectations of students, instructors, administrators, and institutions about writing, teaching, learning, and participation? Where does writing intersect with social, cultural, and educational histories and configurations?

Meier et al. provide compelling examples of how these implicit prevailing questions are embodied in teachers' dilemmas in the classroom: the writing professor who complains about the lack of international student participation in class discussion but is unaware that international students may come from culturally inflected norms that do not reward active engagement; the biology professor who fails to unpack expectations for their students on writing tasks such as "analyze," "synthesize," or "justify"; or the business professor who recognizes different levels of language expertise, yet struggles to develop differentiated instruction.

The answer to these broader questions is the basis of a central question for translingual scholarship and writing pedagogy: Should teachers suppress, tolerate, or encourage the use of (vernacular) language varieties, hybrid semiotic forms, and culturally-diverse epistemic rationales for academic purposes? Even if teachers decide to ignore this question, their pedagogical practices will necessarily embody a particular answer to it. To suppress language varieties responds to subtractive approaches and promotes a process of *acculturation*; to tolerate language varieties draws from additive and accommodative approaches and promotes a process of *enculturation*; and to encourage language varieties draws from critical and heteroglossic approaches and promotes *emancipation* (see Canagarajah, 2006; Flores & Rosa, 2015; Guerra & Shivers-McNair, 2016; Lu, 1992).

Furthermore, a deficit-to-resource turn seems complementary to the speaker-to-listener turn, as Nelson Flores and Jonathan Rosa advocate: a critical move and examination, in pedagogy and research, from the speakers' stigmatized language "to the role of the listening subject in producing 'competent' and 'incompetent' language users" (Flores & Rosa, 2015, p. 167). This turn helps to explain why even students proficient in standardized language may still be labeled as "the other" by a racialized gaze.

New University, New Scholarship: Diverse Profiles beyond Languages

Some findings in translingual research in this volume are similar to what scholars have found in England, Australia, Peru, and Chile when exploring non-traditional students, whether multilingual or not. "We're not regular students. We're the Irregulars," says an international graduate student in U.S. higher education in Hall and Navarro's study; "I have to study twice as much as someone normal," says a non-traditional student in an inclusive program at an elite university in Chile (Ávila Reyes, et al., 2021). Interestingly, both Hall and Navarro and Ávila Reyes et al. draw from a new literacy studies framework that is aimed at social and cultural dimensions of literacy in present-day, increasingly diversified higher education. Social and institutional stigmatization of non-traditional students' skills, cultures, and languages is often internalized by students as part of their student identity, and it decreases their self-esteem and racial self-concept. "I see myself as undeveloped," states an indigenous first-in-family student in an Australian university (Stahl et al., 2020, p. 1495); this stigmatization may even be directed toward the original community or social group by the student (Young, 2014).

This connection between a translingual/transnational student profile with other aspects that intersect with writing instruction in non-traditional students is worth exploring. Outdated, prevailing expectations in higher education, including but not restricted to deficit models based on hegemonic, monoglossic views of language and language varieties, marginalize many non-traditional domestic and international students "as incompetent outsiders," as Meier et al. (this volume) put it. Creating networks of WAC/WID transdisciplinary partnerships and "natural allies" among faculty and administrators is critical for institutional change, Gail Shuck insists (this volume), as well as promoting linguistically inclusive pedagogical practices and reimagining pedagogy in teacher training and professional development (Cavazos et al., this volume). Students might also be strategic allies in institutional settings and sociohistorical contexts where they enact political agency and social change, as in Argentina (Moyano & Natale, 2012) and elsewhere.

In truth, situated studies of literacy and translingual scholarship go beyond topics of writing pedagogy, the maximization of learning gains, or the return of institutional and personal investment. The translingual/transnational lens is more broadly oriented towards social and linguistic justice and support of people's unique identities, trajectories, and well-being, as equity "includes not only eliminating discriminatory practices but also valuing such work in material ways" (Shuck, this volume). According to Zavala (2019), linguistic justice refers to "a language education that empowers oppressed individuals and groups in sociopolitical battles over language" (p. 347; my translation) within broader structural social inequities.

This translingual/transnational lens works similarly for writing research across borders. The import/export, "provincialism" model for knowledge-making is outdated (Donahue, 2009), together with the superficially more liberal additive model of participation in science research (Horner et al., 2011b). If the transnational identities of students are characterized for sustained—sometimes uncomfortable—liminality and the continuous creation of "networks of connective meaning across physical distances, language interactions, and cultural contexts" (Hall & Navarro, this volume), transnational writing research should embrace a "sociology of emergences" (Santos, 2018, p. 15) and "commit to exchange beyond unilateral sharing" (Sharma, this volume). In other words, it should recognize practices, knowledge, and agents from across borders, even if they might confront the very basis of central epistemologies and privileges in knowledge-making (Navarro, 2023). However, such mutually beneficial collaborations among educators and scholars are still to be reported (Sharma, this volume). As Donahue points out, U.S. composition studies are based on the narrative of an American "unique knowledge, expertise, and ownership of writing instruction and writing research" (2009, p. 213). This includes "universal courses, sovereign philosophies and pedagogies, and agreed-on language requirements" (Donahue, 2009, p. 213). This narrative goes together with the narrative of absence, lack, youth, and delay—but expansion and interest—in writing scholarship outside the US.

A translingual/transnational take on writing research means an invitation to engage in dialogue and a desire for exchange (Maldonado-Torres, 2007), and a rejection of a totalitarian approach to knowledge (García & Baca, 2019). The goal is to avoid "importing curricular options in unproductive ways," as Gentil says, and also to advance knowledge on writing teaching and research based on cross-fertilization among traditions. As Donahue suggests (this volume), "U.S. writing studies seems to sometimes 'other' writing instruction and research in countries outside the US that might have different teaching and research traditions."

More than a Language: Beyond Monolingual, Beyond Monodialectical

The collection is marked throughout by criticism of the monolingual myth as an oppressing and simplifying ideology, unrelated to actual linguistic practices (Flores & Rosa, 2015). The monolingual myth is also faulted for stigmatizing language varieties and missing learning and knowledge-making opportunities in multilingual classrooms. However, despite adopting translingual practices in the classroom, it is easy to maintain a traditional implicit take on languages as unique, univocal systems. That is, sometimes a claim to understand two languages (say, English and Spanish) as a continuum of resources and practices that bilingual speakers/writers draw from might involve assuming that there is such a thing as a single "English" and a single "Spanish" in the first place.

In contrast, challenging monodialectal ideologies is central to translingual scholarship and is situated at the core of code-meshing (Canagarajah, 2006; Horner, et al., 2011a; Lee & Alvarez, 2020; Young, 2014). As Hall explains, a translingual approach assumes that "all the languages a person knows can be active in the present moment of reading or writing, that all the components of one's complete communicative repertoire are, at least potentially, simultaneously in play in a mutually re-enforcing manner." Discussion of language varieties within a single language helps to confront a social narrative that undervalues certain language varieties compared to others, racializes some varieties associated with certain underprivileged and stigmatized social and racial groups, and promotes a diglossia that derives in "vernacular speech ghettos" (Canagarajah, 2006, p. 598). Such an approach should be rejected, as Cavazos et al. point out for standard academic Spanish in some programs in the US: "our assessment practices should be rooted from within the transborder student experience rather than imposed by an academic standard, existing outside of or in opposition to those realities" (this volume). Linguistic discrimination is a semi-hidden, semi-indirect means of national, ethnic, racial, or class discrimination (Horner, et al., 2011a; Zavala, 2019). As Flores and Rosa (2015) explain, the negative appraisal of the linguistic practices of language-minoritized populations is typically based on their racial positioning in society—as privileged or underprivileged groups—and it reproduces racial normativity.

Languages include national and local varieties (the "lived language experiences" of students: see Cavazos et al., this volume) that are differently appraised, institutionalized, and used. These tensions within languages impact people's identities, educational histories, job opportunities, and communication practices. In addition, languages include multiple sociolects that correspond to the ways social groups adapt and use language in their activities to signal their identities. Moreover, there are registers within languages that distinguish uses according to contexts (Halliday, 2007). Competing repertoires of registers will have consequences for educational settings: students with more "prestigious" registers (those closer to conventional scholarly communication) will be valued more positively—explicitly or implicitly—in educational and professional settings (Bernstein & Henderson, 2003; Schleppegrell, 2004).

An example of the possibilities for dialogue across fields and traditions is the code-switching/code-meshing controversy, pointed out by Paul Kei Matsuda (2013). Ashanti Vershawn Young rightly confronts a racialized, segregating pedagogical take on code-switching persisting in U.S. educational settings, where "students are instructed to switch from one code or dialect to another . . . according to setting and audience" (2014, p. 2). This definition seems to correspond to what sociolinguists consider "diglossia": "a situation where two genetically related varieties of a language, one identified as the H(igh) (or standard) variety and the other as the L(ow) (or nonstandard) variety, have clearly distinct functions in the community" (Kamwangamalu, 2010, p. 119). In contrast, according to sociolinguists, code-switching means the "alternating use of two or more languages or varieties of a language in the same speech situation" (Kamwangamalu, 2010, p. 116) to convey strategic meanings, to negotiate roles among participants, and to build, claim or identify with social identities. The latter closely resembles the definition of code-meshing in translingual studies: "to combine dialects, styles, and registers" (Young, 2014, p. 6) and "accommodate more than one code within the bounds of the same text" (Canagarajah, 2006, p. 598), ultimately "blending home and school identities, instead of keeping them separate" (Young, 2014, p. 3). Although scholars engage in conversations pertaining to their own settings and traditions, these quotes demonstrate that there is much space for more transnational, transdisciplinary conversations and collaborations. This dialogue would embrace the translingual living subject as the core student in writing teaching pedagogy, as Donahue suggests.

From a more general perspective, the role of specific language instruction remains a disputed domain in translingual scholarship, as some studies and experiences are explicitly situated outside "language-centric programs," as Meier et al. (this volume) maintain, while others vindicate necessary LSP support. Gentil (this volume) adds compelling arguments based on the institutionalization of languages in Canada to explain how the fluidity of language boundaries is sometimes limited. Similarly, Hall and Navarro (this volume) use evidence from interviews to claim that specific language teaching is part of learning writing—and a part that is recognized and demanded by international English-as-an-additional-language writers— together with the WAC/WID emphasized learning of ways of doing and thinking in the disciplines. As Donahue points out, we need "to understand the language relationships as wholly integrated into our questions about literacy, and we thus need to understand language itself, how it functions, what it does" (this volume). A difference-as-resource approach to multilingual, multicultural students does not mean adopting a hands-off approach to language issues (Cox, 2014).

In fact, there are specific linguistic features of languages and language families that distinguish how they conceptualize the world and how those conceptualizations are instantiated through grammatical and discursive means. The "variety, fluidity, intermingling, and changeability of languages," as Horner et al. put it (2011a, p. 305), does not mean that specific structural features of individual languages and language families are unimportant, equivalent, or totally malleable. From a grammatical and psycholinguistic point of view, it is problematic to consider that multi/translingual students use "one linguistic repertoire with features that have been societally constructed as belonging to separate languages" (García & Wei, 2014, p. 2), as Gentil critically points out.

Let us take the system of evidentiality as an example. It is part of the grammar repertoire of several indigenous languages in South America. Quechua speakers explicitly contrast through grammatical means whether what they say has been told to them by somebody else (evidentiality marker *-si*) or has been experienced by them firsthand (evidentiality marker *-mi*) (Adelaar, 1997), among other evidentiality resources which in some indigenous languages can be simultaneously combined (Hasler Sandoval et al., 2020). This grammatical system does not exist in languages such as Spanish or English. Is evidentiality societally constructed as belonging to Quechua for bi/multilingual Quechua/Spanish speakers? This does not seem to be the case, although some multilingual Quechua/Spanish speakers may experience it this way.

More importantly, how would a pedagogy of writing deal with multilingual students without some knowledge and attention to these structural features of languages? How does translanguaging in languages that are not structurally and historically close—such as Spanish/Quechua or Chinese/English—change our take on code-meshing? It is not surprising that, for instance, the pedagogy necessary for teaching Spanish as a second language to Chinese speakers is quite different—and not only for commercial reasons—from the teaching of Spanish to speakers of other languages, as illustrated by the various associations, conventions, journals, and research specifically focused on the Chinese learning community (see, for example, www.sinoele.org).

Thus, the negotiation of language norms and standards, a fundamental principle in a translingual approach (Horner et al., 2011a), is different from the modification of semantic, syntactic, morphological, and phonological language structures. Users of languages and language varieties actively, creatively, and strategically choose between stable-for-now systems of choices and resources for meaning-making (Halliday, 2014). However, these underlying systems are specific to languages and language families, often automatized, and can be freely modified by a single user only to a certain extent, as in the simultaneous centripetal (centralized, conservative) and centrifugal (heteroglossic, creative) language forces that Bakhtin refers to (Bakhtin, 1981).

Needless to say, there are different Mapuzunguns and Quechuas (Hasler Sandoval et al., 2020), as there are multiple Spanishes and Englishes. Structural contrasts may pertain to varieties of the "same" language as well. African American English, for instance, has a durative aspect grammar marker (the naked "be") that does not exist in present-day so-called Standard English (Gee, 2015). When young Leona famously exhibits sophisticated literate devices and grammar means as in "my puppy he always be following me," her teachers misrecognize what she is saying and see her as "deficient"; she eventually is told by an authoritative figure in her early steps into schooling that she does not make sense (Gee, 2015, p. 11).

Beyond controversies on the role of language instruction (Atkinson et al., 2015; Matsuda, 2014), most chapters in this collection agree to quote key references from composition and applied linguistics traditions. According to Donahue, translingual scholarship has "pushed new attention on language in writing, the kind of attention L2 scholars have been advocating" (this volume). Multilingual experiences and skills are considered learning and rhetorical assets; linguistic support is considered together with disciplinary learning and participation; and languages are considered complex political, social, and linguistic dynamic phenomena. This shared view is practical evidence of common scholarly interests in the field, and an enriching example of the collaboration across departments and subfields previously advocated by the translingual program (Horner et al., 2011b).

Discussions on the linguistic basis of translingual research are related to a broader question: what would a linguistically and culturally inclusive pedagogy of translingual/transnational writing be like? Or, in Hall's terms, "how would Writing Trans- the Curriculum be different?" (this volume). As Meier et al. explain, "while there has been increasing interest by rhetoric and composition scholars into translingual approaches across the disciplines, particularly in terms of language development and transfer, gaps remain in terms of what this perspective might look like in practice" (this volume; see also Cox, 2014). Cavazos et al. advance the same argument: "instructors are left wondering about what a translingual approach might look like in practice" (this volume).

As several of the chapters in this collection show, key strategies include 1) "develop[ing] pedagogical tools that support students' sustained examination of language difference" to foster agentive, critical, metalinguistic, transferable skills and rhetorical sensibility; 2) "incorporating alternate modes of communication in the negotiation of meaning" to multiply and acknowledge language modes, varieties, practices, and genres in the classroom; 3) "scaffolding and framing new knowledge in relation to the familiar—including the students' home languages and cultural knowledge" to value funds of knowledge (Moll et al., 1992) and community cultural wealth (Yosso, 2005); and 4) "disrupting taken-for-granted academic and cultural norms" to make teachers' expectations and institutional, disciplinary and linguistic conventions explicit and to a certain extent negotiable (see Meier et al., this volume).

Constructing visual maps of classrooms as culturally inflected spaces or inviting students to translate cultural texts from their home language into English (Meier et al., this volume) are just some possible examples of how these principles can be put to work. As explained above, these principles are of an urgent need for non-conventional students in general, who—as well as international students—now comprise the most substantial part of learners in expanding higher education systems worldwide; that is, these principles are of an urgent need for higher education as it is today.

Further Discussion: Languages, Concepts, Methods

The translingual/transnational take of this collection is implicitly restricted by a shared interest in the role of English in writing instruction. Consequently, several chapters explore how translingual writing instruction establishes complex ties—competition, isolation, collaboration—with TESOL and English for specific purposes. Nevertheless, writing instruction from a translingual/transnational perspective is not restricted, not even mostly related to TESOL or English as a medium of instruction. Perhaps the overrepresentation of English-related transnational writing instruction papers responds to the simple fact that the collection is written in English. What kind of transnational interchanges would emerge if other languages were focused on, as in Zavala's (2019) critical sociolinguistics exploration of the role of indigenous peoples and languages in Peruvian, Spanish-only, higher education institutions?

Similarly, a significant challenge for a translingual/transnational take on writing research and pedagogy is to simply translate technical terms and frameworks to compare our understanding of how pedagogy and research are configured across borders. As Li shows for China, the lack of mentions of a writing-across-the-curriculum approach does not necessarily mean that there is not a complex scenario of approaches to the teaching of discipline-oriented writing; additionally, there is a need for localized terminology, as Sharma suggests.

The methodologies and rationale for knowledge-making used in this collection of chapters are other aspects that deserve attention. They are mostly based on case studies and anecdotal recall of experiences. They use coursework and students' reflections as evidence, although sometimes without going into specifics about corpus/informants' selection, categorization, coding, and qualitative consistency. What is there about the perspective, the field tradition, the parent disciplines, or the conceptualization of the problem that promotes this kind of data collection and argumentation instead of others?

Finally, some of the cases included in this collection could make it appear as if non-Westernized, non-global-North (Rigg, 2007) settings are underdeveloped or lacking. Moreover, they might contribute to the idea that writing/language pedagogy history and development have certain inevitable milestones and principles that are to be reached in all contexts. Evidently, writing instruction and research might have varying degrees of expansion and history in different places. Nevertheless, that does not mean that a collective agreement—based on the premises and histories of central, Northern countries—is to be expected or desired elsewhere.

Acknowledgments

Funding from ANID/ PIA/ Basal Funds for Centers of Excellence FB0003 and FONDECYT 1191069 is gratefully acknowledged. Mary Jane Curry read an early draft of this article and made enriching suggestions.

References

Adelaar, Willem. (1997). *Los marcadores de validación y evidencialidad en quechua: ¿automatismo o elemento expresivo?* [Validation and evidence markers in Quechua: automatism or expressive element?]. *Amerindia, 22*, 3–13.

Adler-Kassner, Linda & Wardle, Elizabeth (Eds.). (2015). *Naming what we know: Threshold concepts of writing studies.* Utah State University Press.

Anderson, Benedict. (2006). *Imagined communities: Reflections on the origin and spread of nationalism* (3rd ed.). Verso.

Atkinson, Dwight, Crusan, Deborah, Matsuda, Paul, Ortmeier-Hooper, Christina, Ruecker, Todd, Simpson, Steve & Tardy, Christine. (2015). Clarifying the relationship between L2 writing and translingual writing: an open letter to writing studies editors and organization leaders. *College English, 77*(4), 383–386.

Ávila Reyes, Natalia, González-Álvarez, & Peñaloza Castillo, Christian. (2013). *Creación de un programa de escritura en una universidad chilena: estrategias para promover un cambio institucional* [Creating a writing program at a Chilean university: strategies to promote an institutional change]. *Revista Mexicana de Investigación Educativa, 18*(57), 537–560.

Ávila Reyes, Natalia, Navarro, Federico & Tapia Ladino, Mónica. (2021). "My abilities were pretty mediocre": Challenging deficit discourses in expanding higher education systems. *Journal of Diversity in Higher Education.* https://doi.org/10.1037/dhe0000366.

Bakhtin, Mikhail. (1981). *The dialogic imagination: Four essays* (Caryl Emerson & Michael Holquist, Trans.; Michael Holquist, ed.). University of Texas Press.

Bazerman, Charles. (2011). The disciplined interdisciplinarity of writing studies. *Research in the Teaching of English, 46*(1), 8–21.

Bernstein, Basil & Henderson, Dorothy. (2003). Social class differences in the relevance of language to socialization. In *Class, codes and control 2: Applied studies towards a sociology of language* (pp. 22–43). Routledge & Kegan Paul.

Canagarajah, A. Suresh. (2002). *Critical academic writing and multilingual students.* University of Michigan Press.

Canagarajah, A. Suresh. (2006). The place of world Englishes in composition: Pluralization continued. *College Composition and Communication, 57*(4), 586–619.

Castro-Gómez, Santiago. (2015). *Decolonizar la universidad. La hybris del punto cero y el diálogo de saberes* [Decolonize the university. The hybris of the zero point and the dialogue of knowledge]. In Zulma Palermo (Ed.), *Des/decolonizar la universidad* (pp. 79–91). Del Signo.

Connor, Ulla, Nagelhout, Ed & Rozycki, William (Eds.). (2008). *Contrastive rhetoric: Reaching to intercultural rhetoric.* John Benjamins.

Cox, Michelle. (2014). In response to today's "felt need": WAC, faculty development, and second language writers. In Terry Myers Zawacki & Michelle Cox (Eds.), *WAC and second language writers. Research towards linguistically and culturally inclusive programs and practices* (pp. 299–326). The WAC Clearinghouse; Parlor Press. https://doi.org/10.37514/PER-B.2014.0551.2.12.

Donahue, Christiane. (2009). "Internationalization" and Composition Studies: Reorienting the discourse. *College Composition and Communication, 61*(2), 212–243.

Flores, Nelson & Rosa, Jonathan. (2015). Undoing appropriateness: Raciolinguistic ideologies and language diversity in education. *Harvard Educational Review, 85*(2), 149–171. https://doi.org/10.17763/0017-8055.85.2.149.

García, Ofelia & Wei, Li. (2014). *Translanguaging: Language, bilingualism, and education.* Palgrave.

García, Romeo & Baca, Damian. (2019). Hopes and visions: the possibility of decolonial options. In Romeo García & Damian Baca (Eds.), *Rhetorics elsewhere and otherwise. Contested modernities, decolonial visions* (pp. 1–48). Conference on College Composition and Communication; National Council of Teachers of English.

Gee, James Paul. (2015). *Literacy and education.* Routledge.

Golson, Emily & Holdijk, Lammert. (2012). The Department of Rhetoric and Composition at the American University in Cairo: Achievements and challenges. In Chris Thaiss, Gerd-Bräuer, Paula Carlino, Lisa Ganobcsik-Williams & Aparna Sinha (Eds.), *Writing programs worldwide: Profiles of academic writing in many places* (pp. 181–188). The WAC Clearinghouse; Parlor Press. https://doi.org/10.37514/PER-B.2012.0346.2.16.

Graves, Roger, Hyland, Theresa & Samuels, Boba. (2010). Undergraduate writing assignments: An analysis of syllabi at one Canadian college. *Written Communication, 27*(3), 293–317. https://doi.org/10.1177/0741088310371635.

Guerra, Juan. (2015). *Language, culture, identity and citizenship in college classrooms and communities*. Routledge.

Guerra, Juan & Shivers-McNair, Ann. (2016). Toward a new vocabulary of motive: Re(con)figuring entanglement in a translingual world. In Bruce Horner & Elliot Tetreault (Eds.), *Crossing divides: Exploring translingual writing pedagogies and programs* (pp. 19–30). Utah State University Press.

Halliday, Michael. (2007). Language and social man. In Jonathan Webster (Ed.), *Language and society. Collected works of M. A. K. Halliday* (Vol. 10) (pp. 65–130). Continuum.

Halliday, Michael. (2014). *An introduction to functional grammar* (Christian Matthiessen, Ed., 4th ed.). Routledge.

Hasler Sandoval, Felipe, Olate Vinet, Aaldo & Soto Vergara, Guillermo. (2020). Origen y desarrollo del sistema evidencial del Mapudungun [Origin and development of the Mapudungun evidential system]. *Círculo de Lingüística Aplicada a la Comunicación, 81*, 9–26. https://doi.org/10.5209/clac.67928.

Horner, Bruce, Lu, Min-Zhan, Royster, Jacqueline Jones & Trimbur, John. (2011a). Language difference in writing: Toward a translingual approach. *College Composition and Communication, 73*(3), 303–321.

Horner, Bruce, NeCamp, Samantha & Donahue, Christiane. (2011b). Toward a multilingual composition scholarship: From English only to a translingual norm. *College Composition and Communication, 63*(2), 269–300.

Kamwangamalu, Nkonko. (2010). Multilingualism and codeswitching in education. In Nancy Hornberger & Sandra Lee McKay (Eds.), *Sociolinguistics and language education* (pp. 116–142). Multilingual Matters.

Lee, Eunjeong & Alvarez, Sara. (2020). World Englishes, translingualism, and racialization in the U.S. college composition classroom. *World Englishes, 39*(2), 263–274. https://doi.org/10.1111/weng.12459.

Lincoln, Yvonna, Lynham, Susan & Guba, Egon. (2017). Paradigmatic controversies, contradictions, and emerging confluences, revisited. In Norman Denzin & Yvonna Lincoln (Eds.), *The SAGE handbook of qualitative research* (5th ed., pp. 213–263). Sage.

Lu, Min-Zhan. (1991). Redefining the legacy of Mina Shaughnessy: A critique of the politics of linguistic innocence. *Journal of Basic Writing, 10*(1), 26–40. https://doi.org/10.37514/JBW-J.1991.10.1.04.

Lu, Min-Zhan. (1992). Conflict and struggle: The enemies or preconditions of basic writing? *College English, 54*(8), 887–913.

Maldonado-Torres, Nelson. (2007). On the coloniality of being: Contributions to the development of a concept. *Cultural Studies, 21*(2–3), 240–270. https://doi.org/10.1080/09502380601162548.

Matsuda, Paul Kei. (2013). It's the wild west out there: A new linguistic frontier in U.S. college composition. In A. Suresh Canagarajah (Ed.), *Literacy as translingual practice: Between communities and classrooms* (pp. 128–138). Routledge.

Matsuda, Paul Kei. (2014). The lure of translingual writing. *Publications of the Modern Language Association of America, 129*(3), 478–483. https://doi.org/10.1632/pmla.2014.129.3.478.

McLeod, Susan. (2000). Translating enthusiasm into curricular change. In Susan McLeod (Ed.), *Strengthening programs for writing across the curriculum* (pp. 5–12). The WAC Clearinghouse. https://wac.colostate.edu/books/landmarks/mcleod_programs/. (Originally published in 1988 by Jossey-Bass)

Melzer, Dan. (2009). Writing assignments across the curriculum: A national study of college writing. *College Composition and Communication, 61*(2), 240–261.

Moll, Luis, Amanti, Cathy, Neff, Deborah & González, Norma. (1992). Funds of knowledge for teaching: Using a qualitative approach to connect homes and classrooms. *Theory into Practice, 31*(2), 132–141.

Moyano, Estela & Natale, Lucía. (2012). Teaching academic literacy across the university curriculum as institutional policy. The case of the Universidad Nacional de General Sarmiento (Argentina). In Chris Thaiss, Gerd Bräuer, Paula P. Carlino, Lisa Ganobcsik-Williams & Aparna Sinha (Eds.), *Writing programs worldwide: Profiles of academic writing in many places* (pp. 23–34). The WAC Clearinghouse; Parlor Press. https://doi.org/10.37514/PER-B.2012.0346.2.02.

Navarro, Federico. (2023). The unequal distribution of research roles in transnational composition: towards illegitimate peripheral participation. In Christiane Donahue & Bruce Horner (Eds.), *Teaching and studying transnational composition*. Modern Language Association.

Navarro, Federico, Ávila Reyes, Natalia, Calle-Arango, Lina & Cortés Lagos, Ana. (2020). *Lectura, escritura y oralidad en perfiles de egreso de educación superior: Contrastes entre instituciones y carreras* [Reading, writing and speaking in higher education graduate profiles: Contrasts across institutions and majors]. *Revista Calidad en la Educación, 52*, 170–204. https://doi.org/10.1075/jerpp.21012.nav

Navarro, Federico, Lillis, Theresa, Donahue, Tiane, Curry, Mary Jane, Reyes, Natalia Ávila, Gustafsson, Magnus, Zavala, Virginia, Lauria, Daniela, Lukin, Annabelle, McKinney, Carolyn, Feng, Haiying & Motta-Roth, Desiree. (2022). Rethinking English as a "lingua franca" in scientific-academic contexts. A position statement. *Journal of English for Research Publication Purposes. 3*(1), 143–153.

O'Day Nicolas, Maureen & Annous, Samer. (2013). Assessing WAC elements in business syllabi. *Business and Professional Communication Quarterly, 76*(2), 172–187. https://doi.org/10.1177/1080569912471709.

O'Shea, Sarah, Lysaght, Pauline, Roberts, Jen & Harwood, Valerie. (2016). Shifting the blame in higher education—social inclusion and deficit discourses. *Higher Education Research & Development, 35*(2), 322–336. https://doi.org/10.1080/07294360.2015.1087388.

Plumb, Carolyn & Scott, Cathie. (2002). Outcomes assessment of engineering writing at the University of Washington. *Journal of Engineering Education, 91*(3), 333–338. https://doi.org/10.1002/j.2168-9830.2002.tb00711.x.

Pozo, Juan Ignacio, Scheuer, Nora, Mateos, Mar & del Puy Pérez Echeverría, María. (2006). *Las teorías implícitas sobre el aprendizaje y la enseñanza* [Implicit theories about learning and teaching]. In Juan Ignacio Pozo, Nora Scheuer, María del Puy Pérez Echeverría, Mar Mateos, Elena Martín & Montserrat de la Cruz (Eds.), *Nuevas formas de pensar la enseñanza y el aprendizaje* (pp. 95–132). Graó.

Prior, Paul & Thorne, Steven. (2014). Research paradigms: Beyond process, product, and social activity. In Eva-María Jakobs & Daniel Perrin (Eds.), *Handbook of writing and text production* (pp. 31–54). Mouton de Gruyter.

Rigg, Jonathan . (2007). *An everyday geography of the Global South*. Routledge.

Ruecker, Todd, Shepherd, Dawn, Estrem, Heidi & Brunk-Chavez, Beth (Eds.). (2017). *Retention, persistence, and writing programs*. Utah State University Press.

Santos, Boaventura de Sousa (2018). *The end of the cognitive empire: The coming of age of epistemologies of the south*. Duke University Press.

Scheurer, Erika. (2015). What do WAC directors need to know about "coverage"? *The WAC Journal, 26*, 7–21. https://doi.org/10.37514/WAC-J.2015.26.1.01.

Schleppegrell, Mary. (2004). *The language of schooling. A functional linguistics perspective*. Lawrence Erlbaum.

Sharma, Shyam. (2018). *Writing support for international graduate students. Enhancing transition and success*. Routledge.

Silva, Tony, Leki, Ilona & Carson, Joan. (1997). Broadening the perspective of mainstream composition studies: Some thoughts from the disciplinary margins. *Written Communication, 14*(3), 398–428. https://doi.org/10.1177/074108839701400300.

Stahl, Garth, McDonald, Sarah & Stokes, Jennifer. (2020). "I see myself as undeveloped": Supporting Indigenous first-in-family males in the transition to higher education. *Higher Education Research & Development, 39*(7), 1488–1501. https://doi.org/10.1080/07294360.2020.1728521.

Williams, Julia. (2001). Transformations in technical communication pedagogy: Engineering, writing, and the ABET engineering criteria 2000. *Technical Communication Quarterly, 10*(2), 149–167. https://doi.org/10.1207/s15427625tcq1002_3.

Woolf, Susi, Zemits, Birut, Janssen, Amanda & Knight, Scott. (2019). Supporting resilience in first year of university: Curriculum, consideration and cooperation. *Journal of Academic Language & Learning, 13*(1), A108-A123.

Yosso, Tara. (2005). Whose culture has capital? A critical race theory discussion of community cultural wealth. *Race Ethnicity and Education, 8*(1), 69–91. https://doi.org/10.1080/1361332052000341006.

Young, Vershawn Ashanti. (2014). Are you part of the conversation? In Vershawn Ashanti Young, Rusty Barret, Y'Shanda Young-Rivera & Kim Brian Lovejoy (Eds.), *Other people's English: Code-meshing, code-switching, and African American literacy* (pp. 1–11). Teachers College Press.

Zavala, Virginia (2019). Justicia sociolingüística para los tiempos de hoy. *Íkala, 24*(2), 343–359. https://doi.org/10.17533/udea.ikala.v24n02a09.

Contributors

Alyssa G. Cavazos is Associate Professor of Rhetoric and Composition in the Department of Writing and Language Studies at the University of Texas Rio Grande Valley. She teaches undergraduate and graduate coursework in writing studies. Her pedagogical and scholarly interests include: language difference in the teaching of writing, translingual writing across communities, professional development, and border rhetorics.

Christiane Donahue, Professor of Linguistics at Dartmouth and member of the Théodile-CIREL research laboratory at l'Université de Lille, France, participates in multiple European research projects, networks, conferences and collaborations that inform her understanding of writing instruction, research, and program development in European and U.S. contexts.

Guillaume Gentil is Professor of Applied Linguistics, Discourse Studies, and French Studies at Carleton University, Ottawa, Canada, and former co-editor of the Journal of Second Language Writing. His research interests in second language writing and bi/pluriliteracy development in professional and postsecondary settings originate from his academic literacy experiences in France, the US, and Canada. His research work has appeared in *Canadian Modern Language Review, Discourse & Society, Journal of English for Academic Purposes, Journal of Second Language Writing, Written Communication*, and several co-edited books.

Jonathan Hall is Professor of English at York College, City University of New York. He is the author (with Heather Robinson and Nela Navarro) of *Translingual Identities and Transnational Realities in the U.S. College Classroom* (Routledge, 2020) His work has appeared in *The WAC Journal, Across the Disciplines*, and elsewhere.

Gene Hammond is Professor of Writing and Rhetoric at the State University of New York at Stony Brook. He has directed the writing program both at Stony Brook and at the University of Maryland as well as chairing the English department at both. He is the author of the texbook *Thoughtful Writing* and of a two-volume biography of Jonathan Swift: *Irish Blow-In* and *Our Dean*.

Marcela Hebbard is a senior lecturer at the University of Texas Rio Grande Valley. She teaches composition, linguistics and teacher preparedness courses. Her research includes language in online writing pedagogy, raciolinguistics, translingual and transnational writing, writing across the curriculum, and teacher preparedness. She has published articles in several academic journals.

José Esteban Hernández is Professor of Hispanic Linguistics at the University of Texas Rio Grande Valley. His research interests include sociolinguistic variation, dialect and language contact, Spanish heritage language, and the construction of identity in contact situations. He has taught courses on language variation and change and the sociolinguistics of U.S Latino communities.

Amy Hodges is Assistant Professor of English at the University of Texas at Arlington, specializing in technical and transnational writing. Her work has appeared in *IEEE Transactions on Professional Communication* and the *Writing Center Journal*. She has also taught technical writing and ESL composition in Qatar and Singapore.

Bruce Horner has served as Endowed Chair in Rhetoric and Composition at the University of Louisville, where he teaches courses in composition, composition theory and pedagogy, and literacy studies. His recent books include *Rewriting Composition: Terms of Exchange, Mobility Work in Composition* (co-edited with Megan Favers Hartline, Ashanka Kumari, and Laura Sceniak Matravers), and *Crossing Divides: Exploring Translingual Writing Pedagogies and Programs*, co-edited with Elliot Tetreault and winner of the 2018 MLA Mina Shaughnessy Prize.

Julia E. Kiernan is Assistant Professor of Communication at Lawrence Technological University. Her research and teaching are intimately linked, and regularly examine the shifting impacts of pedagogical and curricular design in the digital humanities, translingual and transnational writing, environmental humanities, and health humanities. Her work has appeared in a number of peer-reviewed edited collections as well as in the journals *Composition Forum*, *Interdisciplinary Humanities*, *Communication and Language at Work*, *Social Sciences and Humanities Open*, and *Composition Studies*.

Monica (Heejung) Kwon is Assistant Professor at Kanazawa University, Japan where she serves as a member of an academic writing program curriculum committee. She has published articles on English for academic purposes, English as an international language, and corpus studies.

Yongyan Li is Associate Professor in the Unit of Social Contexts and Policies of Education, Faculty of Education, University of Hong Kong. Her areas of research include scholarly practices, academic writing in disciplines, teaching English for research publication purposes, and plagiarism studies in the Chinese context.

Joyce Meier is Associate Professor in Michigan State University's Writing, Rhetoric, and Cultures Department, where she also serves as associate director of the first-year writing program. Her WPA work focuses on teaching multilingual learners; she has published in *Composition Forum*, *English Education*, *The Reading Matrix*, and the *Journal of Global Literacies, Technologies, and Emerging Pedagogies*, along with multiple essays within larger collections.

Federico Navarro has a Ph.D. in linguistics and is Dean and Associate Professor at the Universidad de O'Higgins, Chile. He has been the founding chair of the Latin American Association of Writing Studies in Higher Education. He has led 11 research projects and published more than 100 papers in 12 countries.

Nela Navarro is Associate Director of the Rutgers English Language Institute (RELI), and assistant teaching professor in the English department's writing program. Her research interests include language rights, linguistic justice, trans-lingual pedagogy, new literacies studies, critical pedagogy, writing as sites of recursive memory, educational reform, comparative global education, the role of technology in educational access, human rights, genocide, and peace education.

Crystal Rodriguez has taught composition and rhetoric at South Texas College. Her background in anthropology combined with graduate research cultivated a desire to blend cultural awareness with writing instruction. Her research has centered primarily on first-year composition students' perspectives on language difference.

Geoffrey Schwarz is an institutional research analyst at South Texas College. His research interests include participatory methods, program evaluation, implementation, and race issues in higher education. He has taught sociology at the University of Texas Rio Grande Valley and Texas Southmost College.

Shyam Sharma is Associate Professor and graduate program director in the Program in Writing and Rhetoric at the State University of New York at Stony Brook. His works have appeared in *College Composition and Communication, JAC, Across the Disciplines, Composition Studies, NCTE, Series in Writing and Rhetoric, Hybrid Pedagogy, Kairos, and Professional and Academic English (IELTS SIG)*, and *Routledge*. He has written for the broader public through venues including the *Chronicle of Higher Education* and the *Republica*, a sister publication of *The New York Times* published from South Asia.

Mohammad Shamsuzzaman has been Assistant Professor in the Department of English and Modern Languages at North South University, Bangladesh. He earned his Ph.D. from the University of Canterbury, New Zealand, in 2015. His areas of interest include composition theories and pedagogy, L2 acquisition, and post-colonial studies.

Gail Shuck is Professor of English at Boise State University, where she has directed English language support programs since 2001. She has published in *Composition Studies, WPA: Writing Program Administration*, and several edited collections. She recently published *Plurilingual Pedagogies for Multilingual Writing Classrooms*, co-edited with Kay Losey (Routledge, 2022).

Xiqiao Wang is Assistant Professor in the University of Pittsburgh's composition, literacy, pedagogy, and rhetoric program. Her research on multilingual writing process in the context of global migration has appeared in professional journals such as *Research in the Teaching of English, College Composition and Communication, Journal of Second Language Writing, Journal of Basic Writing*, and *Composition Studies*.

www.ingramcontent.com/pod-product-compliance
Lightning Source LLC
Chambersburg PA
CBHW030230100526
44583CB00013BA/670